Advance Praise for

Paul, Women, and the Meaning of Silence: A Contextual Reading of 1 Corinthians 14:34–35

"In what is possibly the most thorough examination of 1 Corinthians 14:34–35 to date, Alex Carr offers an insightful discussion of the history of research, literary context, historical context, and theological context of this debated text. His knowledge of the topic is vast, his arguments cogent, and his conclusion persuasive. Carr's research will topple several of the popular theories and become the work with which all future scholarship simply must engage."

—Charles L. Quarles, Research Professor of New Testament and Biblical Theology; Charles Page Chair of Biblical Theology, Southeastern Seminary

"After decades of debate and libraries of books on the ministry of women, Alex Carr's study shows there are new insights still to be had from examining the biblical texts afresh. *Paul, Women, and the Meaning of Silence* demonstrates that lexical, literary, historical, and theological factors weigh against Paul's command in 1 Corinthians 14:34 demanding 'absolute silence' of women. Instead, Carr shows that Paul's command enjoins women to temporary silence during a specific time in the church gathering, namely, during the weighing of prophecies. His findings support the authenticity of the text and shed light on the contribution and participation of women in the first century church and today."

—Claire S. Smith, Author of *Pauline Communities as 'Scholastic Communities': A Study of the Vocabulary of 'Teaching' in 1 Corinthians, 1 and 2 Timothy and Titus* (2012)

"1 Corinthians 14:34–35 at first glance appears to silence all women in church, yet 11:5 permits them to pray and prophesy if their heads are covered. A plethora of approaches has developed both to affirm and deny that this is an irreconcilable contradiction. But Alex Carr deftly guides his readers through the maze of options that scholars have developed, showing there is no contradiction at all. A welcome addition to a crowded field of studies."

—Craig L. Blomberg, Distinguished Professor Emeritus of New Testament, Denver Seminary

Paul, Women, and the Meaning of Silence

Studies in Biblical Literature

Hemchand Gossai
General Editor

Vol. 180

The Studies in Biblical Literature series is part of the Peter Lang Humanities list.
Every volume is peer reviewed and meets
the highest quality standards for content and production.

PETER LANG
New York • Berlin • Brussels • Lausanne • Oxford

Alex S. Carr

Paul, Women, and the Meaning of Silence

A Contextual Reading of 1 Corinthians 14:34–35

PETER LANG
New York • Berlin • Bruxelles • Lausanne • Oxford

Library of Congress Cataloging-in-Publication Control Number: 2021056732

Bibliographic information published by **Die Deutsche Nationalbibliothek**.
Die Deutsche Nationalbibliothek lists this publication in the "Deutsche Nationalbibliografie"; detailed bibliographic data are available
on the Internet at http://dnb.d-nb.de/.

ISSN 1089-0645
ISBN 978-1-4331-9489-4 (hardcover)
ISBN 978-1-4331-9491-7 (ebook pdf)
ISBN 978-1-4331-9492-4 (epub)
DOI 10.3726/b19348

© 2023 Alex S. Carr

Peter Lang Publishing, Inc., New York
80 Broad Street, 5th floor, New York, NY 10004
www.peterlang.com

All rights reserved.
Reprint or reproduction, even partially, in all forms such as microfilm,
xerography, microfiche, microcard, and offset strictly prohibited.

Dedicated to my wife, Nicole

thankful for your patience and sacrifices to make this project possible

Table of Contents

List of Figures   xi
Series Editor Preface   xiii
Author Preface   xv
List of Abbreviations   xvii

1   History of Research   1
    General Introduction   1
    History of Research   6
        Literary Context   6
            First Corinthians 14:34–35 Was Inserted by a Later Editor (Interpolation)   6
            First Corinthians 14:34–35 Is a Corinthian Slogan   10
            First Corinthians 14:34–35 Contradicts Paul Elsewhere   11
            First Corinthians 14:34–35 Applies Only to Married Women   14
        Historical Context   14
            Paul Silenced Women because of Their Lack of Education   15
            Paul Silenced Women because of Cultural Restrictions on Speech in Public   16

		Paul Silenced Women because Only Women Were	
		Causing Problems	16
		Theological Context	17
		First Corinthians 14:34–35 Contradicts Paul's Theological Principles	17
		First Corinthians 14:34–35 Contradicts Paul's Practice	18

2   The Literary Context: The Range of ΣΙΓΑΩ as a Basis for Consistency   21
- Introduction   21
- Review of Lexical Works and Dictionaries   21
- Usage in Greek Literature (Narrowed by Date Closest to the New Testament)   24
- Usage in the Old Testament   29
- Usage in the New Testament   32
- Consistency of 1 Cor 14:34–35 within 14:26–40; 12:11; and 11:5   36
- Interpolation and Textual Criticism   58
- Conclusion   67

3   The Historical Context: Consistent Application Then and Now   69
- Introduction   69
- The Multi-cultural Context of Women in the Ancient World   70
  - The Lack of Education Argument   72
  - The Lack of Public Speaking Argument   77
  - The Search for Consistency in Method and Cultural Analysis   81
  - Paul's Consistent Pattern   85
- The Male and Female Problems at Corinth   90
- The Old Testament Law: A Basis for Paul's Teaching in 1 Corinthians   97
- Conclusion   105

4   The Theological Context: Consistency within Pauline Theology and Practice   107
- Introduction   107
- Galatians 3:28   108
- First Timothy 2:11–12 and the Study of Ἡσυχία   120
- Lydia in Acts 16:11–15, 40   133
- Named Women in Romans 16:1–7   135

Euodia and Syntyche in Philippians 4:2–3   150
Nympha in Colossians 4:15   152
Conclusion   155
General Conclusion   156
   Summary   156
   Implications   159

Appendix: ΣΙΓΑΩ in Greek Literature   161
Bibliography   231
Index   259

List of Figures

Figure 1: Usage of σιγάω in Greek Literature (Limited Sample)   25
Figure 2: Ἡσυχία in the LXX   127
Figure 3: Ἡσυχία in Josephus's *Antiquities*   129

Series Editor Preface

More than ever the horizons in biblical literature are being expanded beyond that which is immediately imagined; important new methodological, theological, and hermeneutical directions are being explored, often resulting in significant contributions to the world of biblical scholarship. It is an exciting time for the academy as engagement in biblical studies continues to be heightened.

This series seeks to make available to scholars and institutions, scholarship of a high order, and which will make a significant contribution to the ongoing biblical discourse. This series includes established and innovative directions, covering general and particular areas in biblical study. For every volume considered for this series, we explore the question as to whether the study will push the horizons of biblical scholarship. The answer must be *yes* for inclusion.

In this volume, based on a revised version of the author's Ph.D. dissertation, Alex Carr examines the meaning and role of Paul's reference to the silence of women in I Corinthians 14:34–35. This study will focus primarily on the meaning of σιγάω within the I Corinthians 14:34–35 text and in the larger context of the Bible and the Greco-Roman world. Carr challenges the established scholarly norm that the silence of women in I Corinthians 14:34–35 is inconsistent with the wider Pauline writing. He provides a cogent and detailed overview of the scholarship focusing on the principal proponents and their various literary and theological arguments. Employing literary, historical and their theological interpretations, Carr argues that Paul's use of σιγάω and the role of women as portrayed in his other letters and the church is entirely coherent, and is indeed consistent. He argues that when silence is contextually defined, consistency in Paul is evident. In his examination and assessment of both biblical and extra-biblical texts, Carr notes that only 7.8% of texts may be understood as pointing to *absolute* silence while 75.9% may be construed as *selective* silence. Noting that silence in Paul is not meant to be understood as absolute, Carr provides an exhaustive examination of both texts and contexts to underline his argument and conclusion.

This is an important and significant scholarly examination which might sometimes be viewed as a thorny and divisive issue. This exhaustive investigation will have meaningful implications for both biblical scholarship and the Church. The result is a study that is certain to generate ongoing discourse, and will not only further expand the biblical horizon, but will do so in a direction that invites further conversation.

The horizon has been expanded.

Hemchand Gossai
Series Editor

Author Preface

This book presents a revision of my doctoral dissertation completed under Professor Benjamin L. Merkle at Southeastern Baptist Theological Seminary in May 2021. I thank Dr. Merkle for his own model of scholarship for the church. Several others have reviewed the book, especially my dissertation committee. I am grateful for each one who read the manuscript and offered detailed feedback. Any remaining errors are my own.

I could not have completed this work without the enduring support and love of my wife, Nicole. She is currently pursuing her doctoral degree in Christian missions. I am glad to support her research now as she did for me. This book is dedicated to her.

I am grateful to God for two schools that have shaped my education. Southeastern Baptist Theological Seminary in Wake Forest, North Carolina is a school dedicated to the Great Commission in Matthew 28:16–20. Also, I thank Union University in Jackson, Tennessee. The library staff at each institution were very helpful.

Finally, I give sincere thanksgiving to my Savior Jesus Christ who gives meaning both to this work and my own life. I hope the research edifies his church. To God be the glory.

Alex Shane Carr

Abbreviations

AB	Anchor Bible
ACCS	Ancient Christian Commentary on Scripture
ACNT	Augsburg Commentaries on the New Testament
AcT	*Acta Theologica*
AJA	*American Journal of Archaeology*
ATA	Alttestamentliche Abhandlungen
BA	*Biblical Archaeologist*
BAG	Bauer, Walter, William F. Arndt, and F. Wilbur Gingrich. *Greek-English Lexicon of the New Testament and Other Early Christian Literature.* Chicago: University of Chicago Press, 1957.
BAGD	Bauer, Walter, William F. Arndt, F. Wilbur Gingrich, and Frederick W. Danker. *Greek-English Lexicon of the New Testament and Other Early Christian Literature.* 2nd ed. Chicago: University of Chicago Press, 1979.
BBR	*Bulletin for Biblical Research*
BDAG	Bauer, Walter, Frederick William Danker, W. F. Arndt, and F. W. Gingrich. *Greek-English Lexicon of the New Testament and Other Early Christian Literature.* 3rd ed. Chicago: University of Chicago Press, 2000.

BECNT	Baker Exegetical Commentary on the New Testament
BETL	Bibliotheca Ephemeridum Theologicarum Lovaniensium
BHGNT	Baylor Handbook on the Greek New Testament
Bib	*Biblica*
BibInt	*Biblical Interpretation*
BJS	Brown Judaic Studies
BNP	Cancik, Hubert, and Helmuth Schneider, eds. *Brill's New Pauly: Encyclopaedia of the Ancient World*. 22 vols. Leiden: Brill, 2002–2011.
BNTC	Black's New Testament Commentaries
BR	*Biblical Research*
BSac	*Bibliotheca Sacra*
BSGRT	Bibliotheca Scriptorum Graecorum et Romanorum Teubneriana
BST	The Bible Speaks Today
BT	*The Bible Translator*
BTB	*Biblical Theology Bulletin*
BWANT	Beiträge zur Wissenschaft vom Alten und Neuen Testament
BZNW	Beihefte zur Zeitschrift für die neutestamentliche Wissenschaft
CBC	Cambridge Bible Commentary
CBET	Contributions to Biblical Exegesis and Theology
CBQ	*Catholic Biblical Quarterly*
CEJL	Commentaries on Early Jewish Literature
CNT	Commentaire du Nouveau Testament
ConcC	Concordia Commentary
CRINT	Compendia Rerum Iudaicarum ad Novum Testamentum
CV	*Communio Viatorum*
DNTB	Evans, Craig A., and Stanley E. Porter, eds. *Dictionary of New Testament Background*. Downers Grove, IL: IVP Academic, 2000.
DPL	Hawthorne, Gerald F., and Ralph P. Martin, eds. *Dictionary of Paul and His Letters: A Compendium of Contemporary Biblical Scholarship*. Downers Grove, IL: IVP Academic, 1993.
ÉBib	*Études bibliques*
ECAM	Early Christianity in Asia Minor
EDNT	Balz, Horst, and Gerhard Schneider, eds. *Exegetical Dictionary of the New Testament*. 3 vols. Grand Rapids: Eerdmans, 1990–1993.
EGGNT	Exegetical Guide to the Greek New Testament
EKKNT	Evangelisch-katholischer Kommentar zum Neuen Testament
EvQ	*Evangelical Quarterly*

ExpTim	*Expository Times*
GELS	Muraoka, T. *A Greek-English Lexicon of the Septuagint*. Louvain: Peeters, 2009.
HNT	Handbuch zum Neuen Testament
HR	*History of Religions*
HvTSt	*Hervormde teologiese studies*
IBC	Interpretation: A Bible Commentary for Teaching and Preaching
ICC	International Critical Commentary
JBL	*Journal of Biblical Literature*
JBMW	*Journal for Biblical Manhood and Womanhood*
JETS	*Journal of the Evangelical Theological Society*
JGRChJ	*Journal of Greco-Roman Christianity and Judaism*
JSNT	*Journal for the Study of the New Testament*
JSNTSup	Journal for the Study of the New Testament Supplement Series
JTS	*Journal of Theological Studies*
KEK	Kritisch-exegetischer Kommentar über das Neue Testament (Meyer-Kommentar)
L&N	Louw, Johannes P., and Eugene A. Nida. *Greek-English Lexicon of the New Testament: Based on Semantic Domains*. 2nd ed. 2 vols. New York: United Bible Societies, 1989.
LCL	Loeb Classical Library
LNTS	The Library of New Testament Studies
LSJ	Liddell, Henry George, Robert Scott, and Henry Stuart Jones. *A Greek-English Lexicon*. Oxford: Clarendon, 1996.
MNTC	Moffatt New Testament Commentary
MSJ	*The Master's Seminary Journal*
NA[28]	Aland, Barbara, Kurt Aland, Johannes Karavidopoulos, Carlo M. Martini, and Bruce M. Metzger, eds. *Novum Testamentum Graece*. 28th edition. Institute for New Testament Textual Research. Stuttgart: Deutsche Bibelgesellschaft, 2012.
NAC	New American Commentary
NCB	New Century Bible
NCBC	The New Cambridge Bible Commentary
NCCS	New Covenant Commentary
NEchtB	Neue Echter Bibel
Neot	*Neotestamentica*
NIB	The New Interpreter's Bible
NIBCNT	New International Biblical Commentary on the New Testament

NICNT	New International Commentary on the New Testament
NIGTC	New International Greek Testament Commentary
NIDNTTE	Silva, Moisés, ed. *New International Dictionary of New Testament Theology and Exegesis*. 2nd ed. 5 vols. Grand Rapids: Zondervan, 2014.
NIDOTTE	VanGemeren, Willem A., ed. *New International Dictionary of Old Testament Theology and Exegesis*. 5 vols. Grand Rapids: Zondervan, 1997.
NIVAC	The NIV Application Commentary
NovT	*Novum Testamentum*
NovTSup	Supplements to Novum Testamentum
NTD	Das Neue Testament Deutsch
NTL	New Testament Library
NTM	New Testament Message
NTS	*New Testament Studies*
NTTSD	New Testament Tools, Studies, and Documents
ODCC	Cross, F. L., and E. A. Livingstone, eds. *The Oxford Dictionary of the Christian Church*. 3rd ed. Oxford: Oxford University Press, 1997.
OTP	Old Testament Pseudepigrapha
PNTC	The Pillar New Testament Commentary
PVTG	Pseudepigrapha Veteris Testamenti Graece
SHBC	Smyth & Helwys Bible Commentary
SNTSU	Studien zum Neuen Testament und seiner Umwelt
SP	Sacra Pagina
SR	*Studies in Religion*
StBibLit	Studies in Biblical Literature (Lang)
SwJT	*Southwestern Journal of Theology*
TAM	Tituli Asiae Minoris
TAPA	*Transactions of the American Philological Association*
TEH	Theologische Existenz heute
TENTS	Texts and Editions for New Testament Study
THKNT	Theologischer Handkommentar zum Neuen Testament
TJ	*Trinity Journal*
TKNT	Theologischer Kommentar zum Neuen Testament
TLG	*Thesaurus Linguae Graecae*

TLNT	Spicq, Ceslas. *Theological Lexicon of the New Testament*. Translated and edited by James D. Ernest. 3 vols. Peabody, MA: Hendrickson, 1994.
TNTC	Tyndale New Testament Commentaries
TZ	*Theologische Zeitschrift*
UBSGNT[5]	Aland, Barbara, Kurt Aland, Johannes Karavidopoulos, Carlo M. Martini, and Bruce Metzger, eds. *The Greek New Testament*. 5th ed. Institute for New Testament Textual Research. Stuttgart: United Bible Societies, 2014.
USQR	*Union Seminary Quarterly Review*
WBC	Word Biblical Commentary
WTJ	*Westminster Theological Journal*
WUNT	Wissenschaftliche Untersuchungen zum Neuen Testament
ZECNT	Zondervan Exegetical Commentary on the New Testament

1

History of Research

General Introduction

Paul instructed God's church in Corinth, "Women in the churches are to be silent [σιγάτωσαν], for it is not permitted for them to speak, but let them be in submission, just as also the law says. And if they want to learn anything, let them ask their own husbands at home, for it is shameful for a woman to speak in church" (1 Cor 14:34–35).[1] This book will argue that Paul's intended meaning in 1 Cor 14:34–35 is consistent with the context of 1 Corinthians and the rest of Pauline theology and practice. Some scholars have claimed that the passage is inconsistent with the rest of Paul's writing and practice. This study will primarily focus on the meaning of σιγάω in order to prove consistency.

Chapter One will show the need for this study and the history of research. The history of research will be divided into literary, historical, and theological interpretations of 1 Cor 14:34–35.

Chapter Two will explore the semantic range of σιγάω, including literary arguments in favor of consistency. First, there will be a review of lexical works and dictionaries to discover how they take the term in 1 Cor 14:34. Second, this

---

1   All Scripture translations are my own except where noted.

study will broaden to usage in ancient Greek literature (narrowed by date and priority given to works closest in time to the New Testament). Third, the usage of σιγάω will be discussed throughout the New Testament. Finally, this chapter will show how σιγάω and the silencing of women in the church in 1 Cor 14:34 is consistent with Paul's other comments in 1 Cor 14:26–40 (men and women speaking); 12:11 (the work of the Spirit); and 11:5 (women praying and prophesying). This chapter will be based upon the data in the Appendix with hundreds of occurrences of σιγάω in Greek literature that are in closest proximity to the New Testament. These occurrences will assist in reexamining the context of 1 Corinthians itself.

Chapter Three will compare Paul's words with the Greco-Roman context of women's education and speech. This chapter will explore the historical and cultural arguments, and how they impact a consistent reading and application of Paul's view on women. Concerning methodology, scholars do not always explain how they are consistent in applying background studies with other NT passages in the same way they apply background to gender passages. Chapter Three will attempt to prove three points: (1) Paul gave his instructions within a diverse historical context; (2) men and women were both creating problems in Corinth; and (3) a basis of Paul's instructions is the OT law and not culture. Chapter Three will question the argument that Paul was simply following cultural convention.

Chapter Four will argue for the consistency of 1 Cor 14:34–35 with Pauline theology and practice. This chapter will demonstrate how the passage fits within Paul's theological principles (in Gal 3:28 and 1 Tim 2:9–14) and Paul's practice (in Acts 16:11–16; Rom 16:1–7; Phil 4:2–3; and Col 4:15). Attention to each individual context will show the uniqueness of each passage instead of their contradictions. Paul's use of silence coheres with his overall view of women's participation in the church in his other letters.

The Appendix will list the occurrences of σιγάω in Greek literature that were selected in Chapter Two for review. While not an exhaustive list, the Appendix will bring much needed data to light in order to facilitate additional discussion.

A new look at 1 Cor 14:34–35 is necessary because many scholars assume the passage is inconsistent with the rest of 1 Corinthians and Paul's other letters. This apparent inconsistency is typically argued in relation to literary, historical, and theological arguments. Some writers assume silence is an absolute prohibition in order to create an inconsistency. The range of uses for σιγάω will help explore this question and create some controls on the discussion.

Richard Hays makes his text-critical decisions, in part, on literary and theological arguments concerning inconsistency:

One of the strongest reasons for regarding these verses as an interpolation is that their demand for women to remain silent in the assembly stands in glaring contradiction to 11:2–16, in which Paul teaches that women may in fact pray and prophesy in church as long as they keep their heads appropriately covered.... Furthermore, all the other available evidence indicates that women played an active role in preaching, teaching, and prophesying in the early Pauline communities.[2]

Similarly, Philip B. Payne writes concerning his work on Vaticanus, "This [interpolation theory] is important theologically since it offers a resolution to the notorious difficulty of reconciling vv. 34–35 with Paul's many affirmations of women in vocal ministry and their equal standing with men in Christ."[3] Text-critical discussions are often framed in the context of literary arguments.

Concerning the surrounding literary context of 1 Cor 14:34–35, Joseph Fitzmyer writes (concerning verse 36 also): "These three verses seem to be a self-contained unit, but because they deal with women speaking in cultic gatherings, they have only a general connection with what precedes and follows."[4] Fitzmyer holds to this position despite giving some specific examples of how the context does connect together (e.g., via silence and learning).[5] Likewise, Andreas Lindemann says, "It is clear at any rate that the two rhetorical questions in v. 36 differ stylistically from vv. 34–35, to the extent that the 2nd person plural is used here again (cf. v. 31)."[6] Lindemann's argument is part of his discussion of interpolation. D. W. Odell-Scott writes, "Clearly, the claim made in verses 34 and 35 that women should keep silent in the churches as a sign of their subordination to their husbands conflicts, and in some cases, contradicts what Paul has said elsewhere in First Corinthians (7:4, and 11:11) and other canonical Pauline epistles (Galatians 3:28) regarding the status of women."[7] G. Zuntz makes a similar argument: "Some scholars regard it [1 Cor 14:33b–35] as a Pauline addition;

---

2 Richard B. Hays, *First Corinthians*, IBC (Louisville: John Knox, 1997), 246.
3 Philip B. Payne, "Vaticanus Distigme-obelos Symbols Marking Added Text, Including 1 Corinthians 14.34–35," *NTS* 63 (2017): 606. Payne states this claim again in his conclusion on p. 625.
4 Joseph A. Fitzmyer, S. J., *First Corinthians: A New Translation with Introduction and Commentary*, AB 32 (London: Yale University Press, 2008), 529.
5 Fitzmyer, *First Corinthians*, 528.
6 Andreas Lindemann, *Der erste Korintherbrief*, HNT 9 (Tübingen: Mohr Siebeck, 2000), 320, writes, "Deutlich ist jedenfalls, daß die zweifache rhetorische Frage in V. 36 stilistisch von V. 34.35 abweicht, insofern hier wieder die 2. Pers. Plur. verwendet ist (vgl. V. 31)."
7 D. W. Odell-Scott, "Editorial Dilemma: The Interpolation of 1 Cor 14:34–35 in the Western Manuscripts of D, G and 88," *BTB* 30 (2000): 68.

but the material contradiction with xi.2 ff. lends probability to the view that the passage is not original."[8]

Brian Capper is representative of scholars who see inconsistency between 1 Cor 14:34–35 and the rest of Pauline theology and practice:

> The content and approach of these passages [1 Cor 14:33–36 and 1 Tim 2:11–12] appears drastically to compromise the consistency of the New Testament witness concerning the proper role of women in the worship and leadership of the Christian assembly. The leadership roles of women such as the house-church leaders Nympha (Colossians 4:15) and the patroness-deacon/servant Phoebe (Rom 16:1–2) seem clear to most contemporary interpreters of the New Testament. Similarly, Junia, who appears with Andronicus as kin to Paul and of note amongst the apostles at Rom 16:7, is now frequently granted status as a woman apostle.[9]

These representative scholars clearly show the need to demonstrate consistency across a broad spectrum of issues if 1 Cor 14:34–35 is Pauline. It is necessary to ask if specific New Testament texts are contradictory or complementary. Some assumptions will need to be reexamined. It has become common to assume a definition of silence rather than to defend one.

There has not been any exhaustive study of 1 Cor 14:34–35 and the meaning of σιγάω. This study will be the first time a systematic analysis of σιγάω is created as background to interpreting 1 Corinthians. A quick TLG search provides more than 5,700 occurrences of σιγάω in Greek literature. It is necessary to analyze a representative sample of ancient texts to see how authors expected readers to understand σιγάω in context. No one has provided a comprehensive study that demonstrates consistency throughout 1 Corinthians and Pauline literature in light of what we know about the semantic range of σιγάω. Furthermore, there is a pressing need to answer in detail the common charge of inconsistency based upon the assumption that silence is absolute. When silence is contextually defined, then it opens the way to proving consistency. This study will demonstrate that inaccurate definitions of silence are the cause of the inconsistency.

---

8   G. Zuntz, *The Text of the Epistles: A Disquisition upon the Corpus Paulinum*, The Schweich Lectures of the British Academy 1946 (London: Oxford University Press, 1953), 17.
9   Brian J. Capper, "To Keep Silent, Ask Husbands at Home, and not to Have Authority over Men. Part I (I Corinthians 14:33–36 and I Timothy 2:11–12): The Transition from Gathering in Private to Meeting in Public Space in Second Generation Christianity and the Exclusion of Women from Leadership of the Public Assembly," *TZ* 61.2 (2005): 114–15.

There are some dissertations that relate to 1 Cor 14:34–35 or to the complementarian/egalitarian debate.[10] There are other dissertations on women in the Pauline letters in general.[11] Anna Sui Hluan has written on the interpretation of 1 Cor 14:34–35 for a Myanmar context.[12] There are a few articles that relate to the topic but no full-length treatments. Benjamin Merkle has answered the apparent inconsistency between 1 Cor 11:8–9 and 1 Tim 2:13–14.[13] Since these two passages are not the only verses in dispute, there is a need to broaden the discussion of consistency to include 1 Cor 14:34–35. Wayne Grudem's article distinguishes between the definitions of prophecy and teaching in order to argue for consistency in Paul.[14] He interprets silence as "the women should keep silence during the evaluation of prophecies."[15] Adam Hensley argues for consistency of silence, speech, and submission within 1 Cor 14:26–40, as well as Chapters Eleven to Fourteen in general.[16] He concludes that "the key to understanding Paul's argument lies in recognizing that evaluating prophecy is itself prophetic speech."[17] There is a need to expand the search for consistency in light of the number of scholars who appeal to additional reasons for inconsistency.

---

[10] Marguerite Woodruff, "Underlying Factors Contributing to Paul's Teaching Concerning Women" (PhD diss., Southwestern Baptist Theological Seminary, 1950); William Edward Richardson, "Liturgical Order and Glossolalia: 1 Corinthians 14:26c–33a and its Implications" (PhD diss., Andrews University Seventh-day Adventist Theological Seminary, 1983); Victor Alan Slayman, "1 Corinthians 14:33b–36—The Debate: Biblical Scholarship and the Canon" (PhD diss., Lutheran Theological Seminary at Gettysburg, 1989); Debra Bendel Daniels, "Evangelical Feminism: The Egalitarian-Complementarian Debate" (PhD diss., University of Wisconsin-Madison, 2003); Margaret Elizabeth Köstenberger, "A Critique of Feminist and Egalitarian Hermeneutics and Exegesis: With Special Focus on Jesus' Approach to Women" (ThD diss., University of South Africa, 2006); Clint Miller, "A Comparative Analysis of Wayne Grudem's Complementarian Position and Gordon Fee's Egalitarian Position within the Gender Debate" (PhD diss., New Orleans Baptist Theological Seminary, 2011).

[11] E.g., Leonce F. Rambau, "Paul and His Co-Workers: Equality in Pauline Letters" (PhD diss., The University of Notre Dame, 2014).

[12] Anna Sui Hluan, "Silence in Translation: Interpreting 1 Corinthians 14:34–35 in Myanmar" (PhD diss., University of Otago, 2017).

[13] Benjamin L. Merkle, "Paul's Arguments from Creation in 1 Corinthians 11:8–9 and 1 Timothy 2:13–14: An Apparent Inconsistency Answered," *JETS* 49.3 (2006): 527–48. He argues that women do not have to wear head coverings but that women are not to teach or have authority over a man, writing, "The reason for this distinction is that in 1 Corinthians 11 Paul only indirectly uses the argument from creation to affirm head coverings for women. The direct application of his reasoning is to show that creation affirms gender and role distinctions between men and women—and in the Corinthian context that distinction needed to be upheld through head coverings" (p. 528).

[14] Wayne Grudem, "Prophecy—Yes, But Teaching—No: Paul's Consistent Advocacy of Women's Participation without Governing Authority," *JETS* 30.1 (1987): 11–23.

[15] Grudem, "Prophecy—Yes, But Teaching—No," 23.

[16] Adam D. Hensley, "σιγαω, λαλεω, and ὑποτασσω in 1 Corinthians 14:34 in Their Literary and Rhetorical Context," *JETS* 55.2 (2012): 343–64. He uses the phrase "a rhetorically coherent argument."

[17] Hensley, "σιγαω, λαλεω, and ὑποτασσω," 360.

History of Research

First Corinthians 14:34–35 has had a varied history of research.[18] There is no major consensus regarding how to understand Paul's instructions.[19] In fact, there is not a consensus that Paul even wrote these verses. This section will categorize the various views especially related to the meaning of silence and the charge of inconsistency. The categories will be divided into literary, historical, and theological arguments. The history of interpretation below will be limited to those writers who argue for inconsistency and/or limit the application to the first century. Many views on 1 Cor 14:34–35 are defended on the basis of avoiding an apparent inconsistency.

Literary Context

This section will consider literary arguments involving the charge of inconsistency. First, many scholars argue that someone later inserted the text after Paul wrote the letter (interpolation). Second, the text may be a quotation of the Corinthians themselves. Third, the text contradicts what Paul says elsewhere. Fourth, αἱ γυναῖκες should be translated as married women only, limiting the application of the text.

First Corinthians 14:34–35 Was Inserted by a Later Editor (Interpolation)

There are several writers who state that 1 Cor 14:34–35 (or some variation of the surrounding verses) is a non-Pauline interpolation. They appeal to the manuscript tradition and/or additional literary arguments.[20] E. Earl Ellis has a related

---

18 For a basic overview of the history of interpretation from ancient to modern times, see J. Carl Laney, "Gender Based Boundaries for Gathered Congregations: An Interpretive History of 1 Corinthians 14:34–35," *JBMW* 7.1 (2002): 4–13. Laney intentionally passes over the Middle Ages.

19 Marion L. Soards simply reviews the interpretive options and writes, "One finally cannot decide from the evidence available which of the several suggestions for interpretation is absolutely correct" (*1 Corinthians*, Understanding the Bible Commentary Series [Grand Rapids: Baker, 1999], 307).

20 Johannes Weiss, *Der erste Korintherbrief* (Göttingen: Vandenhoeck & Ruprecht, 1910), xl–xli, 342; Gottfried Fitzer, *Das Weib schweige in der Gemeinde: Über den unpaulinischen Charakter der mulier-taceat-Verse in 1. Korinther 14*, TEH 110 (München: Chr. Kaiser, 1963), 35; Hans Conzelmann, *1 Corinthians*, ed. George W. MacRae, S. J., trans. James W. Leitch (Philadelphia: Fortress, 1975), 246; Gerhard Dautzenberg, *Urchristliche Prophetie: Ihre Erforschung, ihre Voraussetzungen im Judentum und ihre Struktur im ersten Korintherbrief*, BWANT (Stuttgart: W. Kohlhammer, 1975), 270–73; Lindemann, *Der erste Korintherbrief*, 320–21; Hans-Josef Klauck, *1. Korintherbrief*, NEchtB (Würzburg: Echter, 1984), 105–6; Christophe Senft, *La première Épitre de Saint Paul aux Corinthiens*, 2nd ed., CNT 7 (Genève: Labor et Fides, 1990), 182–83; David G. Horrell, *The Social Ethos of the Corinthian Correspondence: Interests and Ideology from 1 Corinthians to 1 Clement* (Edinburgh: T&T Clark, 1996), 194–95; Wolfgang Schrage, *Der erste Brief an die Korinther*, EKKNT (Zürich: Benziger,

view where the verses were ("more likely") written into the margin of the autograph and made its way into the manuscripts later.[21] Roy Ciampa and Brian Rosner ask the question, "With thirty-six words it would be an extraordinarily long 'marginal note'! One wonders how it could fit in the margin of an epistolary papyrus."[22] Interpolation and textual criticism will be explored more below and in Chapter Two.

Gordon Fee is often cited concerning the textual history of 1 Cor 14:34–35 and the interpolation theory. He argues that taking the verses as authentic cannot explain how or why the verses are found in the two locations in the manuscript tradition.[23] He also argues, "The three or four quite non-Pauline moments in this passage, plus the fact that it is otherwise unrelated to anything else in the context, should thus probably settle this issue as a historical phenomenon."[24] However, he later writes, "It is simply a modern invention that someone in the early church would have been troubled by the *placement* of these words in the text, since all who do comment on it never speak to its placement as a difficulty."[25] In other words, when Fee is arguing for interpolation, he appeals to the verses as not relating to their context in any way. Then, when arguing against someone simply moving the verses from the original location to after verse 40, he readily admits that early interpreters had no difficulty with this text in its context.

Jerome Murphy-O'Connor is another proponent of the interpolation theory. He discusses several verses throughout 1 Corinthians as possible interpolations but decides definitively on a phrase (τὸ μὴ ὑπὲρ ἃ γέγραπται) in 4:6 and all of 14:34–35.[26] Suggested interpolations that were not "buttressed by convincing

---

1999), 3:481; Catherine Clark Kroeger, "1 Corinthians," in *The IVP Women's Bible Commentary*, ed. Catherine Clark Kroeger and Mary J. Evans (Downers Grove, IL: InterVarsity Press, 2002), 663; J. Paul Sampley, "The First Letter to the Corinthians," NIB (Nashville: Abingdon, 2002), 10:971; Luise Schottroff, *Der erste Brief an die Gemeinde in Korinth*, TKNT 7 (Stuttgart: Kohlhammer, 2013), 283.

21 E. Earle Ellis, "The Silenced Wives of Corinth (1 Cor 14:34–35)," in *New Testament Textual Criticism and Its Significance for Exegesis: In Honour of Bruce Metzger*, ed. Eldon Jay Epp and Gordon D. Fee (Oxford: Clarendon, 1981), 219. Ryan Donald Wettlaufer places interpolation under the category of conjectural emendation by referring to the interpolation theory arguments found in the commentaries of Richard Hays and Gordon Fee (*No Longer Written: The Use of Conjectural Emendation in the Restoration of the Text of the New Testament, the Epistle of James as a Case Study*, NTTSD 44 [Leiden: Brill, 2013], 3–4).

22 Roy E. Ciampa and Brian S. Rosner, *The First Letter to the Corinthians*, PNTC (Grand Rapids: Eerdmans, 2010), 719.

23 Gordon Fee, *The First Epistle to the Corinthians*, rev. ed., NICNT (Grand Rapids: Eerdmans, 2014), 780–81.

24 Fee, *The First Epistle to the Corinthians*, 781.

25 Fee, *The First Epistle to the Corinthians*, 783 (italics original).

26 Jerome Murphy-O'Connor, "Interpolations in 1 Corinthians," *CBQ* 48 (1986): 81–94.

arguments," according to O'Connor, are 2:6–16; 6:14; 11:3–16; 15:31–32; and 15:44b–48.[27] By contrast, he writes about 1 Cor 14:34–35: "Apart from the manifest contradictions, the principle reason for denying the Pauline authorship of 14:34–35 is the invocation of the authority of the Law to found a moral attitude."[28]

Richard Hays argues for an interpolation based upon a few cumulative factors. In addition to the questions of the manuscript tradition, he claims 1 Cor 14:34–35 is inconsistent with (1) 1 Cor 11:2–16; (2) women in Pauline communities in Rom 16:1–4, 7 and Phil 4:2–3; and (3) how Paul typically refers to church practice and the use of the law.[29] Regarding church practice, Hays writes, "Nowhere else in 1 Corinthians does Paul shift in this way to generalized instruction for the churches at large; indeed, this makes no sense at all from a rhetorical point of view in a letter written to a specific congregation, but it does make sense rhetorically if the passage was added at a later time when the letter was being circulated for the guidance of a wider circle of communities."[30] It is uncertain why Hays makes such a claim in light of 1 Cor 11:16, where Paul does, in fact, appeal to other churches.

Philip Payne makes different arguments for the omission of 1 Cor 14:34–35 throughout his writings. First, he discusses manuscript 88 in relation to a double slash that a scribe placed between 1 Cor 14:40 and the following 1 Cor 14:34–35 (the slash is in the text itself with the words and not in the margin).[31] Manuscript 88 has vv. 34–35 placed after v. 40, but the slash marks show that the scribe of manuscript 88 believed, according to Payne, that the verses were supposed to be after v. 33. Payne then makes an extended argument for how manuscript 88 is evidence for an omission. The scribe of manuscript 88 copied from a non-Western text. Since "no non-Western Greek manuscript supporting this position [vv. 34–35 after v. 40] is known,"[32] then the manuscript must have originally omitted vv. 34–35. He emphasizes this type of logic in his conclusion: "The one other possibility, derivation from a non-Western manuscript with vv. 34–35 after

---

27 O'Connor, "Interpolations in 1 Corinthians," 94.
28 O'Connor, "Interpolations in 1 Corinthians," 91.
29 Hays, *First Corinthians*, 245–47. Horrell, *The Social Ethos of the Corinthian Correspondence*, 194–95, argues in a similar manner.
30 Hays, *First Corinthians*, 246.
31 Philip B. Payne, "MS. 88 as Evidence for a Text Without 1 Cor 14:34–35," *NTS* 44 (1998): 152–58. I agree with Payne who writes, "The words on each side of this double slash are much farther apart than any other adjacent words on this page, so the original scribe must have inserted the double slash before writing vv. 34–5" (p. 152).
32 Payne, "MS. 88 as Evidence for a Text Without 1 Cor 14:34–35," 155.

v. 40, requires the existence of a reading which no surviving non-Western Greek manuscript supports."[33] However, he does not state in his article that no surviving Greek manuscript ever omits 1 Cor 14:34–35.[34]

Second, Payne discusses Vaticanus and argues that the bar + umlaut in the margin shows that the verses were originally omitted (even though the verses are in the actual text).[35] He argues that the bar + umlaut (what he calls distigme-obelos) should be taken together as one symbol. This combined symbol is a reference to "added text."[36] He distinguishes this symbol from a regular paragraph marker. Though he does compare other passages with this symbol, he writes, "1 Cor[inthians] 14.34–35, the text at the gap following the only distigme-obelos in the *Vaticanus* epistles, is the only added text marked by a distigme-obelos to be found in the *Vaticanus* text."[37] Jennifer Shack considers Vaticanus, Fuldensis, and manuscript 88 and concludes, contrary to Payne, that these manuscripts contained 1 Cor 14:34–35.[38]

Another piece of evidence brought forward by proponents of an interpolation is Paul's use of the law.[39] Fee argues that the use of the law in 1 Cor 14:34 is different from Paul's use for the following reasons: (1) there is no specific citation; (2) he never appeals to the law in an absolute manner; and (3) the law itself does not teach women to be silent.[40]

---

33 Payne, "MS. 88 as Evidence for a Text Without 1 Cor 14:34–35," 156.
34 Philip B. Payne does reference this kind of critique in "The Text-Critical Function of the Umlauts in Vaticanus, with Special Attention to 1 Corinthians 14:34–35: A Response to J. Edward Miller," *JSNT* 27.1 (2004): 105–12. His response to Miller shows that he does not take the same nuance in his discussion of texts with vv. 34–35 following v. 40: "Miller states regarding 1 Cor. 14.34–35, 'no known manuscripts omit the passage altogether'. This is factually correct if by 'manuscript' one means documents containing this portion of 1 Cor. 14 and does not mean the different texts contained within the same document. Within textual criticism, however, lists of manuscripts supporting different readings routinely distinguish B* from B^c and sometimes with B'''" (p. 110).
35 Payne, "The Text-Critical Function of the Umlauts in Vaticanus," 105–12. So also Payne, "Vaticanus Distigme-obelos Symbols Marking Added Text," 604–25.
36 Payne's comparison with the LXX and MT is not a perfect parallel for his argument given the different text-critical issues involved between OT and NT textual criticism. It is much easier to argue for an "added text" with the LXX issues than with Greek NT manuscripts. With the LXX there are actual Hebrew manuscripts for comparison, whereas Payne has to speculate regarding what the exemplars would have been with NT manuscripts.
37 Payne, "Vaticanus Distigme-obelos Symbols Marking Added Text," 621 (italics original).
38 Jennifer Shack, "A Text without 1 Corinthians 14.34–35? Not According to the Manuscript Evidence," *JGRChJ* 10 (2014): 90–112. Bruce M. Metzger, *A Textual Commentary on the Greek New Testament*, 2nd ed. (Stuttgart: United Bible Societies, 1994), 499, sees Codex Fuldensis as "ambiguous."
39 Jerome Murphy-O'Connor, *1 Corinthians*, NTM 10 (Wilmington, DE: Michael Glazier, 1979), 133.
40 Fee, *The First Epistle to the Corinthians*, 791; see also Neal M. Flanagan and Edwina H. Snyder, "Did Paul Put Down Women in 1 Cor 14:34–35?" *Foundations* 24.3 (1981): 217.

First Corinthians 14:34–35 is a Corinthian Slogan

There are a number of scholars who take the silencing of women to be Paul's quotation of a Corinthian slogan, which Paul then refutes (often assuming an absolute definition of silence).[41] If correct, this theory would remove any apparent inconsistency. However, the issue here is the creation of an inconsistency in order to appeal to a Corinthian slogan as the solution.

Kirk MacGregor contends, "1 Cor 14:33b–38 is best understood as Paul's quotation and subsequent refutation of the Corinthian men's position that women ought to be silent in the assemblies, a position which originated in the Judaizing faction of the church."[42] MacGregor's reasons are (1) a comparison of ἤ in 1 Cor 14:36 with 1:13; 6:16; 9:6, 8, 10; 11:22, and then 6:2, 9, 19; 10:22; 11:13; (2) μόνος in 14:36; (3) that Corinthian slogans appear elsewhere (according to MacGregor, in 6:12–13; 7:1–2; 8:1, 8; 10:23); (4) it would be inconsistent with 1 Cor 11:3–16 (cf. 14:26, 31); (5) usage in the Apostolic Fathers; and (6) taking the "law" in 14:34 as Jewish oral law. He then says that Paul's theology sets people free from the oral Torah.[43] Thus MacGregor concludes, "Among the Corinthians, rather, it seems clear that 1 Cor 14:33b–35 originated in the Judaizing faction of their church, which stressed obedience to the oral Torah as necessary for salvation and which Paul vehemently opposed."[44] What is key to MacGregor's argument is the criteria upon which he is able to identify a Corinthian slogan. These criteria are "an introducer of new discourse governing the Corinthians quotation and an interjecting term governing the Pauline refutation."[45]

Philip Payne has written a response to MacGregor's claims.[46] Payne himself takes the view that 1 Cor 14:34–35 was a marginal gloss later inserted into the text. He argues against many of MacGregor's claims to support the Corinthian slogan theory. Payne's point-by-point reasoning is more accurate than MacGregor's, even if Payne's overall conclusion is not persuasive. Payne does not see 1 Cor 14:34–35 as the same type of sentences as the other slogans

---

41 Flanagan and Snyder, "Did Paul Put Down Women in 1 Cor 14:34–35?" 218–19; Fitzmyer, *First Corinthians*, 530; Raymond F. Collins, *First Corinthians*, ed. Daniel J. Harrington, S. J., SP 7 (Collegeville, MN: Liturgical, 1999), 517, 522; J. M. Holmes, *Text in a Whirlwind: A Critique of Four Exegetical Devices at 1 Timothy 2.9–15*, JSNTSup 196 (Sheffield: Sheffield Academic, 2000), 237–38.

42 Kirk R. MacGregor, "1 Corinthians 14:33b–38 as a Pauline Quotation-Refutation Device," *Priscilla Papers* 32.1 (2018): 23.

43 MacGregor, "1 Corinthians 14:33b–38," 24–27.

44 MacGregor, "1 Corinthians 14:33b–38," 27.

45 MacGregor, "1 Corinthians 14:33b–38," 26. For seven reasons why the passage is not a Corinthian slogan, see Craig Blomberg, *1 Corinthians*, NIVAC (Grand Rapids: Zondervan, 1994), 280.

46 Philip B. Payne, "Is 1 Corinthians 14:34–35 a Marginal Comment or a Quotation? A Response to Kirk MacGregor," *Priscilla Papers* 33.2 (2019): 24–30.

mentioned in 1 Corinthians. He also refers to manuscript tradition as opposed to MacGregor's reliance upon the latest Greek New Testament editions in where to make the break between 1 Cor 14:33b and 1 Cor 14:34.[47] Payne refers to the 46 occurrences of ἤ in 1 Corinthians to dispute MacGregor's view.[48] He also disputes the male-only interpretation of μόνος by taking it generically. And finally Payne recognizes that the Apostolic Fathers cited 1 Cor 14:34–35 as Paul's view.

First Corinthians 14:34–35 Contradicts Paul Elsewhere

Scholars appeal to various references in 1 Corinthians in order to state that the text of 1 Cor 14:34–35 contradicts Paul elsewhere. These claims can be considered in four categories. First, the text silences women in an absolute manner, and elsewhere Paul does not do so. Second, the text interrupts the context of 1 Cor 14:26–40. Third, it contradicts the Spirit's gifting in 1 Cor 12:11. And fourth, it contradicts women praying and prophesying in 1 Cor 11:5. Each of these positions will be described below.

Marlene Crüsemann takes silence, along with all of vv. 34–35, as "a comprehensive prohibition of public speaking, applying to all Christian women."[49] She makes her argument by appealing to "the double absolute use of the verb λαλεῖν ('to speak')."[50] Then she appeals to the other types of speech in 1 Corinthians 14 and claims that the author is restricting women from these types of speech as well.[51] F. W. Grosheide argues for an absolute restriction on any speaking of women in the worship service. He states that Paul uses the general word for "speak" and so it applies more broadly. He explains that 1 Corinthians 11 where women pray and prophesy does not take place in "official services of the church."[52]

Philip Payne assumes an absolute silence when he writes, "Verses 34–35 silence women in church three times without any qualification."[53] He argues that

---

47 On this point, Payne, "Is 1 Corinthians 14:34–35 a Marginal Comment or a Quotation?" 24, gives seven reasons why the break should happen at 1 Cor 14:34.
48 Depending on the source and textual criticism, the actual number of ἤ may vary slightly. Andreas Köstenberger and Raymond Bouchoc list 49 occurrences (*The Book Study Concordance of the Greek New Testament* [Nashville: Broadman & Holman, 2003], 927).
49 Marlene Crüsemann, "Irredeemably Hostile to Women: Anti-Jewish Elements in the Exegesis of the Dispute about Women's Right to Speak (1 Cor. 14.34–35)," *JSNT* 79 (2000): 21. Cf. p. 20 n. 5 and the "absolute use of λαλεῖν in 1 Cor. 14.34–35." On p. 23, she does see σιγάω in 1 Cor 14:28, 30 as a "temporary silence."
50 Crüsemann, "Irredeemably Hostile to Women," 22.
51 Crüsemann, "Irredeemably Hostile to Women," 22. She takes the verses as an interpolation.
52 F. W. Grosheide, *Commentary on the First Epistles to the Corinthians*, NICNT (Grand Rapids: Eerdmans, 1953), 342.
53 Payne, "Vaticanus Distigme-obelos Symbols Marking Added Text," 617. So also Fee, *The First Epistle to the Corinthians*, 785.

silence would contradict the "all" speaking in 1 Corinthians 14:5, 24 (3x), 26, 31, and that a qualified silence against "disruptive chatter" or "judging prophecies" goes against verse 35.[54]

Scholars occasionally argue for inconsistency based on the immediate literary context. Fee writes concerning 1 Cor 14:34–35, "Thus, this intrusion simply lacks any genuine correspondence with either the larger context (chaps. 12–14) or the immediate argument (vv. 26–40)."[55] Paul writes in 1 Cor 14:26, "What then brothers? When you come together, each one has a psalm, teaching, revelation, tongue, or interpretation? All things must be done for edification." Philip Payne includes 1 Cor 14:26 in his list of how to "reconcile" certain verses with 1 Cor 14:34–35.[56] He gives his reasoning, "Furthermore, 1 Cor 14:26; Col 3:16; and 2 Tim 2:2 describe teaching as an activity enjoined on believers in general."[57] Kirk MacGregor quotes 1 Cor 14:26 along with 14:31 (note its three-fold use of πᾶς), and states, "Further, 14:33b–35 contradicts Paul's central point in 1 Corinthians 14 that in the church everyone, regardless of gender, should be instructed by everyone else."[58] Christophe Senft says that "the expression 'the churches of the saints' is foreign to Paul."[59] Other commentators take 1 Cor 14:34–35 as a "digression,"[60] but not all agree with this assessment.[61] Scholars also question the masculine use of μόνος in 1 Cor 14:36 (ἢ εἰς ὑμᾶς μόνους κατήντησεν;).[62]

Paul's prohibition concerning women is dismissed by some writers as inconsistent with the gifting of the Spirit (writers assume varying definitions of silence when employing this argument).[63] In 1 Cor 12:11 Paul makes a general statement about the Spirit's sovereign will in distributing spiritual gifts to individuals in the church. Hays comments, "Similarly, with respect to the issue of women's public leadership, there are good theological reasons to insist that we should be

---

54 Payne, "Vaticanus Distigme-obelos Symbols Marking Added Text," 617. He also mentions 1 Corinthians 11 and women prophesying (p. 625).
55 Fee, *The First Epistle to the Corinthians*, 785.
56 Philip B. Payne, *Man and Woman, One in Christ: An Exegetical and Theological Study of Paul's Letters* (Grand Rapids: Zondervan, 2009), 219. So also Fee, *The First Epistle to the Corinthians*, 785.
57 Payne, *Man and Woman*, 327.
58 MacGregor, "1 Corinthians 14:33b–38," 26.
59 Senft, *La première épitre de Saint Paul aux Corinthiens*, 183, "L'expression «les Églises des saints» est étrangére á Paul."
60 Craig S. Keener, *1–2 Corinthians*, NCBC (Cambridge: Cambridge University Press, 2005), 118; Ciampa and Rosner, *The First Letter to the Corinthians*, 731.
61 E.g., Ben Witherington III, *Conflict and Community in Corinth: A Socio-Rhetorical Commentary on 1 and 2 Corinthians* (Grand Rapids: Eerdmans, 1995), 288, writes, "Vv. 34f. are, in any case, definitely not a digression."
62 E.g., Flanagan and Snyder, "Did Paul Put Down Women in 1 Cor 14:34–36?" 217.
63 Collins, *First Corinthians*, 515.

guided by Paul's vision of Christian worship in which the gifts of the Spirit are given to *all members of the church, men and women alike*, for the building up of the community."[64] Ben Witherington states directly that "leadership was to be determined primarily by who was called and gifted by the Spirit, and not at all by gender or cultural background."[65] Regardless of which verse one appeals to for the Spirit's work, these scholars must still show how verses on the Spirit do or do not relate to church leadership. First Corinthians 12:11 is one possible verse, but there are often more assumptions than reasoned argumentation when it comes to a synthesis of the New Testament on the Spirit and church leadership.

The apparent inconsistency with 1 Cor 11:5 may be the most-cited reason for dismissing the notion that women may be silenced in 1 Cor 14:34–35.[66] Paul writes in 1 Cor 11:5, "But every woman praying or prophesying with an uncovered head brings shame on her head." Since this statement presupposes that women do pray and prophesy in the church, then absolute silence would be a contradiction in 1 Cor 14:34–35. Jerome Murphy-O'Connor comments, "In the above exposition no notice has been taken of v. 34–35 which prohibit women to speak in church. The reason for this is that they were not written by Paul. If these verses are removed no violence is done to his argument. In fact it gains in clarity. Not only are they not integral to this section, but they contradict 11:4 [*sic*], 13 where Paul takes it for granted that women can speak in church and even assume a leadership role."[67] Jill Marshall contrasts 1 Cor 11:5 and 1 Cor 14:35–35: "I do not assume that Paul is always consistent in his thinking or in how he presents it [his thinking?]. For this reason, I highlight the difficulties in the argument in [1 Cor] 11:2–16 and the possibility that Paul revises his ἐκκλησία as body of Christ

---

64 Hays, *First Corinthians*, 249 (italics original).
65 Witherington, *Conflict and Community in Corinth*, 290.
66 Examples of this common assumption include Lindemann, *Der erste Korintherbrief*, 321; Schottroff, *Der erste Brief an die Gemeinde in Korinth*, 283; Conzelmann *1 Corinthians*, 246; John K. Chow, *Patronage and Power: A Study of Social Networks in Corinth*, JSNTSup 75 (Sheffield: Sheffield Academic Press, 1992), 184 n. 1; Craig Keener, "Women's Education and Public Speech in Antiquity," *JETS* 50 (2007): 748; cautiously Martin Hasitschka, "Die Frauen in den Gemeinden sollen schweigen: 1 Kor 14,33b–36—Anweisung des Paulus zur rechten Ordnung im Gottesdienst," SNTSU 22 (1997): 47 n. 1 ("The interpolation hypothesis is not verifiable, certainly also not refutable"; "Die Hypothese der Interpolation ist nicht beweisbar, freilich auch nicht widerlegbar," p. 53); R. T. France calls the passage "puzzling," in part because of 1 Cor 11:5 (*Women in the Church's Ministry: A Test Case for Biblical Interpretation* [Grand Rapids: Eerdmans, 1995], 53, 55–56); Senft, *La première épitre de Saint Paul aux Corinthiens*, 182.
67 O'Connor, *1 Corinthians*, 133. Archibald Robertson and Alfred Plummer consider 1 Cor 11:5 "may be hypothetical," and so would avoid any possible contradiction with 14:34–35 (*A Critical and Exegetical Commentary on the First Epistle of St Paul to the Corinthians*, 2nd ed., ICC [Edinburgh: T&T Clark, 1953], 324–25).

and different modes of inspired speech."[68] She regularly refers to silence but does not seek to precisely define the term.[69] These claims will be reconsidered throughout Chapter Two, and responses will be given for each of them.

First Corinthians 14:34–35 Applies Only to Married Women

There are some interpreters who take the reference to women in 1 Cor 14:34–35 as referring only to wives.[70] Terence Paige argues that Paul addressed married women who were having casual conversations with people who were not their husbands. This speech to non-relatives could bring shame on an entire household.[71] Paige writes, "That some Christian women were spurning marital relations with their husbands, dispensing with the veil that marked them as modest and virtuous married women, and then having casual conversation with men who were neither husbands nor close relatives was all clearly material for scandal."[72] However, 1 Corinthians does not mention these "casual conversations" being an issue. The context of 1 Corinthians 14 is the public assembly and use of spiritual gifts.

Historical Context

Some scholars limit the application of 1 Cor 14:34–35 to only Corinth or the first century.[73] Some writers do so in general terms concerning the ancient world, and other writers focus on the situation at Corinth in particular. Regarding consistency, they question whether Paul simply followed cultural conventions and if today's culture renders the passage inapplicable (or at least applicable to both

---

68   Jill E. Marshall, *Women Praying and Prophesying in Corinth: Gender and Inspired Speech in First Corinthians*, WUNT 448 (Tübingen: Mohr Siebeck, 2017), 157; cf. 220. She later writes, "After [Paul] categorizes inspired speech and articulates the priority for order, he reverses his acceptance of women praying and prophesying" (p. 212).

69   See, e.g., Marshall, *Women Praying and Prophesying in Corinth*, 2.

70   Blomberg, *1 Corinthians*, 282; Elisabeth Schüssler Fiorenza, *In Memory of Her: A Feminist Theological Reconstruction of Christian Origins* (New York: Crossroad, 1983), 230–31; Robert Scott Nash, *1 Corinthians*, SHBC (Macon, GA: Smyth and Helwys, 2009), 381–82; Finny Philip, "1 Corinthians," in *South Asia Bible Commentary*, ed. Brian Wintle (Rajasthan, India: Open Door Publications, 2015), 1579; David E. Garland, *1 Corinthians*, BECNT (Grand Rapids: Baker Academic, 2003), 667.

71   Terence Paige, "The Social Matrix of Women's Speech at Corinth: The Context and Meaning of the Command to Silence in 1 Corinthians 14:33b–36," *BBR* 12.2 (2002): 217–42.

72   Paige, "The Social Matrix of Women's Speech at Corinth," 240.

73   Robertson and Plummer, *First Epistle of St Paul to the Corinthians*, 327; Ciampa and Rosner, *The First Letter to the Corinthians*, 729–30; Garland, *1 Corinthians*, 673; Carroll D. Osburn, "The Interpretation of 1 Cor. 14:34–35," in *Essays on Women in Earliest Christianity*, ed. Carroll D. Osburn (Eugene, OR: Wipf and Stock, 1993), 1:242.

male and female). For instance, Capper's position is ultimately a historical and cultural argument where Christians "seemed to demand the restriction of women's roles according to prevailing cultural ideals" (he references Plutarch's *Advice to Bride and Groom*).[74] Luise Schottroff does not think the passage belongs to Paul because it agrees with Greco-Roman ideas on women.[75] Three types of historical arguments are described below: the lack of women's education, restrictions on women's speech in public, and the female Corinthian problem.

Paul Silenced Women because of Their Lack of Education

Some scholars argue that women's education in antiquity was limited, which is why Paul specifically silenced women. Craig Keener explains his cultural interpretation as follows:

> More reasonably, women on average were less educated than men, an assertion that no one genuinely conversant with ancient literature would doubt. To be sure, one can collect examples of many educated women in antiquity (normally from wealthier families), but on average women were far less likely to be educated than men.... Most likely the passage addresses disruptive questions in an environment where silence was expected of new learners—which most women were. It also addresses a broader social context in which women were expected not to speak much with men to whom they were not related, as a matter of propriety.[76]

In his article a few years later, Keener explores the actual education of women in antiquity. He adds that women were silenced in 1 Cor 14:34–35 and 1 Tim 2:11–12 "due to first-century women as a rule having less access to education or public speech forums than men."[77] Keener gives examples of educated women, but he calls them exceptions.[78] He refers to Dio Chrysostom, who wrote, "In fact such

---

74 Brian J. Capper, "To Keep Silent, Ask Husbands at Home, and not to Have Authority over Men. Part II (I Corinthians 14:33–36 and I Timothy 2:11–12): The Transition from Gathering in Private to Meeting in Public Space in Second Generation Christianity and the Exclusion of Women from Leadership of the Public Assembly," *TZ* 61.4 (2005): 305; cf. 318–19.
75 Schottroff, *Der erste Brief an die Gemeinde in Korinth*, 283.
76 Craig S. Keener, "Learning in the Assemblies: 1 Corinthians 14:34–35," in *Discovering Biblical Equality: Complementarity without Hierarchy*, ed. Ronald W. Pierce and Rebecca Merrill Groothuis (Downers Grove, IL: InterVarsity Press, 2004), 169, 171. In addition to education, Keener includes "the church's witness in a tense social situation" as another possible reason for Paul's restriction on women; see Craig S. Keener, "Man and Woman," *DPL* 591. Keener also includes 1 Tim 2:9–14 within this educational argument in Craig S. Keener, *Paul, Women and Wives: Marriage and Women's Ministry in the Letters of Paul* (Peabody, MA: Hendrickson, 1992), 107–8.
77 Keener, "Women's Education and Public Speech in Antiquity," 748.
78 Keener, "Women's Education and Public Speech in Antiquity," 749–50.

an ornament [gold earrings] was suitable rather for girls and for sons of Lydians and Phrygians, whereas for sons of Greeks, especially since a god had given the command, nothing else was suitable but education and reason, for it is natural that those who get these blessings should prove to be good men and saviours of the state."[79] Jewish women would have learned in the home and synagogue but not in the schools.[80] Philosophers debated positive and negative arguments for women in education.[81] Keener notes the rarity of women teaching in public (not including inspired speech).[82] Similarly, Leon Morris interprets Paul's prohibition to be discussing "how women should learn (v. 35)." He states, "We must bear in mind that in the first century women were uneducated.... The Corinthian women should keep quiet in church if for no other reason than because they could have had little or nothing worth while to say."[83] Morris's interpretation does not carry the nuance of Keener's view where some women were actually educated.

Paul Silenced Women because of Cultural Restrictions on Speech in Public

Christopher Forbes provides an example of this category of interpretation. He writes, "There existed in the Graeco-Roman world in our period a strong prejudice against women speaking in public, and especially against their speaking to other women's husbands."[84] He cites Plutarch and Marcus Porcius Cato (via Livy), among other references, as "a highly suggestive background against which to interpret Paul's prohibition."[85] Ciampa and Rosner, then, attempt to apply this view to today in light of cultural differences between then and now: "It would be considered shameful for a woman to be restricted from open participation in public conversations."[86]

Paul Silenced Women because Only Women Were Causing Problems

Some writers argue that Paul would have applied his words to both men and women, but due to the historical reconstruction of the situation at Corinth—that is, that women were the problem—then Paul singled out women in this

---

79 Dio Chrysostom, *Ad Alexandrinos* 32.3; Keener, "Women's Education and Public Speech in Antiquity," 750–51.
80 Keener, "Women's Education and Public Speech in Antiquity," 754–56.
81 Keener, "Women's Education and Public Speech in Antiquity," 751–52.
82 Keener, "Women's Education and Public Speech in Antiquity," 756–59.
83 Leon Morris, *1 Corinthians*, rev. ed., TNTC (Grand Rapids: Eerdmans, 1985), 197–98.
84 Christopher Forbes, *Prophecy and Inspired Speech: In Early Christianity and its Hellenistic Environment* (Peabody, MA: Hendrickson, 1995), 274.
85 Forbes, *Prophecy and Inspired Speech*, 276.
86 Ciampa and Rosner, *The First Letter to the Corinthians*, 729.

particular instance. Soeng Yu Li writes, "This means that the men are actually also subjected to this νόμος. The fact that Paul is addressing the women indicates that it was the women who were involved in disturbing speech act.... Since in 14:33b–35 the women were the cause of the problem Paul's remedy has a patriarchal tone."[87] L. Ann Jervis, in adding an additional layer to this argument, says that the problem in Corinth was the "type of speaking the women engaged in rather than that women were the speakers."[88] Furthermore, Paul's answer to this problem was "to resort to the patriarchal values of his society."[89] Thus, Jervis can conclude that the passage is not about women but about "self-focused" speech.[90]

Witherington sees Paul addressing both men and women in the broader context and that "one must assume that he singles these women out for comment because he had heard that some of them were notable violators of these principles."[91] The principles Witherington gives are "respect, submission, and silence of any listener when any prophet is speaking (vv. 28–32)."[92] However, Witherington then includes Keener's argument concerning the lack of women's education as the problem.[93] Pheme Perkins simply states that the passage does not apply today because today's public sector includes women leaders.[94]

Theological Context

Many writers argue for theological inconsistency based upon both Pauline theology and Pauline practice. Some appeal to theological principles such as Gal 3:28 and 1 Tim 2:9–14. Others appeal to specific texts that mention women in the early church, for instance, Acts 16:11–15, Rom 16:1–7, Phil 4:2–3, and Col 4:15.

First Corinthians 14:34–35 Contradicts Paul's Theological Principles

Krister Stendahl discusses Gal 3:28 in his book on the role of women. He says that Gal 3:28 is "directed against what we call the order of creation, and consequently

---

87 Soeng Yu Li, *Paul's Teaching on the Pneumatika in 1 Corinthians 12–14: Prophecy as the Paradigm of ta Charismata ta Meizona for the Future-Oriented Ekklēsia*, WUNT 455 (Tübingen: Mohr Siebeck, 2017), 376. So also L. Ann Jervis, "1 Corinthians 14:34–35: A Reconsideration of Paul's Limitation of the Free Speech of Some Corinthian Women," *JSNT* 58 (1995): 71 (including n. 78).
88 Jervis, "1 Corinthians 14:34–35," 52.
89 Jervis, "1 Corinthians 14:34–35," 72.
90 Jervis, "1 Corinthians 14:34–35," 73.
91 Witherington, *Conflict and Community in Corinth*, 276.
92 Witherington, *Conflict and Community in Corinth*, 276.
93 Witherington, *Conflict and Community in Corinth*, 287.
94 Pheme Perkins, *First Corinthians*, Paideia Commentaries on the New Testament (Grand Rapids: Baker Academic, 2012), 165.

it creates a tension with those biblical passages—Pauline and non-Pauline—by which this order of creation maintains its place in the fundamental view of the New Testament concerning the subordination of women.... [S]omething has happened which transcends the Law itself and thereby even the order of creation."[95] While others may interpret Gal 3:28 differently than Stendahl, many still hold that Gal 3:28 stands at odds with 1 Cor 14:34–35.

At first glance 1 Tim 2:9–14 appears to demonstrate some consistency in Paul's view of women in the church when compared to 1 Cor 14:34–35. However, scholars who disagree with the consistency do so under two broad positions: (1) The two passages refer to different ideas; and (2) Paul did not write one or both of the passages. J. M. Holmes compares 1 Cor 14:34–35 with 1 Tim 2:9–12 and argues that the former is a congregational context and the latter pertains to public life more broadly.[96] Odell-Scott argues that the second-century author of 1 Timothy was reading (or misreading) 1 Cor 14:34–35 as Pauline (when, in fact, according to Odell-Scott, it was a Corinthian slogan).[97]

First Corinthians 14:34–35 Contradicts Paul's Practice

Many scholars read 1 Cor 14:34–35 and argue that other Pauline passages show women in positions of leadership. The passages that they appeal to in order to argue for an inconsistency include Acts 16:11–15, Rom 16:1–7, Phil 4:2–3, and Col 4:15.[98] This position contrasts with the historical view above that the ancient world silenced women and today's culture is different.

Ruth Albrecht is representative of those who take both 1 Tim 2:9–15 and the other New Testament passages listed above as inconsistent with Paul. She writes, "New Testament scriptures draw a contradictory image in regard to the importance and activity of Christian women."[99] Albrecht goes on to list 1 Tim 2:9–15 as early second century, Phoebe as in "a position leading the congregation

---

95 Krister Stendahl, *The Bible and the Role of Women: A Case Study in Hermeneutics*, trans. Emilie T. Sander, Biblical Series 15 (Philadelphia: Fortress, 1966), 32, 34. He connects creation with 1 Cor 14:34–35 on pages 29–30.

96 Holmes, *Text in a Whirlwind*, 190–91. Some take 1 Tim 2:9–14 and 1 Cor 14:34–35 as teaching the same ideas but with both passages silencing women due to a lack of education (for which, see above).

97 David W. Odell-Scott, "In Defense of an Egalitarian Interpretation of 1 Cor 14:34–36: A Reply to Murphy-O'Connor's Critique," *BTB* 17.3 (1987): 102.

98 Capper, "To Keep Silent, Part I," 114–15; Keener, *Paul, Women and Wives*, 237–43; Keener, "Man and Woman," 589–90; Jervis, "1 Corinthians 14:34–35," 56; Hays, *First Corinthians*, 246; Perkins, *First Corinthians*, 164–65.

99 Ruth Albrecht, "Woman," *BNP* 15:710.

as *diákonos*," and Lydia in Acts 16 as "proof that women functioned as the leaders of Christian congregations which gathered in their house."[100]

One dictionary includes Euodia and Syntyche as "female leadership" when commenting on women in various New Testament passages, including 1 Cor 14:34–35 and Phil 4:2–3.[101] Capper refers to Nympha in Col 4:15 in his article on 1 Cor 14:33–36: "Of Nympha of Laodicea we know only that she entertained a church in her home (Col 4:15), but nothing in Paul's mention of her suggests any limitation of her role in this context. The evidence we have concerning Phoebe, Lydia, and Nympha shows that Paul accepted women as much as men in the role of householder-overseers, the leadership class in early Christianity which ultimately evolved to become elders and priests."[102] Capper's statements in themselves are at tension with one another. On the one hand, he mentions "we know only that"; however, on the other hand, Nympha is now "evidence" that Paul had women in leadership roles as householder-overseers.

The above review of literature on 1 Cor 14:34–35 is representative and not exhaustive. Additional writers and claims will be noted below in the appropriate discussions. The review shows the need to reconsider whether 1 Cor 14:34–35 is consistent with Paul. Paul's passage in 1 Cor 14:34–35 will be interpreted via σιγάω in its literary, historical, and theological context.

---

100   Albrecht, "Woman," *BNP* 15:710. She does admit uncertainty as to the exact duties of a deacon.
101   Moisés Silva, ed., "γυνή," *NIDNTTE*, 1:623.
102   Capper, "To Keep Silent, Part I," 131.

2

The Literary Context: The Range of ΣΙΓΑΩ as a Basis for Consistency

Introduction

This chapter will establish the range of meaning of σιγάω. While the presence of semantic range is a common assumption in hermeneutics, it is regularly overlooked in the interpretive possibilities of 1 Cor 14:34. In order to establish an accurate range of σιγάω, this chapter will review lexical works and dictionaries, along with surveying the various uses in biblical and non-biblical literature. This chapter will then discuss the meaning of σιγάω in the context of 1 Corinthians 11–14 in order to confirm Paul's consistent teaching.

Review of Lexical Works and Dictionaries

In his book *A History of New Testament Lexicography*, John Lee not only gives a history of the discipline, but he also provides a helpful list of New Testament lexicons.[1] Lexicons often rely on and update their predecessors,[2] and so it is

---

1 John A. L. Lee, *A History of New Testament Lexicography*, Studies in Biblical Greek 8 (New York: Peter Lang, 2003), 321–26.
2 Lee, *A History of New Testament Lexicography*, 6–8.

unnecessary to include them all in this review. Some lexicons give σιγάω a simple gloss such as "to keep silence" or "schweige" (or with Rom 16:25, "to be kept secret").[3] Other works provide slightly more range of meaning for the term. For example, T. Muraoka gives two options of "to keep silence" and "to stop engaging in activity."[4]

BAG (1957) and BAGD (1979) give the same brief entry of translations such as "say nothing."[5] BDAG (2000) uses the same entry but adds the definition of "to be silent" or "to keep something from becoming known."[6] John Pickering's lexicon shows some of the range of σιγάω when he writes of silence in some contexts as *"generally through prudence"* or *"having respect to consequences."*[7] Pickering's efforts are a step in the right direction (taking in the nuances of different contexts) even if one disagrees with his glosses. LSJ adds an additional section of "metaph[or] of things."[8] The recent *Cambridge Greek Lexicon* provides four basic translations for σιγάω: "be/keep silent," "be silent/be still," "work silently/hold a secret," and "keep quiet about (something)."[9]

The article in *NIDNTTE* lays out some of the facts of σιγάω. That is, there are about 20 occurrences in the LXX (the Appendix lists 18) and ten in the New Testament.[10] There are also two uses of σιγή in the LXX (3 Macc 3:12 and Wis 18:14) and two in the New Testament (Acts 21:40 and Rev 8:1).[11] W. Radl's article in the *Exegetical Dictionary of the New Testament* mentions the various contexts of the verb and corresponding σιγή. He divides the contexts into four sections of Luke/Acts, 1 Corinthians, Rom 16:25, and Rev 8:1. Radl claims that 1 Cor 14:33b–36 is an interpolation that "can easily be extracted from its present

---

3   E.g., Joseph Henry Thayer, "σιγάω," in *A Greek-English Lexicon of the New Testament* (Grand Rapids: Baker, 1977), 574; G. Abbott-Smith, "σιγάω," in *A Manual Greek Lexicon of the New Testament*, 3rd ed. (Edinburgh: T&T Clark, 1937), 405–6; Heinrich Ebeling, "σιγάω," in *Griechisch-deutsches Wörterbuch zum Neuen Testamente* (Hannover: Hahnsche, 1913), 371. Cf. the brief definition in Johannes P. Louw and Eugene A. Nida, "σιγάω," L&N 1:402.
4   T. Muraoka, "σιγάω," *GELS* 621.
5   Walter Bauer, William F. Arndt, and F. Wilbur Gingrich, "σιγάω," BAG 757; Walter Bauer et al., "σιγάω," BAGD 749.
6   Walter Bauer et al., "σιγάω," BDAG 922. Lee, *A History of New Testament Lexicography*, 166, points out that the major distinction of BDAG (2000) from BAG (1957) and BAGD (1979) revolves around providing definitions (and not just glosses). Lee states that about 60 percent of words in the 2000 edition have definitions. Regarding σιγάω, BDAG (2000) updates some of the bibliography.
7   John Pickering, "σιγάω," in *A Comprehensive Lexicon of the Greek Language* (Boston: Wilkins, Carter, and Company, 1847), 1180 (italics original).
8   Liddell, Henry George, Robert Scott, and Henry Stuart Jones, "σιγάω," in *A Greek-English Lexicon* (Oxford: Clarendon, 1996), 1596.
9   J. Diggle et al., "σῑγάω," *The Cambridge Greek Lexicon* 2:1265.
10 Counting can vary slightly depending on which text and variants one chooses.
11 Moisés Silva, ed., "σιγάω," *NIDNTTE* 4:290–92.

context" (the only reason given is that it contradicts 1 Cor 11:5 and the rest of Chapters Twelve and Fourteen).[12] He does not discuss the possible meaning of the term in its context.

Johannes Louw and Eugene Nida's distinctive lexicon provides the following list alongside of σιγάω: σιωπάω, ἡσυχάζω, ἡσυχία, σιγή, φιμοῦμαι, φιμόω, ἐπιστομίζω, and στόμα φράσσω.[13] When considering Louw and Nida's definitions, one should take into account their disclaimer that "there are a host of problems resulting from indeterminacy in the range of referents, fuzzy boundaries, incomplete sets of related meanings, limitations in the corpus and background date, and specialization of meaning due to the uniqueness of the message."[14] Therefore, scholars need to continually build onto their discussions. For example, their definition of σιγάω as "to keep quiet, with the implication of preserving something which is secret"[15] is only occasionally the correct meaning (see the Appendix). Also, σιγάω and other terms for silence do not always allow for nuanced distinctions. In the NT σιωπάω, ἡσυχάζω, ἡσυχία, and σιγή function in very similar ways where, just like σιγάω, the silence is in a specific moment/manner or absolute silence. On the other hand, φιμόω, ἐπιστομίζω, and στόμα φράσσω regularly appear to be much stronger terms (see, e.g., Titus 1:11 and the silencing of false teachers), but the comparison is only a general distinction since Mark 4:39 contains both σιωπάω and φιμόω together as near synonyms. Ultimately, Wayne Grudem's statement holds true, "The answer is that the NT writers often talk about silence in general unrestricted terms while expecting the readers to know from the context which kind of silence is in view."[16] Many scholars who write on 1 Cor 14:34–35 do not pause to ask "which kind of silence is in view."

---

12   W. Radl, "σιγάω; σιγή," *EDNT* 3:242. He follows Dautzenberg for his reasoning.
13   Louw and Nida, L&N 1:402–03. BDAG provides comprehensive NT references: σιωπάω: Matt 20:31; 26:63; Mark 3:4; 4:39; 9:34; 10:48; 14:61; Luke 1:20; 18:39; Acts 18:9; ἡσυχάζω: Luke 14:4; 23:56; Acts 11:18; 21:14; 1 Thess 4:11; ἡσυχία: Acts 22:2; 2 Thess 3:12; 1 Tim 2:11–12; σιγή: Acts 21:40; Rev 8:1; φιμόω: Matt 22:12, 34; Mark 1:25; 4:39; Luke 4:35; 1 Tim 5:18; 1 Pet 2:15; ἐπιστομίζω: Titus 1:11; στόμα φράσσω: Rom 3:19; Heb 11:33; cf. 2 Cor 11:10.
14   Louw and Nida, L&N 1:xx. See the insightful review in Moisés Silva, review of *Greek-English Lexicon of the New Testament: Based on Semantic Domains*, by Johannes P. Louw and Eugene A. Nida, *WTJ* 51 (1989): 163–67.
15   Louw and Nida, L&N 1:402.
16   Wayne Grudem, "Prophecy—Yes, But Teaching—No: Paul's Consistent Advocacy of Women's Participation without Governing Authority," *JETS* 30.1 (1987): 23.

Usage in Greek Literature (Narrowed by Date Closest to the New Testament)

Greek literature clearly shows a range of meaning for σιγάω where one must look at each individual context to decide its meaning. This section will discuss the data found in the Appendix where occurrences are narrowed by date with priority given to works closest in time to the New Testament. The data demonstrates that the majority of instances of σιγάω mean a "selective silence" and not an "absolute silence."[17] Despite the overwhelming data, writers still often assume absolute silence in 1 Cor 14:34.[18] Many writers do not provide a definition for "absolute silence." However, the ones who do define the concept do so without full lexical data. For example, Fee writes, "Despite some protests to the contrary, the 'rule' itself is expressed absolutely. That is, it is given without any form of qualification. Given the unqualified nature of the further prohibition that '*the* women' are not permitted to speak, it is very difficult to interpret this as meaning anything else than all forms of speaking out in public."[19] Fee provides no lexical support for his definition. Texts in the Appendix below (marked absolute silence) typically provide contextual clues for the meaning of absolute silence, which can be in regard to duration, the ability to make a sound, and/or a strong antagonism. For instance, silence can be for a long duration, as in reference to death in the *Lament for Bion*, "As so you, surrounded by silence [σιγᾷ], will be in the earth, while the Nymphs deem it right for the frog to croak for ever."[20] Silence can also be labeled absolute regarding the inability to make a sound as in Hippocrates where patients are unable to speak due to physical ailments.[21] Finally, a strong antagonism can be seen among clear enemies.[22] The context usually provides clues to make absolute silence clear. Therefore, the *absence* of clues from Payne and Fee's perspective

---

17   The idea of this section is similar to the work on κεφαλή in Wayne Grudem, "Does ΚΕΦΑΛΗ ('Head') Mean 'Source' or 'Authority Over' in Greek Literature? A Survey of 2,336 Examples," *TJ* 6 (1985): 38–59.

18   E.g., Philip B. Payne, *Man and Woman, One in Christ: An Exegetical and Theological Study of Paul's Letters* (Grand Rapids: Zondervan, 2009), 217–19, 221, 255–56. While Payne admits silence in 1 Cor 14:28, 30 is "specifically restricted" (p. 256), he does not pursue this option with 1 Cor 14:34.

19   Gordon Fee, *The First Epistle to the Corinthians*, rev. ed., NICNT (Grand Rapids: Eerdmans, 2014), 789–90 (italics original).

20   Moschus, *Lament for Bion*, 105–6. Translations of Greco-Roman authors are from the LCL.

21   E.g., Hippocrates, *Epid.* 3.1.154–58, "She had a cough with signs of coction, but brought up nothing. No appetite for any food the whole time, nor did she desire anything. No thirst, and she drank nothing worth mentioning. She was silent [σιγῶσα], and did not converse at all [οὐδὲν διελέγετο]. Depression, the patient despairing of herself."

22   E.g., *The Life of Adam and Eve*, 12:1–2.

Figure 1. Usage of σιγάω in Greek Literature (Limited Sample; see Appendix).

Usage	Number of Occurrences	Percentage
Sometimes Silent/Silent in a Specific Instance	271	75.9%
Always Silent/Absolute Silence	28	7.8%
Secret/Conceal	25	7%
Not applicable due to no context provided or fragments	16	4.5%
Proverbial Statement	8	2.2%
Descriptive of nature	7	2%
Submission	2	0.6%

is not evidence for their definition. Paul does not give an indication of strong antagonism such as a beating, nor does he say that they cannot make a sound in light of 1 Cor 11:5. In light of the entire set of data, the burden of proof is with the interpreter who takes 1 Cor 14:34–35 to mean absolute silence, since silence in Greek literature often has the same person speaking one moment and silent another moment.

In the Appendix the term σιγάω is quoted a total of 357 times (the 357 occurrences have been chosen for when σιγάω is found between 5 BC–AD 1 to manage the total times the term is found of over 5,700 occurrences in Greek literature).[23] The number of occurrences and percentage of each use are summarized in figure 1.[24]

As noted above in the history of research, many scholars assume the definition of silence to be absolute silence in order to give the impression of inconsistency within Paul's letters. The various definitions of σιγάω presented in the chart above are simply derived from reading different authors who use σιγάω. This method appears fair in light of Grudem's quote above where, again, he writes, "The answer is that the NT writers often talk about silence in general unrestricted terms while expecting the readers to know from the context which kind of silence

---

23   If σιγάω is found in the same context several times, each occurrence is counted as one. For example, in Aristophanes, *Lys.* 507–20, σιγάω is used five times as absolute silence. Therefore, in the chart it will count as five occurrences.

24   The summary here takes into account only the data listed in the Appendix. Fragments that were not quoted would presumably adjust these figures but not in a way as to overturn the overall majority usage.

is in view."[25] The examples below will provide examples for each category in more detail in order to grasp the significance of how σιγάω is actually used.

The usage of σιγάω as absolute silence should especially depend upon contextual clues since this definition only occurs about 7.8 percent of the time. Marlene Crüsemann, as alluded to earlier, takes 1 Cor 14:34–35 as "a comprehensive prohibition of public speaking, applying to all Christian women."[26] She makes her argument by appealing to "the double absolute use of the verb λαλεῖν ('to speak')."[27] Then she appeals to the other types of speech in 1 Corinthians 14 and claims that the author is restricting women from these types of speech as well.[28] She states precisely, "The hermeneutical dilemma posed here is that *either* these texts *or* women theologians can speak and have a place in the church—no third possibility exists."[29] What she does not taken into account is that absolute silence is not the typical definition of σιγάω.[30] Josephus provides an example of absolute silence. His *Jewish War* gives the perspective of Herod, where he "burst out upon [Antipater] to be silent [σιγᾶν]."[31] From Herod's perspective he wished absolute silence, but Antipater later made a speech.[32] Contextual clues are important for recognizing absolute silence since, again, this usage only occurs about 7.8 percent of the time. In the case of Herod, his burst of anger provides this clue.

One should expect σιγάω to mean selective silence about 75.9 percent of the time. This percentage is significant because many Pauline scholars do not start with this assumption. Plutarch and Strabo provide clear representative examples of a selective (and by no means absolute) silence. Plutarch in his work *Concerning Talkativeness* states, "And Ino in Euripides, speaking out boldly concerning herself, says that she knows how to be 'Silent [σιγᾶν] in season, to speak where speech is safe.' For those who have received a noble and truly royal education learn first to be silent [σιγᾶν], and then to speak."[33] There is no possible way for σιγάω to mean absolute silence in this text, and the reader comes across these types of

---

25 Grudem, "Prophecy—Yes, But Teaching—No," 23.
26 Marlene Crüsemann, "Irredeemably Hostile to Women: Anti-Jewish Elements in the Exegesis of the Dispute about Women's Right to Speak (1 Cor. 14.34–35)," *JSNT* 79 (2000): 21. Luise Schottroff also calls silence "comprehensive" or "umfassend" (*Der erste Brief an die Gemeinde in Korinth*, TKNT 7 [Stuttgart: Kohlhammer, 2013], 282).
27 Crüsemann, "Irredeemably Hostile to Women," 22.
28 Crüsemann, "Irredeemably Hostile to Women," 22. She takes the verses as an interpolation.
29 Crüsemann, "Irredeemably Hostile to Women," 20 (italics original).
30 Crüsemann, "Irredeemably Hostile to Women," 23, does see σιγάω in 1 Cor 14:28 and 30 as "temporary silence." She does not explicitly address the inconsistent definition for σιγάω.
31 Josephus, *J.W.* 1.622.
32 Josephus, *J.W.* 1.629–36.
33 Plutarch, *Garr.* 506C.

The Literary Context: The Range of ΣΙΓΑΩ as a Basis for Consistency | 27

examples often in ancient Greek literature. Also, passages like Plutarch's statement prove that σιγάω itself does not *inherently* carry a strong (negative) connotation. In fact, silence in this passage is viewed the opposite of how many today view the term itself.[34] Strabo provides another clear example of how σιγάω would usually have been used:

> Nor yet, surely, was he [Homer] ignorant of peoples that were equally near, some of which he names and some not; for example he names the Lycians and the Solymi, but not the Milyae; nor yet the Pamphylians or Pisidians; and though he names the Paphlagonians, Phrygians, and Mysians, he does not name Mariandynians or Thynians or Bithynians or Bebryces; and he mentions the Amazons, but not the White Syrians or Syrians, or Cappadocians, or Lycaonians, though he repeatedly mentions the Phoenicians and the Egyptians and the Ethiopians. And although he mentions the Alëian plain and the Arimi, he is silent [σιγᾷ] as to the tribe to which both belong.[35]

It is impossible for Strabo to mean Homer is absolutely silent. Strabo is defending Homer from "every man who judges from the poet's failure to mention anything that he is ignorant of that thing uses faulty evidence."[36] In other words, just because Homer did not mention something cannot be used against him regarding what he did mention. Anna Biraschi explains, "Strabo sometimes even justifies Homer's silences; for him they are not signs of ignorance. See 7.3.6–7; 8.3.8; 9.1.5; 9.3.15; 12.3.25 where he states that Homer does not mention some cities because they had not been founded in his time and that then some geographical aspects were not considered important."[37] The types of uses in Plutarch and Strabo demonstrate that σιγάω has a range of meaning, and this fact alone should slow the often-rushed decision to charge Paul with inconsistency on the basis of commanding silence.

It is common in literature for the same person both to speak one moment and be silent another moment, or speak concerning one matter and be silent about another matter. The broader context often makes this distinction clear.

---

34 See fuller context in Plutarch, *Garr.* 505F–506A.
35 Strabo, *Geogr.* 12.3.27.
36 Strabo, *Geogr.* 12.3.27.
37 Anna Maria Biraschi, "Strabo and Homer: A Chapter in Cultural History," in *Strabo's Cultural Geography: The Making of a Kolossourgia*, ed. Daniela Dueck, Hugh Lindsay, and Sarah Pothecary (Cambridge: Cambridge University Press, 2005), 79 n. 14. I would add to Biraschi's references Strabo, *Geogr.* 1.2.29 where Strabo refers to Homer who "keeps silent [σιγῶν] about what is too obvious to mention, or else alludes to it by an epithet."

Discussion of 1 Cor 14:34–35 needs to begin with the data of how σιγάω was used in the ancient world. Can a person both speak and be silent at the same time? Σιγάω is used this way regarding Homer's speech where he speaks about one matter and is silent about another matter. Therefore, it is a valid interpretive option for women's speech.

Silence can also be related to submission, which is significant since Paul combines the two ideas. There are only two examples discovered in the Appendix. One is by Hippocrates: "Let those who look after the patient present the part for operation as you want it, and hold fast the rest of the body so as to be all steady, keeping silence [σιγῶντες] and obeying their superior."[38] The surgeon's assistant is to be silent during the surgical operation, and the context may show the silence to emphasize more of submission. The second is by Josephus: "Joseph, on his side, committing his cause entirely to God, sought neither to defend himself nor yet to render a strict account of what had passed, but silently [σιγῶν] underwent his bonds and confinement, confident that God, who knew the cause of his calamity and the truth, would prove stronger than those who had bound him; and of His providence he had proof forthwith."[39] The silence is the expression and evidence of Joseph's submission to God in the midst of his trials.

The final three meanings of σιγάω can be mentioned briefly since they do not directly apply to 1 Corinthians 14. Closely related to being selectively silent is the idea of concealing or keeping something secret. The secret may or may not be spoken at a future time, as Plutarch writes, "No spoken word, it is true, has ever done such service as have in many instances words unspoken; for it is possible at some later time to tell what you have kept silent [σιγηθέν], but never to keep silent what once has been spoken—*that* has been spilled, and has made its way abroad."[40] Silence can also simply be used in a proverbial sense: "In a council meeting he was asked whether it was due to foolishness or lack of words that he said nothing. 'But a fool,' said he, 'would not be able to hold his tongue [σιγᾶν].'"[41] Finally, silence can be used metaphorically in descriptions of nature or poetry as in Psalm 106:29 LXX: "And he commanded the storm and stopped the wind, and its waves were silenced [ἐσίγησαν]." These final three meanings continue to support the wide-range of σιγάω and the need to closely consider each literary context.

---

38 Hippocrates, *Off.* 6.
39 Josephus, *Ant.* 2.60.
40 Plutarch, *Garr.* 505F (italics original).
41 Plutarch, *Apoph lac.* 220B.

Usage in the Old Testament

The discussion of σιγάω in this section will be limited to the Old Testament (but see the Appendix for additional LXX books). The term occurs ten times in the OT (Exod 14:14; Pss 32:3 [Ps 31:3 LXX]; 39:2 [38:3 LXX]; 50:21 [49:21 LXX]; 83:1 [82:2 LXX]; 107:29 [106:29 LXX]; Eccl 3:7; Isa 32:5; Lam 3:49; Amos 6:10).[42] The term σιγάω translates four different Hebrew terms. The Hebrew word חרשׁ is used in Exod 14:14 and Pss 32:3; 50:21; 83:1. John Oswalt describes חרשׁ in general, "This vb. occurs 47x and is primarily descriptive, reporting the silence of persons in various circumstances."[43] Oswalt also lists several OT references that show diversity of usage and demonstrate the different ways God and people are silent. The term חשׁה is used in Pss 39:2; 107:29 and Eccl 3:7. Regarding Ps 39:2, David is only silent for a temporary period before he references speaking again in the next verse (39:3).[44] Psalm 107:29 is descriptive of nature where waves are "silenced." Ecclesiastes 3:7 is clearly a selective silence: "There is a time to be silent [לַחֲשׁוֹת; σιγᾶν] and a time to speak."[45]

Isaiah 32:5 is likely set within a year before the Assyrian exile in 701 BC.[46] Isaiah 32:1–8 refers to what it will be like with the messianic king. The following is the text of Isa 32:5:

> "And no longer will one say to the foolish to rule, and no longer will helpers say of you, 'Quiet' [Σίγα]." καὶ οὐκέτι μὴ εἴπωσιν τῷ μωρῷ ἄρχειν, καὶ οὐκέτι μὴ εἴπωσιν οἱ ὑπηρέται σου Σίγα (LXX).

> "It will no more be said to the fool 'noble-minded,' and it will not be said 'noble' to the cunning."[47] לֹא־יִקָּרֵא עוֹד לְנָבָל נָדִיב וּלְכִילַי לֹא יֵאָמֵר שׁוֹעַ (MT).

The Hebrew text does not have any corresponding term for silence, which is why the usage in the LXX is more difficult to discern. The Septuagint's addition of the singular σου causes additional confusion. J. J. M. Roberts simply calls Isa 32:5

42　See the Appendix for the text of each passage.
43　John N. Oswalt, "חרשׁ," *NIDOTTE* 2:297.
44　Allan M. Harman, *Commentary on the Psalms*, Mentor (Scotland: Christian Focus Publications, 1998), 170, states, "Finally, he had to break his silence and speak, and the words 'then I spoke with my tongue' bring a dramatic end to the introductory verses."
45　Cf. Eccl 3:1. Scripture quotations are my own unless otherwise noted.
46　Gary V. Smith, *Isaiah 1–39*, NAC 15A (Nashville: B&H, 2007), 538. See p. 539 for the question of a messianic interpretation of Isa 32:1.
47　Cf. ESV: "The fool will no more be called noble, nor the scoundrel said to be honorable."

30 | *Paul, Women, and the Meaning of Silence*

LXX an "odd reading."[48] Abi T. Ngunga and Joachim Schaper explain the LXX of Isaiah in general, "The 'free' renderings by our translator include a significant number of pluses, minuses, lexical choices, variants, neologisms, liberties in word order, and so on. However, scholars have struggled to try to provide plausible factors which might be behind the differences between the Greek text and its Hebrew *Vorlage*."[49] Arie van der Kooij says that the correspondence between the Hebrew and Greek is "unclear," but that "the idea is that one should be silent because one should not dare to contradict a ruler."[50] The best explanation comes from Joseph Ziegler, who writes, "Still Σίγα appears to be a transcription from שׁגע (read as שׁיע). Also here he appears to have started thinking about the Aramaic שׂגא; then he translates from the Vulgate 'great' (= שׂגיא?); at the same time, he became dependent upon Aquila, who here has μεγιστάν."[51] While the LXX may not be the best translation at this point, the usage is still applicable for the present study from the perspective of the Septuagint translator.

Lamentations 3:49 has the Hebrew term דָּמָה: "My eyes are swallowed up with tears, and I will not be silent [תִדְמֶה; σιγήσομαι] to be calm until when the Lord stoops and sees from heaven" (Lam 3:49–50).[52] Lamentations is divided into five sections, with alphabetic acrostics each in Chapters One to Four (Chapter Five does not have an alphabetic acrostic).[53] Lamentations 3 includes both grief and hope (e.g., 3:19–24). Lamentations as poetry[54] should caution against strict

---

48   J. J. M. Roberts, *First Isaiah*, Hermeneia (Minneapolis: Fortress, 2015), 409.
49   Abi T. Ngunga and Joachim Schaper, "Isaiah," in *The T&T Clark Companion to the Septuagint*, ed. James K. Aitken (London: Bloomsbury, 2015), 460.
50   Arie van der Kooij, "The Septuagint of Isaiah and the Issue of Coherence. A Twofold Analysis of LXX Isaiah 31:9B–32:8," in *The Old Greek of Isaiah: Issues and Perspectives: Papers Read at the Conference on the Septuagint of Isaiah, Held in Leiden 10–11 April 2008*, ed. Arie van der Kooij and Michaël N. van der Meer, Contributions to Biblical Exegesis and Theology 55 (Leuven: Peeters, 2010), 42.
51   Joseph Ziegler, *Untersuchungen zur Septuaginta des Buches Isaias*, ATA 12.3 (Münster: Aschendorffschen, 1934), 122, "Weiterhin scheint Σίγα eine Transkr. von שׁגע (aus שׁיע verlesen) zu sein. Auch Hier. scheint an das aram. שׂגא; gedacht zu haben; denn er übersetzt in der Vulg „maior" (= שׂגיא?); zugleich wird er von Aq abhängig sein, der hier μεγιστάν hat." Followed by Moshe H. Goshen-Gottstein, ed., *The Book of Isaiah*, vol. 2., The Hebrew University Bible Project (Jerusalem: Hebrew University, 1981), loc. cit. Thanks to Emanuel Tov and Ken Penner for their correspondence on bibliography.
52   Helpful are Bernard A. Taylor, *Analytical Lexicon to the Septuagint*, exp. ed. (Peabody, MA: Hendrickson, 2009); and T. Muraoka, *A Syntax of Septuagint Greek* (Leuven: Peeters, 2016). In the latter, see esp. p. 295 n. 2.
53   See discussion in Elie Assis, "The Alphabetic Acrostic in the Book of Lamentations," *CBQ* 69.4 (2007): 710–24. Assis writes that the acrostic form "was employed in order to create an unparalleled tension between the deep emotional mode and the contemplated structure, with the aim of conveying the idea that, contrary to the genre of dirges, Lamentations is a rational reflection on the horrifying situation" (p. 717).
54   R. B. Salters, *A Critical and Exegetical Commentary on Lamentations*, ICC (London: Bloomsbury, 2014), 15–17.

definitions of silence referring to speaking or not speaking. In Lam 3:49–50 the mourner would be silent once the Lord "sees," and so theoretically there would be no more weeping (not that the mourner would stop speaking). Paul House writes (referring also to Jer 14:17), "Both passages, then, portray an involved, interceding, determined individual praying persistently for divine help."[55] In prayerful tears he will not be silent.

The term used in Amos 6:10 is הס: "And they will take hold of the members of their households and will prevail upon them to bring out their bones from the house and will say to the heads of the house, 'Is he still with you?' And he will say, 'No longer.' And he will say, 'Quiet [הָס; σίγα], that you may not name the name of the Lord.'" Hans Wolff explains, "'Hush' (הס) is used elsewhere primarily to command silence in the sanctuary where Yahweh is immanent. Here the dominant concern is that Yahweh's name might be mentioned, perhaps in an outcry of lamentation."[56] The interpreter could take silence here in either way—absolute silence or specifically in regard to the name of the Lord.[57] The type of silence specified in Amos 6:10 is כִּי לֹא לְהַזְכִּיר בְּשֵׁם יְהוָה ("that you may not name the name of the Lord").[58] Willem Smelik explains that the phrase הזכיר בשם means swearing by God's name.[59] Douglas Stuart understands silence not as "mere oral formulation, but [it] must concern calling on Yahweh (cf. הזכיר [sic] in Isa 48:1) in prayers of lamentation or the like."[60] The exact interpretation may depend on which other OT passage is considered appropriate to assist in understanding.[61] Amos 6:10 is not conclusive one way or the other for our current thesis since the contextual factors could be taken in either direction of selective silence or absolute silence. Each OT reference of silence demonstrates the wide-range of usage

---

55 Paul R. House, *Lamentations*, WBC 23B (Nashville: Thomas Nelson, 2004), 424.
56 Hans Walter Wolff, *Joel and Amos*, ed. S. Dean McBride, Jr., trans. Waldemar Janzen, S. Dean McBride, Jr., and Charles A. Muenchow, Hermeneia (Philadelphia: Fortress, 1977), 283.
57 See additional comments in the Appendix.
58 Sonja Noll views הס as the opposite of להזכיר in *The Semantics of Silence in Biblical Hebrew*, Studies in Semitic Languages and Linguistics 100 (Leiden: Brill, 2020), 239.
59 Willem F. Smelik, "The Use of הזכיר בשם in Classical Hebrew: Josh 23:7; Isa 48:1; Amos 6:10; Ps 20:8; 4Q504 III 4; 1QS 6:27," *JBL* 118 (1999): 321–32.
60 Douglas Stuart, *Hosea–Jonah*, WBC 31 (Waco, TX: Word, 1987), 364. In Amos 8:3, הס is used in an absolute way, though the LXX does not use σιγάω in this instance. Wolff states, "'Hush!' (הס), the exclamatory imperative demanding strictest silence, suggests the sinister way in which death makes it rounds" (*Joel and Amos*, 320).
61 W. Edward Glenny writes, "'To name the name of the Lord' is used in several different contexts in the Old Testament" (*Amos: A Commentary Based on Amos in Codex Vaticanus*, Septuagint Commentary Series [Leiden: Brill, 2013], 117). He especially highlights, among others, Lev 24:10–23 and Jer 44:24–30 (pp. 117–18).

for σιγάω. Absolute silence should not be assumed when encountered later in the New Testament in light of the varied usage in the Old Testament.

Usage in the New Testament

The NT authors use σιγάω ten times (Luke 9:36; 18:39; 20:26; Acts 12:17; 15:12–13; Rom 16:25; 1 Cor 14:28, 30, 34). Luke describes the transfiguration account in Luke 9:28–36, and concludes, "And after the voice spoke, Jesus was found alone. And they were silent [ἐσίγησαν] and told no one in those days anything that they saw" (9:36). This verse is a clear case of a specific silence regarding both the content and time-frame. They were silent particularly about the transfiguration event itself. If one compares the usage in Luke 9:36 with 1 Cor 14:34, it is significant because it shows women in 1 Corinthians 14 could theoretically be silent regarding one matter but continue speaking in other matters. The apostles were temporarily silent until some point after Jesus's resurrection.

Luke recounts Jesus's journey to Jericho in Luke 18:35–43. Part of the background to Jesus and the blind man's interaction on this journey is in Luke 18:39, "And the ones leading the way were rebuking him that he may be silent [σιγήσῃ], but he cried out all the more, 'Son of David, have mercy on me.'" The ones leading the way wanted the blind man to be silent for a specific moment in time, while Jesus was passing by (Ἰησοῦς ὁ Ναζωραῖος παρέρχεται; Luke 18:37). It is difficult to know if Luke originally used σιγάω. The manuscripts that have σιγάω are B D L P T W Ψ. There is a significant manuscript tradition that has σιωπάω: ℵ A K Q Γ Δ Θ ƒ[1.13] 565 579 700 892 1241 1424 𝔐. Setting aside Luke 18:39, Luke uses σιγάω a total of five times in Luke-Acts. He uses σιωπάω a total of three times (Luke 1:20; 19:40; Acts 18:9).[62] Matthew and Mark use σιωπάω, but they do not use σιγάω. The external evidence (only slightly) leans in favor of σιγάω.[63]

---

62   See BDAG, "σιωπάω," 925.
63   Darrell L. Bock, following Fitzmyer, says that σιγάω "is perhaps original because of better manuscript distribution and absence of harmonization" (*Luke 9:51–24:53*, BECNT [Grand Rapids: Baker Academic, 1996], 2:1512). Bock's argument from manuscript distribution is not clear-cut. Both σιγάω and σιωπάω each have Alexandrian and Byzantine support. Σιγάω also has Western support, but σιωπάω is supported by Θ, which may be Caesarean (?). For manuscript distribution, see Bruce M. Metzger, *A Textual Commentary on the Greek New Testament*, 2nd ed. (Stuttgart: United Bible Societies, 1994), 14–16; and Kurt Aland and Barbara Aland, *The Text of the New Testament: An Introduction to the Critical Editions and to the Theory and Practice of Modern Textual Criticism*, trans. Erroll F. Rhodes, 2nd ed. (Grand Rapids: Eerdmans, 1981), 106–63. Also, the absence of harmonization must be used cautiously because Luke could have simply copied from Matthew or Mark.

In Luke's narrative where Jesus teaches about giving to Caesar what belongs to him and giving to God what belongs to him (Luke 20:19–26), Luke writes, "And they were not able to catch him in his speech in front of the people and, being amazed at his reply, they were silent [ἐσίγησαν]" (20:26). This group of spies (ἐγκαθέτους; 20:20) would have been silent around Jesus after this response to the question about Caesar. The emphasis falls on their inability to offer a reasonable reply. There is no indication that they would have remained silent indefinitely and in every way. Writing on silence in the Gospel of Luke, Michal Dinkler states, "It is important to recognize that in Greek, 'silence' has a wider semantic range than it does in English.... [T]he modern reader ought to understand the Greek phrases and words denoting silence to be located at various points along a communication continuum, rather than assuming that they all refer to the absence of sound."[64] From the Gospel of Luke, there is silence about a certain topic, absolute silence for a moment in time, and silence because of the inability to speak from amazement.

Acts 12 includes Herod's imprisoning of Peter and the miraculous escape. When Peter went to the house of Mary (mother of John Mark) and those inside saw him, then Luke records, "And motioning with his hand to be silent [σιγᾶν], he described [to them] how the Lord led him out of prison and said, 'Tell James and the brothers these things.' And going out, he went to a different place" (12:17). In context this silence is more of lowering one's voice so that others may not hear and expose Peter to the authorities.[65] Keener explains that "silence is needed so he can speak quickly; it may also reduce unwanted neighborhood attention."[66] The desire not to be heard highlights the current atmosphere for Peter, which also explains the ambiguous "he went to a different place" (12:17). Not everyone needed to know where Peter went.[67]

In Acts 15 the apostles and elders were gathered in Jerusalem (15:6). After Peter reported how God had cleansed the Gentiles by faith (15:7–11), then Luke records, "And all the crowd was silent [ἐσίγησεν] and they were listening to Barnabas and Paul reporting what God did in signs and wonders among the Gentiles through them. And after they were silent [σιγῆσαι], James answered saying, 'Men, brothers, listen to me'" (15:12–13). Silence is again during a specific

---

64 Michal Beth Dinkler, *Silent Statements: Narrative Representations of Speech and Silence in the Gospel of Luke*, BZNW 191 (Berlin: Walter de Gruyter, 2013), 45.
65 F. F. Bruce, *The Book of Acts*, rev. ed., NICNT (Grand Rapids: Eerdmans, 1988), 239, refers to the "excited company to make less noise." Though Bruce's main point here is not so much the definition of silence as the evidence of eyewitness testimony.
66 Craig S. Keener, *Acts: An Exegetical Commentary* (Grand Rapids: Baker Academic, 2013), 2:1949.
67 See Keener, *Acts*, 2:1948–49, on the historical details for how Peter could have been heard and discovered if they were not quiet.

occasion while others speak. The example of James shows that a person can be silent and then later speak even in the same assembly. This gathering is analogous to the silence in 1 Cor 14:28, 30 where one was silent so that another could speak.

Paul concludes the book of Romans, "Now to him who is able to establish you according to my gospel and the proclamation of Jesus Christ, according to the revelation of the mystery that was kept secret [σεσιγημένου] for ages past, but now has been manifested and made known[68] through the prophetic writings, according to the command of the eternal God for the obedience of faith for all nations. To the only wise God, through Jesus Christ, be glory forever. Amen" (Rom 16:25–27).[69] The conclusion would have reminded the readers of the beginning of the letter in Rom 1:1–7 with the similar wording.[70] The revelation of the mystery is the gospel (cf. Rom 1:1–2, and the repetition of κατά in Rom 16:25). Douglas Moo explains σιγάω, writing, "Here Paul reflects a motif typical in apocalyptic: the hiddenness of God's plan and purposes. This hiddenness, as Paul will make clear in v. 26, does not mean that one could have no knowledge of the content of the mystery. What it means, rather, is that one could not fully understand it nor—and this is the special emphasis—experience it."[71] The term in Romans 16:25 proves a semantic range for σιγάω.[72] Though few would deny a semantic range for σιγάω, the range of meaning is often forgotten in the discussions.[73] Thus, a definition cannot be assumed but must be contextually defined in each instance.

---

68 See Thomas R. Schreiner, *Romans*, 2nd ed., BECNT (Grand Rapids: Baker Academic, 2018), 786–87 on translating τε and the two participles φανερωθέντος and γνωρισθέντος.

69 The text of Rom 16:25–27 is omitted by Greek manuscripts F G 629. It is located after Rom 14:23 in L Ψ 0209^vid 1175 1241 1505 1881 𝔐. It is located after Rom 15:33 in 𝔓^46. It is located after both Rom 14:23 and 15:33 in manuscript 1506. It is located after both Rom 14:23 and 16:23 in A P 5 33 104 2805. It concludes Rom 16 in 𝔓^61 ℵ B C D 81 365 630 1739 2464. See discussion in Schreiner, *Romans*, 789–90, and Metzger, *A Textual Commentary on the Greek New Testament*, 470–73, 476–77. Metzger specifically points out that 𝔓^61 is fragmentary, and so the text could theoretically have been located elsewhere in the papyrus in addition to Rom 16 (p. 471 n. 2). For the argument that the correct location is at the end of Rom 15 (following 𝔓^46), see Philip W. Comfort, *New Testament Text and Translation Commentary: Commentary on the Variant Readings of the Ancient New Testament Manuscripts and How They Relate to the Major English Translations* (Carol Stream, IL: Tyndale House, 2008), 477–80.

70 Schreiner, *Romans*, 790.

71 Douglas J. Moo, *The Letter to the Romans*, 2nd ed., NICNT (Grand Rapids: Eerdmans, 2018), 955. James D. G. Dunn, *Romans 9–16*, WBC 38B (Dallas: Word, 1988), 915, says that σιγάω is "clearly a divine passive."

72 For a general (i.e., not limited to σιγάω) discussion of silence in relation to Rom 16:25, see L.-M. Dewailly, "Mystère et silence dans Rom 16:25," *NTS* 14 (1967): 111–18.

73 See, e.g., the limited options for 1 Cor 14:34–36 given in Grant R. Osborne, "Hermeneutics and Women in the Church," *JETS* 20 (1977): 343–44.

The two uses of σιγή in the NT (Acts 21:40; Rev 8:1) are worth noting. In Acts 21:27–36, Paul was in Jerusalem and had been the center of an uproar. Paul spoke to the tribune and requested to address the people (21:37–40). Luke records that "when there was a great silence [πολλῆς δὲ σιγῆς γενομένης] he addressed (them) in the 'Hebrew' language" (21:40).[74] As Paul began to speak, Luke writes, "they granted even more silence [μᾶλλον παρέσχον ἡσυχίαν]" (22:2). The crowd did not quietly listen to Paul's speech for long before they began shouting again (22:22–23). Luke's use of σιγή is clearly a momentary silence for a specific purpose. The comparison of Acts 21:40 with 22:2 may show that σιγή was only a general silence with some possible mumbling in the crowd at Acts 21:40 and a greater intensity of silence in 22:2. If so, then there were different levels of silence that depended upon how quiet the crowd wanted to be to hear Paul speak. One might say the crowd went from silently listening (21:40) to sympathetic listening (22:2).[75]

John describes the opening of the seventh seal when "there was silence in heaven for about half an hour [ἐγένετο σιγὴ ἐν τῷ οὐρανῷ ὡς ἡμιώριον]" (Rev 8:1). Even an eschatological silence has a specified time-frame where the participants are silent. Grant Osborne lists no less than eight interpretations of silence for Rev 8:1.[76] Osborne sums up his view, "In short, there are two primary reasons for this dramatic pause: the hushed expectancy of God's judgment about to unfold, and the liturgical silence of heaven in light of the incense and the prayers of the saints in 5:8; 6:9–11; and 7:3–4."[77] The place of Rev 8:1 within the structure of Revelation sheds light on the significance of this silence. Revelation refers to the final judgment throughout the book in the seventh seal, seventh trumpet, and seventh bowl (8:1–5; 11:15–19; 16:17–21).[78] It is noteworthy that all four elements of thunder, rumblings, lightning, and earthquakes are mentioned together in

---

74 On the question of Hebrew vs. Aramaic dialect, see Ken M. Penner, "Ancient Names for Hebrew and Aramaic: A Case for Lexical Revision," *NTS* 65 (2019): 412–23. Penner persuasively argues for a revision in BDAG to opt for "Hebrew." Contrast Darrell L. Bock, *Acts*, BECNT (Grand Rapids: Baker Academic, 2007), 658, who thinks Acts 21:40 is "a likely reference to Aramaic."

75 Cf. I. Howard Marshall, *Acts: An Introduction and Commentary*, TNTC 5 (Downers Grove, IL: IVP Academic, 1980), 373.

76 For details and discussion, see Grant R. Osborne, *Revelation*, BECNT (Grand Rapids: Baker Academic, 2002), 336–38.

77 Osborne, *Revelation*, 338. Robert H. Mounce writes, "We are reminded of the prophetic injunction, 'The LORD is in his holy temple; let all the earth be silent before him' (Hab 2:20; cf. Zeph 1:7–8; Zech 2:13)" (*The Book of Revelation*, rev. ed., NICNT [Grand Rapids: Eerdmans, 1977], 170). Note that σιγάω is not used in Hab 2:20 (LXX has εὐλαβέομαι, "reverence") even though it theoretically could have been used (cf. LXX/MT in Amos 6:10).

78 For a discussion of the recapitulation vs. telescopic views for the structure of Revelation, see Robert L. Thomas, "The Structure of the Apocalypse: Recapitulation or Progression?" *MSJ* 4 (1993): 45–66. Thomas argues for the telescopic view.

Rev 8:5; 11:19; 16:18 (cf. 4:5). G. K. Beale refers to silence as related to the final judgment.[79]

Each of these New Testament references above has demonstrated the semantic range of σιγάω. Absolute silence is not the usual meaning, even if occasionally it may be. The uses of σιγάω in both the OT and NT should serve as a foundation by which to judge how scholars interpret 1 Cor 14:34 and what they assume about the definition of silence. Passages like Rev 8:1 prove that there is nuance and complexity to the term despite the common assumptions today.

Consistency of 1 Cor 14:34–35 within 14:26–40; 12:11; and 11:5

First Corinthians 12–14 is one argument regarding exercising spiritual gifts in the local church. Being led by the Spirit relates directly to being under the lordship of Christ (12:1–3). The same Holy Spirit gives spiritual gifts to each person for the church's edification (12:4–11). By one Spirit all are baptized into one body, and so they suffer and rejoice together regardless of their specific role. God has ordered specific roles and the people for those roles (12:12–31a). Regardless of gifting, spiritual work is nothing unless there is love for others (12:31b–13:3). Paul defines what this love is, such as being patient with others, and explains that love is superior to other spiritual matters (13:4–13). Prophecy is superior to speaking in tongues because prophecy builds up the church and not only the individual (14:1–5). Paul wants them to focus on building up the church as they seek to be spiritual, and simply speaking in tongues does not accomplish this edification (14:6–12). If one does speak in tongues, one should pray for the interpretation so that the other person in the church can be built up (14:13–19). Prophecy is superior to tongues in bringing unbelievers to repentance and faith (14:20–25). Paul then concludes his argument in 1 Cor 14:26–40, which will be discussed below in detail (in addition to 1 Cor 12:11 and 11:5). This analysis will demonstrate how Paul's teaching in 1 Cor 14:34–35 is consistent with the rest of his comments in the surrounding literary context.

---

79   G. K. Beale, *The Book of Revelation: A Commentary on the Greek Text*, NIGTC (Grand Rapids: Eerdmans, 1999), 446–54.

First Corinthians 14:26

Paul writes in 1 Cor 14:26, "Then, how is it, brothers [τί οὖν ἐστιν, ἀδελφοί], when you come together, each one has a psalm, each one has a teaching, each one has a revelation, each one has a tongue, each one has an interpretation. Let all things be done for edification." Paul addresses a problem in 1 Cor 14:26. He does not provide instructions on worship where every member *ought* to have the *same* gift. Paul says that "each one has" something to say (ἔχω is mentioned five times), which sets up the emphasis to exercise spiritual gifts for the sake of edification. The end of this section, in 1 Cor 14:40, also shows emphasis on the way the church service ought to be done, that is, correctly and orderly. The Spirit distributes gifts especially for the common good of the church (1 Cor 12:7; cf. 14:3–5, 12). Edification is a criterion against which to measure the exercising of spiritual gifts in the church.

Scholars have various interpretations for 1 Cor 14:26 that may be viewed on a spectrum: from Paul simply stating what people do in church,[80] to Paul showing what ought to be done in church,[81] to Paul actually commanding each one to bring something.[82] The view that Paul is referring to a Corinthian problem in 1 Cor 14:26 is sometimes not even considered as an option. For example, Craig Keener provides an either/or option: "Whether this is descriptive, or more likely, Paul's ideal, the regulating principle is edifying all those present (14:26)."[83] Could Paul not have stated a problem in 1 Cor 14:26 and then answered it in the following verses? While each element of speech can be found elsewhere in the New Testament, as Keener mentions, the immediate context weighs more in favor of describing a problem in the Corinthian's church service.[84] When a Corinthian

---

80 George T. Montague, *First Corinthians*, Catholic Commentary on Sacred Scripture (Grand Rapids: Baker Academic, 2011), 249–50.
81 Fee, *The First Epistle to the Corinthians*, 764. Contrast Timothy A. Brookins and Bruce W. Longenecker, *1 Corinthians 10–16: A Handbook on the Greek Text*, BHGNT (Waco, TX: Baylor University Press, 2016), 122, who state that the occurrences of ἔχω point to interruptions.
82 Waldemar Kowalski, "Does Paul Really Want All Women to Be Silent?" *Asian Journal of Pentecostal Studies* 201 (2017): 171. There are other views, e.g., B. J. Oropeza uses 1 Cor 14:26 to emphasize gifts for women (*1 Corinthians*, A New Covenant Commentary [Eugene, OR: Cascade, 2017], 190); Harold R. Holmyard III thinks "each one" refers to males ("Does 1 Corinthians 11:2–16 Refer to Women Praying and Prophesying in Church?" *BSac* 154 [1997]: 462).
83 Craig S. Keener, *1–2 Corinthians*, The New Cambridge Bible Commentary (Cambridge: Cambridge University Press, 2005), 117.
84 David E. Garland states that 1 Cor 14:26 is a "hypothetical scenario" that is not real (*1 Corinthians*, BECNT [Grand Rapids: Baker Academic, 2003], 657). Since Paul does address real problems elsewhere, then it is more likely that the reference in 1 Cor 14:26 is a real situation. For example, compare 1 Cor 11:17 (which shares συνέρχομαι with 14:26), "because you come together not for the better but for the worse."

problem is ignored in 1 Cor 14:26, then some scholars interpet ἕκαστος as emphasizing every individual's participation (though, again, the emphasis of the text is edification). For example, Richard Hays comments, "In verses 26–33, Paul sketches a picture of a free-flowing community gathering under the guidance of the Holy Spirit in which 'each one' contributes something to the mix."[85] Others slightly shift "each one" to "all," as in Martin Hasitschka's comment, "Paul first gives a foundational instruction in v. 26. In the worship service of the church all ['alle'] the participants should bring a different contribution (a psalm, teaching, revelation, tongue, interpretation) for 'building'/for 'edification' (οἰκοδομή) to serve the church, what a glance at v. 3 also means words of comfort (παράκλησις)."[86] Often these slight shifts in language cause the interpretation to move further away from Paul addressing a problem to Paul giving "foundational instruction" on worship.

However, James Moffatt rightly says, "Paul is not drawing up any order of worship."[87] It is very possible that Paul opens 1 Cor 14:26 with the phrase "what then is it, brothers" (τί οὖν ἐστιν, ἀδελφοί) because he is addressing a problem. Paul's references to the practices of the Corinthians cannot automatically be interpreted as an endorsement, just as in Paul's reference to their baptizing on behalf of the dead (1 Cor 15:29). When scholars assume Paul endorses the Corinthian practice in 1 Cor 14:26, then the assumption is used to contradict silence in 1 Cor 14:34. The phrase (τί οὖν ἐστιν) also appears in 1 Cor 3:4–5 with the problem of division: "For when someone says, 'I am of Paul.' And another, 'I am of Apollos.' Are you not being merely human? Who then is [τί οὖν ἐστιν] Apollos? And who is Paul? Servants through whom you have believed, and to each one as the Lord has given." This cross-reference does not prove that 1 Cor 14:26 is addressing a problem, but it does show that the phrase can sometimes be found in the context of addressing an issue in Corinth. Paul does answer a problem with τί οὖν ἐστιν in 1 Cor 14:15 regarding the problem of praying in a tongue while one's mind is unfruitful (1 Cor 14:14). Paul answers to pray with one's mind also (1 Cor 14:15). The Corinthian problems should at least be included

---

85   Richard B. Hays, *First Corinthians*, IBC (Louisville: John Knox, 1997), 241.
86   Martin Hasitschka, "Die Frauen in den Gemeinden sollen schweigen: 1 Kor 14,33b–36—Anweisung des Paulus zur rechten Ordnung im Gottesdienst," SNTSU 22 (1997): 48, "In V. 26 gibt Paulus zunächst eine grundsätzliche Weisung. Beim Gottesdienst der Gemeinde sollen alle unterschiedlichen Beiträge, die die Teilnehmer darin einbringen (Psalm, Lehre, Offenbarung, Zungenrede, Auslegung), zum 'Aufbau'/ zur 'Erbauung' (οἰκοδομή) der Gemeinde dienen, was im blick auf V. 3 auch Trost (παράκλησις) und Zuspruch bedeutet."
87   James Moffatt, *The First Epistle of Paul to the Corinthians*, MNTC (New York: Harper and Brothers, 1900), 227.

in the possible meaning when discussing 1 Cor 14:26. The three-fold command to silence in 1 Cor 14:28, 30, 34 is part of the answer to the problems in 1 Cor 14:26. Paul will move onto describing the answers more fully in 1 Cor 14:27–40 to the implicit problems in 14:26.

First Corinthians 14:27–30

First Corinthians 14:27–30 shows that mention of σιγάω can be consistent with Paul because references of silence in 1 Cor 14:28 and 14:30 are clearly not absolute silence. Paul first states, "If anyone speaks in a tongue, two or at most three at a time and in turn, and let one interpret. Now if there is not an interpreter, let him be silent in church, and let him speak to himself and to God" (1 Cor 14:27–28). Silence and speaking are in the same sentence, which then could not mean absolute silence. Paul then says, "And let two or three prophets speak and let the others judge. Now if the other one sitting receives a revelation, let the first one be silent. For you all are able, each one, to prophesy, in order that all may learn and all be encouraged" (1 Cor 14:29–31). The one silenced temporarily was allowed to prophesy, as the final sentence states "each one, to prophesy." Since these two most immediate uses of σιγάω are a temporary silence within the church service, it is very likely that Paul's use in 1 Cor 14:34 would be a specific type of silence.

Therefore, when Paul mentions σιγάω for a third time in 1 Cor 14:34, absolute silence would need to be proven and not assumed. Again, inconsistency in Paul often depends upon an absolute definition of silence. Wolfgang Schrage depends on this absolute definition of σιγάω in order to argue for an interpolation theory. In the middle of several reasons for his position, he claims σιγάω is absolute and unconditional in 1 Cor 14:34 and not in 1 Cor 14:28, 30, due to the latter verses being conditional with ἐάν as well as the "imposition of quotas ('two or three')."[88] In other words, for Schrage, Paul would have had to include ἐάν and a limitation of "two or three" in 1 Cor 14:34 in order for him to silence

---

88 Wolfgang Schrage, *Der erste Brief an die Korinther*, EKKNT (Zürich: Benziger, 1999), 3:483, states, "Certainly also tongues should be 'silent,' if there is no interpretation given (v 28), and also prophetic speech should be 'silent' (again in the singular), if another receives a revelation (v 30), but such occur as conditional regulations with ἐάν before *occasional* 'silences' and the imposition of quotas ('two or three'), here imposes an unconditional and absolute speaking ban (cf. λαλεῖν)" (italics original); "Gewiß soll auch der Glossolale »schweigen«, wenn keine Auslegung gegeben wird (V 28), und auch der prophetisch Redende soll es (beidemal der Singular), wenn ein anderer eine Offenbarung empfängt (V 30), doch statt solch konditionierter Regelungen mit ἐάν über ein *zeitweises* Schweigen und der Kontingentierungen (»zwei oder drei«) wird hier ein unkonditioniertes und absolutes Redeverbot verhängt (vgl. zu λαλεῖν)."

women in a conditional manner. However, based upon the data in the Appendix, a conditional silence should be the assumed starting point unless context dictates otherwise.

Paul highlights the question of speaking with λαλέω six times (1 Cor 14:27, 28, 29, 34, 35, 39). Paul's instructions concerning speech should be viewed in the same way as Ecclesiastes 3:7, where "there is a time to be silent and a time to speak" (καιρὸς τοῦ σιγᾶν καὶ καιρὸς τοῦ λαλεῖν). Silence is commanded if there is no interpreter (1 Cor 14:28), but the person can still speak ("let him speak to himself and to God"). In other words, silence in 1 Cor 14:28 cannot be absolute silence.[89] This fact makes it at least possible that 1 Cor 14:34 is not absolute silence either.

First Corinthians 14:29–30 mirrors 14:27–28, and the overlapping terms are in bold below:

1 Corinthians 14:27–28: εἴτε γλώσσῃ τις λαλεῖ, κατὰ **δύο ἢ** τὸ πλεῖστον **τρεῖς** καὶ ἀνὰ μέρος, καὶ εἷς διερμηνευέτω **ἐὰν δὲ** μὴ ᾖ διερμηνευτής, **σιγάτω** ἐν ἐκκλησίᾳ, ἑαυτῷ δὲ λαλείτω καὶ τῷ θεῷ.

1 Corinthians 14:29–30: προφῆται δὲ **δύο ἢ τρεῖς** λαλείτωσαν καὶ οἱ ἄλλοι διακρινέτωσαν **ἐὰν δὲ** ἄλλῳ ἀποκαλυφθῇ καθημένῳ, ὁ πρῶτος **σιγάτω**.

In 1 Cor 14:27–28 there needs to be an interpreter, while in 14:29–30 there are others who judge the prophecies. Just as in 1 Cor 14:28, the silence here in 1 Cor 14:30 is a specific silence and not absolute. The first two uses of σιγάω in this context are often forgotten or ignored when writers come to 1 Cor 14:34. For example, Christine Walde writes, "The commandment for silence, which the apostle Paul (I Cor 14,34f.) imposes on women in church, aims in a different direction as a means for discrimination (cf. also corresponding statements in pagan texts, for example Eur. HF 534 f.)."[90] Walde comments without any reference to silencing others in 1 Cor 14:28 and 14:30. This omission is significant since Walde would need to state why silence in 1 Cor 14:34 is "a means for discrimination" but not so in 1 Cor 14:28 and 14:30.

---

89   Keener, *1–2 Corinthians*, 118, writes, "Like tongue-speakers (14:28) and prophets (14:30), women were to remain 'silent' under some circumstances." So there can be some agreement on how to interpret σιγάω among some writers on all sides. However, the historical reconstruction and application varies, which will be discussed later. It is unclear how Keener on the one hand connects 1 Cor 14:28, 30, and 34, but on the other hand still claims that "the digression in 14:34–35 is so disjunctive in its context that some argue plausibly that it is a post-Pauline interpolation" (p. 117).

90   Christine Walde, "Silence," *BNP* 13:455.

The Literary Context: The Range of ΣΙΓΑΩ as a Basis for Consistency | 41

Here in 1 Cor 14:29 the concept of judging arises (καὶ οἱ ἄλλοι διακρινέτωσαν), which is an important contextual clue in interpreting silence. Paul helpfully explains that "the spirits of prophets are subject to the prophets" (1 Cor 14:32), which implies discernment among prophecies. One might say that 1 Cor 14:37 is itself a call for discernment where they recognize (ἐπιγινώσκω) what Paul writes is truly from the Lord. Paul has already made the issue of judging key throughout his letter (1 Cor 2:15; 4:1–5; 5:3, 12–13; 6:1–6; 10:14–16, 29; 11:13, 28–34; 12:10). Judging has a range of meaning and is dependent upon the related topic. When it is related to speech, it often has the idea of discernment of what is true or false (1 Cor 10:14–16; 11:13; 12:10; 14:29).[91] When it is a matter of conscience, then judgment is suspended (1 Cor 10:29). When it is a matter of ethics, then judgment is allowed, as long as it is inside the church (1 Cor 5:3, 12–13). Inside the church, there is an additional consideration: if a church member judges himself rightly, then there is no need for judgment by others (1 Cor 2:15; 11:28–34; cf. 4:1–5). When Paul considers how eschatology applies to the idea of judging, then the church is shown to be in a better position than human courts to wisely adjudicate everyday matters and to refrain from declaring final judgment on someone's motives (4:1–5; 6:1–6).[92] This emphasis of judging rightly throughout 1 Corinthians, including Chapter Fourteen, lends support to those who say silence in 1 Cor 14:34 is specifically regarding the judgment of prophecy. While both men and women may prophesy, D. A. Carson argues that silence means that women "may *not* participate in the oral weighing of such prophecies."[93] If true,

---

91   Combining 1 Cor 12:10 with 1 Cor 14:32 helps to see that speech is likely in view in 1 Cor 12:10, and hence categorized here with speech.

92   1 Corinthians 4:1–5 is a difficult text to synthesize with the rest of 1 Corinthians. However, the answer lies somewhere regarding present and future judgment and motives of the heart, specifically in relation to each servant belonging to God. See Thomas R. Schreiner, *1 Corinthians: An Introduction and Commentary*, TNTC 7 (Downers Grove, IL: IVP Academic, 2018), 98–100; and Mark Taylor, *1 Corinthians*, NAC 28 (Nashville: B&H, 2014), 110–15.

93   D. A. Carson, "'Silence in the Churches': On the Role of Women in 1 Corinthians 14:33b–36," in *Recovering Biblical Manhood and Womanhood: A Response to Evangelical Feminism*, ed. John Piper and Wayne Grudem (Wheaton, IL: Crossway, 1991), 151 (italics original). Alan F. Johnson by contrast asks, "Further, if the issue is simply women/wives' sifting of male prophets' messages, then why wouldn't Paul permit women to sift the messages of women prophets and restrict them only from evaluating male prophets" (*1 Corinthians*, The IVP New Testament Commentary [Downers Grove, IL: InterVarsity Press, 2004], 274). This hypothetical question can be answered by clarifying that the authoritative action itself (evaluation in the public assembly) is what is prohibited, and not just the object of evaluation, the male or female prophet. In any case, Paul does refer to women-to-women ministry in Titus 2:3–5.

42 | *Paul, Women, and the Meaning of Silence*

then there would be no charge of inconsistency with the rest of Paul's statements because σιγάω is not absolute silence.⁹⁴

First Corinthians 14:31–33

A closer look at submission (ὑποτάσσω) and learning (μανθάνω) in 1 Cor 14:31–32 will demonstrate a more complete understanding of σιγάω, since these three terms are found together in 1 Cor 14:34–35. First Corinthians 14:31–33 mirrors 14:34 (just like the previous verses above mirrored each other in 1 Cor 14:27–30). Paul goes from each person in general (1 Cor 14:31; καθ' ἕνα) to women in particular (1 Cor 14:34; αἱ γυναῖκες). Next, there is the mention of submission in both 1 Cor 14:32 and 14:34. Finally, Paul appeals to either God (1 Cor 14:33a) or the law (1 Cor 14:34)—the former with γάρ and the latter with καθώς. If this parallelism is correct, then ἐκκλησία is found at the seam between 1 Cor 14:33 and 14:34. The parallelism reinforces that 1 Cor 14:34 is not a digression or out of context.⁹⁵

Paul provides an important explanation concerning submission in 1 Cor 14:32: "the spirits of the prophets are subject to the prophets" (καὶ πνεύματα προφητῶν προφήταις ὑποτάσσεται), where the two references to prophets are the same people.⁹⁶ Fitzmyer sums up well that the Christian prophets' ability to control themselves stood in contrast to the un-controlled pagan worship.⁹⁷ Comparing 1 Cor 14:32 with 1 Cor 14:34 is important because the first use of submission has an indirect object, whereas the second use of submission does not have an indirect object. Eckhard Schnabel summarizes the differences of opinion: "The demand for submission is differently interpreted: submission is a

---

94 There is a question as to the identity of ἄλλος in 1 Cor 14:29 (cf. also the term in 1 Cor 14:30). These "others" judging prophecy could be the church in general or other prophets. See discussion in Christopher Forbes, *Prophecy and Inspired Speech in Early Christianity and its Hellenistic Environment* (Peabody, MA: Hendrickson, 1995), 265–69; and Elim Hiu, *Regulations Concerning Tongues and Prophecy in 1 Corinthians 14:26–40: Relevance Beyond the Corinthian Church*, LNTS 406 (New York: T&T Clark, 2010), 120–22. While I take the judging as coming from the church in general, the question if women may judge prophecy still depends on the interpretation of 1 Cor 14:34 (so Forbes, *Prophecy and Inspired Speech*, 269).

95 Contrast Walter Klaiber, *Der erste Korintherbrief*, Die Botschaft des Neuen Testaments (Neukirchen-Vluyn: Neukirchener Theologie, 2011), 232, who writes, "In V. 34f Paul abruptly reaches to a new topic: women are not allowed to speak in the church but should be silent"; "In den V. 34f greift Paulus unvermittelt ein neues Thema auf: Frauen dürfen in den Gemeindeversammlungen nicht sprechen, sondern sollen schweigen."

96 So Brookins and Longenecker, *1 Corinthians 10–16*, 125–26.

97 Joseph Fitzmyer, *First Corinthians: A New Translation with Introduction and Commentary*, AB 32 (New Haven: Yale University Press, 2008), 526–27.

question of (1) under the order of the church, that is, under the order of public worship; (2) under the order of God, that is, society; (3) under apostolic instructions; (4) under the husband."[98] The first solution appears most likely where submission is to the church, and in particular the male leadership in the church during the evaluation of prophecy.[99] The submission is not simply to husbands from 1 Cor 14:35 because in that verse they are simply to "ask" their husbands at home, whereas 1 Cor 14:34 regards submission in the local church (cf. submission to prophets in 1 Cor 14:32). It is uncertain whether the scribe of Codex Alexandrinus inserted τοῖς ἀνδράσιν in 1 Cor 14:34 to mean husbands in particular or men in general. The principle of male headship is taught elsewhere (e.g., Eph 5:22–24; 1 Tim 2:12).[100] It should be noted that the entire church was to be submissive to the church leaders. First Corinthians 16:15–18 states: "Now I urge you, brothers, you know the household of Stephanas, that they are the firstfruits of Achaia and they devoted themselves to service among the saints so that you also be subject to [ὑμεῖς ὑποτάσσησθε] such ones and to all the ones who assist and labor. Now I rejoice at the coming of Stephanas and Fortunatus and Achaicus, because these supplied that which was lacking in you, for they refreshed my spirit and yours. Therefore, recognize such ones." Not only is submission to church leaders made explicit here in 1 Cor 16:16, but there is also overlap with "recognizing" certain ones in the church (1 Cor 14:37; 16:18). It is likely that Stephanas was in some sort of leadership position in Corinth, even if the exact details are not known.[101] Hensley writes, "Just as the 'spirits of prophets' are subject to prophets, so now Paul commands the women to subject their prophetic speech to the evaluation of other prophets."[102]

Clarifying the evaluation of prophecies in relation to submission helps to explain the two (seemingly opposite) uses of μανθάνω in 1 Cor 14:31, 35. Walter

---

98   Eckhard J. Schnabel, *Der erste Brief des Paulus an die Korinther*, Historisch-theologische Auslegung, Neues Testament 4 (Wuppertal: Brockhaus, 2006), 847, states, "Die Aufforderung zur Unterordnung wird unterschiedlich erklärt: Es handelt sich um die Unterordnung 1. unter die Gemeindeordnung bzw. unter die Ordnung des Gottesdienstes; 2. unter die Ordnung Gottes bzw. der Gesellschaft; 3. unter die apostolischen Anweisungen; 4. unter den Ehemann."

99   Cf. Schreiner, where he takes silence as reference to asking questions that challenged male headship (*1 Corinthians*, 297–98).

100   See Grudem, "Does ΚΕΦΑΛΗ ('Head') Mean 'Source' or 'Authority Over' in Greek Literature?" 51, 57. The former page lists the results of κεφαλή in Greek literature, and the latter page discusses Eph 5:22–24.

101   Benjamin L. Merkle, *The Elder and Overseer: One Office in the Early Church*, StBibLit 57 (New York: Peter Lang, 2003), 101–4. cf. 1 Cor 1:16.

102   Adam D. Hensley, "σιγαω, λαλεω, and ὑποτασσω in 1 Corinthians 14:34 in Their Literary and Rhetorical Context," *JETS* 55.2 (2012): 351.

Klaiber lists the question of learning in these two verses as one reason Paul's words seem "surprising."[103] In the first instance all were allowed to learn in the church, but in the second instance the women were told to ask their husbands at home if they wanted to learn anything. The first occurrence is learning in general in the church as everyone spoke to one another. But the second is referring to learning more if a woman disagreed with the judgment of prophecy from one of the male leaders. To engage in this type of disagreement could begin to assert authority over a male leader in the church (contrary to 1 Tim 2:12). Asking questions at home did not mean absolute silence in church because women were free to speak in church in other ways that did not portray a lack of submission to male church leadership. Thus, a specific silence in church is consistent with submission and learning in this passage.

First Corinthians 14:34

Interpreting σιγάω has at least two challenges.[104] First, "silence" is a common word in English, and so many commentators simply assume a general definition without considering the range of usage. Second, there is a tendency to import modern sensibilities into the ancient text. For example, Margaret Mitchell says, "In the strongest possible language, the text issues the dual commands 'let them be silent' and 'let them be subordinated' in the assemblies."[105] However, in the ancient world, σιγάω could have included stronger language, and in fact, sometimes did (see, e.g., Aristophanes *Lys.* 507–20 where silence is paired with reference to getting a beating). Luise Schottroff employs the same type of rhetorical strategy as Mitchell when Schottroff writes three times that the language of 1 Cor 14:34–38 is "radical."[106] Schottroff does not specify exactly what made Paul's word radical. From Schottroff's own perspective, "the content is congruent with Greco-Roman conservative ideology of women."[107] Does Schottroff only mean that the words are "radical" from a modern perspective? If so, how can Schottroff use a modern view to conclude that Paul did not write these words? To say that σιγάω is the

---

103 Klaiber, *Der erste Korintherbrief,* 232–33, says, "Diese Aussage [1 Cor 14:34] überrascht aus ganz verschiedenen Gründen" (p. 232). Klaiber lists five total reasons that he thinks this passage is surprising.
104 The law will be discussed below in Chapter Three under the historical context.
105 Margaret Mitchell, "1 Cor 14:33B–36: Women Commanded to Be 'Silent' in the Assemblies," in *Women in Scripture: A Dictionary of Named and Unnamed Women in the Hebrew Bible, the Apocryphal/Deuterocanonical Books, and the New Testament,* ed. Carol Meyers (Grand Rapids: Eerdmans, 2000), 477.
106 Schottroff, *Der erste Brief an die Gemeinde in Korinth,* 282–83.
107 Schottroff, *Der erste Brief an die Gemeinde in Korinth,* 283, writes, "inhaltliche Kongruenz mit römisch-hellenistischer konservativer Frauenideologie."

"strongest possible language" or "radical" are modern sensibilities and should not be used to prove the authenticity or meaning of Paul's ancient words.

The Appendix shows that σιγάω typically means a specific silence. In the case of 1 Cor 14:34, the specific silence relates to the evaluation of prophecy since the immediate context (e.g., 1 Cor 14:32) includes evaluation.[108] However, James Greenbury systematically challenges the evaluation of prophecy view in his article "1 Corinthians 14:34–35: Evaluation of Prophecy Revisited."[109] He lists the following five reasons against this interpretation, mentioned here in summary fashion: (1) prophecy itself is more authoritative than evaluation of prophecy (women can prophesy, and so why deny them evaluation?); (2) learning at home in 1 Cor 14:35 does not seem to fit this view (according to Greenbury, v. 35 shows women did not understand the prophecies); (3) διακρίνω is a silent evaluation by the congregation; (4) λαλέω is unqualified and cannot mean evaluation; and (5) this view is modern and has not been detected by ancient interpreters to fit the flow of the passage, and verse 29 is too distant to provide a contextual clue.[110] These reasons will be addressed in turn.

First, the idea that prophecy itself is more authoritative than judging goes against 1 Cor 14:32 where the spirits of the prophets are subject to the prophets. The ones prophesying are submitting to those judging. Also, when Greenbury appeals to texts such as 1 Cor 12:28 and the hierarchy of gifted persons,[111] those judging prophecy are not listed, so the passage is not relevant to the question at hand.

Second, Greenbury's statement about 1 Cor 14:35 and women not understanding the prophecies in the first place is an unproven assumption,[112] and so in itself is not evidence against the evaluation view. Paul gives the reason he tells them to ask their husbands: "for it is shameful for a woman to speak in church" (1 Cor 14:35b).

---

108 Several writers hold to the judgment of prophecy view, such as, Simon J. Kistemaker, *Exposition of the First Epistles to the Corinthians* (Grand Rapids: Baker, 1993), 512; James B. Hurley, "Did Paul Require Veils or the Silence of Women? A Consideration of I Cor. 11:2–16 and I Cor. 14:33b–36," *WTJ* 35 (1973): 217, 219; Margaret E. Thrall, *I and II Corinthians*, CBC (Cambridge: Cambridge University Press, 1965), 102; Grudem, "Prophecy—Yes, But Teaching—No," 23; and, as already quoted above, Carson, "Silent in the Churches," 151. Cf. William D. Mounce, *Pastoral Epistles*, WBC 46 (Nashville: Thomas Nelson, 2000), 118, who says, "1 Cor 14:34–35 prohibits a certain type of speech, perhaps the authoritative evaluation of a prophet's message."
109 James Greenbury, "1 Corinthians 14:34–35: Evaluation of Prophecy Revisited," *JETS* 51.4 (2008): 721–31.
110 Greenbury, "1 Corinthians 14:34–35," 731.
111 Greenbury, "1 Corinthians 14:34–35," 724.
112 Greenbury, "1 Corinthians 14:34–35," 726.

Third, Greenbury writes emphatically, "Therefore, to suggest that judging of prophecies was expressed audibly during the assemblies is to read more into Paul's words than he actually says."[113] However, earlier he had explained, "The word [διακρίνω] can denote either audible speaking or silent appraisal."[114] In his discussion, he does not prove which category 1 Cor 14:29 falls under, as many of his arguments are themselves arguments from silence (contrast, e.g., 1 Cor 11:31 with 1 Cor 6:5; for clearly audible uses elsewhere, see Jas 2:4 and Jude 9).

Fourth, Greenbury writes, "Yet now in verses 34–35 he uses λαλεῖν in its unqualified form."[115] However, it is qualified by the intervening mention of submission in 1 Cor 14:34, which also connects it back to 1 Cor 14:32.

Fifth, Greenbury makes the claim that there is too much distance between 1 Cor 14:34–35 and 1 Cor 14:29 to connect the evaluation of v. 29 to the silence in v. 34. However, the idea of evaluation is also implicit in the submission of one prophet to another mentioned in 1 Cor 14:32. Greenbury's argument that the evaluation of prophecy view is only a modern interpretation is significant.[116] If only ancient views were correct, then several views on 1 Corinthians, including the interpolation theory, would be wrong. Some older writers may have been close to interpreting silence in connection with evaluating prophecy. For example, Wolfgang Musculus, a 16th century Reformed theologian,[117] writes in his commentary on 1 Corinthians, "Now the apostle has plainly not disallowed the speaking of words generally, as if women were permitted to say nothing whatsoever. Rather, he has disallowed that kind of speaking where public deliberations or judicial cases are officially discussed and treated in assemblies of men in the churches and in the marketplace, where men come together, not women."[118] Musculus rules out the typical general view of σιγάω where women are banned from saying anything. "Public deliberations or judicial cases" are more than evaluating prophecy, but could it include this idea? Another writer John Colet

---

113   Greenbury, "1 Corinthians 14:34–35," 729.
114   Greenbury, "1 Corinthians 14:34–35," 727.
115   Greenbury, "1 Corinthians 14:34–35," 729.
116   Hiu specifies who he thinks first noted the evaluation of prophecy view as Margaret Thrall's 1965 commentary (Hiu, *Regulations Concerning Tongues and Prophecy in 1 Corinthians 14:26–40*, 147). See her view in Thrall, *I and II Corinthians*, 102.
117   J. Wayne Baker, "Musculus, Wolfgang," *The Oxford Encyclopedia of the Reformation* 3:103–4.
118   Text is taken from Scott M. Manetsch, ed., *1 Corinthians*, Reformation Commentary on Scripture: New Testament 9a (Downers Grove, IL: IVP Academic, 2017), 345. For general remarks, see Scott M. Manetsch, "(Re)Constructing the Pastoral Office: Wolfgang Musculus's Commentaries on 1 and 2 Corinthians," in *On the Writing of New Testament Commentaries: Festschrift for Grant R. Osborne on the Occasion of His 70th Birthday*, ed. Stanley E. Porter and Eckhard J. Schnabel, TENTS 8 (Leiden: Brill, 2013), 253–66.

(1466?–1519)[119] states, "Let the prophets, the spiritual men who are endowed with divine understanding, interpret on particular points the readings that are heard. Where there are several prophets, let each yield to a judgment that is better. Prophecies, to be sure, are understood by prophets, and rightly interpreted, they move men wondrously and transport them to Christ. In these matters let women be silent in the church and in the assembly of saints. Let them learn at home from their husbands."[120] Colet's words "in these matters" leaves open the question of his intended reference. He provides additional insight on his view of 1 Cor 11:5 in relation to 1 Cor 14:34–35 when he writes,

> [Paul's] teaching is that in a society composed of men and women, the latter should have their heads covered, the former uncovered, when praying or prophesying.... To prophesy means here to teach and interpret the scriptures and revelations, and this belongs only to men, at least in a men's church. In a church of women, there is nothing to keep women from prophesying; for holy monastic women are all of them, in this sense, man-like women. In this place, however, Paul intentionally restricts himself to the covering and veiling of the head, intending to speak later more explicitliy in their own place of prayer and of prophecy, which is a declaration by the Spirit of reality, truth, and meanings. For women he now ordains and commands the veil; afterwards, he ordains and commands silence.[121]

It is not certain just how much Colet intended women to be silent in the churches, especially with his distinction of "a church of women." It is likely that Colet would have seen women's silence as necessary during the evaluation of prophecy. Also, it is likely that Colet would not have banned women from all speech. What is not certain is where exactly Colet is located in-between a specific silence and absolute silence.

First Corinthians 14:35–36

A proper view of σιγάω removes the need to appeal to a Corinthian slogan. Nonetheless, this view should still be addressed since Paul *certainly* quotes the

---

119   Precise dating is not certain. See F. L. Cross and E. A. Livingstone, eds., "Colet, John," *ODCC*, 3rd ed., 375.
120   Bernard O'Kelly and Catherine A. L. Jarrott, *John Colet's Commentary on First Corinthians: A New Edition of the Latin Text, with Translation, Annotations, and Introduction*, Medieval & Renaissance Texts & Studies 21 (Binghamton, NY: Center for Medieval & Early Renaissance Studies, 1985), 275.
121   O'Kelly and Jarrott, *John Colet's Commentary on First Corinthians*, 221, 225.

48 | *Paul, Women, and the Meaning of Silence*

Corinthians in 1 Cor 1:12; 3:4; 15:12 (the text itself says as much).[122] Paul *may* quote the Corinthians in 1 Cor 7:1 (less likely, but still potentially in 8:1, 4). These verses contain textual clues that a quotation might be the case. Several other texts, including 1 Cor 14:34–35, are named by various scholars as being a Corinthian slogan, which most of them are likely not slogans. For the present purpose, the emphasis will be on the question of 1 Cor 14:34–35 as a Corinthian slogan.

Discussion of Kirk MacGregor (above in Chapter One) provided many of the reasons scholars appeal to a Corinthian slogan theory. Some scholars emphasize the masculine interpretation of 1 Cor 14:36. For instance, Neal Flanagan and Edwina Snyder state matter-of-factly, "In the original Greek it [μόνος] is masculine. Paul is now talking to the *men*, where we would expect just the opposite."[123] There are objections against taking 1 Cor 14:36 as masculine only, in addition to other objections to the slogan theory.[124] First, even some scholars who deny Pauline authorship do not hold to this position. Richard Hays refers to Corinthian slogans and states that "this explanation is farfetched in the extreme. There is no indication in the text that Paul is quoting anything (unlike 7:1) or that the Corinthians held such views about women; furthermore, the other Corinthian views cited by Paul are always short slogans, not extended didactic arguments."[125]

Second, there is no unanimity on which texts are considered slogans throughout 1 Corinthians. Jay Smith writes, "Moreover, probably no verse in 1 Corinthians is *universally recognized* as a Corinthian slogan."[126] Smith gives a visual representation of the mixed references among seven major commentators.[127]

---

122 Daniel C. Arichea, who argues for the Corinthian slogan theory, writes, "It is not unusual in 1 Corinthians for Paul to quote the opinion of his adversaries and then to refute them. While these opinions are not marked as such in the Greek text, they can nevertheless be identified through exegesis and discourse analysis" ("The Silence of Women in the Church: Theology and Translation in 1 Corinthians 14.33b–36," *BT* 46.1 [1995]: 107). This statement is partially incorrect. Paul does explicitly mark opinions in 1 Cor 1:12; 3:4; 15:12.

123 Neal M. Flanagan and Edwina H. Snyder, "Did Paul Put Down Women in First Corinthians 14:34–36?" *Foundations* 24.3 (1981): 217 (italics original). Flanagan and Snyder provide additional reasons in their article, but they conclude with this reason twice (cf. pp. 217 and 219).

124 See above in the history of research where Philip Payne refutes a number of points related to the Corinthian slogan theory. Some scholars simply dismiss the theory in general. E.g., Christian Wolff, *Der erste Brief des Paulus an die Korinther*, THKNT 7 (Leipzig: Evangelische Verlagsanstalt, 1996), 344, writes, "But v. 36 is not formulated as a contradiction" ("Aber V.36 ist nicht als Widerspruch formuliert").

125 Hays, *1 Corinthians*, 248.

126 Jay E. Smith, "Slogans in 1 Corinthians," *BSac* 167 (2010): 74 (italics original).

127 Smith, "Slogans in 1 Corinthians," 87.

The Literary Context: The Range of ΣΙΓΑΩ as a Basis for Consistency | 49

Third, there are no agreed upon objective criteria on which to prove a Corinthian slogan. Travis Smith set out to argue for a specific set of criteria.[128] Where does Smith ultimately derive his criteria? He writes, "Based upon the *progymnasmata* (preliminary exercises, or rhetorical exercise handbooks), the extant rhetorical handbooks, and the five generally accepted slogans (1 Corinthians 1:12 [cf. 3:4]; 6:12 [cf. 10:23]; 6:13; 7:1; 8:1ff), we will establish a [*sic*] tentative criteria in order to identify embedded Corinthian slogans."[129] The use of "generally accepted slogans" as a basis for figuring out what is a slogan is begging the question.[130] If one used only certain texts where Paul makes it explicit (1 Cor 1:12; 3:4; 15:12), then 1 Cor 14:34–35 is clearly not a slogan.

Fourth, the particle ἤ in itself does not prove the slogan theory. Carson explains, "The brute fact is this: *in every instance in the New Testament where the disjunctive particle in question is used in a construction analogous to the passage at hand, its effect is to reinforce the truth of the clause or verse that precedes it.*"[131] Regardless of if one agrees completely with Carson,[132] the fact is that the particle can easily be found to reinforce a previous argument (e.g., 1 Cor 9:6 [which includes μόνος!]), and therefore, the particle in 1 Cor 14:36 does not support the slogan theory.[133]

---

128 Travis Lee Smith, "Towards Establishing Criteria for Identifying Corinthian Slogans and Their Application to 1 Corinthians 14:34–35 and 15:29" (ThM thesis, Dallas Theological Seminary, 2006).
129 Smith, "Towards Establishing Criteria for Identifying Corinthian Slogans," 6–7.
130 Smith, "Slogans in 1 Corinthians," 74, admits this fact.
131 Carson, "Silent in the Churches," 151 (italics original).
132 For interaction with Carson, see J. M. Holmes, *Text in a Whirlwind: A Critique of Four Exegetical Devices at 1 Timothy 2.9–15*, JSNTSup 196 (Sheffield: Sheffield Academic Press, 2000), 231–32.
133 There is a second type of argument from Ben Witherington who says the function of rhetorical questions means that the questions cannot support a slogan theory. He refers to Duane F. Watson, "1 Corinthians 10:23–11:1 in the Light of Greco-Roman Rhetoric: The Role of Rhetorical Questions," *JBL* 108.2 (1989): 301–18. In Watson's article, the function of rhetorical questions are as follows: (1) Rhetorical questions as recapitulation; (2) as anticipation; (3) as argumentation; (4) as figures of thought (aiding in argumentation and emphasis); and (5) as ornament. Ben Witherington III, *Conflict and Community in Corinth: A Socio-Rhetorical Commentary on 1 and 2 Corinthians* (Grand Rapids: Eerdmans, 1995), 288 n. 51, says, "If this reading is correct, then it rules out the view that vv. 34f. are a quotation and that the questions respond to the quotation." Witherington has not considered all of 1 Corinthians when assessing the full value of Watson's categories. In 1 Cor 1:12–13, Paul clearly refers to Corinthian slogans and then follows them up with rhetorical questions (and thus, rhetorical questions do *not* rule out 1 Cor 14:34–35 as a quotation). Since 1 Corinthians contains both rhetorical questions in response to slogans and questions in line with Watson's categories (e.g., 1 Cor 9:1), then the issue over a Corinthian slogan must be decided somewhere else other than that of rhetorical questions.

50 | *Paul, Women, and the Meaning of Silence*

Fifth, similar to the particle ἤ, the term μόνος *in itself* cannot prove that Paul is referring only to men, and thus to a Corinthian slogan in 1 Cor 14:34–35.[134] In Phil 4:15 Paul references εἰ μὴ ὑμεῖς μόνοι (plural, masculine term), and in context this reference is clearly referring to the entire church (men and women) at Philippi.[135] Furthermore, as Philip Payne has written, "Its 'you only' far more naturally contrasts with 'all the churches' (V. 33)."[136] In sum, several reasons fail to prove a Corinthian slogan exists in 1 Cor 14:35–35, and the answer to apparent inconsistencies lies elsewhere—in particular in a proper understanding of σιγάω.[137]

First Corinthians 14:37–40

If 1 Cor 14:34–35 is original (as argued below in "Interpolation and Textual Criticism"), then 1 Cor 14:37–38 confirms that the instructions for women still refer to the issue of prophecy. Paul writes immediately after 1 Cor 14:34–36, "If anyone considers himself to be a prophet or spiritual, let him recognize what I write to you that it is a command of the Lord. But if anyone disregards it, he is disregarded" (1 Cor 14:37–38). The conclusion (1 Cor 14:39–40) also includes mention of prophecy. First Corinthians 14:37 refers to evaluation of a prophet (in this case, evaluating what Paul is saying), and further confirms the contextual meaning of σιγάω.[138] Paul presents himself here as a prophet giving a command of the Lord.[139] In 1 Cor 14:38, if there is any so-called spiritual person

---

134   Chris Ukachukwu Manus relies heavily upon a certain understanding of the particle ἤ and the term μόνος ("The Subordination of the Women in the Church: 1 Cor 14:33b–36 Reconsidered," *Revue Africaine de Théologie* 8 [1984]: 183–95).

135   This reference in Philippians also shows the issue in Pheme Perkin's view on 1 Cor 14:36, "Therefore the expression is best considered a general reinforcement of Paul's authority to introduce rules. The masculine plural adjective indirectly indicates that the apostle envisages male leaders as responsible for administering church affairs" (Pheme Perkins, *First Corinthians*, Paideia Commentaries on the New Testament [Grand Rapids: Baker Academic, 2012], 165). In other words, the adjective itself does not demonstrate this assertion about male leaders.

136   Philip B. Payne, "Is 1 Corinthians 14:34–35 a Marginal Comment or a Quotation? A Response to Kirk MacGregor," *Priscilla Papers* 33.2 (2019): 25. Payne's observation is correct, but he uses this observation for an entirely different conclusion (the inauthenticity of 1 Cor 14:34–35).

137   For seven succinct reasons why 1 Cor 14:34–35 is not a Corinthian slogan, see Craig Blomberg, *1 Corinthians*, NIVAC (Grand Rapids: Zondervan, 1994), 279–80.

138   Hensley, "σιγαω, λαλεω, and ὑποτασσω," 349, explains, "The logic runs thus: since true prophets submit to the evaluation of other prophets, the Corinthians ought to submit to Paul's judgment if they, too, aspire to be 'spiritual' or 'prophets.' Thus, the nearest context of 1 Cor 14:34 (i.e. verses 29–37) is saturated with the differentiation between prophetic speech and its prophetic evaluation."

139   Command here is taken generally. Some manuscripts have the plural κυριου εισιν εντολαι (D¹ K L Ψ 81 104 365 630 1175 1505 2464 𝔐).

in the church who does not recognize that what Paul writes is the Lord's command, then the church is commanded not to recognize that person as spiritual.[140] The meaning of the "command of the Lord" is not easy to understand, but the inability to interpret the exact reference does not negate the rest of the context of 1 Cor 14:37–40 supporting a specific understanding of σιγάω.[141] Paul concludes this section encouraging the exercise of spiritual gifts within good order (1 Cor 14:39–40). Good order would presumably be based upon following Paul's instructions within 1 Corinthians 12–14.

First Corinthians 12:11

Scholars sometimes appeal to various texts about the Spirit when arguing for a particular interpretation of 1 Cor 14:34. Based upon certain interpretations of the Spirit's work, scholars attempt to show inconsistency with any restriction on a woman's speech. However, no text on the Spirit precludes certain restrictions concerning how church leadership functions. Paul writes in 1 Cor 12:11, "Now all these things [i.e., spiritual gifts] are produced by one and the same Spirit, who distributes to each one individually just as he wills." David Garland sets up the question the way many writers ask, "If tongues and prophecy are spiritual gifts, and if each individual is allotted gifts as the Spirit chooses (12:11)—presumably without regard to gender, social status, or race—why should women with these

---

140   I am taking the subject of the first ἀγνοέω in 1 Cor 14:38 as the church. The second use of the verb ἀγνοέω I take as an imperative (instead of indicative) due to the external evidence of the manuscripts, which include 𝔓⁴⁶ and B; though, Metzger, *A Textual Commentary on the Greek New Testament*, 500, argues that the external evidence favors the indicative. See discussion in Paul D. Gardner, *1 Corinthians*, ZECNT (Grand Rapids: Eerdmans, 2018), 638 n. 37, 639–40. Cf. Garland, *1 Corinthians*, 674, who writes, "If they do not recognize his instructions as valid, then they are invalidated as prophets and as spiritual persons" (though Garland goes on to refer more to God's judgment). See also Taylor, *1 Corinthians*, 362, who notes, "The phrase 'If anybody thinks' appears now for the third time in the letter. The phrase occurs in three of the major argumentative sections of the letter as a rebuke to those who consider themselves to be wise (3:18), knowledgeable (8:2), and spiritual (14:37)."

141   Christian Stettler's article is helpful in understanding the issues involved with the phrase κυρίου ἐστὶν ἐντολή ("The 'Command of the Lord' in 1 Cor 14,37—a Saying of Jesus?" *Bib* 87 [2006]: 42–51). Stettler reviews why the phrase should be understood in relation to a saying of Jesus and not simply from Paul's apostolic authority. From Stettler's comparison with the rest of 1 Corinthians, I think it is very plausible that Paul refers to Jesus's teaching. Stettler continues to try to pinpoint this teaching to Jesus's command to love (= mutual edification), and this view also is very possible. What is doubtful is Stettler's view that 1 Cor 14:(33b)34–35 is not part of the command due to the interpolation theory (p. 44). Contrast F. F. Bruce, who explains that the command of the Lord "is not a question of appealing to something laid down by Jesus in the course of his ministry (as in 7.10, 25), but of the dominical authority by which the apostle speaks" (*1 and 2 Corinthians*, NCB [Grand Rapids: Eerdmans, 1971; repr., 1983], 136).

gifts be silent in the assembly?"[142] As mentioned before, Ben Witherington states directly that "leadership was to be determined primarily by who was called and gifted by the Spirit, and not at all by gender or cultural background."[143] The details of each text about the Spirit must be considered before pronouncing that gender is *never* a factor. And often a look at the specific details causes scholars to admit what is "presumed" (as Garland does).

Gordon Fee's book *Gospel and Spirit* takes particular issue with how the Spirit relates to women in ministry. He writes, "The Spirit is unconscious of race, sex, or rank. He gifts whom he wills for the common good (1 Cor 12:7, 11)."[144] If this claim about the Spirit were completely accurate, how could Paul *at any time in history* have restricted women in any way (e.g., 1 Cor 11:2–16)? Fee even references, "[D]ivinely ordained hierarchical structures—which can only be found after, not before, the Fall."[145] This view misses several clues in Genesis 2 of Adam's leadership.[146] Appeal to the Spirit's work is often presented in absolute terms (without any nuance on sometimes being silent). However, people gifted by the Spirit in 1 Cor 14:28, 30 are also told to be silent—and one does not appeal to the Spirit's work in order to void the commands in those verses. The way Fee presents the Spirit as proving his position comes to a methodological problem. Can anyone simply appeal to the Spirit to justify a statement? For example, Jeffrey S. Siker writes, "Above all, I believe the Spirit of God has led me to see lesbian and gay Christians as sisters and brothers in Christ. When I witness something of the prophetic and healing ministry of gay and lesbian Christians as they reach out to people with whom most of us still feel uncomfortable, what can I do but praise God for God's Spirit at work in ministering to those most despised by our society and church?"[147] Siker's way of appealing to the Spirit in order to justify

---

142 Garland, *1 Corinthians*, 665. C. K. Barrett, *A Commentary on the First Epistle to the Corinthians*, BNTC (Peabody, MA: Hendrickson, 1993), 332, who argues in a different way regarding the Spirit and 1 Cor 14:34–35, writes, "Paul did not write verses 34 f. They were added later as a marginal note ... at a time when good order was thought more important than the freedom of the Spirit." Barrett's statement implies a certain reconstruction of early church history (early spiritual gifts vs. later organized church ministry). Merkle has provided a more balanced picture from the data of the New Testament (i.e., both spiritual gifts and organized church leadership at the early stages of Pauline ministry) in Merkle, *The Elder and Overseer*, 67–119.

143 Witherington, *Conflict and Community in Corinth*, 290. Cf. Raymond F. Collins, *First Corinthians*, SP 7 (Collegeville, MN: Liturgical, 1999), 515; Oropeza, *1 Corinthians*, 190.

144 Gordon D. Fee, *Gospel and Spirit: Issues in New Testament Hermeneutics* (Peabody, MA: Hendrickson, 1991), 137; cf. 64–65.

145 Fee, *Gospel and Spirit*, 45.

146 For an introduction on this question, see Kenneth Mathews, *Genesis 1–11:26*, NAC 1A (Nashville: B&H, 1996), 219–22.

147 Jeffrey S. Siker, "Gentile Wheat and Homosexual Christians: New Testament Directions for the Heterosexual Church," in *Biblical Ethics and Homosexuality: Listening to Scripture*, ed. Robert L. Brawley (Louisville: Westminster, 1996), 144.

this particular biblical hermeneutic is no different in method with the way others argue with regard to women in the church. The issue is not that a certain view of women will lead to affirming homosexuality, but the issue is that the methods overlap at significant points.

Adam Hensley's article, by contrast, interprets the Spirit's will in 1 Corinthians 12–14 as consistent with Paul's silencing of women. He writes,

> Indeed, by insisting on the Spirit's will in distribution of charismata, chapter 12 may already contain the latent criticism soon to become explicit in chapter 14: some or many at Corinth are actually contravening the Spirit's will through their exercise of self-appointed gifts. Once again, the character of 14:34 coheres with Paul's broader desire in chapters 12–14 that the Corinthians let the Spirit determine the distribution of gifts (12:11) rather than claim every kind of speaking gift for themselves (14:26).[148]

The statement in 1 Cor 12:11 (cf. 12:18) is a general one and does not specify exactly how the Spirit distributes the gifts. The context (12:4–10) shows the Spirit gives different gifts to different people (in contrast to the argument that the Spirit gives the same gifts to men and women).

Schrage connects the Spirit's gifting with a certain interpretation of 1 Cor 14:26. He appeals to ἕκαστος in 1 Cor 14:26 in connection with the term in 1 Cor 12:7 when he mentions that the Spirit "gifts every Christian equally [or without discrimination]."[149] Paul writes in 1 Cor 12:7, "Now each one [ἑκάστῳ] is given the manifestation of the Spirit for the common good." The combination of 1 Cor 12:7 and 14:26 via ἕκαστος blurs the meaning of each passage in its own context (see comments above on 1 Cor 14:26). Furthermore, 1 Cor 12:7 states that the Spirit gifts each person, but it does not state that each is gifted the same. Hensley answers Schrage by appealing to the Spirit's will in 1 Cor 12:11 and stating, "Thus, there are no intrinsic grounds here to rule out gender differentiation in the distribution of charismata."[150] In addition, if silencing a person

---

148   Adam D. Hensley, "σιγαω, λαλεω, and ὑποτασσω," 355.
149   Schrage, *Der erste Brief an die Korinther*, 3:484, comments, "However, above all: 12:11ff primarily goes to the work of the Spirit in the church, who gifts each Christian equally (cf. ἕκαστος in 12:7 and last in 14:26), not to delegate or deny a position or divide by specific gender, (and) to lay down greater differentiation between specific functions of man and woman is completely distant"; "Vor allem aber: Da es nach 12,1ff in der Gemeinde primär um das Wirken des Geistes geht, der jeden Christen unterschiedslos beschenkt (vgl. das ἕκαστος 12,7 und zuletzt 14,26), nicht um zu delegierende bzw. zu verwehrende Ämter oder gar deren geschlechtsspezifische Aufteilungen, liegt eine Differenzierung zwischen spezifischen Funktionen des Mannes und der Frau völlig fern."
150   Hensley, "σιγαω, λαλεω, and ὑποτασσω," 353. Taylor, *1 Corinthians*, 255, appeals to creation in order to argue for "gender distinction . . . in the exercise of the gifts," even when gifted by the Spirit.

or group of people contradicts the Spirit's gifting, then how can Paul consistently silence other groups in 1 Cor 14:28, 30? Silence in these two verses is usually not disputed.

First Corinthians 11:5

Paul's command for women to be silent in regard to judging prophecies is consistent with women's ability to pray and prophesy, despite the oft-repeated assertion that 1 Cor 14:34 contradicts 1 Cor 11:5. Flanagan and Snyder represent how many view the two passages: "It [1 Cor 14:34–36] appears to contradict the picture of women praying and prophesying in church which Paul has already given and approved of in 1 Corinthians 11:5.... Is Paul, in Chapter 14, saying 'No' to a question—women speaking in church—to which he has already responded 'Yes' in chapter 11? Will the real Paul speak up?"[151] The authors do not provide evidence concerning the apparent contradiction.

Dieter Zeller uses λαλέω as a reason why there is a contradiction between 1 Cor 11:5 and 14:34. He writes, "Now in this framework the jussive is embedded where the first (σιγάτωσαν v. 34a) is evidently linked to the silence regulation in v. 28a, 30. So one would think that the women are forbidden to speak in any tongues or prophetic speech in the assembly; but λαλεῖν in v. 34b is general and probably also embraces teaching and public prayer. Thus the ban stands in clear contradiction to 11:5 where women's prayer and prophecy in the church service is not a problem."[152] Zeller creates the problem of inconsistency for σιγάω by attributing "teaching and public prayer" within the scope of λαλέω. However, even λαλέω can be contextually defined.[153] In 1 Cor 14:26–40, the term refers specifically to speaking in tongues (14:27, 28, 39) and speaking by prophecy (14:29). It is possible that λαλέω refers to speaking in judgment of prophecy in 1 Cor 14:34–35. At a minimum, if Paul limits λαλέω in any way in this broader

---

151 Flanagan and Snyder, "Did Paul Put Down Women in First Corinthians 14:34–36?" 216–17.
152 Dieter Zeller, *Der erste Brief an die Korinther*, KEK 5 (Göttingen: Vandenhoeck & Ruprecht, 2010), 444, states, "In diesen Rahmen nun sind die Jussive eingebettet, wovon der erste (σιγάτωσαν V. 34a) sichtlich an die Schweigegebote V. 28a.30 anknüpft. Von daher sollte man denken, dass den Frauen in den Versammlungen vor allem Glossolalie und prophetische Rede untersagt sind; aber das λαλεῖν in V. 34b ist allgemeiner, es umfasst wohl auch Lehre und öffentliches Gebet. So steht das Verbot in deutlichem Widerspruch zu 11,5, wo das Betten und Prophezeien der Frau im Gottesdienst der Gemeinde nicht das Problem ist."
153 E. Earle Ellis writes, "Likewise, the 'speaking' (14:34, λαλεῖν) almost certainly refers, as it does throughout the section, to the exercise of pneumatic gifts" ("The Silenced Wives of Corinth [1 Cor 14:34–35]," in *New Testament Textual Criticism and Its Significance for Exegesis: In Honour of Bruce Metzger*, ed. Eldon Jay Epp and Gordon D. Fee [Oxford: Clarendon, 1981], 218).

The Literary Context: The Range of ΣΙΓΑΩ as a Basis for Consistency | 55

literary context, then the contradiction to 1 Cor 11:5 must be revisited. Christian Wolff discusses λαλέω while explaining the correlation between 1 Cor 11:5 and 14:33b–36. For Wolff the command to silence and λαλέω (1 Cor 14:34) and asking questions at home (14:35) revolve around "interrupting questions" in the church service.[154] While Wolff rejects the prophecy view,[155] the interrupting questions view still demonstrates a contextual reading of σιγάω and λαλέω. By contextual reading, I mean limiting the scope of these terms by the context and not viewing the terms in an absolute sense. Furthermore, some women could have started to assess prophecy simply by posing questions.

Friedrich Lang gives an overview of many German commentators in how they attempt to reconcile 1 Cor 14:34–35 with 11:5. He explains that many interpreters divide the two passages between public and private worship (e.g., Bachmann),[156] that Paul only makes a concession in 1 Cor 11:5 (Lietzmanns), that the silence is only on interrupting questions (Delling, Wendland, Wolff), or that 1 Cor 14:33b–36 is a later insertion (Conzelmann, Dautzenberg, Fitzer).[157] The oft-repeated point of contradiction between 1 Cor 11:5 and 14:34 should be assessed more critically in light of these varying opinions. In other words, a contradiction needs to be proven and not simply stated (as in Flanagan and Snyder's article above). Ultimately, when σιγάω is no longer defined in absolute terms, then the two passages do not contain any inherent contradiction.

---

154   Wolff, *Der erste Brief des Paulus an die Korinther*, 344, 346, "Dazwischenfragen."
155   Wolff, *Der erste Brief des Paulus an die Korinther*, 345, notes, "These observations stand against the attempted solution that Paul in v. 33bff. was against the participation of women in the judgment of prophecies (v. 29) (women should not come to assess the comments from men in this situation)"; "Diese Beobachtungen stehen dem Lösungsversuch entgegen, wonach sich Paulus in V.33bff. gegen die Beteiligung von Frauen an der Einschätzung von Prophezeiungen (V.29) wendet (Frauen sollen nicht in die Situation kommen, Äußerungen von Männern zu beurteilen)."
156   So also Gregory J. Lockwood, *1 Corinthians*, ConcC (Saint Louis: Concordia, 2000), 533–34; Holmyard, "Does 1 Corinthians 11:2–16 Refer to Women Praying and Prophesying in Church?" 461–72.
157   Friedrich Lang, *Die Briefe an die Korinther*, NTD (Göttingen: Vandenhoeck & Ruprecht, 1986), 200, writes, "In der Auslegung sind verschiedene Deutungsvorschläge gemacht worden, um den Widerspruch dieser Verse zu 11,5 zu vermeiden. 1) Manche Ausleger (z.B. Ph. Bachmann) weisen das Beten und Prophezeien von 11,5 nicht dem Gemeindegottesdienst, sondern der Hausandacht zu.... 2) Die Vermutung H. Lietzmanns, Paulus habe in 11,5 das Prophezeien nur widerwillig geduldet und bringe in 14,33–36 siene wahre Meinung zum Ausdruck, traut dem Apostel eine taktische Konzession zu, die im Widerspruch zu seiner eigentlichen theologischen Auffassung steht. 3) Zahlreiche Ausleger entnehmen dem V. 35, daß das Redeverbot nicht das inspirierte Beten und Prophezeien, sondern nur ein störendes Dazwischenfragen im Gottesdienst betreffe (G. Delling; H. D. Wendland; Ch. Wolff).... 4) Aus den genannten Gründen verdient m.E. die Annahme den Vorzug, daß der Abschnitt V.33b–36 als Einschub eines Schreibers aus der Situation der Pastoralbriefe zu beurteilen ist (H. Conzelmann; G. Dautzenberg; G. Fitzer)." Lang includes 1 Cor 14:33b and 14:36, but the specific verses can vary depending on the commentator.

56 | *Paul, Women, and the Meaning of Silence*

Additional solutions have been offered. Keith Burton claims that Paul references men and women in 1 Cor 11 but husbands and wives in 1 Cor 14 (including silencing specifically wives in 1 Cor 14:34).[158] He appeals especially to 1 Cor 14:35 to justify his translation of wives in 1 Cor 14:34.[159] He does not entertain a definition of σιγάω in its context. Anders Eriksson takes the silence as directed against women tongue speakers.[160] Eriksson writes in reference to 1 Cor 11:2–16 and 1 Cor 14:34, "In principle women may prophesy, but the particular group of women tongue speakers in Corinth should literally 'shut up.' "[161] There is no contextual reason why the term ought to be translated "shut up." The previous two uses of σιγάω (1 Cor 14:28, 30) provide sufficient evidence that Paul is not speaking harshly to women in particular. Greek literature also shows that the translation "shut up" is found in contexts where there is reason for a strong response. For example, Seth said to the beast in *The Life of Adam and Eve*, "Shut your mouth and be silent [σίγα], and keep away from the image of God until the day of judgment." Then the beast said to Seth, "See, I stand off, Seth, from the image of God."[162] In addition to the hostile relationship between Seth and the beast, there is the additional emphasis on absolute silence with the phrase κλεῖσαί σου τὸ στόμα ("shut your mouth"). This type of hostility is not present in 1 Cor 14:34–35, and so σιγάω should not be translated as "shut up."

A final solution is one where 1 Cor 11:5 itself is reinterpreted. Noel Weeks takes the view that 1 Cor 11:5 does *not* provide permission for women to pray or prophesy, and so there is no inconsistency with silencing women prophets in 1 Cor 14:34.[163] One of the reasons provided by Weeks revolves around the type of

---

158 Keith A. Burton, "1 Corinthians 11 and 14: How Does a Woman Prophesy and Keep Silence at the Same Time?" *Journal of the Adventist Theological Society* 10 (1999): 268–84.
159 Burton, "1 Corinthians 11 and 14," 281. For why 1 Cor 14:34 should not be translated with "wives," see Antoinette Clark Wire, *The Corinthians Women Prophets: A Reconstruction through Paul's Rhetoric* (Minneapolis: Fortress, 1990), 156, who writes, "Yet the phrase is appropriate not only for wives, since daughters, widows, and women slaves are just as subordinate to the man of the house. Nor can we assume that Paul excludes from his restrictions the exceptional woman who lives alone or with other women just because he concedes that women may ask men questions at home."
160 Anders Eriksson, " 'Women Tongue Speakers, Be Silent': A Reconstruction through Paul's Rhetoric," *BibInt* 6 (1998): 80–104.
161 Eriksson, "Women Tongue Speakers, Be Silent," 92. Eriksson claims, "The regulation for the women is an absolute prohibition of public speaking: Let the women be silent (σιγάτωσαν)" (p. 91).
162 Translation from *OTP*. For the Greek text with variants, see Johannes Tromp, *The Life of Adam and Eve in Greek: A Critical Edition*, PVTG 6 (Leiden: Brill, 2005), 132–34. In the Appendix, there are a few other occasions of absolute silence that can be translated "shut up." Usually there are obvious contextual clues for this interpretation (e.g., Josephus, *J.W.* 1.622; Aristophanes, *Lys.* 507–20).
163 Noel Weeks, "Of Silence and Head Covering," *WTJ* 35 (1972): 21–27; cf. John H. Fish III, "Women Speaking in the Church: The Relationship of 1 Corinthians 11:5 and 14:34–36," *Emmaus Journal* 1.3 (1992): 214–51.

dative for ἀκατακάλυπτος in 1 Cor 11:5, as he notes, "In the interpretation of v. 5 the sense of the dative ἀκατακαλύπτῳ is crucial. It is generally taken as a dative of accompanying circumstances. The comitative dative is historically linked with the instrumental dative."[164] Weeks goes on to state that translating "by means of the unveiling of the head" will "obtain a different sense and one in line with Paul's argument."[165] However, there are at least three reasons why Weeks' argument with the dative is not convincing. (1) Weeks does not go on to explain the accusative form of ἀκατακάλυπτος in 1 Cor 11:13 ("Judge among yourselves, is it proper for a woman to pray to God uncovered [ἀκατακάλυπτον]?"); (2) the dative can just as easily be taken as a simple dative of manner, which does not provide a clue as to the overall interpretation;[166] and (3) the context of 1 Cor 11:2–16 continually discusses the issue of a head covering for women but does not specifically go on about the issue of prayer or prophecy. In other words, Weeks has to assume Paul takes issue with prayer itself rather than the manner of prayer.

Many scholars (e.g., Flanagan and Snyder) depend on σιγάω meaning absolute silence in 1 Cor 14:34 as they claim Paul or the author of the text is inconsistent. If they did not assume absolute silence, then rhetorical statements such as "Will the real Paul speak up" would fall flat.[167] Adolphus Chinedu Amadi-Azuogu explicitly states that σιγάω is absolute silence—even appealing to the "lexical meaning" (see above on the review of lexical works for a different view).[168] Schnabel, by contrast, points out that σιγάω is not to be taken in an absolute

---

164 Weeks, "Of Silence and Head Covering," 25–26 (iota subscript added).
165 Weeks, "Of Silence and Head Covering," 26.
166 For agreement on the dative of manner, see Andreas J. Köstenberger, Benjamin L. Merkle, and Robert L. Plummer, *Going Deeper with New Testament Greek: An Intermediate Study of the Grammar and Syntax of the New Testament*, rev. ed. (Nashville: B&H Academic, 2020), 134 n. 46; and Daniel B. Wallace, *Greek Grammar Beyond the Basics: An Exegetical Syntax of the New Testament* (Grand Rapids: Zondervan, 1996), 161–62.
167 Flanagan and Snyder, "Did Paul Put Down Women in First Corinthians 14:34–36?" 217. Of all the sources consulted on 1 Cor 14:34, most of the highly-sensational comments come from egalitarian writers. For example, Gordon D. Fee, writing of those who might disagree with his point, says, "Moreover, and to put it strongly, anyone who thinks otherwise can only be accused of knowing very little at all about textual criticism" ("On Women Remaining Silent in the Churches: A Text-Critical Approach to 1 Corinthians 14:34–35," in *Evangelical Scholarship, Retrospects and Prospects: Essays in Honor of Stanley N. Gundry*, ed. Dirk R. Buursma, Katya Covrett, and Verlyn D. Verbrugge [Grand Rapids: Zondervan, 2017], 185).
168 Adolphus Chinedu Amadi-Azuogu, *Gender and Ministry in Early Christianity and the Church Today* (Lanham, MD: University Press of America, 2007), 79–80. Arthur Rowe, "Silence and the Christian Women of Corinth: An Examination of 1 Corinthians 14:33b–36," *CV* 33 (1990): 60, states that σιγάω has a "contextual limitation" that is "despite the absolute style and lexical meaning of the word." This type of clarification is unnecessary when words often have a range of meaning.

sense.[169] Schnabel's view coheres with σιγάω in 1 Cor 14:28, 30. Strikingly, Andreas Lindemann does not think the view of "women can prophesy and also be silent" to be a possibility.[170] However, the term throughout Greek literature shows a person can speak and be silent. Hensley is correct that "there is nothing in chapter 11 to suggest that Paul gives blanket permission for women to exercise all forms of prophecy without qualification."[171] Women pray and prophesy in 1 Cor 11:5 but a certain type of prophecy (judgment) is limited by σιγάω in 1 Cor 14:34.

Interpolation and Textual Criticism

The thesis statement concerning Pauline consistency assumes Pauline authorship of 1 Cor 14:34–35. The interpolation theory, if true, would nullify this thesis. Therefore, it is important to consider the merits of this theory. Furthermore, the interpolation theory demands attention because of how often writers repeat it. Gottfried Fitzer is often referred to for interpolation but sometimes without engaging his arguments. For example, what is not pointed out is that Fitzer also includes minor variants as reason for suspicion. He discusses at length minor variants throughout 1 Cor 14:34–35, and then he pairs this discussion with the dislocation issue.[172] He then concludes, "The text-critical result leads first only to suspicion."[173] However, if minor variants were evidence for suspicion, then most of the New Testament (and other ancient literature) would be suspect.

Text-critical decisions for the interpolation theory are often supported by an appeal to the literary argument of a potential contradiction. For instance, Hans-Josef Klauck, who takes 1 Cor 14:34 as an interpolation, states, "Even if one keeps

---

169   Schnabel, *Der erste Brief des Paulus an die Korinther*, 846, writes, "Da Paulus in 11,5 vorausgesetzt hatte, dass Frauen in der Gemeinde beten und prophezeien, kann sich „schweigen" night generell und absolut auf jeden Wortbeitrag von Frauen beziehen."

170   Andreas Lindemann, *Der erste Korintherbrief*, HNT 9 (Tübingen: Mohr Siebeck, 2000), 241, notes, "[N]ach Tomson, Paul 137 könnte das προφητεύειν der Frau auch stumm ("silent") erfolgt sein (womit die Spannung zu 14,34f. ausgeglichen wäre), aber das ist ausgeschlossen." Specifically, Peter J. Tomson states, "But there is no reason to suppose that prayer and prophecy should always be aloud when practiced in the community" (*Paul and the Jewish Law: Halakha in the Letters of the Apostle to the Gentiles*, CRINT [Minneapolis: Fortress, 1990], 137).

171   Hensley, "σιγαω, λαλεω, and ὑποτασσω," 355.

172   Gottfried Fitzer, *Das Weib schweige in der Gemeinde: Über den unpaulinischen Charakter der mulier-taceat-Verse in 1. Korinther 14*, TEH 110 (München: Chr. Kaiser, 1963), 6–9.

173   Fitzer, *Das Weib schweige in der Gemeinde*, 8, states, "Das textkritische Ergebnis führt zunächst nur auf einen Verdact."

the verse as from Paul, one must say: the NT does not speak with a unified voice about the participation of a woman in church life."[174] However, since 1 Cor 14:34 is consistent with the context and normal usage of σιγάω, this literary argument should not be used to omit the passage. There are at least three ways to look at the problems of the interpolation theory:[175] (1) the problem of external evidence; (2) the problem of how an editor could have inserted the text; and (3) the problem of literary evidence. The literary concerns already mentioned above answer the last problem. So this section will focus on the problems of external evidence and a supposed editor.[176]

The Problem of External Evidence for Interpolation

All Greek manuscripts that contain 1 Corinthains 14 have the words of 1 Corinthians 14:34–35. Also, the only Greek manuscripts that move the words from their present location (after 1 Cor 14:33) to the end of 1 Cor 14:40 are D (6th cent.), F (9th cent.), G (9th cent.), 0319 (9th cent.), 88 (12th cent.), and 915 (13th cent.).[177] Antoinette Wire does not view manuscript 88 as an independent

---

174 Hans-Josef Klauck, *1. Korintherbrief*, NEchtB (Würzburg: Echter, 1984), 106, writes, "Selbst wenn man die Verse dem Paulus beläßt, muß man sagen: Das NT spricht über die Beteiligung der Frau am Gemeindeleben nicht mit einer Stimme." In order for Klauck to make such a claim, he argues that 1 Cor 14:34 is "an absolute, universal speaking ban for women in the church service"; "ein uneingeschränktes, allgemeines Redeverbot für Frauen in der Gemeindeversammlung" (p. 105).

175 The impetus for looking at this issue from this angle comes from L. Ann Jervis, "1 Corinthians 14.34–35: A Reconsideration of Paul's Limitations of the Free Speech of Some Corinthian Women," *JSNT* 58 (1995): 51–59.

176 The problem of the origin of the interpolation theory could also be discussed, though the origin of a theory neither proves nor disproves a theory. Terence Paige incorrectly states that the German commentator J. Weiss first proposed a non-Pauline interpolation ("The Social Matrix of Women's Speech at Corinth: The Context and Meaning of the Command to Silence in 1 Corinthians 14:33b–36," *BBR* 12.2 [2002]: 218). Instead, Karin B. Neutel discusses the origin of interpolation in her recent article "Women's Silence and Jewish Influence: The Problematic Origins of the Conjectural Emendation on 1 Cor 14.33b–35," *NTS* 65 (2019): 477–95. She explains that the theory originated with Dutch minister Jan Willem Straatman in 1863. Neutel writes about Straatman, "His subsequent two-volume work, *Kritische studiën over den 1en Brief van Paulus aan de Korinthiërs* ('Critical Studies on the 1st Letter of Paul to the Corinthians') is devoted to the argument that 1 Corinthians is corrupt not only in chapter 15, but also in many other places, including 1 Cor 14.33b–35" (p. 481). There is a general lack of concern in 1 Corinthians literature about the origin of interpolation and about Straatman's own methodology. See also the discussion in Bart L. F. Kamphuis et al., "Sleepy Scribes and Clever Critics: A Classification of Conjectures on the Text of the New Testament," *NovT* 57 (2015): 87–88.

177 For a list and discussion of these manuscripts (and Latin manuscripts), see Curt Niccum, "The Voice of the Manuscripts on the Silence of Women: The External Evidence for 1 Cor 14.34–35," *NTS* 43 (1997): 247–52. For the debate on manuscript F, see Jeffrey John Kloha, "A Textual Commentary on Paul's First Epistle to the Corinthians" (PhD diss., The University of Leeds, 2006), 4:1196 n. 115. Some scholars label the ninth century manuscript 0319 (Codex Sangermanensis) as manuscript

witness, but it is instead a "rebound from the 'Western' tradition.... [And] the scribe's slashes and marginal marks in ms 88 represent the final demise of the 'Western' placement of the women's silencing."[178] A final piece of data is the textual marker(s) in Codex Vaticanus where there is a line above the first alpha in αι γυναικες at 1 Cor 14:34; and the line protrudes slightly out into the left margin. Then directly to the left and above this line is an umlaut at 1 Cor 14:33.[179] Finally, Vaticanus at 1 Cor 14:40 does have some text-division markings, but they do not appear to be related to the markings at 1 Cor 14:33.[180] What the bar and umlaut mean has been debated in the recent history of studying umlauts in Vaticanus.

Edward Gravely's work on Vaticanus provides a history of the study of umlauts up through 2007.[181] Philip B. Payne's 1995 article serves as the impetus for this discussion where he mentions "27 'bar-umlaut' sigla in the Vaticanus

E. Labeling 0319 as E can cause confusion as to what manuscript is meant since the manuscript E (today) refers to manuscripts containing the Gospels and Acts (E07 and E08). Note that the Latin portion of this manuscript is labeled with a lowercase e. Scholars who refer to E as placing 1 Cor 14:34–35 after 1 Cor 14:40 include Johann Salomo Semler, *Paraphrasis in Primam Pavli ad Corinthios Epistolam: Cvm Notis, et Latinarvm Translationvm Excerptis* (Halae Magdebvrgicae: Impensis Carol. Herm. Hemmerde, 1770), 384; Constantinus Tischendorf, *Novum Testamentum Graece*, vol. 2, 8th ed. (Lipsiae: Giesecke & Devrient, 1872), 547 (see also Tischendorf's "Notantur Interim" at the beginning of volume 2, which has no page numbers, but he does clearly list E as Codex Sangermanensis); Philip B. Payne, "Fuldensis, Sigla for Variants in Vaticanus, and 1 Cor 14.34–5," *NTS* 41 (1995): 240; Wire, *The Corinthians Women Prophets*, 149; Niccum, "The Voice of the Manuscripts on the Silence of Women," 249; and E.-B. Allo, *Saint Paul: Première épitre aux Corinthiens*, 2nd ed., ÉBib (Paris: J. Gabalda, 1956), 372, who writes, "Les versets 34 et 35 ont été mis après le v. 40, à la fin du chapitre, par D, E, F, G, 93, Ambr." I am uncertain why Allo also refers to manuscript 93 since 93 has vv. 34–35 in the traditional location after v. 33. See manuscript 93 at https://ntvmr.uni-muenster.de/manuscript-workspace. Those who list neither manuscript E nor 0319 in discussion of 1 Cor 14:34 include NA[28]; UBSGNT[5]; Kloha, "A Textual Commentary on Paul's First Epistle to the Corinthians," 4:1196; and Fee, *The First Epistle to the Corinthians*, 780. The classification of manuscript 0319 should be preferred over E to avoid confusion. For the most up-to-date list of classifications, see J. K. Elliott, *A Bibliography of Greek New Testament Manuscripts*, 3rd ed., NovTSup 160 (Leiden: Brill, 2015); and www.uni-muenster.de/INTF. They both refer to manuscript 0319 in their general classifications and lists.

178 Wire, *The Corinthians Women Prophets*, 151. Likewise, Niccum states that Codex Sangermanensis is a copy of D and thus "has no textual value where Claromontanus is extant" ("The Voice of the Manuscripts on the Silence of Women," 249).
179 See 1474A at the Vatican's website: https://digi.vatlib.it/view/MSS_Vat.gr.1209. The website www.csntm.org was also consulted for certain manuscript checks.
180 Thanks to Edward Gravely for explaining that there does not appear to be a relationship in this case between the markings at 1 Cor 14:40 and the distigmai at 1 Cor 14:33. Personal email, 1 April, 2020.
181 Edward D. Gravely, "The Text Critical Sigla in Codex Vaticanus" (PhD diss., Southeastern Baptist Theological Seminary, 2009), 7–15. He ends with the article concerning umlauts in the Gospel of Mark in Christian-Bernard Amphoux, "Codex Vaticanus B: Les Points Diacritiques des Marges de Marc," *JETS* 58.2 (2007): 440–66.

NT."[182] Some of Payne's work on umlauts has already been discussed above.[183] A key question is if the scribe[184] intended the bar and umlaut as actually one symbol or two separate symbols. Curt Niccum argues that Payne "confused two separate markings" in his discussion of the "bar umlaut."[185] Niccum also shows that the transposition to after verse 40 was in a localized tradition, and that the traditional order is found in some Latin witnesses.[186] He concludes,

> No extant MS offers evidence of an original omission of 1 Cor 14.34–35. Furthermore, the external evidence precludes viewing the attestation of the two known readings as equal. One cannot speak of the "Western" reading in competition with the "Eastern". Far from being balanced, the transposition occurs in only a few, closely related MSS from northern Italy spread abroad in the Middle Ages by Irish monastics. No other reading has claim to being "original" other than that preserving the traditional sequence of verses.[187]

J. Edward Miller understands the bar + umlaut to be distinct symbols, noting, "While the umlaut siglum is peculiar to Vaticanus, the bar is not."[188] Miller calls Payne's view on the bar + umlaut unique among ancient manuscripts.[189] Jennifer Shack provides a reevaluation of Codex Vaticanus, Codex Fuldensis, and manuscript 88, and she comes to drastically different conclusions than Payne.[190] In

---

182 Payne, "Fuldensis, Sigla for Variants in Vaticanus, and 1 Cor 14.34–5," 251. Epp discusses Payne's writings approvingly in E. J. Epp, "Text-Critical, Exegetical, and Socio-Cultural Factors Affecting the Junia/Junias Variation in Romans 16,7," in *New Testament Textual Criticism and Exegesis: Festschrift J. Delobel*, ed. A. Denaux, BETL 161 (Leuven: Leuven University Press, 2002), 240–42.
183 See the history of research in Chapter One.
184 Gravely, "The Text Critical Sigla in Codex Vaticanus," 96, writes, "The evidence is overwhelmingly in favor of a date for the umlauts close to the time of the construction of the codex." See the evidence compiled especially in Philip B. Payne and Paul Canart, "The Originality of Text-Critical Symbols in Codex Vaticanus," *NovT* 42.2 (2000): 105–13. Kloha gives an important clarification whereas Payne and Canart "have demonstrated that the umlauts in B are written in the same ink as that used by the original hand, they have not decisively demonstrated that the bars are also linked to the original hand" (Kloha, "A Textual Commentary on Paul's First Epistle to the Corinthians," 2:513, n. 161).
185 Niccum, "The Voice of the Manuscripts on the Silence of Women," 244.
186 For a list of the Latin manuscripts that include the traditional order, see Niccum, "The Voice of the Manuscripts on the Silence of Women," 252–53.
187 Niccum, "The Voice of the Manuscripts on the Silence of Women," 254.
188 J. Edward Miller, "Some Observations on the Text-Critical Function of the Umlauts in Vaticanus, with Special Attention to 1 Corinthians 14.34–35," *JSNT* 26.2 (2003): 219. For Payne's reply to several of Miller's points, see Philip B. Payne, "The Text-Critical Function of the Umlauts in Vaticanus, with Special Attention to 1 Corinthians 14:34–35: A Response to J. Edward Miller," *JSNT* 27.1 (2004): 105–12.
189 Miller, "Some Observations on the Text-Critical Function of the Umlauts in Vaticanus," 220.
190 Jennifer Shack, "A Text without 1 Corinthians 14.34–35? Not According to the Manuscript Evidence," *JGRChJ* 10 (2014): 90–112.

Payne's more recent article in 2017, he revisited 1 Cor 14:34–35.[191] Payne makes several assertions, one of which is the measurements of the horizontal bars: "Eight of the twenty-eight bars adjacent to distigmai are different from the other twenty in four respects: 1. They extend, on average, almost twice as far into the margin as the other twenty. 2. They are, on average, almost one third longer than the other twenty."[192] However, in 2019 Jan Krans (in general) and Richard Fellows (in particular) have cautioned against this criterion.[193] Krans writes, "Surely, Payne thinks he has found such a clue in what he regards as significant differences in length of the horizontal strokes, but here all sorts of alarm bells should go off since we are talking only fractions of millimetres in a text that is handwritten."[194] Furthermore, Fellows measured the bars and came up with different measurements than Payne.[195] After reviewing Fellows's measurements, Payne remeasured the bars on the IPZS facsimile of Vaticanus and wrote, "My new, more precise measurements are much closer to Fellows's measurements."[196] The external evidence for an interpolation is slim. Witherington correctly states, "The two verses are found after v. 40 in a few manuscripts and other textual authorities, but displacement is no argument for interpolation."[197] The external evidence is not a strong case for interpolation.

The Problem of How an Editor Could Have Inserted the Text

Interpreters who take 1 Cor 14:34–35 as original to Paul in its traditional location must answer how the text could have been *dislocated*. On the other hand, those who take the text as an interpolation must answer how it could have been originally omitted and then later added into the text *and* have no manuscript evidence for the omission. Holmes writes, "Even if the passage is judged to be non-Pauline,

---

191   Philip B. Payne, "Vaticanus Distigme-obelos Symbols Marking Added Text, Including 1 Corinthians 14.34–5," *NTS* 63.4 (2017): 604–25.
192   Payne, "Vaticanus Distigme-obelos Symbols Marking Added Text, Including 1 Corinthians 14.34–5," 623. Payne's third and fourth points do not refer to measurements.
193   Jan Krans, "Paragraphos, Not Obelos, in Codex Vaticanus," *NTS* 65 (2019): 252–57; Richard G. Fellows, "Are There Distigme-Obelos Symbols in Vaticanus," *NTS* 65 (2019): 246–51.
194   Krans, "Paragraphos, Not Obelos, in Codex Vaticanus," 255.
195   He provides graphic comparisons in Fellows, "Are There Distigme-Obelos Symbols in Vaticanus," 248, 250.
196   Payne's response can be found at https://www.pbpayne.com/wp-content/uploads/2021/07/Critique-of-Fellows-Krans-Vaticanus-Distigme-Obelos-Denials.pdf. Quotation from page 4. Accessed Oct 25, 2022. This article is not currently published in any academic journal. I want to thank Philip Payne for his email correspondence.
197   Witherington, *Conflict and Community in Corinth*, 288.

it is not necessarily post-Pauline.... Paul's geographically wide influence, as well as that of his close associates, including a number of women, makes it improbable that only the interpolated version would be reflected in extant MSS."[198] How could this insertion originally have been placed into the text? This problem is the opposite way to ask Gordon Fee's concern, "It should be noted finally that all those who have expressed vigorous disagreement here have consistently and conveniently avoided asking and answering the ultimate text-critical questions of the 'how' and 'why'—that material which appears to be in no way related to the surrounding context should find its way into *two significantly different places* in the manuscript tradition."[199] Three years later Fee argued that this issue of the "how" question is "certainly the most damning of all" for a traditional reading.[200] Contrary to Fee's assertion that this question has been avoided, both sides have provided their "how" answers (just because one does not agree with an answer does not justify charging another group as "avoiding" the issue). It remains a challenge for Fee and others to provide a plausible explanation on how there is not a single surviving Greek manuscript that omits this passage.[201]

Wire plausibly explains that the dislocation of 1 Cor 14:34–35 may have happened by accidental haplography as the scribe's eye moved from ἐκκλησίαις in 1 Cor 14:33b to ἐκκλησίᾳ at end of 1 Cor 14:35.[202] Hiu comments regarding Wire's theory of haplography, "We would contend that this answers Fee's quest for an 'adequate answer' as to the existence of the Western reading if 14.33–35 were originally Pauline."[203] Wire's explanation also answers Jacobus Petzer when he writes, "From a transcriptional point of view, there seems no apparent reason why a scribe, who had in front of him a copy of the first Corinthian epistle in

---

198   Holmes, *Text in a Whirlwind*, 227.
199   Fee, *The First Epistle to the Corinthians*, 780 (italics original).
200   Fee, "On Women Remaining Silent in the Churches," 185.
201   Kloha writes, "Fee does not cite any evidence of any other gloss or marginal note which has crept into the text from an early edition of the *Corpus*" ("A Textual Commentary on Paul's First Epistle to the Corinthians," 2:539).
202   Wire, *The Corinthians Women Prophets*, 151. Of course, there is the intervening phrase τῶν ἁγίων at the end of 1 Cor 14:33. This explanation is more plausible than the explanation that the text was simply moved by an early copyist because of the apparent contradiction with 1 Cor 11:2–16 (see Joël Delobel, "Textual Criticism and Exegesis: Siamese Twins?" in *New Testament Textual Criticism, Exegesis, and Early Church History: A Discussion of Methods*, ed. Barbara Aland and Joël Delobel, CBET [Kampen, The Netherlands: Kok Pharos, 1994], 111).
203   Hiu, *Regulations Concerning Tongues and Prophecy in 1 Corinthians 14:26–40*, 142. For a different answer, see David W. Bryce, " 'As in All the Churches of the Saints': A Text-Critical Study of 1 Corinthians 14:34, 35," *Lutheran Theological Journal* 31 (1997): 31–39, who argues that Marcion could have been the one who edited 1 Cor 14:34–35.

which the passage appeared after verse 33, should have transposed it to the end of the chapter (or *vice versa* of course)."[204]

The work by J. M. Ross should also be noted as a partial answer. He discusses five other examples where a passage appears in varying locations in the manuscript tradition (Matt 23:14; Luke 22:43–44; Luke 23:17; John 7:53–8:11; and Rom 16:25–27).[205] In each of these passages there is a manuscript tradition that (1) has the text in one location; (2) has the text in a different location; and (3) has the text omitted. A convenient layout of the evidence and discussion can be found at the appropriate places in Philip Comfort's textual commentary.[206] The passages that Ross cites contrast with Fee's assertion that John 7:53–8:11 is "the only other 'displacement' that might legitimately be brought into this discussion."[207] Fee should not omit other variants in the New Testament where sentences are dislocated. Of course, only one of Ross's passages is Pauline, but it is beneficial to consider all passages since the question is one of scribal habits and not just Pauline practice. Ross concludes, "Consideration of particular cases seems to show that while the occurrence of a single word in different places is a sign (though not a proof) of its spuriousness, the varying location of a longer passage is a pointer towards (though not a guarantee of) its genuineness."[208] I tend to disagree with this type of conclusion. However, what can be learned from Ross's article is that dislocation *can* happen and the text *can* still be genuine—whether one takes one or more of these passages as genuine.[209] Furthermore, *some manuscripts omit the words in each of these passages* (unlike 1 Cor 14:34–35). Interpolation cannot ultimately be proven by dislocation.

There are several problems with positing an interpolation editor, especially the farther away chronologically one claims the interpolation happened from the time of the autograph (an editor in the late first-century is more plausible than an editor in the late second-century). L. Ann Jervis provides several reasons against a later editor, especially "interpolation-by-a-Pastoral-type-editor."[210] She mentions the "tensions" between 1 Corinthians and the Pastoral Epistles.[211] One would

---

204 Jacobus H. Petzer, "Reconsidering the Silent Women of Corinth—a Note on 1 Corinthians 14:34–35," *Theologia Evangelica* 26 (1993): 133.
205 J. M. Ross, "Floating Words: Their Significance for Textual Criticism," *NTS* 38 (1992): 153–56.
206 Comfort, *New Testament Text and Translation Commentary*, 69–70; 233–35; 238; 285–88; 477–80.
207 Fee, "On Women Remaining Silent in the Churches," 178.
208 Ross, "Floating Words," 156.
209 It is likely the doxology in Romans 16 is original (see discussion above).
210 Jervis, "1 Corinthians 14.34–35," 54.
211 Jervis, "1 Corinthians 14.34–35," 53–54.

also need to explain the editor's choice of location.[212] The choice of location is often used as reason why these verses should *not* be in the text. Jervis perceptively writes, "There remains this conundrum: the editor presumably added his words to Paul's discussion of prophecy because he was concerned about women's speaking in such circumstances, but why then did he leave untouched Paul's words in 1 Cor 11.2–16?"[213] In other words, the interpolation theory fails by its own criteria. Gerhard Dautzenberg writes confidently, "The deutero-Pauline and the Pastoral Epistles especially show the concern of post-Pauline generations to authorize through the apostle the household codes and church traditions. By this trend the update itself was inserted into the church tradition in 1 Cor 14:26–40 through the interpolation of the silence regulation for the women."[214] In other words, as the editing and updating of Paul's letters went on, then some editors attempted to align these updates with Paul and some accidentally became associated as from Paul.[215] Dautzenberg writes in favor of the interpolation theory with unproven historical assumptions (e.g., deutero-Pauline) and no manuscript evidence. He discusses at length the interpolation theory confidently despite his own admission that "there are no textual witnesses in which our verse is not contained."[216]

The interpolation theory also blurs two different categories: (1) that Paul did not write the passage and (2) that an editor inserted it. Reasons given for non-Pauline authorship are often also assumed as the same reasons for an editor who inserted the 1 Cor 14:34–35 text. However, non-Pauline authorship and a later editor are two different issues. Arguing against Pauline authorship and arguing for an editor are two different arguments that should have differing reasons. For example, one might use theological inconsistency to state that Paul did not write these words. However, an editor presumably already believed in silencing women

---

212   Jervis, "1 Corinthians 14.34–35," 54.
213   Jervis, "1 Corinthians 14.34–35," 55.
214   Gerhard Dautzenberg, *Urchristliche Prophetie: Ihre Erforschung, ihre Voraussetzungen im Judentum und ihre Struktur im ersten Korintherbrief,* BWANT (Stuttgart: W. Kohlhammer, 1975), 272, states, "Gerade die Deuteropaulinen und die Pastoralbriefe beweisen das Interesse der nachpaulinischen Generationen an durch den Apostel autorisierten Haustafeln und Gemeindeordnungen. In diesen Trend würde sich die Aktualisierung der Gemeindeordnung 1 Kor 14, 26–40 durch den Einschub des Schweigegebotes für die Frauen einfügen."
215   Cf. also Dautzenberg, *Urchristliche Prophetie,* 271, who writes, "The intention behind the editing and updating of the authentic Pauline epistles in each period was to orient it around the word of the Apostles"; "Hinter der Herausgabe und Aktualisierung der echten Paulusbriefe in jener Zeit steht der Wille, sich am Wort des Apostels zu orientieren."
216   Dautzenberg, *Urchristliche Prophetie,* 271, writes, "Es gibt keine Textzeugen, die unsere Verse nicht enthalten."

in the church and so might insert the words regardless of theological consistency. Considering again Richard Hays's comments, he writes,

> One of the strongest reasons for regarding these verses as an interpolation is that their demand for women to remain silent in the assembly stands in glaring contradiction to 11:2–16, in which Paul teaches that women may in fact pray and prophesy in church as long as they keep their heads appropriately covered.... Furthermore, all the other available evidence indicates that women played an active role in preaching, teaching, and prophesying in the early Pauline communities.[217]

Hays refers to an interpolation (i.e., someone other than Paul inserted the words) based upon, for example, the active role of women. However, it stands to reason that an editor would have believed the words in 1 Cor 14:34–35. Hays could have said that these are possible reasons against Pauline authorship. But Hays has blurred the lines between non-Pauline authorship and authorship by someone else.

It is plausible to interpret 1 Cor 14:34–35 within Paul's writings, theology, and practice in light of the problems with the interpolation theory. Many scholars today are voicing concerns over the interpolation theory. The concern grows when one claims an editor far away from the autograph changed the text.[218] E. Ellis writes, "However, no MS lacks the verses and, in the absence of some such evidence, the modern commentator has no sufficient reason to regard them as a post-Pauline gloss."[219] Similarly, Alan Johnson writes, "Were it not for the content of the verses, it is difficult to imagine anyone arguing against their authenticity on textual grounds—though admittedly I would welcome this as the solution if it were appropriate."[220] The semantic range of σιγάω is a much simpler alternative. The quantity and distribution of the external evidence show that the most likely option is 1 Cor 14:34–35 came from Paul's pen. The historical and

---

217 Richard B. Hays, *First Corinthians*, IBC (Louisville: John Knox, 1997), 246.
218 This concern includes debates within the egalitarian position that argue against the merits of the interpolation theory over against other views of 1 Cor 14:34. See David W. Odell-Scott, "In Defense of an Egalitarian Interpretation of 1 Cor 14:34–36: A Reply to Murphy-O'Connor's Critique," *BTB* 17.3 (1987): 100–3. Odell-Scott changed his view of where the passage should start from v. 33b to v. 34 (p. 100).
219 Ellis, "The Silenced Wives of Corinth (1 Cor 14:34–35)," 220. Ellis's own view is that the text was originally a marginal note in the autograph (p. 219). His main piece of evidence comes from 1 Corinthians having an amanuensis (1 Cor 16:21). Cf. Stephen C. Barton, "Paul's Sense of Place: An Anthropological Approach to Community Formation in Corinth," *NTS* 32 (1986): 229–30.
220 Johnson, *1 Corinthians*, 271.

theological sections below will provide additional data against other arguments for interpolation.

Conclusion

Scholars have often claimed that 1 Cor 14:34–35 is inconsistent with its literary context, including but not limited to 1 Cor 14:26–40; 12:11; and 11:5. In order to respond to this charge, I have examined the meaning of σιγάω in Greek lexicons, Greek literature, and the Old and New Testaments. There has not been an exhaustive study of σιγάω, and therefore, the examples of σιγάω in the Appendix are essential to any interpretation of 1 Cor 14:34. The majority of uses of σιγάω throughout Greek literature clearly show a meaning of "selective silence" and not "absolute silence."

The majority use of selective silence was used to reexamine the literary context in 1 Corinthians. The statement of 1 Cor 14:26 ("Then, how is it, brothers, when you come together, each one has a psalm, each one has a teaching, each one has a revelation, each one has a tongue, each one has an interpretation. Let all things be done for edification.") is shown to set up the problem in the Corinthian assembly. This interpretation answers writers who think this passage shows each person speaking in contradiction to the silence in 1 Cor 14:34. Furthermore, the silence in 1 Cor 14:34 was seen to be the same selective silence as the men in Corinth from 1 Cor 14:28, 30. The type of selective silence for women is explained to be regarding the judgment of prophecy. The judgment of prophecy view also helps to see how silence is consistent with 1 Cor 11:5 where women are described as praying and prophesying. The work of the Spirit in 1 Cor 12:11 ("Now all these things [i.e., spiritual gifts] are produced by one and the same Spirit, who distributes to each one individually just as he wills.") does not preclude certain regulations of silence either regarding men in 1 Cor 14:28, 30 or women in 1 Cor 14:34.

The interpolation view of 1 Cor 14:34–35, that Paul did not actually write the two verses originally, was included in the analysis since the thesis of consistency assumes Pauline authorship. Some problems were discussed including the external evidence and how an editor could have inserted the passage. This chapter has demonstrated that Paul's selective silence of women (in the judgment of prophecy) is consistent with the rest of the literary context of 1 Corinthians 12–14 and 1 Cor 11:5.

3

The Historical Context: Consistent Application Then and Now

Introduction

Paul's intended meaning in 1 Cor 14:34–35 is consistent with the context of 1 Corinthians and the rest of Pauline theology and practice. By contrast, some scholars claim that 1 Cor 14:34–35 is inconsistent with the rest of Paul's writing based upon historical arguments. The arguments of why women would have been silenced are: (1) because in the Greco-Roman world women lacked education and public speaking opportunities; (2) because women were causing the problems in the church at Corinth; or (3) because an editor inserted the words since Paul would not have used the law (νόμος) in this manner. In order to demonstrate that Paul is consistent in 1 Cor 14:34–35, this chapter will respond by (1) reexamining ancient education and public speaking, and examining the Pauline pattern of mixing transcultural principles with cultural references; (2) reviewing the letter of 1 Corinthians in order to show both male and female problems in Corinth (along with Paul's appeal to "all the churches"); and (3) arguing that Paul varied his use of the law in his writing.[1]

---

1   A discussion of νόμος ("law") could be placed in a theological chapter or historical chapter. This discussion is placed with historical and cultural considerations because a basis of Paul's teaching is the νόμος and this basis ultimately answers the foundation of a cultural argument. Namely, Paul was primarily

The Multi-cultural Context of Women in the Ancient World

Writers sometimes claim that Paul was merely following cultural convention when he silenced women in the church. For example, they argue that Paul silenced women because of women's lack of education or public speaking in the ancient world.[2] Roy Ciampa and Brian Rosner assert, "Paul's suggestion that the women ask *their own husbands at home* reflects that cultural context where a man could be expected to be better informed/educated than his wife and was understood to be the proper channel of information to the wife."[3] Broadly speaking, writers like Ciampa and Rosner assume a monolithic cultural context instead of dynamic and fluid cultural contexts. They refer to "that cultural context" (singular!) as if the ancient cultures were monolithic. They go on to discuss differences with "modern Western societies" (plural!) in order to apply the passage differently.[4] Robert Yarbrough asks a simple question for today: "What society and which church?"[5] While the early church did not see the exact same issue of denominations as we have today, the same question of "what society" could be asked for the ancient world. What exactly was the culture of first century Corinth? Was Corinth thoroughly Roman? Or was Corinth Roman with an appreciation of her Greek past?[6] There is also the question of how to apply the comparison. On the one hand, Ciampa and Rosner take this view to mean Paul's words do not apply today in the same way, but on the other hand, Luise Schottroff takes cultural convention as a

---

thinking of the Old Testament and not his culture when he prohibited women from speaking in certain contexts.

2   On the question of women in the ancient world, Carolyn Osiek writes, "The present wave of interest in women in the ancient world might be traced back to beginnings in the late 1960s and early 70s, coinciding with the rise of feminist consciousness in academia, though certainly there were earlier studies of biblical women as well" ("Women in the Ancient Mediterranean World: State of the Question New Testament," *BR* 39 [1994]: 57).

3   Roy R. Ciampa and Brian S. Rosner, *The First Letter to the Corinthians*, PNTC (Grand Rapids: Eerdmans, 2010), 729 (italics original). David E. Garland thinks that "Paul's instructions are conditioned by the social realities of his age and a desire to prevent a serious breach in decorum" (*1 Corinthians*, BECNT [Grand Rapids: Baker Academic, 2003], 673).

4   Ciampa and Rosner, *The First Letter to the Corinthians*, 729; cf. James G. Sigountos and Myron Shank, "Public Roles for Women in the Pauline Church: A Reappraisal of the Evidence," *JETS* 26.3 (1983): 294.

5   Robert W. Yarbrough, "Familiar Paths and a Fresh Matrix: The Hermeneutics of 1 Timothy 2:9–15," in *Women in the Church: An Interpretation and Application of 1 Timothy 2:9–15*, ed. Andreas J. Köstenberger and Thomas R. Schreiner, 3rd ed. (Wheaton, IL: Crossway, 2016), 236. In Yarbrough's original context, he was showing the difficulty of simply referring to one society or a particular church (denomination) in order to interpret the meaning and application of Scripture.

6   See discussion in Robert S. Dutch, *The Educated Elite in 1 Corinthians: Education and Community Conflict in Graeco-Roman Context*, LNTS (London: T&T Clark International, 2005), 45–56.

reason why Paul did not write 1 Cor 14:34–35.[7] In other words, scholars can use the same comparison for two different interpretations of background materials. A scholar can even look at the same background materials and conclude that Paul was being counter-cultural instead of following culture.[8]

Some scholars are recognizing the multi-cultural context of women in the ancient world. Lynn Cohick writes, "Some male authors lament the perceived boldness of women speaking and acting in public while other writers praise certain women's public deeds and speeches—and this during the same basic time frame. Thus, while we can trace through the Roman period a general increase in autonomy for women, we should not imagine this change as a straight-line trajectory."[9] Similarly, Susan Hylen notes, "This strange variety seems to be a regular feature of Roman life: the 'rules' do not always align neatly with the evidence of practice. There are explicit prohibitions of women's participation in certain activities or roles, along with evidence that women not only did these things, but did them with approval."[10] One reason for the discrepancy of different views of women in the ancient world may be the challenge of synthesizing literary and legal sources with inscriptions (analogous to Hylen's "rules" versus "practice").[11] For example, Plutarch states, "For a woman ought to do her talking either to her husband or through her husband, and she should not feel aggrieved if, like the flute-player, she makes a more impressive sound through a tongue not her own."[12] But an inscription from Corinth shows a woman, though mentioned as a sister and not wife, with a major role in honoring a certain Cornelius Philiscus. The woman's name is Calpurnia Frontina (Καλπουρνία Φροντεῖνα ἡ

---

7   Luise Schottroff, *Der erste Brief an die Gemeinde in Korinth*, TKNT 7 (Stuttgart: Kohlhammer, 2013), 283, writes, "The main arguments for the non-Pauline origin of 14:34–35 (14:34–38) are for myself the following:... content agreement with Greco-Roman conservative ideology of women"; "Die Hauptargumente für die nicht-paulinische Herkunft von 14,34–35 (14, 34–38) sind für mich also folgende:... inhaltliche Kongruenz mit römisch-hellenistischer konservativer Frauenideologie" (Schottroff lists 4 other reasons for a non-Pauline origin).
8   Gregory J. Lockwood, *1 Corinthians*, ConcC (Saint Louis: Concordia, 2000), 511.
9   Lynn H. Cohick, *Women in the World of the Earliest Christians: Illuminating Ancient Ways of Life* (Grand Rapids: Baker Academic, 2009), 29.
10 Susan E. Hylen, "Modest, Industrious, and Loyal: Reinterpreting Conflicting Evidence for Women's Roles," *BTB* 44 (2014): 9. Cf. Bruce W. Winter, *Roman Wives, Roman Widows: The Appearance of New Women and the Pauline Communities* (Grand Rapids: Eerdmans, 2003), 6–7.
11 Cf. Winter, *Roman Wives, Roman Widows*, 181, who quotes J. Rives, "Rives commented on what was true for all the Empire when he wrote: 'The importance of women in civic life is another aspect of the ancient world that is known almost entirely from inscriptions, since literary and legal sources depict women as largely relegated to private life....' Unlike literary evidence these official inscriptions recorded the actual public offices held by these women in the East."
12 Plutarch, *Conj. praec.* 142D. Greco-Roman translations are from the LCL.

ἀδελ[φή]).[13] Inscriptions honoring Cornelius were also set up by other men and not just Calpurnia.[14] The Corinthian inscription and Plutarch's statement bring contrasting views of the speech of women in the ancient world.

An additional inscription may be relevant to the situation of women in the ancient world since Corinth has a possible reference to a woman as a priestess. The inscription states, "To Polyaena, daughter of Marcus, priestess of Victory. The high priest [Publius] Licinius Priscus Juventianus, [while still living, (set up this monument)] with the official sanction of the city council to (this) excellent woman."[15] The inscription is not without debate regarding the identity of the woman Polyaena and the date of the inscription. Winter dates the inscription to the late first century or middle second century.[16] Nonetheless, the city of Corinth would have had all the diversity of a major city, which should give caution to any broad and general statements on women in 1 Corinthians.[17]

The Lack of Education Argument

Scholars often refer to women's education in the ancient world. In Chapter One it was noted that Craig Keener is one of the proponents of the lack of education view for why Paul would have silenced women in the church.[18] Regarding 1 Cor 14:34–35 in particular, Keener writes that "Paul was addressing relatively uneducated women who were disrupting the service with irrelevant questions."[19] Some commentators follow Keener's suggestion but with caution. Alan Johnson

---

13 See text in Benjamin Dean Meritt, *Corinth: Greek Inscriptions 1896–1927*, vol. 8, part 1 (Cambridge: The American School of Classical Studies at Athens, Harvard University Press, 1931), 59–60 no. 80. The text is second century AD. See discussion in Benjamin Powell, "Greek Inscriptions from Corinth," *AJA* 7.1 (1903): 49–51.

14 Meritt, *Corinth: Greek Inscriptions 1896–1927*, 61–62 nos. 82 and 83.

15 Text and discussion in John Harvey Kent, *Corinth: The Inscriptions 1926–1950*, vol 8, part 3 (Princeton: The American School of Classical Studies at Athens, 1966), 89 no. 199. For inscriptions, though debatable, of Jewish women priestesses outside of Corinth, see Bernadette J. Brooten, *Women Leaders in the Ancient Synagogue: Inscriptional Evidence and Background Issues*, BJS 36 (Atlanta: Scholars, 2020), 73–77.

16 Winter, *Roman Wives, Roman Widows*, 90 n. 68. For reference to temples in Corinth (belonging to Asclepius, Athena, Apollo, Demeter and Persephone, Aphrodite, the imperial cult and another temple of unknown identity), see J. R. McRay, "Corinth," *DNTB* 228–29.

17 For a description of ancient Corinth, see Strabo, *Geogr* 8.22–23; and Jerome Murphy-O'Connor, "The Corinth that Saint Paul Saw," *BA* 47 (1984): 147–59.

18 Craig Keener, "Women's Education and Public Speech in Antiquity," *JETS* 50 (2007): 747–59; Craig S. Keener, "Learning in the Assemblies: 1 Corinthians 14:34–35," in *Discovering Biblical Equality: Complementarity without Hierarchy*, ed. Ronald W. Pierce and Rebecca Merrill Groothuis (Downers Grove, IL: InterVarsity Press, 2004), 169, 171.

19 Craig S. Keener, *Paul, Women and Wives: Marriage and Women's Ministry in the Letters of Paul* (Peabody, MA: Hendrickson, 1992), 70.

states that "*perhaps* Craig Keener is right,"[20] and Ben Witherington writes that "Keener *may be right* in saying that a pedagogical problem is involved here. Those asking questions were not yet educated enough in the school of Christ to know what was and was not appropriate in Christian worship."[21] While Johnson and Witherington use cautious language due to some uncertainty of the ancient world and women's education, other writers state matters more matter-of-factly. For instance, B. J. Oropeza concludes his comments on 1 Cor 14:34–35 by claiming, "We add to this that, unlike the ancient patriarchal world, women in our own era can receive the same biblical and theological education that men do. They are just as competent as men, then, to lead a church, teach in a classroom, or preach from the pulpit."[22] Oropeza does not give any discussion of ancient education in his commentary despite his strong assertion. In fact, he discussed instead Jewish women leaders of synagogues.[23] A final example of appealing to ancient education is James Estep who draws several parallels between Paul and his Greco-Roman context of education. Estep concludes ambiguously that Paul's view is "difficult for a twenty-first century audience to comprehend."[24] The use of educational differences in order to dismiss Paul's command (or change the application to men and women today) has a significant weakness, that is, Paul himself based his command not on culture but on the OT law. Yet, aside from this main weakness, there are also additional concerns with the education view itself. Commentators usually do not frame the discussion of ancient education comprehensively enough, and they often do not discuss how they apply their methodology consistently with rest of the NT commands. Both of these concerns of how to interpret the ancient world will be discussed below.

First, women's education varied in the ancient world, and they were not completely cut off from knowledge. Quintilian, commenting on elementary education, writes,

> As to the parents, I should wish them to be as highly educated as possible. (I do not mean only the fathers. We are told that the eloquence of the Gracchi owed

---

20　Alan F. Johnson, *1 Corinthians*, The IVP New Testament Commentary (Downers Grove, IL: InterVarsity Press, 2004), 274 (italics added).

21　Ben Witherington III, *Conflict and Community in Corinth: A Socio-Rhetorical Commentary on 1 and 2 Corinthians* (Grand Rapids: Eerdmans, 1995), 287 (italics added).

22　B. J. Oropeza, *1 Corinthians*, A New Covenant Commentary (Eugene, OR: Cascade, 2017), 193–94.

23　Oropeza, *1 Corinthians*, 193–94.

24　James Riley Estep, Jr., "Women in Greco-Roman Education and Its Implications for 1 Corinthians 14 and 1 Timothy 2," in *Women in the Biblical World: A Survey of Old and New Testament Perspectives*, ed. Elizabeth A. McCabe (Lanham: University Press of America, 2011), 2:90.

much to their mother Cornelia, whose highly cultivated style is known also to posterity from her letters; Laelia, Gaius Laelius' daughter, is said to have echoed her father's elegance in her own conversation; and the speech delivered before the triumvirs by Hortensia, the daughter of Quintus Hortensius, is still read—and not just because it is by a woman.) However, those who have not been lucky enough to learn themselves should not for that reason take less trouble about their sons' teaching; on the contrary, it should make them all the more careful in other matters.[25]

Keener's comments in his article do not give full justice to the women in Quintilian's passage. Keener writes, "Men also valued educated mothers, though especially for their contribution to their sons' eloquence."[26] Keener's comment is true of Cornelia, but the other two women mentioned are referred to on their own merits. Keener does admit, "Philosophers and other intellectuals often supported the ideal of women's education and trusted their ability to learn."[27] This statement is contrary to the impression left by others who simply appeal to the lack of women's education in the ancient world.[28]

When commentators refer to ancient education for 1 Cor 14:34, which educational system are they referring to? Robert Kaster explains, "Indeed, *all* the evidence presented in this paper is consistent with one view only: that there were throughout the Empire schools of all shapes and kinds, depending on local needs, expectations, and resources. And in a world without centralized direction of education of any sort, that is only what we should expect."[29] Quintilian writes on education and assumes some distinction, writing, "Turning to verbs, who is so ignorant as not to know their voices, moods, persons, and numbers? These matters almost belong to the elementary school and to everyday knowledge."[30] So were women in the ancient world not educated in basic elementary school, or just higher learning? Kent Yinger explains the problem, "The variety

---

25 Quintilian, *Inst.* 1.1.6–7.
26 Keener, "Women's Education and Public Speech in Antiquity," 750.
27 Keener, "Women's Education and Public Speech in Antiquity," 751. Keener refers, e.g., to Plutarch, *Conj. praec.* 48.
28 For additional examples of women's education, though outside of Corinth, see Mary R. Lefkowitz and Maureen B. Fant, *Women's Life in Greece and Rome: A Source Book in Translation*, 3rd ed. (Baltimore, MD: Johns Hopkins University Press, 2005), 166–70.
29 Robert A. Kaster, "Notes on 'Primary' and 'Secondary' Schools in Late Antiquity," *TAPA* 113 (1983): 346 (italics original). View part of the organization of ancient education on p. 337 in graph form, which is debated.
30 Quintilian, *Inst.* 1.4.27. See discussion in Kaster, "Notes on 'Primary' and 'Secondary' Schools in Late Antiquity," 339.

and contradictory nature of depictions of first-century AD Jewish education in standard handbooks is bewildering.... The difference lies in the sources used and in the interpretation of these sources."[31] He continues, "Most of the Jewish populace in first-century Palestine had no access to institutional education."[32] He helpfully refers to Acts 4:13 and John 7:14–15.[33] In Acts, Luke writes, "Now perceiving the confidence of Peter and John and understanding that the men were uneducated and untrained, they were amazed. And they recognized them that they had been with Jesus" (Acts 4:13). Thomas Kraus argues that the description ἀγράμματοί εἰσιν καὶ ἰδιῶται (uneducated and untrained) is not a hendiadys.[34] He also states that, from the standpoint of the religious leaders, Peter and John would have been "of minor education, just laymen."[35] Darrell Bock interprets, "In this context, it is religious instruction that is primarily meant."[36] Since the religious leaders likely referred to religious education, though broader education could also be meant, any reference to women in the church being "uneducated" needs to clarify whether all education or just religious education is intended. Furthermore, Acts 4:13 shows that a simple appeal to ancient education in order to explain 1 Cor 14:34 is not sufficient. John makes a similar statement regarding Jesus, "And already Jesus went up in the middle of the feast to the temple and was teaching. Then the Jews were amazed, saying, 'How does this one know letters since he has no learning?'" (John 7:14–15). John's Gospel shows that ancient education was more complex than simply men were educated and women were not. Commentators who refer to the lack of education usually do not specify which education the women were missing.

Second, proponents of the lack of education view do not consistently apply this method. J. M. Holmes asks why did Paul prohibit all women and not just uneducated women? And why did Paul not silence uneducated men?[37] Paul described the social status of the men and women in the Corinthian church as

---

31 Kent L. Yinger, "Jewish Education," in *The World of the New Testament: Cultural, Social, and Historical Contexts*, ed. Joel B. Green and Lee Martin McDonald (Grand Rapids: Baker Academic, 2013), 325.
32 Yinger, "Jewish Education," 327.
33 Yinger, "Jewish Education," 328.
34 Thomas J. Kraus, "'Uneducated', 'Ignorant', or even 'Illiterate'? Aspects and Background for an Understanding of ΑΓΡΑΜΜΑΤΟΙ (and ΙΔΙΩΤΑΙ) in Acts 4.13," *NTS* 45 (1999): 444–46, 449.
35 Kraus, "'Uneducated', 'Ignorant', or even 'Illiterate'?" 448.
36 Darrell L. Bock, *Acts*, BECNT (Grand Rapids: Baker Academic, 2007), 195.
37 J. M. Holmes, *Text in a Whirlwind: A Critique of Four Exegetical Devices at 1 Timothy 2.9–15*, JSNTSup 196 (Sheffield: Sheffield Academic Press, 2000), 206. Part of Benjamin L. Merkle's critique of the education view in the parallel passage of 1 Tim 2:13–14 is wondering why Paul did not just refer to education ("Paul's Arguments from Creation in 1 Corinthians 11:8–9 and 1 Timothy 2:13–14: An Apparent Inconsistency Answered," *JETS* 49.3 [2006]: 545–46).

"not many were wise according to the flesh, not many were powerful, not many were of noble birth" (1 Cor 1:26). This statement likely gives a window into how many men and women had access to higher education in that particular congregation. If education was the main issue, Paul seemingly would have also silenced some of the men. Instead, Paul clarified that the issue was disorder, not education (1 Cor 14:26, 40). Thus, he gave instructions on silence to both males and females (1 Cor 14:28, 30, 34).

Even if one could describe the cultural context with precision, would that automatically change the application today? Consistency in applying this method is an important hermeneutical issue. If a scholar emphasizes the Greco-Roman or Jewish background to the Lord's Supper, should the modern church then dismiss the Lord's Supper as culturally-bound? Or at least adjust the church's practice to the modern preference to fast food? J. Robertson McQuilkin explains that "if a cultural factor not alluded to in Scripture itself is introduced, the potential is almost limitless for setting aside biblical teaching which we do not like on the basis of some cultural reason that would make it dispensable."[38] Scholars who appeal to cultural background material in order to change the application for the modern church usually do not add an explanation showing how this method is not "limitless." Köstenberger explains, "To insist fallaciously that occasionality equals cultural relativity renders in the ultimate analysis any divine revelation to humanity impossible, since such revelation by necessity occurs in a cultural, circumstantial context. Thus, the question is not whether a given teaching is *occasional* in nature but whether it is *limited to the occasion* by the biblical writer or other textual or contextual factors."[39] In other words, Köstenberger challenges every interpreter not to simply explain that "gender passages" are set within occasional documents but also to explain how the biblical writer or other clues limit the application. Paul does show a willingness to change his cultural habits in relation to evangelism (1 Cor 9:19–23) but not on how the church is structured. Paul's varied usage of silence in 1 Cor 14:26–40 regarding both men and women

---

[38] J. Robertson McQuilkin, "Problems of Normativeness in Scripture: Cultural Versus Permanent," in *Hermeneutics, Inerrancy, and the Bible*, ed. Earl D. Radmacher and Robert D. Preus (Grand Rapids: Zondervan, 1984), 233.

[39] Andreas Köstenberger, "Gender Passages in the NT: Hermeneutical Fallacies Critiqued," *WTJ* 56 (1994): 273 (italics original). Douglas J. Moo, "The Interpretation of 1 Timothy 2:11–15: A Rejoinder," *TJ* 2 (1981): 219, writes, "The point, then, is this: *the isolation of local circumstances as the occasion for a particular teaching does not, by itself, indicate anything about the normative nature of that teaching*" (italics original). For additional discussion, see Benjamin L. Merkle, "Are the Qualifications for Elders or Overseers Negotiable?" *BSac* 171 (2014): 179–81.

in the church can consistently be applied today as in the ancient world when both similarities and differences are rightly judged.[40]

The Lack of Public Speaking Argument

Some writers make blanket statements about women's silence in the ancient world in regard to public speech. Commenting on 1 Cor 14:33b–35, Kim Riddlebarger claims, "In Greco-Roman culture, women did not speak or say anything in public (except to other women)."[41] Aside from the main critique of displacing Paul's own reasoning (the OT law), this claim is too broad to be helpful in searching through the data. How the data is framed is important, which will be discussed below.

Keener's article mentioned above also has some important information about women and public speaking, but his article raises questions about how to frame and use the primary source data. For example, Keener quotes Sophocles's *Ajax* about a conversation between Ajax and Tecmessa, daughter of Teleutas. Keener simply states, "'Silence,' one classical hero warned his concubine, 'makes a woman beautiful.'"[42] Keener opens up the possibility of misunderstanding by quoting this passage in a section on public speaking. The woman was being silenced because she was objecting to Ajax, not because she was speaking in public. And, the idea of silence itself comes with a complex history. Silence was also directed towards men as a virtue in antiquity. For instance, Euripides states, "A thinking man is better silent [σιγᾶν] than when fallen into company. I wish I may be neither friend nor companion to the man who believes his thoughts are self-sufficient while deeming his friends slaves."[43] Silence as a virtue continued throughout the centuries. Apollonius of Tyana states,

> Apollonius to his pupils: Take great care not to say what you should not. For it is the absolute mark of an uncultured person not to be unable to stay silent [σιγεῖν] and to blurt out improprieties. Apollonius to the same. Talkativeness causes many a mistake, but silence [σιγᾶν] is safe. Apollonius to Euphrates. The best people use the fewest words. That is why, if chatterers felt as much annoyance as they cause, they would not make long speeches.[44]

---

40 When comparing the ancient world with today, a scholar has the choice to emphasize the differences, the similarities, or both. See Philip Richter, "Social-Scientific Criticism of the New Testament: An Appraisal and Extended Example," in *Approaches to New Testament Study*, ed. Stanley E. Porter and David Tombs, JSNTSup 120 (Sheffield: Sheffield Academic Press, 1995), 271.
41 Kim Riddlebarger, *1 Corinthians*, The Lectio Continua (Powder Springs, GA: Tolle Lege, 2013), 396.
42 Keener, "Women's Education and Public Speech in Antiquity," 756–57; quoting Sophocles, *Ajax* 293.
43 Euripides, *Fragments* 29.
44 Apollonius of Tyana, *Letters* 92–94.

78 | *Paul, Women, and the Meaning of Silence*

Just because Ajax made a point about women being silent does not necessarily mean that they did not speak in public. Silence could apply to both men and women.

Women in antiquity (or women and public speaking) can be so broad a topic that a problem arises of omitting counter-evidence or relegating counter-evidence to a footnote. Keener discusses men who avoided speaking with women in public, and appeals, for example, to Sirach 9:9. While Keener did discuss some Jewish literature, why is there no reference to the book of Judith, which has a woman making public speeches?[45] Judith speaks to the elders of the city, and the elders respond well to her (8:10–36; cf. 10:6–10). Judith speaks to the men of the Assyrians (10:11–17), as well as to Holophernes himself (11:1–12:9). Judith then returns to her people and speaks to all of them about the victory (13:11–14:10). Judith finally sings a song before all Israel (16:1–17).[46] While the historicity of the account may be a question, the text itself gives no indication that Judith's public speeches were viewed negatively.[47] Keener's discussion of Jewish literature could have made mention of Judith.

Keener did mention some women speaking, but he relegated certain texts to footnotes. In Keener's main text, he mentions Valerius Maximus's "only three examples" of women speaking in public, who were Maesia of Sentinum, Carfania, the wife of Senator Licinius Buccio, and Hortensia, daughter of Q. Hortensius.[48] Keener frames the discussion in a way that highlights the exceptional nature of women speaking in public. However, he relegated additional evidence to the contrary to a footnote. He notes,

> Under duress, women sometimes pleaded before judges (e.g. *Pesiq. Rab Kah.* 15:9; *Song Rab.* 5:16, §2) and might request or win special consideration on account of their gender (*P. Ryl.* 114, line 5; Alciphron *Courtesans* 4 [Bacchis to Phrynê], 1.31, §4; cf. Lysias *Or.* 32.11–18, §§506–511). Under such duress, women likewise pleaded with Marcius to spare Rome in Appian, *Hist. rom.* 2.5.3; Plutarch, *Coriol.* 34.2. Yet Mediterranean laws were prejudiced even against women as witnesses (e.g. Justinian, *Inst.* 2.10.6; Josephus, *Ant.* 4.219).[49]

---

45 For contrasts of Sirach and Judith, see Richard J. Coggins, *Sirach*, Guides to Apocrypha and Pseudepigrapha (Sheffield: Sheffield Academic, 1998), 90.
46 Text used from Deborah Gera, *Judith*, CEJL (Berlin: de Gruyter, 2014).
47 On questions of date and historicity, see Gera, *Judith*, 26–44. Gera dates the text to 100 BC.
48 Keener, "Women's Education and Public Speech in Antiquity," 757; referring to Valerius Maximus, *Memorable Doings and Sayings* 8.3.
49 Keener, "Women's Education and Public Speech in Antiquity," 757 n. 66.

The Jewish references that Keener cites do not give any hint that women pleading before judges was exceptional. One states, "Said R. Berekhiah, 'There was the case of a woman whose kettle was stolen. She went to complain about it to the judge, and found the kettle sitting on his stove' "; and, "Said R. Levi, 'There was the case of a woman who bribed a judge with a silver lamp.' "[50] Another text states, "Said R. Yudan [b. R. Simeon], 'The matter may be compared to a widow who was complaining to a judge about her son.' "[51] Not only did Keener place P. Ryl. 114 in a footnote, but there is additional evidence of women petitioning judges throughout the papyri.[52] P. Ryl. 120.1–5, from AD 167, records (though fragmented), "To Archias, priest and exegetes of Hermopolis Magna, from …, daughter of … and …, of Hermopolis, registered in the quarter of …, with my representative, for the purposes of this petition, Demetrius son of … also called Heliodorus, whose mother is Helene, of Hermopolis, registered in the quarter of the Eastern …, who is writing on my behalf as I am illiterate."[53] Though she is illiterate, men could also be called illiterate.[54] P. Ryl. 122.14–15 (AD 127) records, "I, Hermione daughter of Dionysius, have presented this petition through Menodorus my agent."[55] Even if women spoke through mediators, they still were able to bring their concerns to judges. The impression that women's voices were not somehow heard in the ancient world in public is not correct. Finally, Keener's reference to Josephus's discussion of Deuteronomy (*Ant.* 4.219), in the quotation above, is unclear in how it directly relates to Mediterranean law. Furthermore, the actual practice of women as witnesses may have varied from the written law. For example, P. Ryl. 136.1–12 (AD 34) states, "To Gaius Arrius

---

50 Pesiq. Rab Kah. 15:9. Translation from Jacob Neusner, *Pesiqta deRab Kahana: An Analytical Translation*, BJS 123 (Atlanta: Scholars, 1987), 2:11.
51 Song Rab. 5:16. Translation from Jacob Neusner, *Song of Songs Rabbah: An Analytical Translation*, BJS 198 (Atlanta: Scholars, 1989), 2:129.
52 P.Ryl. 114.1–6, dated to AD 280–81, states, "To …, the most illustrious praefect, from Aurelia Artemis daughter of Paesius, of the village of Thraso in the Arsinoïte nome. Perceiving your love of equity, my lord praefect, and your care for all, especially women and widows, I approach you praying to obtain your aid" (lines 1–6). Aurelia goes on to provide details of her case in this text. Dating, text, translation, and commentary are found in J. de M. Johnson, Victor Martin, and Arthur S. Hunt, eds., *Catalogue of the Greek Papyri in the John Rylands Library Manchester* (Manchester: Manchester University Press, 1915), 2:97–100. The editors provide extensive discussion on the reference to Aurelia (p. 99).
53 Johnson, Martin, and Hunt, eds., *Catalogue of the Greek Papyri in the John Rylands Library Manchester*, 2:111–13 (ellipses in original).
54 P. Ryl. 122.22–24 states, "I, Tyrannus son of Hephestion, have written for him, as he is illiterate." Johnson, Martin, and Hunt, eds., *Catalogue of the Greek Papyri in the John Rylands Library Manchester*, 2:115–16.
55 Johnson, Martin, and Hunt, eds., *Catalogue of the Greek Papyri in the John Rylands Library Manchester*, 2:115–16.

Priscus, chief of police, from Papus son of Papus. In the month of Pachon of the 20th year of Tiberius Caesar Augustus, as I was talking to Ancherimphis and his wife Thenapunchis, a door-keeper of Euhemeria in the division of Themistes, concerning the tin cups and . . . and other utensils and the 60 dr. of silver which they thievishly carried off from my house, he subjected me to no common outrage."[56] Why did the victim name a woman in a robbery claim?

What is usually missed in this discussion of women and public speech is the fact that women could rebel against the ideal. It is not correct to state, as Riddlebarger does above, that women did not speak in public. It would be more accurate to say that women did sometimes speak in public even though some men did not want them to. Furthermore, there were some men who were not as concerned about women speaking in public, as Livy's *History of Rome* demonstrates. Stephen Simon, referring to women protesting in the street in Livy's history, writes that Cato the Censor "reacted very negatively to actions of these women."[57] Simon only quotes the portion of Livy's history on women where Cato questions the conduct of the women in the streets.[58] The main point here involves Cato's statement, "Frankly, I was blushing somewhat a moment ago when I came into the Forum through the midst of a crowd of women.. . . . I would have said: 'What sort of conduct is this, all this running out into public places, blocking streets and accosting other women's husbands? Couldn't you all have asked your own husbands the very same thing at home?' "[59] But Livy's work continues when Lucius Valerius responds to Cato by saying,

> The consul, however, has spent more words on criticizing married women than he has on rebutting our proposal, to the point of making it unclear whether the behavior for which he was reproaching the women came naturally or was motivated by us.. . . Now, what is so strange about the women's action in coming into the streets in large numbers over a matter that concerns them? Have they never appeared in public before? I shall open your own *Origins* to contradict you. Listen to how often they have done it, and always, you will see, for the common good.[60]

---

56   Johnson, Martin, and Hunt, eds., *Catalogue of the Greek Papyri in the John Rylands Library Manchester*, 2:133 (ellipses in original).
57   Stephen J. Simon, "Women Who Pleaded Causes Before the Roman Magistrates," *Classical Bulletin* 66 (1990): 79.
58   Simon refers to Livy, *History of Rome*, 24.2.1–14, but the reference is to 34.2.1–14.
59   Livy, *History of Rome*, 34.2.8–10.
60   Livy, *History of Rome*, 34.5.3, 7–8.

Subsequently, Valerius describes additional actions by women.[61] After the rest of Valerius's speech, Livy states, "On the day after these speeches for and against the law were delivered a considerably larger crowd of women flooded into the streets. En masse they all blockaded the doors of the Bruti, who were for vetoing the proposal of their colleagues, and they did not give up until the veto they had threatened was withdrawn by the tribunes."[62] Thus, one gets a wrong impression of women in the ancient world if a writer only quotes Cato and not Lucius Valerius. Not only does Keener rely on Stephen Simon's limited quotation of Livy (quoting only Cato), but Christopher Forbes uses the same limited quotation as well (without also quoting Lucius Valerius).[63]

Some writers on Greco-Roman backgrounds are not as precise as Keener, who explains, "An egalitarian conclusion need not follow automatically from such very general premises, but neither should the egalitarian case be dismissed on the specific basis of a denial of the likelihood of these premises."[64] Many writers do automatically follow with egalitarian conclusions simply after describing some aspects of the ancient world without either exploring counter-evidence or wondering if the same methodology would be problematic with non-gender texts.[65] Two writers who have attempted to discuss methodology in relation to Bible passages on women are Grant Osborne and William Webb, who will be considered in the next section.

The Search for Consistency in Method and Cultural Analysis

A recurring theme in hermeneutics, not least regarding gender passages, is appeal to the cultural situation in order to nullify or adjust the biblical command. Some writers simply discuss the cultural background without discussing methodology and so leave open the question of methodological consistency.[66] The cultural situation is important for reconstructing the original setting and for word studies.

---

61   Livy, *History of Rome*, 34.5.8–13.
62   Livy, *History of Rome*, 34.8.1–2.
63   Keener, "Women's Education and Public Speech in Antiquity," 757 n. 65; Christopher Forbes, *Prophecy and Inspired Speech in Early Christianity and its Hellenistic Environment* (Peabody, MA: Hendrickson, 1995), 275–76.
64   Keener, "Women's Education and Public Speech in Antiquity," 747.
65   Gillian Clark writes in a way that implies *any* ancient problem will be different from modern concerns, and so one does not need to apply 1 Cor 14:34 the same. Gillian Clark, "The Women at Corinth," *Theology* 85 (1982): 261, concludes, "But we need not let first-century anxieties restrict the twentieth-century use of women in ministry: they had different problems at Corinth."
66   E.g., Preston T. Massey, "Women, Talking and Silence: 1 Corinthians 11.5 and 14.34–35 in the Light of Greco-Roman Culture," *JGRChJ* 12 (2016): 127–60.

However, what is often forgotten is that, as John Davis helpfully clarifies, the "God of the Bible is the Lord of culture, not its victim."[67] One could argue that most or all of the biblical books are occasional documents. Simply appealing to the specific situation into which God spoke does not automatically void God's commands. There must be additional reasons for setting aside a biblical command than simply a blanket appeal to culture. Grant Osborne provides some parameters between timeless and cultural references in Scripture. Osborne notes, "We dare not isolate the passages on women in the Church from the other Biblical injunctions. What we need is a series of covering laws to distinguish the eternal core from the cultural application in all the commands of Scripture and *then* apply these to the sections on women in the church."[68] His general principles are (1) interpret narrative in light of didactic sections; (2) a "systematic" discussion of a topic should be used to interpret "incidental references"; and (3) interpret passages in light of historical and literary contexts.[69] If Osborne's method is followed, then these principles would apply to the silence of women in the church by using passages like 1 Tim 2:9–14 and 1 Cor 14:34–35 (didactic passages) to interpret narrative passages like women in Romans 16 or women in the book of Acts. Also, systematic discussion of men and women (such as 1 Tim 2:9–14) should be used to interpret the incidental reference in Gal 3:28. Even if one disagrees with Osborne's interpretive principles, he at least clearly states his method. Interpreting passages consistently is one of the challenges. For example, how is one consistent with interpreting the New Testament on both women and homosexuality? Passages on women and homosexuality are more apt comparisons than slavery since questions about women or homosexuality inherently involve gender but slavery did not.[70] William Webb has attempted to answer these kinds of questions in his important book *Slaves, Women and Homosexuals: Exploring the Hermeneutics of Cultural Analysis*.[71] It will be shown below that Webb himself is inconsistent in how he applies his own method.

---

67 John Jefferson Davis, "Some Reflections on Galatians 3:28, Sexual Roles, and Biblical Hermeneutics," *JETS* 19 (1976): 207.
68 Grant R. Osborne, "Hermeneutics and Women in the Church," *JETS* 20 (1977): 338 (italics original).
69 Osborne, "Hermeneutics and Women in the Church," 338–39.
70 It is possible to consistently reject slavery today, while still seeing commands to women and homosexuals as transcultural. When Genesis 1–2 is viewed as normative, then one sees man's leadership in the garden of Eden, but one does not see either slavery or male/male relationships. Furthermore, there is no command in the NT that calls for slavery, even though the NT regulates it.
71 William J. Webb, *Slaves, Women and Homosexuals: Exploring the Hermeneutics of Cultural Analysis* (Downers Grove, IL: InterVarsity Press, 2001).

Webb attempts to argue consistently that the homosexual passages apply the same way in both ancient culture and modern culture, but one must move from the biblical ethics on slavery and women towards an "ultimate ethic."[72] In other words, he interprets passages on homosexuality and women differently, but is Webb's view methodologically consistent? His book is important because one might argue that to move beyond the Bible's words on women opens up the question of moving beyond the Bible's words on homosexuality. Put another way, if the cultural changes can alter the application of women in ministry, why can cultural changes not alter the application of homosexuality? Webb claims, "My point is simply that our modern culture must not determine the outcome of any cultural/transcultural analysis of Scripture."[73] Here Webb denies the centrality of cultural change to influence what the "ultimate ethic" is regarding the three groups of people: slaves, women, and homosexuals. However, he later writes, "The comparative outcome is this: *the homosexual texts are in a different category than the women and slavery texts.* The former are almost entirely transcultural in nature, while the latter are heavily bound by culture."[74] So Webb does lean heavily on the cultural distinctions despite his claim to the contrary. His conclusion on texts regarding women in particular states that "it is reasonable to say that much of the portrait of patriarchy within Scripture contains culturally bound components and is not uniformly transcultural in nature."[75] However, what if one finds transcultural elements in passages regarding women?

Webb discusses Genesis 1–2 and how it may or may not apply to texts on women. Five out of his six arguments are cultural arguments. In essence, Webb argues that Genesis 1–2 does not apply transculturally because most of Genesis 1–2 is cultural, including primogeniture and the agricultural setting.[76] His sixth reason is that the new creation texts in the NT seem "to displace or supersede the patriarchy found in the first-creation story."[77] Webb's analysis about Genesis 1–2 shows that his hermeneutic is not simply about "movement," but that it is

---

72 On ultimate ethic, see Webb, *Slaves, Women and Homosexuals*, 31–33.
73 Webb, *Slaves, Women and Homosexuals*, 246.
74 Webb, *Slaves, Women and Homosexuals*, 252 (italics original).
75 Webb, *Slaves, Women and Homosexuals*, 248.
76 The way Webb discusses Genesis 1–2 here differs significantly with his teaching on homosexuality in another book where he begins by using Genesis 1–2 to show how the Bible does not support homosexuality (with no disclaimer that Genesis 1–2 has cultural elements). See William J. Webb, "Gender Equality and Homosexuality," in *Discovering Biblical Equality: Complementarity without Hierarchy*, ed. Ronald W. Pierce and Rebecca Merrill Groothuis (Downers Grove, IL: InterVarsity Press, 2004), 402–3.
77 Webb, *Slaves, Women and Homosexuals*, 249.

also about the question of applying cultural elements in Scripture. If he can show that Genesis 1–2 is mostly cultural, then he can reapply the passage in an altogether different manner. The problem of consistency arises when one compares Webb's analysis of Genesis 1–2 and women to his analysis of homosexuals. Each time he mentions the cultural elements in relation to homosexuality in the Bible in his conclusion, he dismisses the concept and moves to other criteria (such as the rest of Scripture).[78] For example, he writes, "The cultural environment and Israel's theocratic setting may have influenced the severity of the Old Testament penal code, which called for the death penalty for homosexual behavior. Yet, the inherent *negative assessment* of homosexual activity itself retains a transcultural dimension."[79] In sum, Webb treats cultural elements differently depending on if he is referring to women or homosexuals.

Likewise, his use of "movement" is different in relation to women and homosexuals. Regarding women he writes, "*Nonetheless, what should be clear is that a redemptive-movement hermeneutic beckons for change.*"[80] But regarding homosexuals he states, "We need to journey with the redemptive spirit of the text and always move in a direction toward which the whole of Scripture taken together points."[81] In other words, there is no major change that the movement "beckons for" in relation to homosexuality. When Webb is referring to women, he emphasizes the culture, but when he is referring to homosexuals, he emphasizes the texts of Scripture ("the whole of Scripture"). It should also be noted that Webb's view of going up "the ladder of abstraction" and the question of cultural versus transcultural elements are closely intertwined in his argument.[82] So if there is a problem with how he views cultural versus transcultural elements, then his view of movement will need to be adjusted. Despite Webb's contribution, there still remains significant problems with the cultural argument used for passages involving gender and the same argument used for passages about homosexuality.

In practice, writers often rely heavily on the cultural argument whether speaking about women or homosexuality. They often do so without the nuance of Webb's argumentation. Two different writers referring to women or homosexuality can be seen using the same method of argumentation. For instance, Jean Héring claims, "It is permissible to suppose that in our own day, when women

---

78 Webb, *Slaves, Women and Homosexuals*, 250–52.
79 Webb, *Slaves, Women and Homosexuals*, 251 (italics original).
80 Webb, *Slaves, Women and Homosexuals*, 250 (italics original).
81 Webb, *Slaves, Women and Homosexuals*, 251.
82 See the combination in William J. Webb, "The Limits of a Redemptive-Movement Hermeneutic: Focused Response to T. R. Schreiner," *EvQ* 75.4 (2003): 335–37.

enjoy all rights and shock no one by speaking in public, the restriction enjoined by the Apostle no longer has the same force."[83] Victor Furnish writes (with the same method), "But what Paul accepted as a matter of course about homosexual behavior, we can no longer take for granted."[84] Methodologically, the two statements are the same. The issue is not if egalitarian conclusions on women lead to the moral acceptance of homosexuality, but whether there is any difference in methodology. There is a better alternative to examining cultural elements within biblical commands, which will now be examined.

Paul's Consistent Pattern

Paul's writing is consistent throughout his letters in the way he blends cultural references with what is applicable for all the churches. Benjamin Merkle, in his article demonstrating consistency between 1 Cor 11:8–9 and 1 Tim 2:13–14, provides a significant explanation that deserves full quotation. He writes,

> Groothuis claims, "It is inconsistent to regard the dress code in 1 Timothy 2:9 as culturally relative and, therefore, temporary, but the restrictions on women's ministry in 2:12 as universal and permanent" (*Good News* 214). But this argument fails to take note of the context of Paul's teaching since Paul clearly gives us the principle underlying his prohibitions when he says, "I want women to adorn themselves with proper clothing, modestly and discreetly" (1 Tim 2:9). Before he gives the culturally relative prohibitions, Paul first gives the universal principle behind them: women are to dress modestly and discreetly. Therefore, although the prohibitions of wearing braided hair, gold, pearls, and expensive clothing are culturally relative, the previous stated principle is not. Paul is not saying that tending to one's hair, wearing jewelry, or wearing clothes is wrong (note that Paul specifically says "expensive clothing" [ἱματισμῷ πολυτελεῖ]). Rather, he is saying that modesty and discreetness should be maintained when giving consideration to how one appears in public. It is misleading, then, to claim that the dress code in 1 Timothy 2 is culturally relative without acknowledging that Paul does give us a transcultural principle. Furthermore, there are other examples where we find culturally relative issues mixed with transcultural

---

83 Jean Héring, *The First Epistle of Saint Paul to the Corinthians*, trans. A. W. Heathcote and P. J. Allcock (London: Epworth, 1962), 155. See the French version, Jean Héring, *La première épître de saint Paul aux Corinthiens*, CNT 7 (Neuchatel: Delachaux & Niestlé, 1949), 130, "Il est permis de supposer que dans notre civilisation contemporaine, où les femmes, jouissant de tous les droits, ne choquent personne en prenant la parole en public, la restriction prévue par l'apôtre n'a plus la même raison d'être," where the conclusion could be translated "no longer has a reason to be."
84 Victor Paul Furnish, *The Moral Teaching of Paul* (Nashville: Abingdon, 1979), 80.

86 | *Paul, Women, and the Meaning of Silence*

principles (e.g. 1 Cor 16:20). To simply appeal to the context where a culturally relative issue exists and then claim that the whole context must be dealing with such issues is not good exegesis.[85]

Merkle's explanation can be applied outside of 1 Timothy 2 and 1 Corinthians 11. The main point here is Merkle's statement that "there are other examples where we find culturally relative issues mixed with transcultural principles (e.g. 1 Cor 16:20)." In other words, there is a Pauline pattern of mixing cultural and transcultural statements. Thus, a writer cannot dismiss an entire text simply by pointing out some of the cultural elements. Merkle's view will be expanded by looking at other analogous statements and then applying this view to 1 Cor 14:34–35.

Merkle points to 1 Cor 16:20 as another example of mixed cultural and transcultural principles. Paul states, "Greet one another with a holy kiss" (1 Cor 16:20). The Greek text is Ἀσπάσασθε ἀλλήλους ἐν φιλήματι ἁγίῳ, which is found again in Rom 16:16 and 2 Cor 13:12 (in 2 Cor 13:12 the final phrase is transposed as ἐν ἁγίῳ φιλήματι). Paul writes in 1 Thess 5:26 a similar statement, Ἀσπάσασθε τοὺς ἀδελφοὺς πάντας ἐν φιλήματι ἁγίῳ ("Greet all the brothers with a holy kiss"). Paul states only the transcultural principle in Phil 4:21 by omitting the kiss, "Greet all the saints in Christ Jesus." Keener discusses the cultural element of kissing, but he does not state that the text no longer applies today. Keener refers to how modern Christians "express sibling affection differently."[86] Keener naturally sees a transcultural principle that is closely related to kissing, even if kissing is not used. If Groothuis's hermeneutic were correct (in Merkle's quote above), then one could charge Keener with being inconsistent in seeing kissing as cultural but affection as universal and permanent. In fact, part of Groothuis's evidence of inconsistency is that "all of these instructions are part of the same paragraph, the same flow of thought...."[87] If Groothuis's interpretive principles were applied to 1 Cor 16:20 then the entire greeting would have to be either completely cultural or completely transcultural.

The slavery texts are more debated than Christian greetings. However, if one interprets the slavery texts with the mixture of cultural and transcultural

---

85 Merkle, "Paul's Arguments from Creation in 1 Corinthians 11:8–9 and 1 Timothy 2:13–14," 548 n. 74. The quote from Groothuis comes from Rebecca Merrill Groothuis, *Good News for Women: A Biblical Picture of Gender Equality* (Grand Rapids: Baker, 1997), 214. Groothuis wrote "restriction" (singular).

86 Craig S. Keener, *1–2 Corinthians*, New Cambridge Bible Commentary (Cambridge: Cambridge University Press, 2005), 141.

87 Groothuis, *Good News for Women*, 214.

elements in mind, then interpretation becomes more consistent. Paul writes in his letter to the Ephesians,

> Slaves, obey your masters according to the flesh with fear and trembling in sincerity of your heart as to Christ, not according to eye-service as people pleasers, but as slaves of Christ, doing the will of God from the heart, serving with goodwill as to the Lord and not to men, knowing that whatever good each one does, this he will receive from the Lord whether slave or free. And masters, do the same for them, ceasing the threats, knowing that the Lord, both theirs and yours, is in heaven, and there is no partiality with him. (Eph 6:5–9)[88]

The cultural and transcultural elements are together in the same unit. Culturally, slavery and slave-ownership have changed throughout time.[89] However, the rest of the passage includes transcultural attitudes and theology that apply across the generations. The transcultural elements include the manner of working unto the Lord, treating others without sinful anger, and recognizing the Lordship of Christ in relationships. Even the metaphor of "slaves of Christ" has applicability for the modern church.[90] For example, Paul contrasts obedience as a slave of Christ in contrast to pleasing other people (ὑπακούετε . . . μὴ . . . ὡς ἀνθρωπάρεσκοι ἀλλ' ὡς δοῦλοι Χριστοῦ; Eph 6:5–6). The following participial phrase after "slaves of Christ" (ποιοῦντες τὸ θέλημα τοῦ θεοῦ ἐκ ψυχῆς; Eph 6:6) may also define what the metaphor means, where Paul refers to the slave as "doing the will of God from the heart." Certainly, the Lord's impartiality still applies today, in every situation, as it did in the ancient world.[91] Paul refers to end-time judgment with the basis of "there is no partiality with God" (Rom 2:11). The transcultural elements are not changed from one cultural to another. Neither can the entire passage be dismissed simply because it includes slavery since the theology of the Lord's impartiality clearly spans generations.

---

88 Cf. Col 3:22–4:1; 1 Tim 6:1–2; Phlm. For discussion of the Greek text, see Benjamin L. Merkle, *Ephesians*, EGGNT (Nashville: B&H Academic, 2016), 201–7.
89 Slavery varied in different cultures even within the ancient world itself. J. A. Harrill writes, "The term 'Greco-Roman slavery' thus proves problematic. Evidence from the Greek period cannot be used as background for the Roman period of the NT authors" ("Slavery," *DNTB* 1125).
90 See, e.g., Murray J. Harris, *Slave of Christ: A New Testament Metaphor for Total Devotion to Christ*, New Studies in Biblical Theology (Downers Grove, IL: IVP Academic, 1999), 148–56. Harris notes, "No metaphor that is used to picture the believer's relationship to Christ or God can or should be applied at every point of the comparison" (p. 148). Regardless of agreement with Harris's exegesis, interpreters can ask what aspects of slavery are the biblical authors using to teach the church about her relationship to Christ.
91 For references, see BDAG, 887.

Even passages that are thoroughly cultural still have transcultural principles in them. For instance, Paul's states in the letter to Titus, "When I send Artemas to you or Tychicus, hurry to come to me in Nicopolis, for I have decided to winter there. Diligently assist Zenas the lawyer and Apollos on their journey that there is no lack for them. And also let our people learn to give attention to good works for necessary needs that they may not be unfruitful" (Titus 3:12–14). Paul refers to specific names, an ancient city, and ancient travel plans. The amount of cultural references outnumbers the references to transcultural principles. Still, Paul ends with the transcultural principle in Titus 3:14 that informed his comments, namely, good works (cf. Titus 3:8). The transcultural principle remains intact today even if it finds expression in different names and places today. To complete the Groothuis quote above, she writes, "All these instructions are part of the same paragraph, the same flow of thought, and are elements of an epistle that was written, not as a general 'church manual' applicable to all churches everywhere, but specifically for Timothy with respect to his assigned task of dealing with the false teaching in the Ephesian church at that time."[92] Of course, one could easily substitute the name Titus for Timothy in Groothuis's quotation. However, Groothuis's interpretive principles would not be clear for Titus 3:12–14. Would the culturally-conditioned words to Titus mean it is inconsistent to apply doing good works today? It is better to say that Paul mixes cultural and transcultural principles throughout his letters and even commands. Andreas Köstenberger explains a fallacy that makes "the arbitrary distinction between passages conveying a 'general principle' and those of 'limited application.'"[93] In other words, scholars themselves can be inconsistent when claiming one passage is universal and another passage is of limited application. By what criteria do they make these distinctions? It is axiomatic to say that all of Paul's letters were written to a particular group, in a particular time, and for a particular occasion. Yet, Roger Nicole writes, "In 1 Corinthians 14:34–35 we have a case of a fairly evidential ad hoc prescription.... In principle Paul's concern to avoid cultural disrepute would apply today to both men and women, though in Corinth at this time it was clearly specifically applicable to the women involved."[94] Nicole does not clearly state criteria by which to determine when a passage is ad hoc and when one is not. Nicole previously admitted that Scripture was originally given to those in the

---

92 Groothuis, *Good News for Women*, 214.
93 Köstenberger, "Gender Passages in the NT: Hermeneutical Fallacies Critiqued," 273.
94 Roger Nicole, "Biblical Hermeneutics: Basic Principles and Questions of Gender," in *Discovering Biblical Equality: Complementarity without Hierarchy*, ed. Ronald W. Pierce and Rebecca Merrill Groothuis (Downers Grove, IL: InterVarsity Press, 2004), 362.

ancient Near East and Greco-Roman world.[95] Since the original context of *any* biblical passage could be defined as ad hoc, then what other criteria can Nicole use to interpret 1 Cor 14:34–35? The better alternative is to see a mixture of cultural and transcultural elements in Paul's letters for each passage.

What might be the cultural and transcultural principles in 1 Cor 14:34? Craig Blomberg says, "The timeless principle in this passage [1 Cor 14:33–38], as in 11:2–16, seems to be male leadership and wifely submission in home and church; the culturally specific outworking in first-century Corinth was the silencing of wives during this one aspect of the worship service."[96] How does Blomberg decide that the silence was culturally specific? Blomberg does not state if the silence in 1 Cor 14:28 and 14:30 is also cultural. Anne Blampied writes, "The latter statement [silence] was only Paul's application of this principle [order] to one of the groups at Corinth who were disrupting the worship service."[97] She goes on to state that Paul's words do not limit women today.[98] Blampied's reference to silence only being for those in Corinth ignores the rest of Paul's wording in 1 Cor 14:34. Paul describes the silence for women "in the churches" (plural; ἐν ταῖς ἐκκλησίαις). The reference to all the churches will be considered below. Blampied also does not state if submission still applies today. What is certain, in light of several other passages in Scripture, is that submission is transcultural, as Blomberg articulates.[99] Silence is likely, though not certainly, also transcultural. If the issue was the judging of prophecy (as argued in Chapter Two), then silence was inherently bound up with submission. Furthermore, if silence were a culturally-bound command, then 1 Cor 14:28 and 14:30 should also be taken as no longer applicable in the same way today. The most likely option for a cultural reference is the mention of shame in 1 Cor 14:35. Shame might be culturally-specific while other references in the passage can be transcultural (though, honor and shame might also be universal).[100] Since it has been shown that Paul mixes cultural and transcultural references in his letters, shame as a cultural reference

---

95 Nicole, "Biblical Hermeneutics: Basic Principles and Questions of Gender," 360–61.
96 Craig L. Blomberg, "Applying 1 Corinthians in the Early Twenty-First Century," *SwJT* 45 (2002): 35.
97 Anne Blampied, "Paul and Silence for 'the Women' in 1 Corinthians 14:34–35," *Studia Biblica et Theologica* 13 (1983): 164.
98 Blampied, "Paul and Silence for 'the Women' in 1 Corinthians 14:34–35," 165.
99 Cf. Gen 2:18–25; 3:20; Eph 5:22–33; 1 Tim 2:11–14; 1 Pet 3:1–7.
100 Halvor Moxnes, "Honor and Shame," in *The Social Sciences and New Testament Interpretation*, ed. Richard L. Rohrbaugh (Peabody, MA: Hendrickson, 1996), 19, writes "Notions about honor and shame exist in virtually all cultures. But in many Western societies these terms play a minor role in descriptions of prominent social values."

does not automatically change the entire section. Simply finding a cultural reference in 1 Cor 14:34–35 does not void the passage or, more broadly, 1 Cor 14:26–40.[101]

Paul provided his basis of silencing women in the church, which was the OT νόμος (see discussion of νόμος below). Since Paul explicitly stated his basis for his words in 1 Cor 14:34–35, then appeal to the Greco-Roman background as a basis may be insufficient. Any claim that Paul regulated the speech of women on the basis of his culture *alone* misses the very words of the passage (καθὼς καὶ ὁ νόμος λέγει in 1 Cor 14:34). Nonetheless, before discussing the law, one additional argument must be addressed.

The Male and Female Problems at Corinth

Some writers claim Paul's words in 1 Cor 14:34–35 applied to Corinth alone and not to other churches or today. L. Ann Jervis explains the focus on women in Corinth: "I have argued that Paul responded to 'the women' alone because their speaking, rather than that done by any of the men, was disrupting the communal expression of prophesy. Yet in the process of convincing his converts to change their behavior he was willing to resort to the patriarchal values of his society."[102] Oropeza likewise states, "[W]e surmise that the only reason Paul does not silence men or husbands from chatting in the Corinthian setting is because they were not the problem."[103] Oropeza does not attempt to prove this statement despite the many references to women and men in Corinth (e.g., 1 Cor 14:26, 28, 30). Oropeza's introduction to 1 Corinthians discusses the problems of the entire church in Corinth without giving any hint that there was a female only problem.[104] F. F. Bruce shows how some limit the application when he says,

---

101 Finding a principle that distinguishes between what is normative and not normative is a challenge. McQuilkin's view is that "the historic context of a teaching is normative only if Scripture treats it that way, whereas the cultural context is normative unless Scripture treats it as limited" ("Problems of Normativeness in Scripture: Cultural Versus Permanent," 237). George W. Knight agrees with McQuilkin's thesis. See George W. Knight III, "A Response to Problems of Normativeness in Scripture: Cultural Versus Permanent" in *Hermeneutics, Inerrancy, and the Bible*, ed. Earl D. Radmacher and Robert D. Preus (Grand Rapids: Zondervan, 1984), 243–53. While McQuilkin's view is a good attempt, it still leaves room for debate about what Scripture limits. His entire essay shows the challenge any scholar faces in answering what is normative.

102 L. Ann Jervis, "1 Corinthians 14.34–35: A Reconsideration of Paul's Limitation of the Free Speech of Some Corinthian Women," *JSNT* 58 (1995): 72.

103 Oropeza, *1 Corinthians*, 191.

104 Oropeza, *1 Corinthians*, 9–10.

"Much of the teaching in this chapter [1 Corinthians 14] is relevant only to such exceptional circumstances as prevailed in the church of Corinth."[105] Yet Bruce does not consider the conflict of his interpretation with Paul's "churches" (plural) refferences in 1 Cor 14:33–34 (he notes the debate of the placement for 1 Cor 14:33b).[106] The comments below will demonstrate that Paul addressed both male and female problems in Corinth and viewed his comments as applicable beyond Corinth.

Paul directly indicated what the problems were in Corinth throughout 1 Corinthians. In fact, a review of 1 Corinthians demonstrates that men were also disrupting the church in Corinth. Paul begins his letter by defining the key issue in the Corinthian church as quarreling that led to division (1 Cor 1:11–12).[107] The Corinthian quarreling was itself a result of spiritual immaturity (1 Cor 3:1–4). The Corinthians took wealth as an example of being spiritual, following cultural values in exalting wealth (1 Cor 4:8).[108] Some in the church were questioning if Paul was going to visit them (1 Cor 4:18; cf. 9:3), and Paul in return challenged their speech (λόγος; 1 Cor 4:19). Since some interpreters focus on the women's speech in 1 Cor 14:34 and deny men were disrupting prophecy (as Jervis does above), then Paul's explanation in 1 Cor 4:19 of the Corinthian problem becomes more significant evidence against this view. The problem was not only with speech and division, but the Corinthians also had a sexual immorality problem (1 Cor 5:1–2, 6). Paul's concern for lawsuits in 1 Cor 6:1–8 is described in such a way that shows lawsuits, too, may have been a Corinthian problem. The division and lack of discernment was evident in the taking of the Lord's supper (1 Cor 11:17–34). Not only was the Lord's supper not practiced well, but there were, at least at times, several people talking in the service (1 Cor 14:26). Theologically, Paul states directly that "some have no knowledge of God" (1 Cor 15:34), which refers at least to knowledge of the resurrection (1 Cor 15:12, 35). This summary of Paul directly describing the problems in Corinth makes clear that women were not the only problem in the worship service.[109] Even Antoinette Wire, who writes

---

105 F. F. Bruce, *1 and 2 Corinthians*, NCB (Grand Rapids: Eerdmans, 1971; repr., 1983), 137; see also Roy A. Harrisville, *1 Corinthians*, ACNT (Minneapolis: Augsburg, 1987), 243–44; and Catherine Kroeger and Richard Kroeger, "Strange Tongues or Plain Talk?" *Daughters of Sarah* 12.4 (1986): 12–13.
106 Bruce, *1 and 2 Corinthians*, 135.
107 On the question of how many divisive factions the Corinthians had, if any, see discussion in Dutch, *The Educated Elite in 1 Corinthians*, 17–20.
108 Thomas R. Schreiner, *1 Corinthians: An Introduction and Commentary*, TNTC 7 (Downers Grove, IL: IVP Academic, 2018), 101–2; Keener, *1–2 Corinthians*, 45.
109 I interpret 1 Cor 1:10 as the purpose statement of the letter. Paul writes, "Now I urge you, brothers, through the name of our Lord Jesus Christ, that you all speak the same and there be no divisions among you, but be restored in the same mind and in the same mind-set" (1 Cor 1:10).

on Corinthian women prophets, does not see the women as the only problem in Corinth. Wire says, "It needs to be stated that the Corinthian women prophets are only one part of Paul's audience; other parts could also be reconstructed in this way."[110] Wire's investigation into the women in Corinth demonstrates the limits on focusing only on women.[111] For some reason, Paul directed his comments to the women in 1 Cor 14:34–35, but his comments were not because only women were causing problems in Corinth.

The instruction in 1 Cor 14:34–35 is in the broader context of 1 Cor 14:26–40, which refers to both men and women, including problems in the assembly. The problems and the other uses of silence included men since Paul addresses the entire church (1 Cor 14:26, 28, 30, 33a, 38). Paul writes concerning both men and women, "Then, how is it, brothers, when you come together, each one has a psalm, each one has a teaching, each one has a revelation, each one has a tongue, each one has an interpretation. Let all things be done for edification" (1 Cor 14:26). Then he gives a specific silence to men and women in 1 Cor 14:28 and 14:30. This literary context proves that women were not the only problem in the church service. Furthermore, the speech problems throughout 1 Corinthians were not limited to women only. So Paul must have had another reason for referring to women in 1 Cor 14:34–35. That reason was the OT law.

Scholars who seek to limit Paul's words in 1 Cor 14:34–35 must take into account the phrase "all the churches" (1 Cor 14:33) and "in the churches" (1 Cor 14:34). Despite Paul's terminology, Daniel Arichea says, "In other words, detaching v 33b from vv 34–35 allows for the possibility that what Paul is writing here is not meant to be a rule for all the churches, but only for the Corinthian church."[112] Arichea mentions the plural churches in 1 Cor 14:33, but he omits the plural "churches" in 1 Cor 14:34 from his interpretation. If detaching 1 Cor 14:33b with the plural "churches" could limit Paul's words only to Corinth, then how does Arichea interpret the plural "churches" in 1 Cor 14:34? Since Paul repeats

---

110   Antoinette Clark Wire, *The Corinthian Women Prophets: A Reconstruction through Paul's Rhetoric* (Minneapolis: Fortress, 1990), 9. Wire does, however, see the women prophets as playing a "key role" in opposing Paul (p. 184).

111   Wire also states regarding speech and knowledge in Corinth, "There is no sign that any part of the church is being excluded from Paul's description, least of all its prophets" (*The Corinthian Women Prophets*, 40).

112   Daniel C. Arichea, "The Silence of Women in the Church: Theology and Translation in 1 Corinthians 14.33b–36," *BT* 46.1 (1995): 104. Likewise, Arichea writes, "One effect of connecting v 33b with vv 34–35 is to make the injunction to silence a general rule of wide application, which means that it is valid not only for the Corinthian Christians but also for other Christian communities during Paul's time" (p. 103).

the church in the plural in 1 Cor 14:33 and 14:34, then the question of where the text is divided is not relevant for the question of wider application.

Philip Payne correctly notes that "these two verses [1 Cor 14:34–35] were consistently represented in the mss. as a separate paragraph and not grouped with 14.33b."[113] Some have interpreted this fact to mean that the first phrase of "as in all the churches of the saints" (1 Cor 14:33b) goes with the statement that God is a God of peace (1 Cor 14:33a).[114] Then the second phrase of "in the churches" (1 Cor 14:34) goes with women being silent. Aḷesja Lavrinoviča argues the same point as Payne for the placement of 1 Cor 14:33b, but she includes the question of "exegetical implications" on if 1 Cor 14:33b goes with what precedes or what follows. For example, Lavrinoviča refers to D. A. Carson, who argues that "little is changed in the interpretation of verses 34–35, since the phrase 'in the churches' (in the plural) is found *in verse 34*."[115] But then Lavrinoviča refers to Arichea's article quoted above that limits Paul's words.[116] Lavrinoviča discusses the external evidence in favor of connecting 1 Cor 14:33b with 14:33a. However, Lavrinoviča does not give her own conclusive position on the "exegetical implications" despite discussing the debate. Carson is correct that there is little interpretive value in the placement of 1 Cor 14:33b since the plural churches appears again in 1 Cor 14:34.[117]

The question as to whether Paul would have limited his words only to Corinth needs to be argued from 1 Corinthians more broadly since Paul refers to the church(es) throughout his letter, including in 1 Cor 14:34. Paul alternates between a singular and plural reference to the church throughout this letter to the Corinthians. The term ἐκκλησία occurs 22 times in 1 Corinthians with 16

---

113 Philip B. Payne, "Fuldensis, Sigla for Variants in Vaticanus, and 1 Cor 14.34–5," *NTS* 41 (1995): 251. I examined some manuscripts to confirm this statement, including ℵ A B D L Ψ 33 1175. Payne places $\mathfrak{P}^{46}$ as evidence of a break at 1 Cor 14:34. While the papyrus has ὡς next to εἰρήνη (though with a slash above ὡς) in 1 Cor 14:33b, the reference to women in 1 Cor 14:34 is cut off at the bottom left portion of $\mathfrak{P}^{46}$. Aḷesja Lavrinoviča takes $\mathfrak{P}^{46}$ as evidence that 1 Cor 14:33b goes with 14:33a due to slash marks above some of the words, which show a break in thought. Lavrinoviča also says that there may be a slash mark after "the saints," but I am unable to see any slash. Additional study of $\mathfrak{P}^{46}$ and 1 Corinthians may be needed. See discussion in Aḷesja Lavrinoviča, "1 Cor 14.34–5 without 'in All the Churches of the Saints': External Evidence," *NTS* 63 (2017): 375–76.
114 Contra NA[28].
115 D. A. Carson, "'Silent in the Churches': On the Role of Women in 1 Corinthians 14:33b–36," in *Recovering Biblical Manhood and Womanhood: A Response to Evangelical Feminism*, ed. John Piper and Wayne Grudem (Wheaton, IL: Crossway, 1991), 141 (italics original).
116 Lavrinoviča, "1 Cor 14.34–5 without 'in All the Churches of the Saints': External Evidence," 371.
117 That is, the interpretive value is slight for the debate on the silencing of women. There is value in understanding Paul's point about God being a God of peace in all the churches.

times in the singular and six times in the plural.[118] None of these passages were limited to Corinth, with the possible exception of 1 Cor 11:18. Paul viewed most of his comments in 1 Corinthians to apply more broadly outside of Corinth. Paul opens his letter by saying, "Paul called an apostle of Christ Jesus through the will of God and Sosthenes our brother. To the church of God which is in Corinth [τῇ ἐκκλησίᾳ τοῦ θεοῦ τῇ οὔσῃ ἐν Κορίνθῳ], sanctified in Christ Jesus, called saints, with all the ones who call on the name of our Lord Jesus Christ in every place [σὺν πᾶσιν τοῖς ἐπικαλουμένοις τὸ ὄνομα τοῦ κυρίου ἡμῶν Ἰησοῦ Χριστοῦ ἐν παντὶ τόπῳ], their (Lord) and ours" (1 Cor 1:1–2). Paul had other churches in mind when he wrote Scripture since he used σύν to connect the church in Corinth with everyone else claiming Jesus as Lord. Kenneth Bailey asks the question, "Paul states openly and boldly that *this letter is addressed to the entire church.* Is he serious?"[119] Bailey answers affirmatively that Paul was serious because (1) ancient interpreters saw Paul as addressing "*the whole church*"; (2) the letter shows an overall coherence, and Paul brings to bear his own theology on the problems; (3) Paul leaves out what may have been specific to Corinth in 1 Cor 11:34 ("Now concerning the rest, I will instruct when I come"); and (4) other churches would have had questions about most of the topics since they are common issues.[120] In light of 1 Cor 1:1–2, scholars need explicit textual reasons why Paul would have not seen his instructions apply more broadly to churches in the first century. Simple appeal to Greco-Roman background material is not sufficient to limit Paul's words to Corinth alone. Paul again makes another connection between Corinth and other churches: "For this reason I sent Timothy to you, who is my beloved child and faithful in the Lord, who will remind you of my ways in Christ [Jesus], just as I teach everywhere in every church [πανταχοῦ ἐν πάσῃ ἐκκλησίᾳ]" (1 Cor 4:17). Why would his later discussion on spiritual gifts in 1 Corinthians 12–14 be different?

---

118 The singular of ἐκκλησία is found in 1 Cor 1:2; 4:17; 6:4; 10:32; 11:18, 22; 12:28; 14:4, 5, 12, 19, 23, 28, 35; 15:9; 16:19 and the plural in 1 Cor 7:17; 11:16; 14:33, 34; 16:1, 19. Andreas Köstenberger and Raymond Bouchoc, *The Book Study Concordance of the Greek New Testament* (Nashville: Broadman & Holman, 2003), 920. While 1 Cor 4:17 is singular, the meaning is distributive because of the use of πᾶς ("just as I teach everywhere in every [πάσῃ] church"). Cf. 1 Cor 1:2 ("with all the ones who call on the name of our Lord Jesus Christ in every place, their Lord and ours").

119 Kenneth E. Bailey, *Paul through Mediterranean Eyes: Cultural Studies in 1 Corinthians* (Downers Grove, IL: IVP Academic, 2011), 23 (italics original). For a critique of Bailey's overall commentary, see Massey, "Women, Talking and Silence," 139–40.

120 Bailey, *Paul through Mediterranean Eyes*, 23–27. Bailey refers to "*the whole church*" (italics original) on p. 23. Bailey admits the fourth point contains an assumption, but the assumption is reasonable. Cf. also Kenneth E. Bailey, "The Structure of 1 Corinthians and Paul's Theological Method with Special Reference to 4:17," *NovT* 25.2 (1983): 152–81.

When Paul was writing about lawsuits in the church, he states, "Then if you have everyday cases, do you appoint those who are of no account in the church [ἐν τῇ ἐκκλησίᾳ]" (1 Cor 6:4)? While this specific use of ἐκκλησία referred to Corinth, the broader instruction on lawsuits would certainly have applied to the other churches. Paul supported his teaching from broader eschatological truths (the church will judge the world and angels in 1 Cor 6:2–3).

Paul sometimes uses very broad language with the singular use of ἐκκλησία, which demonstrates that his words could apply beyond Corinth even when the singular was used. For example, Paul writes, "Therefore, whether you eat or drink or whatever you do, do everything [πάντα] for the glory of God. And giving no offense to Jews ['Ιουδαίοις] and Greeks ['Έλλησιν] and the church of God [τῇ ἐκκλησίᾳ τοῦ θεοῦ], just as I also please everyone in every way [πάντα πᾶσιν] not seeking my own benefit but the benefit of many [πολλῶν], in order that they may be saved" (1 Cor 10:31–33). Paul also uses universal language when he states that "God placed in the church [ἐν τῇ ἐκκλησίᾳ] first apostles, second prophets, third teachers, then workers of power, then gifts of healing, helpful deeds, administration, kinds of tongues" (1 Cor 12:28; cf. Paul's apostleship and the church in 15:9). Thus, the singular use of church could also apply beyond Corinth from Paul's perspective.

Paul uses the term ἐκκλησία nine times in 1 Corinthians 14, which contains several theological principles that applied broadly across churches in the Greco-Roman world. Paul specifically refers to the edification of the church in 1 Cor 14:4–5, 12. Paul states in 1 Cor 14:4 that "the one who prophesies edifies the church [ἐκκλησίαν [θεοῦ]]." Greek manuscripts F and G add θεοῦ ("of God") to the reference to church, which would apply broadly. In 1 Cor 14:12 Paul points out the Corinthians specifically (καὶ ὑμεῖς) regarding the need for edification, but directing his comments at Corinth does not negate the edification principle for all churches. Paul demonstrates the principle of edification in his own practice when he says that "in the church [ἐν ἐκκλησίᾳ] I would rather speak five words with my mind, in order that I may instruct others, than countless words in a tongue" (1 Cor 14:19). This latter reference of Paul's wish to speak clearly in church shows that his teaching can apply beyond Corinth even if one discusses the speech problems that Corinth was experiencing. In the same way, appealing to speech problems in 1 Cor 14:34 does not automatically change Paul's position on the silence of women in church.

Paul continues, "Now if there is not an interpreter, let him be silent in church [ἐν ἐκκλησίᾳ], and let him speak to himself and to God. And let two or three prophets speak and let the others judge. Now if the other one sitting receives a revelation, let the first one be silent (implied: ἐν ἐκκλησίᾳ)" (1 Cor 14:28–30). The silencing of tongue-speakers in 1 Cor 14:28 fits with the theological principles of peace and order in 1 Cor 14:33, 40. There is no textual reason to think that the silence in 1 Cor 14:28 would be limited to Corinth. The same broad applicability is true for the silencing of prophets in 1 Cor 14:30 with ἐν ἐκκλησίᾳ implied from 1 Cor 14:28. The silence in 1 Cor 14:34, with churches in the plural, connects to the same concept of order as silence in 1 Cor 14:28, 30. Why, then, would Paul's teaching in 1 Cor 14:34 only apply to Corinth? Paul's instructions reaching beyond Corinth is also supported by the use of πᾶς in 1 Cor 14:33 ("as in all [πάσαις] the churches of the saints").[121] The reference to church, singular, in 1 Cor 14:35 appears to be to contrast with the home. It is possible that 1 Cor 14:35 could refer to only Corinth, especially with the reference to shame, but in light of all the other references throughout 1 Corinthians, Paul's words may still reach beyond Corinth. Paul's concluding remarks about the churches of Galatia and Asia (ταῖς ἐκκλησίαις τῆς Γαλατίας; αἱ ἐκκλησίαι τῆς Ἀσίας) support the view that the church in Corinth was far from being isolated from the theology and practice of other churches (1 Cor 16:1, 19). Paul commanded Corinth to do the same collection as Galatia (1 Cor 16:1). Paul also speaks concerning the love the churches had for one another—in this case, in the form of a greeting (1 Cor 16:19). The network of the churches in the ancient world, in addition to the circulation of Paul's letters, provides a reasonable probability that Paul's instructions on women in the church would have been discussed beyond Corinth.[122]

The one use of ἐκκλησία that might have been limited to Corinth (from Paul's perspective) is 1 Cor 11:18. Paul explains the problem in Corinth about the Lord's supper by saying, "For, first, when you come together in church [ἐν ἐκκλησίᾳ] I hear that there are divisions among you, and I partially believe it" (1 Cor 11:18). The reference is clearly to the church in Corinth. Even in this passage, however, there are instructions that are universally valid (e.g., remembering Jesus's body and blood in 1 Cor 11:23–26). Paul appeals to their understanding of the church of God in 1 Cor 11:22, which could be either a reference to Corinth or, more likely, all the churches. The majority of references to the church in 1

---

121 Graham Clarke, "'As in All the Churches of the Saints' (1 Corinthians 14.33)," *BT* 52 (2001): 146–47, gives the plausible interpretation that "as in all the churches of the saints" in 1 Cor 14:33b modifies "the spirits of the prophets are subject to the prophets" in 1 Cor 14:32, making the reference to God's peace parenthetical.

122 Since I do not accept the interpolation theory (see Chapter Two above), I think that the text of 1 Cor 14:34–35 would have been included in the copies for other churches.

Corinthians reach beyond the geographical location of Corinth, at least from Paul's perspective.

Therefore, it is concluded that Paul's words concerning silence applied to the church in Corinth and beyond in the first century. The singular or plural use of ἐκκλησία does not itself determine if something is limited to Corinth, but instead this determination comes from the overall usage of ἐκκλησία. Paul was consistent in his comments about women in all the churches. Since Paul's silence of women was also based upon the law, then the law will now be considered.

The Old Testament Law: A Basis for Paul's Teaching in 1 Corinthians

Interpreters of Paul's use of the law sometimes assume that Paul could not have appealed to the law in general as a basis for his instruction. As stated in Chapter One, Jerome Murphy-O'Connor defended the interpolation theory by saying, "Apart from the manifest contradictions, the principle reason for denying the Pauline authorship of [1 Cor] 14:34–35 is the invocation of the authority of the Law to found a moral attitude."[123] O'Connor even claims, without further explanation, that "Paul never appeals to the Law in this manner."[124] It will be shown below that O'Connor's absolute statement is not supported by Paul's varied usage. Wolfgang Schrage, also a proponent for the interpolation theory, states, "Added to the non-Pauline expressions: καθὼς καὶ ὁ νόμος λέγει may surely be remembered as a completely unique quotation formula in Paul (compared to) other Pauline quotation introductions such as καθὼς γέγραπται. In addition, Paul cites a quotation from the Old Testament in the approximately 75 remaining places where he uses a quotation formula (cf. also the example in v. 27 [sic]). A quotation from the Old Testament here [in 1 Cor 14:34] is already impossible because a ban on a woman's speech is not found anywhere in the law."[125] Schrage's argument is more

---

123 Jerome Murphy-O'Connor, "Interpolations in 1 Corinthians," *CBQ* 48 (1986): 91; see also Harrisville, *1 Corinthians*, 244. By contrast, Raymond F. Collins, *First Corinthians*, SP 7 (Collegeville, MN: Liturgical,1999), 516, sees the vocabulary and syntax of 1 Cor 14:33b–36, including the reference to the law, as showing that Paul did write the passage. E.g., he appeals to 1 Cor 9:8.

124 O'Connor, "Interpolations in 1 Corinthians," 91. Cf. David E. Garland, *1 Corinthians*, BECNT (Grand Rapids: Baker Academic, 2003), 673, who sees Paul's appeal to the law as "incidental to Paul's argument rather than foundational" (quoting Rowe).

125 Wolfgang Schrage, *Der erste Brief an die Korinther*, EKKNT (Zürich: Benziger, 1999), 3:484, writes, "Unpaulinische Wendungen kommen hinzu: καθὼς καὶ ὁ νόμος λέγει erinnert zwar an andere paulinische Zitateinleitungen wie καθὼς γέγραπται, ist aber in Wahrheit eine bei Paulus völlig singuläre Zitationsformel. Außerdem wird an jeder der ca. 75 übrigen Stellen, die eine *formula quotationis*

nuanced than O'Connor's statements. However, Schrage does not refer back to Paul's similar quotation formula in 1 Cor 9:8 (ἢ καὶ ὁ νόμος ταῦτα οὐ λέγει). Furthermore, there are examples where Paul does not actually cite the OT quotation but the reader should know the general reference. Paul speaks of the church by the Spirit fulfilling the law (Rom 8:4) and then later explains it to be the law of love with OT quotations (Rom 13:8–10). The same strategy is seen when one compares Gal 5:14 (law with an OT quotation) with Gal 6:2 (the law of Christ referenced in general). Nonetheless, a closer look at Paul's use of the law in 1 Cor 14:34 is necessary in light of the concerns represented by O'Connor and Schrage.

Scholars have debated what Paul might have intended by his general appeal to the law in 1 Cor 14:34. Elim Hiu summarizes the main views of what the law might refer to in 1 Cor 14:34: (1) Gen 3:16; (2) Gen 2:18–24; (3) the Pentateuch; (4) the entire OT; (5) Rabbinic tradition; (6) Paul's own teaching; or (7) some unwritten teaching of Jesus.[126] A general (universal or Greco-Roman) reference to law should be added to Hiu's list (8).[127] Options 5–8 do not align with Paul's most common uses of the law. Option 6 might be persuasive if it were not for the function of καί in 1 Cor 14:34. Anne Blampied claims that Paul's own words are what is meant by νόμος, but Blampied ignores the use of καί where Paul is adding the support from the law to his statement, not equating his words with the law (καθὼς καὶ ὁ νόμος λέγει).[128] Option 1, where Eve is told "he will rule over you" (καὶ αὐτός σου κυριεύσει), is often discussed but not convincing.[129] Options 2–4 are much more likely since they fit with Paul's use of the law elsewhere without the negative connotation of Gen 3:16.[130]

When searching for the reference to the OT, it should be noted that the closest referent is submission and not silence (ἀλλ' ὑποτασσέσθωσαν, καθὼς καὶ ὁ νόμος λέγει).[131] Simon Kistemaker persuasively explains that the law refers to

---

    bieten, auch tatsächlich ein Zitat aus dem Alten Testament angeführt (vgl. als Beispiel V 27), was hier schon darum unmöglich ist, weil von einem Redeverbot für die Frau im Gesetz nirgendwo etwas steht." Perhaps Schrage intended to reference 1 Cor 14:21 instead of 14:27, since the former has an OT citation.

126 Elim Hiu, *Regulations Concerning Tongues and Prophecy in 1 Corinthians 14:26–40: Relevance Beyond the Corinthian Church*, LNTS 406 (New York: T&T Clark, 2010), 145–46.

127 See this argument in Harm W. Hollander, "The Meaning of the Term 'Law' (ΝΟΜΟΣ) in 1 Corinthians," *NovT* 40 (1998): 127–30. Contrast Joseph A. Fitzmyer, who says that "there is not even a hint that Paul is thinking of Roman law" (*First Corinthians: A New Translation with Introduction and Commentary*, AB 32 [New Haven: Yale University Press, 2008], 531–32).

128 Blampied, "Paul and Silence for 'The Women' in 1 Corinthians 14:34–35," 158.

129 E.g., C. K. Barrett, *A Commentary on the First Epistle to the Corinthians*, BNTC (Peabody, MA: Hendrickson, 1993), 330.

130 The connotation of silence and submission in 1 Cor 14:28–35, 40 is positive from Paul's perspective.

131 Fitzmyer also sees the reference of the law to submission, but he relies upon Gen 3:16 (*First Corinthians*, 532).

Gen 2:18–24, with Adam created first and Eve as helper. He also recalls the use of Genesis 2 in 1 Cor 6:16 and 1 Cor 11:8–9.[132] Genesis 2–3 includes hints of Adam's leadership.[133] Wayne Grudem provides the broader context when he states, "Paul elsewhere appeals to the OT to establish the idea of male headship and female submission to male leadership (see 1 Cor 11:8–9; 1 Tim 2:13), and it is therefore certainly possible to see him as appealing to the OT to support a distinction in authority in judging prophecies as well."[134] A general reference to man's leadership could be in view not only from Gen 2:18–24 but also from the Pentateuch or the OT in general (options 2–4 are complementary). With so many interpretive options, O'Connor's view above ("the principle reason for denying the Pauline authorship of 14:34–35 is the invocation of the authority of the Law to found a moral attitude") should not be accepted too quickly.[135]

Comparing Paul's varied uses of νόμος is helpful.[136] Paul's own question in Rom 3:27 shows that the term νόμος possesses a range of meanings (διὰ ποίου νόμου;). Paul also refers to "another" law in Rom 7:23 (ἕτερον νόμον). While the Mosaic law is the most typical reference, Paul's meaning of the law could vary in the following ways:

- The law of sin and death that produces sin and leads to death (Rom 8:2; cf. 7:8)
- The Mosaic law that is holy, spiritual, and good (Rom 7:12, 14, 16)
- A reference to the Jewish people (Rom 4:16; 1 Cor 9:20)
- A shorthand for the Old Testament used with the prophets (Rom 3:21)
- The Mosaic law fulfilled in Jesus (Rom 10:4)
- The Mosaic law fulfilled in the church by the Spirit (Rom 8:4; 13:8, 10; Gal 5:14)
- The law of faith (Rom 3:27)

---

132 Simon J. Kistemaker, *Exposition of the First Epistle to the Corinthians* (Grand Rapids: Baker, 1993), 512–13. Cf. Mark Taylor, *1 Corinthians*, NAC 28 (Nashville: B&H, 2014), 355.
133 Schreiner, *1 Corinthians*, 298.
134 Wayne Grudem, "Prophecy—Yes, But Teaching—No: Paul's Consistent Advocacy of Women's Participation without Governing Authority," *JETS* 30.1 (1987): 22.
135 Again, O'Connor, "Interpolations in 1 Corinthians," 91.
136 Paul uses νόμος in his letters the following times: Rom (74x); 1 Cor (9x); 2 Cor (zero); Gal (32x); Eph (1x); Phil (3x); Col (zero); 1 Thess (zero); 2 Thess (zero); 1 Tim (2x); 2 Tim (zero); Titus (zero); Phlm (zero). See Köstenberger and Bouchoc, *The Book Study Concordance of the Greek New Testament*. There is a variant where Frank Thielman says, "The reading νόμῳ at [1 Cor] 7:39 is clearly secondary" ("The Coherence of Paul's View of the Law: The Evidence of 1 Corinthians," *NTS* 38 [1992]: 235 n. 3). Thielman appears correct even though there is significant external evidence supporting the addition of the law at 1 Cor 7:39.

- God's moral law, which includes the Mosaic law, referred to as the law of God, law of Christ, or law of the Spirit of life (Rom 7:22, 25; 8:2, 7; Gal 6:2)[137]

Paul's overall uses of the law in 1 Corinthians are consistent with his uses in his letters. Paul uses νόμος in reference to God's moral law, even as found in the Mosaic law, in four out of nine occasions in 1 Corinthians (9:8–9; 14:21, 34). Three times Paul uses law as a reference for the Jews and once as reference to being under the Mosaic law (1 Cor 9:20). The power of sin, which uses the Mosaic law, is found once (15:56). Given Paul's varied usage, especially in 1 Corinthians, his general reference to the law in 1 Cor 14:34 would not have come as a surprise to the Corinthians. If a scholar questions the usage of the law in 1 Cor 14:34, then the comparable use of the law in 1 Corinthians 9 must also be questioned. A closer look at Paul's use of the OT law in 1 Corinthians will be considered below.

The closest example for 1 Cor 14:34 in Paul's first letter to the Corinthians is 1 Cor 9:8–9 where Paul writes, "Do I say these things according to man, or does not the law also say these things? For in the law of Moses it is written, 'Do not muzzle an ox when it is threshing.' Is God concerned for the oxen?" Paul is discussing material support for ministers (1 Cor 9:10–11). In both 1 Cor 9:8–9 and 14:34 Paul supports what the church should do based, in part, on the law. The support is partial because Paul clarifies that the law "also" (καί) states the command. The following shows both passages and the function of καί,

ἢ καὶ ὁ νόμος ταῦτα οὐ λέγει (1 Cor 9:8)

καθὼς καὶ ὁ νόμος λέγει (1 Cor 14:34)

Paul provides extra support from the law in his instructions to the church at Corinth. Roy Ciampa and Brian Rosner explain that the use of Deut 25:4 in 1 Cor 9:9 "is another example of Paul's use of Scripture as a guide for Christian conduct.... Thus, it is not merely a matter of acceding to an affirmation of Paul's apostolic authority on this subject, but rather of learning to understand how scriptural authority should inform our ethical understanding with respect to such

---

137 My understanding of Paul and the law comes especially from Brian S. Rosner, *Paul and the Law: Keeping the Commandments of God*, New Studies in Biblical Theology (Downers Grove, IL: InterVarsity Press, 2013).

issues."[138] They see Paul using the lesser to the greater Jewish argument.[139] They go on to say that Paul "probably has the Genesis creation narratives in mind" with his use of the law in 1 Cor 14:34.[140] Therefore, to state that the appeal to the law in 1 Cor 14:34 is not characteristic of Paul is not correct. The law can show timeless principles about what God expects of his creation, as Paul asks, "Is God concerned for the oxen?" (μὴ τῶν βοῶν μέλει τῷ θεῷ; 1 Cor 9:9).[141]

Paul's reference to the law in 1 Cor 14:21 shows that the law does not necessarily have to refer to the Mosaic law. Paul quotes Isa 28:11–12 in 1 Cor 14:21, "In the law [ἐν τῷ νόμῳ] it is written that by foreign tongues and by foreign lips I will speak to this people, and not even then will they obey me, says the Lord." The LXX of Isa 28:11–12 is as follows: διὰ φαυλισμὸν χειλέων διὰ γλώσσης ἑτέρας, ὅτι λαλήσουσιν τῷ λαῷ τούτῳ λέγοντες αὐτῷ τοῦτο τὸ ἀνάπαυμα τῷ πεινῶντι καὶ τοῦτο τὸ σύντριμμα, καὶ οὐκ ἠθέλησαν ἀκούειν. There are several textual issues with this quotation, but for the current purpose Paul clearly refers in some form to the prophet Isaiah.[142] The context in 1 Cor 14:21 refers to mature thinking about tongues (1 Cor 14:13–25). When Paul quotes Isaiah, he then states "so" (ὥστε) in 1 Cor 14:22 in order to link the OT quotation to his current explanation on how to think about tongues (and prophecy) in the church. The relevant point is that Paul supported the practice of tongues and prophecy in the Corinthian church with reference to OT law construed broadly with the OT prophets. Paul gives the result of the Lord's statement where the Isaiah quotation became a sign in the Corinthian church (εἰς σημεῖον; 14:22).[143] Grudem explains that a sign in the OT (LXX) and NT refers to "an indication of God's attitude" that can be either negative or positive (or both).[144] Paul expected the Corinthian church to exercise spiritual gifts in accordance with his understanding of signs, which reached back to the OT law in Isaiah.

In 1 Cor 9:21 Paul refers to being under the law of Christ (ἔννομος Χριστοῦ), which Paul equates with the law of God (μὴ ὢν ἄνομος

---

138   Roy E. Ciampa and Brian S. Rosner, "1 Corinthians," in *Commentary on the New Testament Use of the Old Testament*, ed. G. K. Beale and D. A. Carson (Grand Rapids: Baker Academic, 2007), 721–22.
139   Ciampa and Rosner, "1 Corinthians," 720–21.
140   Ciampa and Rosner, "1 Corinthians," 743.
141   For additional argumentation on the use of the law without using allegory, see D. Instone Brewer, "1 Corinthians 9:9–11: A Literal Interpretation of 'Do Not Muzzle the Ox'," *NTS* 38 (1992): 554–65.
142   See the textual discussion with references in Ciampa and Rosner, "1 Corinthians," 741.
143   Daniel B. Wallace shows that ὥστε means "the outcome or consequence of an action" and gives John 3:16 as an example where the result of God's love meant that he gave his son (*Greek Grammar Beyond the Basics: An Exegetical Syntax of the New Testament* [Grand Rapids: Zondervan, 1996], 677).
144   Wayne Grudem, "1 Corinthians 14.20–25: Prophecy and Tongues as Signs of God's Attitude," *WTJ* 41.2 (1979): 389.

θεοῦ).¹⁴⁵ Paul appealed to being under some type of νόμος to guide how he lived his evangelistic life. Ho Hyung Cho, who wrote his dissertation on the law of Christ in Gal 6:2, explains that "scholars argue about the phrase ἔννομος Χριστοῦ from two broad perspectives: a written law in comparison with the Mosaic law or a metaphorical expression."¹⁴⁶ Cho takes the preposition ἐν in ἔννομος as "under the influence of."¹⁴⁷ Schreiner rightly interprets the law of Christ (Gal 6:2; 1 Cor 9:21) as love for one another.¹⁴⁸ He also clarifies, "However, Romans 13:8–10 guards us from oversimplifying the nature of Christ's law, for love is expressed when believers fulfill moral norms. The law of Christ is exemplified by a life of love, but such love is expressed in a life of virtue."¹⁴⁹ Therefore, the "law of God" or "law of Christ" referred to being under the "law of love" in the way Paul related to each person or group. Love allowed flexibility with cultural norms, such as food laws, but love was consistent with submission to God's timeless moral norms, such as in Rom 13:9. Or, as Frank Thielman argues, "His [Paul's] claim not to be ἄνομος θεοῦ but ἔννομος Χριστοῦ in v. 21 further demonstrates his concern to limit his talk about being flexible on legal matters to those matters which do not touch upon moral issues."¹⁵⁰ Paul appealed to the law of Christ to guide his conduct as a Christian (1 Cor 9:21).

Paul also appeals to the OT as a basis for ethics throughout 1 Corinthians in the way he quotes OT passages. Paul did not want the Corinthians to boast in anyone other than Christ, "in order that just as it is written [ἵνα καθὼς γέγραπται],

---

145 On the many questions raised by 1 Cor 9:21, see Ho Hyung Cho, "Another Look at ἔννομος Χριστοῦ in 1 Corinthians 9:21," *ExpTim* 130.2 (2018): 62–71. Cho's introduction to the issues is helpful, but his overall thesis is doubtful that the phrase means "the principle (of the new era) created by Christ" (p. 71).
146 Cho, "Another Look at ἔννομος Χριστοῦ in 1 Corinthians 9:21," 63.
147 Cho, "Another Look at ἔννομος Χριστοῦ in 1 Corinthians 9:21," 67.
148 Thomas R. Schreiner, *40 Questions About Christians and Biblical Law*, ed. Benjamin L. Merkle, 40 Questions (Grand Rapids: Kregel, 2010), 101–4.
149 Schreiner, *40 Questions About Christians and Biblical Law*, 102. Though the "law of Christ" is interpreted here in the manner of love and ethics, the phrase is highly debated. John Riches provides a helpful church history survey for the phrase in Gal 6:2 (*Galatians Through the Centuries*, Wiley-Blackwell Bible Commentaries [Oxford: Wiley-Blackwell, 2013], 285–88). He also notes, "Clearly there are links between this verse [Gal 6:2] and 5:14, which speaks of the whole law being fulfilled in one word, the command in Lev 19:18 to love one's neighbour" (p. 288). For a concise list of interpretations, see Craig S. Keener, *Galatians: A Commentary* (Grand Rapids: Baker Academic, 2019), 269–70 (where Keener lists interpretations on law as in a "principle," a messianic Torah, Scripture promises fulfilled in Jesus, loving God and neighbor, the teaching of Jesus, the example of Jesus, the law of Moses reinterpreted, the fruit of the Spirit, or any combination of these views). For additional discussion (and partial summary), see Douglas J. Moo, *Galatians*, BECNT (Grand Rapids: Baker Academic, 2013), 376–78. Moo writes that "'the law of Christ' refers, in direct counterpart to 'the law of Moses,' to the broadly ethical demand of the gospel" (p. 378).
150 Thielman, "The Coherence of Paul's View of the Law," 245.

'Let the one who boasts boast in the Lord'" (1 Cor 1:31).[151] This command comes from a summary of LXX Jer 9:22–23 (ET 9:23–24).[152] Paul also called the Corinthians to look at their calling in 1 Cor 1:26, which is associated with the OT quotation in 1 Cor 1:31. Continuing with the theme of boasting, Paul writes, "[F]or it is written [γέγραπται], 'He catches the wise in their trickery.' And again, 'The Lord knows the thoughts of the wise that they are useless.' So (ὥστε) let no one boast in men" (1 Cor 3:19b–21a). The OT quotations (Job 5:13 and LXX Ps 93:11 [ET 94:11]) are associated with the previous statement about not being deceived with worldly wisdom (1 Cor 3:18–19), via γέγραπται γάρ in 3:19, and the quotations are associated with the following statement about not boasting in people, via ὥστε in 3:21.[153] Paul called for church discipline regarding a member inside the church based upon the refrain from Deuteronomy, "Remove the wicked person from yourselves" (1 Cor 5:13). Paul did not provide any introductory formula, but he clearly appeals to Deuteronomy. The Greek text of 1 Cor 5:13 is nearly identical to the LXX of Deut 17:7; 19:19; 21:21; 22:21, 24; 24:7.[154] These passages in Deuteronomy cover ethical topics such as idolatry (Deut 17:2–7), false witnesses (19:15–21), a rebellious son (21:18–21), sexual immorality (22:20–21, 23–24), and stealing (24:7). Paul explains to the Corinthians why sexual immorality with a prostitute is wrong on the basis of Gen 2:24, "[Or] do you not know that one who joins himself to a prostitute is one body? For it says [γάρ φησίν] the two will become one flesh. Now the one who joins himself to the Lord is one spirit. Flee sexual immorality" (1 Cor 6:16–18a). Timothy Brookins and Bruce Longenecker explain that γάρ "clarifies, via a quotation from LXX Gen 2:24, the grounds on which the foregoing is said."[155] Paul continues in his letter, "Circumcision is nothing and uncircumcision is nothing, but keeping God's commands" (7:19). Here keeping God's commands does not mean being circumcised. Paul is perhaps referring to the general law of love.[156] Finally, Paul

---

151 The quotation formula is not easy to understand. Perhaps it is an ellipsis, for which see Timothy A. Brookins and Bruce W. Longenecker, *1 Corinthians 1–9: A Handbook on the Greek Text*, BHGNT (Waco, TX: Baylor University Press, 2016), 41.
152 Fitzmyer, *First Corinthians*, 165.
153 Brookins and Longenecker, *1 Corinthians 1–9*, 88–89.
154 Ciampa and Rosner, "1 Corinthians," 709. Cf. Deut 17:12; 22:22. The refrain in Deuteronomy is καὶ ἐξαρεῖς τὸν πονηρὸν ἐξ ὑμῶν αὐτῶν, and 1 Cor 5:13 is ἐξάρατε τὸν πονηρὸν ἐξ ὑμῶν αὐτῶν. Deuteronomy 17:12 and 22:22 replaces ὑμῶν αὐτῶν with Ισραηλ.
155 Brookins and Longenecker, *1 Corinthians 1–9*, 147.
156 Philip la Grange du Toit interprets 1 Cor 7:19 differently in line with especially Gal 5:3 and Rom 2:25 that "between the lines Paul is saying that believers should not bother with circumcision, for if they do, they might as well do the whole Torah and subject themselves to the old epoch before Christ again" ("Paul's Reference to the 'Keeping of the Commandments of God' in 1 Corinthians 7:19," *Neot*

provides a hermeneutical guideline for the Corinthians reading the Mosaic law, "Now these things happened to them as an example, but were written for our instruction [ἐγράφη δὲ πρὸς νουθεσίαν ἡμῶν], for whom the end of the ages has arrived" (10:11). Paul clearly appealed to the OT law to support Christian ethics throughout 1 Corinthians.

Paul's appeal to the law in general in 1 Cor 14:34 would not have been unusual in light of the other uses of the law throughout 1 Corinthians. Thielman is close to denying Pauline authorship of 1 Cor 14:34–35, but he still writes, "If it is authentic, however, the reference to the law is consistent with the positive attitude which Paul has displayed so far [in 1 Corinthians]."[157] Brian Rosner helpfully explains, "The question to ask in these cases is not *which bits* of the law are still useful, but *in what sense* is the law valuable for Christians. In short, Christians are instructed by the law, but not as Jewish law. Instead, Paul models reading the Law of Moses as prophecy and as wisdom."[158] Rosner provides several examples of how Paul referred to the law to teach Christian wisdom.[159] Throughout his book Rosner attempts to teach a hermeneutic of repudiation, replacement, and reappropriation of the law in Paul. Even Craig Keener admits that "Paul sometimes does refer to the whole law as teaching something in a general way."[160] Keener views the law (whether in general or from creation) as supporting submission. The difference in interpretation comes with how Keener views a husband's submission.[161] First Corinthians 14:34 easily fits within Paul's overall understanding of the law.

O'Connor's view of 1 Cor 14:34 mentioned at the beginning of this section is also found in his commentary on 1 Corinthians.[162] His commentary would have been an excellent place to elaborate on his view of Paul and the law. Instead, he provides very little comment on his position of the use of the law in 1 Corinthians

---

49.1 [2015]: 43). If 1 Cor 7:19 were removed from consideration, the overall thesis of Paul's varied use of the law in 1 Corinthians still remains. Cf. 1 Cor 7:19 with Gal 5:6; 6:15.

157   Thielman, "The Coherence of Paul's View of the Law," 247 n. 43. The full quotation is, "I take the next reference to be [1 Cor] 15.56 rather than 14.34. The objections to accepting 14.34–35 as authentic seem to me slightly to outweigh arguments for its authenticity. The passage fits awkwardly into the surrounding context, whose focus is on the merits of prophecy and the pitfalls of tongues, and moves enigmatically to the end of the chapter in the western textual tradition. If it is authentic, however, the reference to the law is consistent with the positive attitude which Paul has displayed so far." Although Thielman does not technically deny Pauline authorship of 1 Cor 14:34–35, he aligns himself closer to scholars who deny Pauline authorship than those who accept Pauline authorship.

158   Rosner, *Paul and the Law*, 40–41 (italics original).

159   Rosner, *Paul and the Law*, 159–205.

160   Keener, *Paul, Women and Wives*, 86.

161   Keener, *Paul, Women and Wives*, 87.

162   Jerome Murphy-O'Connor, *1 Corinthians*, NTM 10 (Wilmington, DE: Michael Glazier, 1979), 133.

The Historical Context: Consistent Application Then and Now | 105

in several relevant places, such as comments on 1 Cor 5:13; 6:16; and 14:21.[163] He does not even mention Deuteronomy in his comments on 1 Cor 5:13. He translates 1 Cor 9:21 by saying it means "the law which is God" and "the law which is Christ," though the genitives could be interpreted differently.[164] He writes, without much explanation, on 1 Cor 9:8–9, "The first two arguments are *based on* commonsense (v. 7–8a) and on the Law of Moses (v. 9–12a)."[165] He explains the references to Deuteronomy as "a simple argument from the lesser to the greater."[166] How can O'Connor question the use of the law in 1 Cor 14:34 but not have the same problem with the use of the law in 1 Cor 9:8–9? O'Connor is inconsistent in how he comments on the law throughout 1 Corinthians.

It has been demonstrated that Paul's appeal to the law in 1 Cor 14:34 is consistent with the way he appeals to the law throughout 1 Corinthians and his other letters. The term νόμος has a range of meaning depending on the context. First Corinthians 14:34 is not the only place that Paul appealed to the law for moral guidance. Thus, one cannot claim 1 Cor 14:34 is inconsistent (or non-Pauline) without also questioning other Pauline passages (such as 1 Cor 9:8–9).

Conclusion

It has been argued so far that Paul is consistent with his use of silence in 1 Corinthians despite some literary and historical claims. Some scholars claim Paul only silenced women in Corinth because of the Greco-Roman culture where women lacked education or public speaking opportunities. However, this chapter took a closer look at these historical arguments and found the complexity of the ancient education system absent in many of these claims. Furthermore, women did sometimes have public speaking opportunities in the ancient world. Thus, Paul did not silence women on the basis of a cultural reason but on the basis of the Old Testament law.

The consistency of using cultural arguments was called into question in this chapter. Specifically, if one appeals to the ancient context of women in order to adjust or reject Paul's silence of women in the church, is one consistent in using ancient contexts in other biblical passages? The examples considered were passages regarding homosexuality. If one appeals to ancient culture in order to deny

---

163 O'Connor, *1 Corinthians*, 44–45, 53, 130.
164 O'Connor, *1 Corinthians*, 90. He claims the genitive can only be taken in the way he presents.
165 O'Connor, *1 Corinthians*, 86 (italics added for emphasis).
166 O'Connor, *1 Corinthians*, 86.

the meaning or application of women's silence in the church, consistency would require the same hermeneutic regarding homosexuality. The answer to the hermeneutical challenge of consistently interpreting Paul's writings is to recognize a mixture of cultural and transcultural elements in many of his passages. If Paul regularly mixed cultural with transcultural elements, then one cannot dismiss an entire passage simply by referring to one cultural element in the text.

Another historical argument was examined in which women were claimed to be the primary problem in the Corinthian assembly. Paul silenced women, some argue, because they were the problem instead of the men. Furthermore, others argue that Paul only meant the silence for the Corinthian church and not other churches. However, a review of Paul's first letter to the Corinthians gave evidence that both women and men were causing problems in the church. And Paul referred to the churches (singular and plural) throughout his letter, indicating that he intended his instructions to be applicable beyond Corinth.

The basis of the Old Testament law as the reason for Paul's instructions is itself debated. Some scholars think that Paul could not have written 1 Cor 14:34–35, because he would never have appealed to the law as a basis for Christian ethics. Yet, Paul's use of the law in 1 Cor 14:34–35 is consistent with his other references to the law since νόμος itself has a range of meaning depending on the context. Paul exhibits a varied usage of the law, including as a basis for Christian ethics in certain places (even in 1 Corinthians). Literary and historical contexts have been considered. The broader theological context remains.

4

The Theological Context: Consistency within Pauline Theology and Practice

Introduction

John Barclay is representative of scholars who see inconsistency between 1 Cor 14:34–35 and Paul's broader theology and practice. He writes, "But as it stands the passage [1 Cor 14:33b–36] seems to presuppose that women in all Paul's churches were wholly silent, which hardly fits what we know of women leaders in Pauline congregations (e.g. Rom 16:1–2, 3–5, 7; Phil 4:2)."[1] Barclay assumes that σιγάω means "wholly silent" in his charge that it does not "fit." The literary context and examination of Greek data in the ancient world has already shown that σιγάω has a range of meanings; thus, Barclay's presupposition needs to be proven and not assumed. Paul's writings and the book of Acts still need to be examined in order to see if there is consistency in his theology and practice. The discussion will be divided between Paul's theological principles in Gal 3:28 and 1 Tim 2:11–12 and Paul's practice in Acts 16:11–15, 40, Rom 16:1–7, Phil 4:2–3, and

---

1 John Barclay, "1 Corinthians," in *The Oxford Bible Commentary: The Pauline Epistles*, ed. John Muddiman and John Barton (Oxford: Oxford University Press, 2001), 121. Barclay claims there are only two options: inconsistency or interpolation.

Col 4:15.[2] Acts 18:24–28 will also be considered due to Paul's mention of Prisca and Aquila in Rom 16:3–5a. These passages have been selected because they are the ones usually cross-referenced in discussion of women's silence in the church.

Galatians 3:28

Paul's silencing of women in 1 Cor 14:34 is consistent with Gal 3:28, where he writes, "There is neither Jew nor Gentile, there is neither slave nor free, there is not male and female, for you all are one in Christ Jesus."[3] Unsurprisingly, Gal 3:28 has been variously interpreted. This section will review the different perspectives regarding the methodology, interpretation, and original context of Gal 3:28. It will be concluded that Gal 3:28 and 1 Cor 14:34 cannot be contradictory because both passages have a different meaning and function. Any charge of contradiction must be argued on the basis of Paul's original meaning and not future (secondary) applications.

Scholars often make brief reference to Gal 3:28 ("no male and female") in order to challenge the *prima facie* meaning of 1 Cor 14:34. Occasionally, this brief reference to Gal 3:28 does not fully consider the original context of Gal 3–4. For example, Walter Klaiber discusses 1 Cor 14:34 at length but only gives one concluding sentence on Gal 3:28. He writes, "As a matter of principle there is also the question if the silent regulation for women does not contradict what Paul fundamentally says in Gal 3:28 about the equal rights of women and men in Christ."[4] What does he mean by equal rights? More importantly, why should there be a contradiction in two passages with two different original contexts and topics?

---

[2] Paul likely wrote his letters in the order of Galatians, Romans, Philippians, Colossians, and then 1 Timothy. See the helpful summary chart in Andreas J. Köstenberger, L. Scott Kellum, and Charles L. Quarles, *The Cradle, the Cross, and the Crown: An Introduction to the New Testament*, 2nd ed. (Nashville: B&H Academic, 2016), 474. Philippians may have been written before Colossians (see p. 641). The book of Acts would have been written in the early 60s (pp. 391, 393–95).

[3] Paul shifts from οὐκ … οὐδέ for Jew/Gentile/slave/free to οὐκ … καί for male/female, and this change is reflected in my translation. This shift may be due to the LXX translation of Gen 1:27. See F. F. Bruce, *The Epistle to the Galatians: A Commentary on the Greek Text*, NIGTC (Grand Rapids: Eerdmans, 1982), 189; David A. deSilva, *Galatians: A Handbook on the Greek Text*, BHGNT (Waco, TX: Baylor University Press 2014), 77.

[4] Walter Klaiber, *Der erste Korintherbrief*, Die Botschaft des Neuen Testaments (Neukirchen-Vluyn: Neukirchener Theologie, 2011), 234, says, "Prinzipiell ist auch zu fragen, ob ein Schweigegebot für Frauen nicht dem widerspricht, was Paulus grundsätzlich in Gal 3,28 über die Gleichstellung von Frauen und Männern in Christus sagt."

Different Views of Galatians 3:28

The different views on Gal 3:28 may be viewed in three general ways: gender is no longer significant or applicable in regard to (1) sex, (2) sociology, or (3) soteriology.[5] The first view interprets "there is not male and female" to mean biological sex differentiation no longer exists or matters. Removing biological differences reads the words of Paul over-literally. The second view on the sociological context emphasizes the social implications of Gal 3:28 over against the original soteriological context (view three). Since views (1) and (2) do not emphasize the original soteriological context, there is a question how they differ hermeneutically. How far should one press the sociological implications? The third view emphasizes the original context of salvation and inheritance, reading the verse in its literary context. This view seeks to apply the passage in a way that coincides with the original soteriological meaning. Representatives of each view will be noted below.

Some writers take Paul in Gal 3:28 as removing any sexual differentiation. Hans Dieter Betz writes that Paul used a pre-formed tradition with the phrase "there is not male and female," and that the meaning is "the metaphysical removal of the *biological* sex."[6] Betz even claims the background is "an androgynous Christ-redeemer" myth.[7] The androgynous view is also in Wayne Meek's essay where he writes,

> Now, however, the Nag Hammadi texts have reminded us of the extent to which the unification of opposites, and especially the opposite sexes, served in early Christianity as a prime symbol of salvation. To be sure, in the second- and third-century gnostic texts this symbolism flourishes in some bizarre forms which are not always clear to us, but the notion itself had an important place much earlier—in the congregations founded by Paul and his school.[8]

Wayne Meeks is able to make such a statement by disregarding the literary context of Gal 3:28 and claiming a baptismal formula so that the literary context

---

5   For a general review of the literature on Gal 3:28, see D. Francois Tolmie, "Tendencies in the Interpretation of Galatians 3:28 Since 1990," *AcT* 34 (2014): 105–29. For specific reasons for a pre-Pauline baptismal formula (though unpersuasive), see Martinus C. de Boer, *Galatians: A Commentary*, NTL (Louisville: Westminster John Knox, 2011), 245–46.
6   Hans Dieter Betz, *Galatians: A Commentary on Paul's Letter to the Churches in Galatia,* Hermeneia (Philadelphia: Fortress, 1979), 196 (italics original).
7   Betz, *Galatians*, 199.
8   Wayne A. Meeks, "The Image of the Androgyne: Some Uses of a Symbol in Earliest Christianity," *HR* 13 (1974): 165–66.

no longer controls the application.⁹ Furthermore, Meeks claims that what is described in Gal 3:28 "reverses" the division of the sexes in Gen 2:21–22 where the Lord made woman from the rib of man.¹⁰ Similarly, in Jeremy Punt's article the "blurring of gender roles" is evidence for the queer interpretation.¹¹ How can Punt read Paul in this way? By way of metaphors in Scripture.¹² Punt claims to give attention to the literary context, but there is not much detail provided.¹³ This omission is significant because a way to argue against Punt's interpretation is to appeal to the immediate literary context of Gal 3:28 as a control.

A number of writers take a sociological view of Gal 3:28, especially as it relates to women's roles in leadership in the church. Attention to the literary context varies among these interpreters. Elisabeth Fiorenza writes that gender is "abolished" with Gal 3:28.¹⁴ She then clarifies, "In a similar fashion the biological-sexual-legal differences between men and women remain but gender roles and their cultural-religious significance are no longer valid for the Christian community."¹⁵ It is not clear how exactly she makes these clarifications (i.e., biological and legal restrictions) after declaring everything abolished. Singling out roles, as Fiorenza does, appears arbitrary given the original literary context of Gal 3:28. Caroline Cutler seeks to provide evidence that Gal 3:28 is applied sociologically by appealing to Gal 2:11–14 where Peter separated himself from the Gentiles and Paul rebuked him.¹⁶ This comparison ignores that Gal 2:11–14 illustrates the phrase that "there is neither Jew nor Gentile" and not in reference to gender. But by way of method, Craig Keener writes, "One can hardly say that Gal. 3:28 addresses 'only' salvation as if salvation itself lacks transformative implications for relationships. One cannot fully isolate 3:28 from relevance to social contexts since social conflict

---

9   Meeks, "The Image of the Androgyne," 180–83. He also claims, "When early Christians in the area of the Pauline mission adapted the Adam-Androgyne myth to the eschatological sacrament of baptism, they thus produced a powerful and prolific set of images" (p. 207). Joseph A. Marchal applies Gal 3:28 to intersexuality partly based upon a baptismal formula view ("Bodies Bound for Circumcision and Baptism: An Intersex Critique and the Interpretation of Galatians," *Theology and Sexuality* 16.2 [2010]: 163–82).

10 Meeks, "The Image of the Androgyne," 185.

11 Jeremy Punt, "Power and Liminality, Sex and Gender, and Gal 3:28: A Postcolonial, Queer Reading of an Influential Text," *Neot* 44.1 (2010): 157 (Punt is quoting B. J. Brooten).

12 Punt, "Power and Liminality, Sex and Gender, and Gal 3:28," 162.

13 Punt, "Power and Liminality, Sex and Gender, and Gal 3:28," 140–41.

14 Elisabeth Schüssler Fiorenza, "Women in the Pre-Pauline and Pauline Churches," *USQR* 33.3 (1978): 158.

15 Fiorenza, "Women in the Pre-Pauline and Pauline Churches," 158.

16 Caroline Schleier Cutler, "New Creation and Inheritance: Inclusion and Full Participation in Paul's Letters to the Galatians and Romans," *Priscilla Papers* 30.2 (2016): 21–29.

informs the entire letter."[17] However, even if one refers to the implications, why does this method demand that the only true implication is including women in church leadership? Gal 2:11–14 does not discuss the issue of church leadership.

If the interpreter is moving from text to implications, one example of applying the soteriological view of Gal 3:28 is evangelism (which would seem to fit more of the immediate literary context of Gal 3:23–4:7). By analogy, Jesus showed himself as the Messiah to a Samaritan woman in John 4:1–42. The disciples marveled that Jesus was speaking to a woman (4:27). Likewise, Paul likely was the one who evangelized the slave Onesimus (see Philemon). Evangelism for all people is a way to show that the church believes that there are no social barriers to becoming sons of God.[18] Therefore, not applying Gal 3:28 to women's roles in the church does not mean that the text is not applied at all. Galatians 3:28 can be applied in a way that is closer to the topics at hand in the letter to the Galatians.

Paul Jewett discusses the differences between the three couplets in Gal 3:28, stating that "these three categories are not alike in every respect."[19] Jewett explains the difference as "an ordinance of creation" for men and women.[20] Despite Jewett's distinctions, he relies heavily upon the analogy to slavery in application to men and women. Jewett writes, "Had the church, through the centuries, interpreted 'neither slave nor free' in Galatians 3:28 in terms of the explicit implementation in the New Testament, the institution of slavery would never have been abolished. The same is true of woman's liberation."[21] However, the New Testament does contain statements that point towards the abolition of slavery. For example, Paul writes, "You were called as a slave, let it be of no concern to you, but if also you are able to be free, rather make use of it. For the slave who is called by the Lord is a freedperson of the Lord. Likewise, the free who is called is a slave of Christ. You were bought with a price, do not become slaves of men. Brothers, let each one remain in the sight of God in this (calling) in which he was called" (1 Cor 7:21–24; cf. Phlm). Similar statements are not made about women in

---

17   Craig S. Keener, *Galatians: A Commentary* (Grand Rapids: Baker Academic, 2019), 315. Cf. Gordon D. Fee, *Galatians: Pentecostal Commentary*, Pentecostal Commentary Series (Blandford Forum, Dorset, UK: Deo, 2007), 140–43.
18   Colossians 3:5–11 is a passage where the context spells out the implications of there being no "Gentile and Jew, circumcised and uncircumcised, barbarian, Scythian, slave, free, but Christ is everything and in everything" (3:11). The implications are specifically moral implications. Greek manuscripts D* F G 629 add the variant ἄρσεν καὶ θῆλυ.
19   Paul K. Jewett, *Man as Male and Female: A Study in Sexual Relationships from a Theological Point of View* (Grand Rapids: Eerdmans, 1975), 143.
20   Jewett, *Man as Male and Female*, 143.
21   Jewett, *Man as Male and Female*, 148.

the New Testament. Furthermore, Jewett's quote compares freedom from slavery with "woman's liberation." Does Jewett intend to mean that any submission in the New Testament is similar to the oppression of slavery? The New Testament often portrays submission in a positive manner. The assumptions behind Jewett's analogy to slavery are not how the New Testament portrays women in the church as compared to slavery. Jewett then discusses how the church should go beyond what Paul socially implemented, using general language like "to all the manifold variety of associations in our communal existence as men and women."[22] Since Jewett appeals to creation but then goes beyond the NT text, what then limits the application only to heterosexual men and women?

Hans-Joachim Eckstein appears close to a middle position between the sociological view and the soteriological view. Eckstein gives significant attention to the original context of salvation in regard to male and female but then makes a few ambiguous references to social implications.[23] The ambiguity relates to how far and in what specific ways the implications should be pursued. Eckstein concludes his section on Gal 3:28, stating, "But there is primarily not yet the question of different distribution of roles within social relationships, but the question of position and dignity, which is described as completely equal rights before God."[24] Eckstein's discussion emphasizes the relationship to God as children or sons/daughters of God. But what does Eckstein mean by "not yet" in reference to roles? Not yet from the perspective of the early church or not yet for the modern reader? Eckstein appears to be taking a moderate position in the debate by explaining the original context but leaving the door open to the social consequences. Ambiguous statements are a problem in much of the Gal 3:28 literature because one is left not knowing how far to take the open social implications.

Writers who comment on Gal 3:28 in relation to salvation and its original context include Ronald Fung and David McWilliams. Fung argues that readers should not go beyond the original context of Gal 3:28 to roles, and the male

---

22 Jewett, *Man as Male and Female*, 147–48 (quote on p. 148).
23 Hans-Joachim Eckstein, *Christus in Euch: Von der Freiheit der Kinder Gottes: Eine Auslegung des Galaterbriefes*, Neukirchener Theologie (Göttingen: Vandenhoeck & Ruprecht, 2017), 125–29.
24 Eckstein, *Christus in Euch*, 129: "Dabei geht es zunächst noch nicht um die Frage der verschiedenen Rollenverteilung innerhalb der gesellschaftlichen Verhältnisse, sondern um die Frage der Stellung und Würde, die vor Gott als völlig gleichberechtigt beschrieben wird." Cf. the ambiguity in Pierre Bonnard, *L'Épitre de Saint Paul aux Galates*, CNT 9 (Neuchatel, Paris: Delachaux & Niestlé, 1953), 79. Bonnard mentions three senses that Paul could have meant (moral, ecclesiastical, and Christological senses) and then states, "Not any of these senses are excluded"; "Aucun de ces sens n'est exclu." The question, then, is if there is *any* sense where someone could limit the reference to male and female. While many would disagree with, for example, the androgynous view, the same writers exclude any clarifications otherwise.

and female distinction goes back to creation (unlike the other two couplets).[25] McWilliams's comment sheds light on the challenge of broad application: "In addition, a consistent application of this sort of argument [an egalitarian argument] might do away with all offices in the church."[26] In other words, if there is an issue of men having authority over women, then there could potentially be an issue with anyone having authority over anyone else. A closer look at the literary context of Gal 3:28 will bring needed controls on the debate.

The Original Context of Galatians 3:28

Galatians 3:28 fits into its own literary context in at least three ways. First, the reference to no male or female fits broadly into the discussion of the gospel and salvation in relation to history, theology, and ethics.[27] After Paul gives an introduction (Gal 1:1–4), he moves into a discussion of the gospel and his personal history (1:5–2:21). Then Paul explains the gospel in relation to the Spirit, the promise to Abraham, the law, faith and sonship/inheritance, and freedom (3:1–5:1).[28] Finally, Paul explains ethics in relation to faith, love, and the Spirit (5:2–6:10). Paul gives a conclusion about the cross and suffering (6:11–18). Second, Gal 3:28 fits more narrowly within Gal 3:1–5:1. In this section Paul is seeking to show who are the children of God and offspring of Abraham who receive the promise of the Spirit. This section is clearly about justification by faith in Christ regarding salvation (e.g., Gal 3:6). Third, the reference to no male and female directly relates to the question of faith and sonship in regard to receiving divine inheritance (Gal 3:23–4:7). Salvation is in view.

Paul argues against "works of the law" (Gal 2:16), and especially male circumcision (5:2–6, 11–12; 6:12–15). The issue of circumcision is the historical context in order to understand *why* Paul would mention male and female. Troy Martin rightly refers to Gen 17:9–14 in order to explain all three antitheses (Jew/Greek, slave/free, male/female).[29] Genesis 17:9–14 refers to God's words to Abraham about every male born in his house or bought with his money being circumcised as a sign of the covenant. Martin also responds to Krister Stendahl's

---

25 Ronald Y. K. Fung, *The Epistle to the Galatians*, NICNT (Grand Rapids: Eerdmans, 1988), 176 n. 44.
26 David B. McWilliams, *Galatians*, A Mentor Commentary (Ross-shire, Great Britain: Mentor, 2009), 140.
27 My outline of Galatians (history, theology, ethics) makes only slight adjustments to the outline in Timothy George, *Galatians*, Christian Standard Commentary (Nashville: Holman, 2020), 55.
28 The phrase Ὦ ἀνόητοι Γαλάται at Gal 3:1 helps understand a major division within the letter.
29 Troy W. Martin, "The Covenant of Circumcision (Genesis 17:9–14) and the Situational Antitheses in Galatians 3:28," *JBL* 122 (2003): 111–25.

assumptions on the "tension" that Gal 3:28 creates.[30] Martin says, "Stendahl's comment assumes that the male/female antithesis in Gal 3:28 is taken from Gen 1:27 and abolishes the order of creation. The present essay proposes instead that this antithesis is taken from the covenant of circumcision, stipulated in Gen 17:9–14, and that Gal 3:28 abolishes not the order of creation but the communal distinctions established by this covenant."[31] R. A. Cole explains that the problem in Galatia was teaching that one must keep the law of Moses in order to be saved, similar to the opposition at the Jerusalem Council in Acts 15:1, 5.[32] In contrast to male circumcision, there is no male and female regarding Christians being "Abraham's offspring, heirs according to promise" (Gal 3:29). Being an heir is clearly the immediate context of Gal 3:28. The language of "sons of God" (3:26) implies an inheritance. Being "heirs according to promise" (3:29) is a continuation of the statement about male and female in 3:28 (see δέ at 3:29). Paul then explains his reference to an heir (4:1) and how adoption as sons means one is an heir through God (4:5–7).[33] Therefore, the male and female reference in Gal 3:28 must be interpreted in light of the inheritance of salvation.[34]

Reading Gal 3:28 within its immediate context of Gal 3:23–4:7 makes the original context of salvation abundantly clear. Paul states,

> Now before faith came, we were guarded under the law, being confined until the coming faith to be revealed, so that the law became our guardian until Christ, in order that we might be justified by faith. Now when faith came, we were no longer under a guardian. For you are all sons of God through faith in Christ Jesus. For whoever has been baptized into Christ has put on Christ. There is neither Jew nor Gentile, there is neither slave nor free, there is no male and female, for you all are one in Christ Jesus. Now if you are of Christ then you are Abraham's offspring, heirs according to the promise. Now I say as

---

30   See above in Chapter One history of research on Stendahl.
31   Martin, "The Covenant of Circumcision (Genesis 17:9–14) and the Situational Antitheses in Galatians 3:28," 118 n. 25.
32   R. Alan Cole, *Galatians: An Introduction and Commentary*, 2nd ed., TNTC 9 (Downers Grove, IL: IVP Academic, 1989), 31. For discussion of the North and South Galatian theories, and which favors the South Galatian theory, see Cole, *Galatians*, 20–26.
33   There are eight different textual variants regarding God and/or Christ in relation to being an heir. See Bruce M. Metzger, *A Textual Commentary on the Greek New Testament*, 2nd ed. (Stuttgart: United Bible Societies, 1994), 526–27, who lists the variants and opts for κληρονόμος διὰ θεοῦ.
34   The literary context of inheritance and adoption clearly shows why Paul would include the phrase "male and female," contra Wayne Litke who claims that "the phrase has no bearing on Paul's argument in this portion of Galatians" ("Beyond Creation: Galatians 3:28, Genesis and the Hermaphrodite Myth," *SR* 24 [1995]: 174). Just as Litke, Meeks also claims that Gal 3:28 does not bear resemblance to its context ("The Image of the Androgyne," 181).

long as the heir is a child, he is in no respect different than a slave though he is master of all things, but he is under guardians and managers until the time set by the father. So also we, when we were children, were enslaved under the elementary ideas of the world. But when the fullness of time had come, God sent his Son, being born from woman, being born under the law, in order that he may deliver the ones under the law, in order that we might receive adoption. And because you are sons, God sent the Spirit of his Son into our hearts, who cries, "Abba, Father," so that you are no longer a slave but a son, and if a son, also an heir through God. (Gal 3:23–4:7)

The language of salvation and inheritance is thoroughly embedded into the literary context of Gal 3:28. Paul explains the relationship between faith, the law, and sonship (Gal 3:23–29). Then he gives an illustration about being an heir in the ancient world (4:1–2). Last, he explains the meaning of the illustration in what he means by sonship and being an heir through God (4:3–7).[35] Paul intended the reference to gender to explain inheriting salvation. Peter Schemm, who argues for a contextual reading of male and female, explains, "Under the Old Testament law, Greeks, slaves, and females did not enjoy the right of land and property inheritance directly. In the New Covenant, however, salvation is described with the metaphor of inheritance as that which anyone may personally receive."[36] This view provides a reasonable solution as to why Paul would include the statement on "no male and female" and wait until other occasions to address the roles of men and women in the church.

The term κληρονόμος, which occurs three times in Galatians, occurs 15 times in the New Testament.[37] The implications of being an heir in Paul's letters are associated with living by the Spirit in good works and not by the flesh in sin

---

35 This way of dividing the text helps to answer the question of which background is being used—Jewish, Greek, or Roman. In general, the Jewish background is being used in relation to Paul's main points about the law and sonship. However, the illustration in Gal 4:1–2 is a Greco-Roman background. Thomas R. Schreiner, commenting on Gal 4:2, states, "Perhaps Paul interweaves exodus and Greco-Roman traditions here" (*Galatians*, ZECNT [Grand Rapids: Zondervan, 2010], 266). On the Greco-Roman background to inheritance, see John K. Goodrich, "'As Long as the Heir Is a Child': The Rhetoric of Inheritance in Galatians 4:1–2 and P. Ryl. 2.153," *NovT* 55 (2013): 61–76. Bradley R. Trick argues specifically for a Greek background to adoption (*Abrahamic Descent, Testamentary Adoption, and the Law in Galatians: Differentiating Abraham's Sons, Seed, and Children of Promise*, NovTSup 169 [Leiden: Brill, 2016], 151–61). For a summary on the background issue, see Schreiner, *Galatians*, 265 n. 1.

36 Peter R. Schemm, Jr., "Galatians 3:28—Prooftext or Context?" *JBMW* 8 (2003): 27.

37 BDAG, 548. Matt 21:38; Mark 12:7; Luke 20:14; Gal 3:29; 4:1, 7; Rom 4:13–14; 8:17 [2x]; Tit 3:7; Heb 1:2; 6:17; 11:7; Jas 2:5. Keener writes, "Rules regarding women's inheritance varied geographically and culturally" (*Galatians*, 305). Cf. Num 27:1–11; 36.

(Rom 8:12–17; Titus 3:1–11). These same implications are also seen in Gal 5:16–6:10. Bernard Lategan writes that Gal 3:28 "is consistent with the precepts of an alternative symbolic universe and prepares the ground for the ethical implications for believers that will be elaborated in Chapters five to six."[38] However, Lategan's following "pragmatic implications" explains nothing in Gal 5–6, but instead he speaks generally about "far-reaching social consequences" and "far-reaching implications."[39] Salvation permeates the discussion of κληρονόμος throughout the other NT letters (Heb 1:1–4; 6:17; 11:7; Jas 2:5; cf. Rom 4:13). Therefore, interpreters who read Gal 3:28 within its literary context and then more broadly within inheritance language will not think Gal 3:28 must contradict 1 Cor 14:34. While it is argued here that the best approach is the soteriology view, there still remains the need to see if the sociological view contains any inconsistency in method.

Methodological Consistency?

What hermeneutical criteria distinguish view 1 (removal of sexual distinctions) from view 2 (removal of sociological barriers)? Another way of asking this question would be: is Gal 3:28 limited in any way in its modern-day application? If so, how? This section will discuss the problems with hermeneutical discussions of Gal 3:28 and the similarities between egalitarian and queer hermeneutics.

There are at least two problems with some discussions of Gal 3:28. The first problem is many commentaries do *not* discuss Gal 3:28 within the literary context of Gal 3:23–4:7. Instead commentaries often go directly to social implications. Some simply go immediately to attacking another interpretation. G. Walter Hansen writes, "When men exclude women from significant participation in the life and ministry of the church, they negate the essence of the gospel."[40] Hansen does not elaborate on the literary context in his commentary. Ben Witherington emphasizes the social context over against other areas.[41] Witherington refers the reader to his journal article on Gal 3:28, and in the article he laments the lack of

---

38 Bernard C. Lategan, "Reconsidering the Origin and Function of Galatians 3:28," *Neot* 46.2 (2012): 283.
39 Lategan, "Reconsidering the Origin and Function of Galatians 3:28," 285.
40 G. Walter Hansen, *Galatians*, IVP New Testament Commentary Series (Downers Grove, IL: InterVarsity Press, 1994), 113. He also writes, "Equality in Christ is the starting point for all truly biblical social ethics. The church that does not express this equality and unity in Christ in its life and ministry is not faithful to the gospel" (p. 112).
41 Ben Witherington III, *Grace in Galatia: A Commentary on Paul's Letter to the Galatians* (Grand Rapids: Eerdmans, 1998), 278–81 (his emphasis can be seen from his use of "social consequences," "social transformation," and "social implications," on pp. 278–79).

attention to the context. However, Witherington does not discuss the immediate literary context of inheritance even in his article.[42] Witherington instead attempts to "mirror-read" the letter to the Galatians.[43] He writes, "The answer may have been the one offered in rabbinic Judaism—they [women] must marry and bear children and thus by their connection to a circumcised husband (or son) assume a place in the covenant community."[44] Since circumcision was especially a *male* problem in Galatians (see, e.g., Gal 2:3 with Titus and Gal 2:11–14 with Peter), there may be other reasons for Paul's appeal to male and female in Gal 3:28, such as inheritance language.

The second problem is the conflation of meaning and application.[45] In 1994 Andreas Köstenberger discussed hermeneutics specifically related to gender passages since interpretations and methods vary among evangelical scholars.[46] He specifically points out that "the line between the ancient and the contemporary horizons is often blurred."[47] Even more difficult is when there is supposedly more than one original meaning. Adewale Adelakun argues, "In opinion, both Egalitarians and Complementarians are right in their interpretations of the verse but are wrong in its applications."[48] It is unclear how both sides can be right in their interpretations of the original meaning.

The interpretive methods employed by the sociological view of Gal 3:28 are similar to the methods used by some queer readings. Certain arguments from Gal 3:28 could, if true, be applied to the moral acceptance of homosexuality. In Chapter Three the question of cultural arguments in relation to the question of women and homosexuality was explored, but here the focus will be on Gal 3:28 in particular. For instance, Richard Cleaver, who argues for the morality of homosexuality, writes, "I use the term *gender* to mean the system of social meanings that our society attaches to the biological categories of male and female—categories

---

42 Ben Witherington III, "Rite and Rights for Women—Galatians 3:28," *NTS* 27 (1981): 593–604.
43 On the pros and cons of mirror-reading, see Andrew David Naselli, *How to Understand and Apply the New Testament: Twelve Steps from Exegesis to Theology* (Phillipsburg: P&R, 2017), 171–73; and John M. G. Barclay, "Mirror-Reading a Polemical Letter: Galatians as a Test Case," *JSNT* 31 (1987): 73–93. Barclay's explanation of a statement's frequency and consistency (pp. 84–85) should cause one to hesitate to make male/female historical reconstructions in Galatians.
44 Witherington, "Rite and Rights for Women—Galatians 3:28," 595.
45 Some may view meaning and application as inherently the same. However, it is good to maintain a distinction in order to adjudicate between different interpretations.
46 Andreas Köstenberger, "Gender Passages in the NT: Hermeneutical Fallacies Critiqued," *WTJ* 56 (1994): 259–83.
47 Köstenberger, "Gender Passages in the NT," 281.
48 Adewale J. Adelakun, "Complementarians Versus Egalitarians: An Exegesis of Galatians 3:28 from Nigerian Cultural Perspective," *Ogbomoso Journal of Theology* 17.3 (2012): 92.

that Paul tells us in Gal. 3:28 have no more meaning 'in Christ Jesus.' This set of expectations is woven into a structure of oppression we call 'patriarchy.'"[49] The similarities with the way evangelical egalitarians argue is clear, for example, with the rhetoric of "oppression" and the appeal to "patriarchy." Similarly, James Nelson discusses Gal 3:28 and social implications in order to conclude that one must look at the Bible broadly and remember that "particular biblical statements about human sexuality are inevitably historically conditioned."[50] Disregarding "particular biblical statements" because they are "historically conditioned" is not unique to queer readings. From a different angle, Richard Longenecker states, "But Paul speaks in Galatians without any qualification or reservations."[51] A queer reading would agree with Longenecker's statement. If Paul intended for there to be no qualification whatsoever, then a scholar could make the case for the acceptance of homosexuality based upon Gal 3:28. If someone claims that the rest of Scripture prohibits homosexuality, then we are back to qualifying Gal 3:28 with reservations, which is not what Longenecker states. Faith Martin says, "Galatians 3:28 is quite clear. There is little doubt about the point Paul is making: In Christ we are all the same—we are equal with one another."[52] General comments about sameness in relation to gender could easily be used in a queer reading of the text. Sameness in gender in what manner? Several scholars push back on the idea that Gal 3:28 can mean any type of gender elimination.[53] Tom Schreiner explains that Paul "does not claim that maleness and femaleness are irrelevant in every respect."[54] Schreiner's point about "in every respect" contrasts sharply with Longenecker's "without any qualification." At creation God referred to all that he had made as "very good," which included male and female before the Fall (Gen 1:27, 31).

---

49 Richard Cleaver, *Know My Name: A Gay Liberation Theology* (Louisville: Westminster John Knox, 1995), 27 (italics original). This section explores and elaborates on William J. Webb, *Slaves, Women and Homosexuals: Exploring the Hermeneutics of Cultural Analysis* (Downers Grove, IL: InterVarsity Press, 2001), 88 n. 37. Webb also has a convenient bibliography on the acceptance of homosexuality (pp. 288–89).
50 James B. Nelson, *Embodiment: An Approach to Sexuality and Christian Theology* (Minneapolis: Augsburg, 1978), 51. Nelson also claims that Paul's eschatology "did not have a transformative effect upon social relationships in the present time" (p. 51).
51 Richard N. Longenecker, *New Testament Social Ethics for Today* (Grand Rapids: Eerdmans, 1984; repr., Vancouver: Regent College Bookstore, 1995), 75.
52 Faith McBurney Martin, "Galatians 3:28," *Priscilla Papers* 9 (1995): 1.
53 E.g., Douglas J. Moo, *Galatians*, BECNT (Grand Rapids: Baker, 2013), 254; John R. W. Stott, *The Message of Galatians*, BST (Downers Grove, IL: InterVarsity Press, 1968), 100.
54 Schreiner, *Galatians*, 259.

William Webb, who has already been discussed in Chapter Three regarding his cultural analysis, attempts to answer the question why Gal 3:28 applies to women's equality issues but does not apply in the same way to homosexual equality. It is worth noting that his language changes from how he discusses women to how he discusses homosexuals in his section on Gal 3:28. He explains that Gal 3:28 had social implications for Gentiles and slaves, and so he asks, "Why should it not today for females?"[55] When explaining how Gal 3:28 may or may not apply to homosexuals, he does not ask the same rhetorical question. He instead states, "The important qualifier is that the movement in a seedbed text must be in the *same direction of movement set by Scripture* as evidenced in the movement of other same-topic texts relative to the broader social context."[56] He continues with different language: "Thus one cannot argue the kind of forward projection from the seed idea of Galatians 3:28 using extrapolated implications for subsequent generations based upon what happened in Paul's day in raising the status of Gentiles. That kind of trajectory *only works with slaves and women*, if one is to extrapolate the original intent of the verse."[57] Finally, he mentions, "A case would first have to be made from biblical texts outside of this verse that attempt to break down the social stigma of a particular area."[58] The nuanced language that Webb uses for homosexuals is not used in relation to Gal 3:28 and other texts involving women. Furthermore, when speaking about women, Webb can argue straight from Gal 3:28, but when speaking about homosexuals he appeals to other passages of Scripture. In other words, Webb's biblical starting points are different where "other Scripture" informs homosexuality and the application of Gal 3:28, whereas Gal 3:28 is a starting point that informs other Scripture passages regarding women. Why, then, can other texts about women not inform Gal 3:28, as Webb allows regarding homosexuals? And can some argue against "extrapolated implications" or "secondary deduction" regarding women and Gal 3:28, as Webb does with homosexuals?[59] In sum, Webb has different criteria depending on which group he is discussing.

When applications of Gal 3:28 are unleashed completely from their original literary context, then there is the question of how far these applications should or

---

55 Webb, *Slaves, Women and Homosexuals*, 87. This type of argument was already made by Bruce, *The Epistle to the Galatians*, 190.
56 Webb, *Slaves, Women and Homosexuals*, 88 (italics original).
57 Webb, *Slaves, Women and Homosexuals*, 89 (italics added for emphasis).
58 Webb, *Slaves, Women and Homosexuals*, 90.
59 For use of "secondary deduction" language in the homosexual debate, see Webb, *Slaves, Women and Homosexuals*, 90.

can go. Dale Martin argues for a queer reading of Gal 3:28 by separating original meaning from application. Martin explains, "In this case, Christians could be gendered in many different ways. I am not saying that this is the 'historical-critical' meaning of the text. I am saying that it is no *more* 'unhistorical' or 'anachronistic' than the overwhelmingly dominant interpretations current today. And I am also saying that it is just as supportable by appeals to 'the text itself.' "[60] Certain readings that move from the original context of Gal 3:28 to social implications regarding women's church leadership positions must answer how they do not go farther into Martin's view of applying the text to the dissolving of sexuality (and how they do so consistently). By contrast, Timothy George can explain, "The propriety of women leaders in the church must be decided through careful exegesis of those passages that touch on that issue. Galatians 3:28 cannot legitimately be used either as evidence or counterevidence in this debate. It is regrettable that recent discussions of this theme have obscured the amazing good news Paul set forth in this verse."[61] George offers some controls on how to apply the passage to the modern day without using the same argumentation of queer readings.

There is nothing in the immediate literary context of Gal 3:28 that contradicts 1 Cor 14:34–35. Paul did not contradict himself but made different points for different contexts. A specific silencing of women in 1 Cor 14:34 is consistent with Paul's view of men and women in Gal 3:28 since each passage has its own function and meaning. Paul's words in 1 Cor 14:34 can only be claimed to contradict Gal 3:28 by appeal to debatable *applications*. Scholars should no longer cross-reference Gal 3:28 in order to contradict 1 Cor 14:34 in light of the various views of Gal 3:28 itself. Scholars also will need to clarify if the charge of contradiction regards the original meaning of Gal 3:28 and/or a particular application.

First Timothy 2:11–12 and the Study of Ἡσυχία

Paul's principles in 1 Cor 14:34–35 are consistent with his theological principles in 1 Tim 2:9–14. More specifically for σιγάω, Paul is consistent in both letters regarding silence in that 1 Cor 14:34 is a more specific application of the

---

60   Dale B. Martin, *Sex and the Single Savior: Gender and Sexuality in Biblical Interpretation* (Louisville: Westminster John Knox, 2006), 89 (italics original).
61   George, *Galatians*, 321.

broader principle found in 1 Tim 2:11–12.[62] The term for silence in 1 Tim 2:11–12 is ἡσυχία, repeated twice "emphasizing silence."[63] This section will analyze the meaning of ἡσυχία and demonstrate consistency in regard to Paul's view of silencing women in the church.[64] He is consistent in that neither text speaks of absolute silence. Both passages speak of a specific silence in relation to a particular speech.

Despite Robert Karris's claim that 1 Cor 14:34–35 is not parallel to 1 Tim 2:12, there are good reasons to see the texts as parallel. Karris writes, "But before 1 Tim 2:12 can qualify as an interpretive parallel to 1 Cor 14:34–35, two criteria have to be met: (1) the vocabulary and literary contexts should be similar; (2) the historical situations should be similar. Criterion one is not quite met. Although both passages contain exhortations, 1 Cor 14:34–35 uses the verb *lalein* whereas 1 Tim 2:12 uses *didaskein* ('to teach')."[65] Karris's focus on the general difference of vocabulary misses several literary similarities that cannot be accidental if Paul was the author of both texts. Origen, by contrast, saw the need to keep the two texts together. Origen's explanation of 1 Cor 14:34–35 refers to 1 Tim 2:12, stating that Paul "says concerning the woman that she may not be ruler over the word of man" (εἴρηται περὶ τοῦ μὴ τὴν γυναῖκα ἡγεμόνα γίνεσθαι τῷ λόγῳ τοῦ ἀνδρός).[66] Origen saw the benefit of 1 Timothy 2 in explaining 1 Corinthians 14. The general parallels are obvious when viewed together:

---

62 On the relationship of these two letters, E. Earle Ellis writes, "All this suggests a common tradition or an existing regulation to which both passages are indebted rather than a direct literary relationship, whether that relationship is conceived of as an interpolation of elements of 1 Tim. 2:11–3:1a into 1 Cor. 14:34–5 (Weiss) or a construction of 1 Timothy 2 from 1 Corinthians 14" ("The Silenced Wives of Corinth (1 Cor. 14:34–5)," in *New Testament Textual Criticism: Its Significance for Exegesis: Essays in Honour of Bruce M. Metzger*, ed. Eldon Jay Epp and Gordon D. Fee [Oxford: Clarendon, 1981], 214–15). I view both letters as Pauline with 1 Timothy written after 1 Corinthians. The concern of this chapter is consistency and not literary dependency. The results of this chapter may have implications for literary dependency, but theological consistency does not hinge upon dependency.

63 Ray Van Neste, *Cohesion and Structure in the Pastoral Epistles*, JSNTSup 280 (London: T&T Clark International, 2004), 38.

64 Luke Timothy Johnson also sees consistency between the two passages, and he writes that silence in 1 Tim 2:11–12 has "a broader connotation" than in 1 Cor 14:34. However, he does not expand on his position (*The First and Second Letters to Timothy: A New Translation with Introduction and Commentary*, AB [New York: Doubleday, 2001], 206).

65 Robert J. Karris, "Women in the Pauline Assembly: To Prophesy, but Not to Speak?" in *Women Priests: A Catholic Commentary on the Vatican Declaration*, ed. Leonard Swidler and Arlene Swidler (New York: Paulist, 1977), 206.

66 My translation. Greek text from Claude Jenkins, "Origen on 1 Corinthians, IV," *JTS* 10.37 (1908): 42. Greek manuscript 1915 can be viewed at https://ntvmr.uni-muenster.de. For more information, see Benjamin A. Edsall, *The Reception of Paul and Early Christian Initiation: History and Hermeneutics* (Cambridge: Cambridge University Press, 2019), 127 n. 5; and Korinna Zamfir, "Women Teaching—Spiritually Washing the Feet of the Saints? The Early Christian Reception of 1 Timothy 2:11–12," *Annali di Storia dell'esegesi* 2 (2015): 361.

> αἱ γυναῖκες ἐν ταῖς ἐκκλησίαις σιγάτωσαν οὐ γὰρ ἐπιτρέπεται αὐταῖς λαλεῖν, ἀλλ᾽ ὑποτασσέσθωσαν, καθὼς καὶ ὁ νόμος λέγει. εἰ δέ τι μαθεῖν θέλουσιν, ἐν οἴκῳ τοὺς ἰδίους ἄνδρας ἐπερωτάτωσαν αἰσχρὸν γάρ ἐστιν γυναικὶ λαλεῖν ἐν ἐκκλησίᾳ. (1 Cor 14:34–35)
>
> γυνὴ ἐν ἡσυχίᾳ μανθανέτω ἐν πάσῃ ὑποταγῇ διδάσκειν δὲ γυναικὶ οὐκ ἐπιτρέπω οὐδὲ αὐθεντεῖν ἀνδρός, ἀλλ᾽ εἶναι ἐν ἡσυχίᾳ. (1 Tim 2:11–12)

Paul used words that are identical, similar, and different between these two passages. The identical words are γυνή, ἐπιτρέπω, μανθάνω, and ἀνήρ. The similar terms are σιγάω/ἡσυχία, ὑποτάσσω/ὑποταγή, and λαλέω/διδάσκω (the latter terms connected by ἐπιτρέπω). The differences between the passages include ἐκκλησία, οἶκος, ἐπερωτάω, and αἰσχρός in 1 Corinthians and πᾶς and αὐθεντέω in 1 Timothy. Paul must have been intentional to create so much overlap within such a short amount of space. This observation shows that σιγάω and ἡσυχία may well function in similar ways. Paul silenced women broadly in regard to teaching men (applying it to the situation in Ephesus), and then he applied the silence specifically to judging prophecies of men (applying it to the situation in Corinth). Nonetheless, scholars do not have a consensus on the definition of ἡσυχία.

J. N. D. Kelly combines an absolute silence interpretation of 1 Cor 14:34 with silence in 1 Tim 2:11–12. He writes, "In [1 Cor 14:33–36] he absolutely forbids women to address the congregation and imposes silence on them. In the same way he adds here [1 Tim 2:12], I do not allow a woman to teach … she ought to keep quiet."[67] He applies absolute silence to 1 Timothy 2 by referring to 1 Corinthians 14 ("in the same way"). He provides no evidence for this interpretation.[68] Many writers do not see absolute silence in 1 Tim 2:11–12.[69] Robert Yarbrough writes that ἡσυχία "rarely refers to a blanket prohibitive policy against spoken expression."[70] Even more pointedly, A. Schlatter writes, "ἐν ἡσυχίᾳ cannot

---

[67] J. N. D. Kelly, *A Commentary on the Pastoral Epistles: Timothy I and II, Titus* (San Francisco: Harper & Row, 1960), 68.

[68] While it is common in commentaries to be brief due to space constraints, a specific view of a passage should come with at least reference to evidence. All the more reason in Kelly's case since very few argue for an absolute silence in 1 Timothy 2 even if they do so in 1 Corinthians 14.

[69] E.g., Andreas J. Köstenberger, *1–2 Timothy and Titus*, Evangelical Biblical Theology Commentary (Bellingham, WA: Lexham, 2020), 113; Ben Witherington III, *Letters and Homilies for Hellenized Christians: A Socio-Rhetorical Commentary on Titus, 1–2 Timothy and 1–3 John* (Downers Grove, IL: IVP Academic, 2006), 226; Robert W. Yarbrough, *The Letters to Timothy and Titus*, PNTC (Grand Rapids: Eerdmans, 2018), 172.

[70] Yarbrough, *The Letters to Timothy and Titus*, 172. Though more work needs to be done on Greco-Roman literature, I have not found a single instance where ἡσυχία refers to absolute silence. Yarbrough does not give any example for it either.

mean that she learn in silence, just as the ἡσύχιος βίος [see 1 Tim 2:2] for the church was not intended as a mute existence and word-less life."[71] A specific silence in both 1 Cor 14:34 and 1 Tim 2:11–12 shows consistency in regard to Paul's instructions regarding women's speech in the church. If 1 Tim 2:11–12 was interpreted as absolute silence then it would contradict 1 Cor 14:34–35.

The main debate regarding the meaning of ἡσυχία is between Douglas Moo and Philip Payne. In Moo's first article, he writes that the term "can denote either 'silence' (cf. Acts 22:2) or 'quietness' (2 Thess 3:12), but in a context having to do with teaching and learning, the former is more likely."[72] Payne then responded to Moo's article in order to argue for the meaning of "quiet" and against "silence." Payne sums up his reasoning in three ways: "(1) the usual NT meaning of ἡσυχία is 'quiet'; (2) elsewhere in Paul's letters ἡσυχία denotes 'quiet' and another term, σιγάω, is used to denote 'silence'; (3) the context of 1 Tim 2:11–12 supports the translation 'quiet' since 'quiet' forms a natural pair with 'submission' in 2:11 and a natural contrast to αὐθεντεῖν in 2:12."[73] It is important to note on Payne's first point that he claims, "All of the main Greek lexica including LSJ, BAG, Moulton-Milligan, and Thayer give 'quiet' as the primary meaning for ἡσυχία."[74] Moo's rejoinder replied to each of Payne's three points and questioned Payne's use of Greek lexicons, his claim of σιγάω (a verb) and how it relates to ἡσυχία (a noun), and the "subjective consideration" of how ἡσυχία is read in context.[75] Significantly, Moo explains, "What Payne apparently means when he says that the lexicons give 'quiet' as the 'primary meaning' is that they list it first."[76] Payne wrote a surrejoinder to Moo and adjusted his argument slightly, "As long as the positive connotation of ἡσυχία is understood, either 'quietness' or 'silence' is an adequate rendering."[77] While he still prefers the translation "quietness," he now states that "silence" is a possibility.[78] Payne omits discussion of Moo's concern

---

71 A. Schlatter, *Kirche der Griechen im Urteil des Paulus: Eine Auslegung seiner Briefe an Timotheus und Titus*, 2nd ed. (Stuttgart: Calwer, 1958), 88: "ἐν ἡσυχίᾳ kann nicht heißen, sie lerne schweigend, wie auch mit dem ἡσύχιος βίος für die Gemeinde nicht ein stummes Dasein und wortloses Leben gewünscht war."
72 Douglas J. Moo, "1 Timothy 2:11–15: Meaning and Significance," *TJ* 1 (1980): 64.
73 Philip B. Payne, "Libertarian Women in Ephesus: A Response to Douglas J. Moo's Article, '1 Timothy 2:11–15: Meaning and Significance,'" *TJ* 2 (1981): 170.
74 Payne, "Libertarian Women in Ephesus," 169.
75 Douglas J. Moo, "The Interpretation of 1 Timothy 2:11–15: A Rejoinder," *TJ* 2 (1981): 198–99.
76 Moo, "The Interpretation of 1 Timothy 2:11–15: A Rejoinder," 198.
77 Philip B. Payne, "The Interpretation of 1 Timothy 2:11–15: A Surrejoinder," in *What Does the Scripture Teach about the Ordination of Women: A Study Commissioned by the Committee on Ministerial Standing*, Part 2 (Minneapolis: The Evangelical Free Church of America, 1986), 99.
78 Payne, "The Interpretation of 1 Timothy 2:11–15: A Surrejoinder," 100.

124 | *Paul, Women, and the Meaning of Silence*

over his use of lexicons. In Payne's book, he responded to the second and third points mentioned above but again did not respond to Moo's significant concern over the use of lexicons.[79] Neither Moo nor Payne closely consider broader Greek usage.[80] A broader look at ἡσυχία is needed, and the overlap with σιγάω will be seen below.

No one has written an exhaustive study of ἡσυχία in the ancient world, and commentators typically give little attention to this term, perhaps due to the other debates in 1 Timothy 2:9–15.[81] TLG lists over 6,000 occurrences in Greek literature. BDAG is a good place to start because ἡσυχία is simply divided into two main definitions. The term is either "quietness, rest" or "silence."[82] "Peace" needs to be added as a third definition due to military contexts, which BDAG does not make explicit. Strabo demonstrates a military context: "Again, about the time of the wars with Hannibal, they were deprived of their freedom, although later they received a colony of Romans, and are now living at peace [ἡσυχίαν ζῶσι] and better than before."[83] While peace and tranquility permeate Greek literature regarding ἡσυχία, C. H. Peisker goes too far in writing, "The primary meanings in Greek literature, 'rest, peace, tranquility,' are those present in the NT."[84] For in Acts 22:2 ἡσυχία is glossed as silence. Luke writes of Paul, "And when they

---

[79] Philip B. Payne, *Man and Woman: One in Christ: An Exegetical and Theological Study of Paul's Letters* (Grand Rapids: Zondervan, 2009), 315. Payne is often meticulous in his debates, which makes this omission more significant.

[80] Others have written on the topic, but they also omit broader usage. Schreiner originally took ἡσυχία as silence but later changed his position to quietness (cf. Thomas R. Schreiner, "An Interpretation of 1 Timothy 2:9–15: A Dialogue with Scholarship," in *Women in the Church: A Fresh Analysis of 1 Timothy 2:9–15*, ed. Andreas J. Köstenberger, Thomas R. Schreiner, and H. Scott Baldwin [Grand Rapids: Baker, 1995], 123–24; and Thomas R. Schreiner, "An Interpretation of 1 Timothy 2:9–15: A Dialogue with Scholarship," in *Women in the Church: An Interpretation and Application of 1 Timothy 2:9–15*, ed. Andreas J. Köstenberger and Thomas R. Schreiner, 3rd ed. [Wheaton, IL: Crossway, 2016], 187 n. 103). William D. Mounce, *Pastoral Epistles*, WBC 46 (Nashville: Thomas Nelson, 2000), 118–19, provides four reasons for a quiet definition. The most formidable argument is that Paul's own usage favor's quiet (appealing to 2 Thess 3:12, plus the verb form in 1 Thess 4:11). If one broadens out to the NT (or Greek literature), the possibility of a different definition changes. When appealing to Pauline usage, the small sample size is problematic for coming to a definitive definition.

[81] Thanks to Charles Bumgardner for his insight regarding bibliography for the Pastoral Epistles. For a specialized bibliography on 1 Tim 2:9–15, see Köstenberger and Schreiner, eds., *Women in the Church*, 359–90. The closest discussion of some length is Ceslas Spicq, "ἡσυχάζω, ἡσυχία, ἡσύχιος," *TLNT* 2:178–83. Other than a number of good (selective) ancient references, the weakness of Spicq's discussion lies in its overall organization. For example, Spicq's conclusion in summing up the range of meanings does not completely correspond to his overall article.

[82] BDAG, 440. Cf. the three definitions of "quiet circumstances, silence, and quiet living" in Johannes P. Louw and Eugene A. Nida, L&N 2:116.

[83] Strabo, *Geogr* 6.3.4. Translations of Greco-Roman authors are from the LCL.

[84] C. H. Peisker, "ἡσυχία, ἡσυχάζω, ἡσύχιος," *EDNT* 2:125.

The Theological Context: Consistency within Pauline Theology and Practice | 125

heard that he addressed them in the Hebrew language, they granted even more silence [μᾶλλον παρέσχον ἡσυχίαν]." But in 2 Thess 3:12 the term refers to a tranquil lifestyle where Paul writes, "Now to such ones we command and urge in the Lord Jesus Christ that they eat their own bread by working with tranquility [μετὰ ἡσυχίας]." There are no other occurrences of ἡσυχία in the NT except for 1 Tim 2:11–12. The verb ἡσυχάζω has the same division between "silence" and "tranquility," though more often it is simply "silence."[85] The two adjectival occurrences of ἡσύχιος are "tranquil."[86] The LXX contains a similar range of glosses (see Figure 2 below).[87]

The term ἡυσχία overlaps with σιγάω in that they both mean a selective silence in certain contexts. The following example from Philo, *That the Worse Attacks the Better*, provides evidence that ἡσυχία can function similar to σιγάω:

> And because a tongue and a mouth and organs of speech have been allotted to you, do not blurt out [ἐκλάλει] all things, even those which are secrets; for there are places where it is good to refrain from speech; and it seems to me that those who have learned to speak [λέλειν] have learned also to be silent [ἡσυχάζειν], since the same faculty renders us capable both of exercising speech and of refraining from its exercise; and those who talk about things they should not, appear to me to display not power of speech [λόγων] but weakness in keeping silent [ἡσυχίας]. So let us make it our earnest endeavor to bind up each of the openings which we have mentioned with the adamantine chains of self-control. For Moses says elsewhere (Numb. xix. 15) that "every open vessel which had no covering bound upon it, is unclean," implying that wretchedness is due to the different parts of the soul having been left loose and gaping and unfastened, while proper ordering of life and speech is the result of these being kept close and tight.[88]

When one compares Philo with what has already been observed (see Chapter Two and the Appendix), then either Greek term, ἡσυχία or σιγάω, can suffice when referring to knowing when to speak and when to be silent. Another example comes from Dionysius of Halicarnassus:

> For a time quiet [ἡσυχᾷ] and silence [σιγή] prevailed in both armies, and then there was shouting by both sides together and alternate exhortations to the

---

85 Luke 23:56 (rest), 1 Thess 4:11 (tranquil), and Luke 14:4; Acts 11:18; 21:14 (silence). BDAG, 440.
86 1 Peter 3:3; 1 Tim 2:2. BDAG, 440–41.
87 E.g., cf. Job 34:29 and Josh 5:8 in the LXX.
88 Philo, *Worse* 102–03; cf. Philo, *Worse* 42.

combatants; and there were vows and lamentations and continual expressions of every other emotion experienced in battle, some of them caused by what was either being enacted or witnessed by each side, and others by their apprehensions of the outcome; and the things they imagined outnumbered those which actually were happening.[89]

Dionysius uses the noun form of σιγάω in what may be a hendiadys. Both terms are contrasted with "shouting" and other forms of speech.

The same author can use ἡσυχία to mean both silence and peace. Josephus, on the one hand, writes, "The Dalmatians, too, who have so often reared their heads for liberty, whose constant defeats have only led them to muster their forces for a fresh revolt, do they not now live in peace [ἡσυχίαν] under a single Roman legion?"[90] On the other hand, he can write,

> When they have taken their seats in silence [ἡσυχίας], the baker serves out the loaves to them in order, and the cook sets before each one plate with a single course. Before meat the priest says a grace, and none may partake until after the prayer. When breakfast is ended, he pronounces a further grace; thus at the beginning and at the close they do homage to God as the bountiful giver of life. Then laying aside their raiment, as holy vestments, they again betake themselves to their labours until the evening. On their return they sup in like manner, and any guests who may have arrived sit down with them. No clamour or disturbance ever pollutes their dwelling; they speak in turn, each making way for his neighbour. To persons outside the silence [σιωπή] of those within appears like some awful mystery; it is in fact due to their invariable sobriety and to the limitation of their allotted portions of meat and drink to the demands of nature.[91]

In the latter text, Josephus describes the Essenes and their rituals. There is clear overlap with σιωπῇ (another term similar to σιγάω). Even if a quiet demeanor is included, the description of the Essenes demonstrates that ἡσυχία includes the temporary absence of words ("silence"). Furthermore, Josephus shows that an author is not limited to one definition of the term ἡσυχία (contrast above Payne's focus on Paul's usage).

To provide more evidence that ἡσυχία can overlap in meaning with σιγάω, the chart below will summarize the data in the LXX and in Josephus's *Antiquities*.

---

89   Dionysius of Halicarnassus, *Ant. rom.* 3.19.1.
90   Josephus, *J.W.* 2.370–71.
91   Josephus, *J.W.* 2.130–33.

Figure 2. Ἡσυχία in the LXX[a].

LXX Reference	Meaning of ἡσυχία	Context
Joshua 5:8	Tranquility (while healing)	Joshua circumcised men of Israel, and they remained in the camp until healed
1 Chronicles 4:40	Quiet (not at war)	Description of the land itself to shepherd flocks
1 Chronicles 22:9	Quiet (not at war)	Military context of Solomon's reign
Esther 4:17w	Quiet living (in private as opposed to public)	Esther's prayer referencing her days of silence
1 Maccabees 9:58	Living in peace (not at war)	Military context of Jonathan
2 Maccabees 12:2	Quiet living	Government leaders not letting Judeans live a quiet life
2 Maccabees 14:4	Temporary silence or selective silence	Alcimus takes a day to be quiet, then speaks to King Demetrius
Proverbs 7:9	Quiet (of the night)	Foolish son meeting the adulterous woman (folly) at night
Proverbs 11:12	Selective silence	Proverb showing wisdom in knowing when to be silent
Job 34:29	Selective silence	Elihu speaking about God, when God is silent
Sirach 28:16	Peaceful living	A proverb on not finding peace and quiet
Ezekiel 38:11	Quiet living (not at war)	The Lord quotes Gog as saying that he will come against people living in quiet and peace

[a] Translations in this section taken from Albert Pietersma and Benjamin G. Wright, eds., *A New English Translation of the Septuagint: And the Other Greek Translations Traditionally Included under that Title* (New York: Oxford University Press, 2007). The Greek text is from Rahlfs and Hanhart.

The LXX has three clear examples (out of 12 total uses) of a "selective silence" meaning for ἡσυχία, which is similar to the main usage of σιγάω. Second Maccabees 14:3–5 states,

> Now a certain Alcimus, who had formerly been high priest but had willfully defiled himself in the times of separation, realized that there was no way for him to be safe or to have access again to the holy altar and went to King Demetrius

in about the one hundred fifty-first year, presenting to him a crown of gold and a palm and, besides these, some of the customary olive branches from the temple. During that day he kept quiet [καὶ τὴν ἡμέραν ἐκείνην ἡσυχίαν ἔσχεν], but he seized the right moment for his own folly when he was invited by Demetrius to a meeting of the council and was asked in what condition and counsel the Judeans were he replied to this.

Robert Doran explains the silence before the king: "The author portrays Alcimus as clever in his use of silence.... Whereas in 1 Macc 7:5–7 a group of people led by Alcimus blurt out their accusation against Judas, here the author focuses on the individual, Alcimus, who restrains himself until asked."[92] Proverbs 11:12 has the same meaning of silence: "A person who lacks sense scorns citizens, but an intelligent man keeps quiet [ἀνὴρ δὲ φρόνιμος ἡσυχίαν ἄγει]." Also Job 34:29 has the same meaning: "And he [God] will furnish quiet [καὶ αὐτὸς ἡσυχίαν παρέξει], and who can condemn?" Definitions such as "quiet demeanor" and "tranquility" do not accurately portray the meaning of ἡσυχία in these contexts. While selective silence is not the dominant meaning of ἡσυχία, it is a necessary translation when the context demands. The need to be open to this meaning is demonstrated even more fully in Josephus.

---

92 Robert Doran, *2 Maccabees: A Critical Commentary*, Hermeneia (Minneapolis: Fortress, 2012), 268.

Figure 3. Ἡσυχία in Josephus's *Antiquities*.

Antiquities Reference	Meaning	Context
1.274–75	Selective silence	Isaac not blessing Esau after blessing Jacob.
3.67–68	Selective silence	Raguel (i.e., Jethro) not saying anything that would hinder someone from coming to Moses
5.235–36	Stop talking to listen	Jotham quiets the crowd to speak to them
5.330	Temporary silence	Boaz, with Ruth at his feet, paused from speaking until daybreak
7.127–28	No quiet (war)	Ammanites war against the Hebrews
8.263	Quiet life	King Roboamos lived "in great quiet and fear" as opposed to "an illustrious commander"
8.275–76	Stop talking to listen	Abias requests everyone "to hear him in quiet," and Josephus comments that Abias spoke "when silence was obtained"
8.351–52	(The land) is quiet	God spoke to Elijah after he "heard the earth rumble" and then quietness
9.79–80	Quiet (general silence)	The Syrians had left their tents and so the silence was because no one was present when the lepers arrived
9.156–57	General quiet	Celebration in the palace, but quiet in the city because of the death of Othlia
9.193–96	Selective silence	Amasias told the prophet to be quiet concerning his prophetic message that made Amasias angry
9.222–24	Selective silence	Ozias (Uzziah) told the priests to be quiet when they tried to prevent him from offering sacrifice
11.260–62, 266	Temporary silence	A eunuch waits to speak about the cross (σταυρός) prepared for Mordecai
14.46–47	Keep peace	Military context where Pompey told Aristobulus and Hyrcanus to keep the peace until Pompey could settle matters later
14.171	Selective silence	The Sanhedrin did not know what to do with Herod when Herod appeared before them

(Continued)

Figure 3. Continued

Antiquities Reference	Meaning	Context
14.413	Not live at peace	Herod chose not to live at peace for the moment but continued to engage in war
15.116	Live at peace	Athenion's decision to remain at peace is contrasted with his other decision to attack (war)
16.258–60	General quietness (associated with sadness)	There was "silence and sadness" in Herod's palace due to current circumstances
16.375–78	Selective silence	Tiro speaks about what others kept silent about
18.245	Tranquil life	Herod spoke of a tranquil life as opposed to seeking a kingdom

Josephus used ἡσυχία to mean a temporary or specific silence in ten out of twenty occurrences in his *Antiquities*. These ten occurrences in *Antiquities* provide significant overlap with σιγάω. Josephus's work demonstrates that the context decides the meaning of the term, and one may not appeal simply to the "primary" meaning. To quote only two examples, Josephus writes,

> Now one day when there was a public festival at Shechem and the people were all assembled there, his brother Jotham—the one who, as we said, had escaped—ascended Garizin, the mountain which rises above the city of Shechem, and shouting so as to be heard by the crowd if they would but listen to him quietly [ἡσυχίαν], begged them to attend to what he had to say. Silence [σιγῆς] being established, he told them how the trees, once gifted with a human voice, held a meeting and besought a fig-tree to rule over them.[93]

The example above shows the relationship with the noun form of σιγάω in the same paragraph. The second example is also clear:

> But one of them, an old soldier named Tiro, who had a son of the same age as Alexander, his friend, spoke out freely about all the things that the others had secretly felt but had kept silence about [ἡσυχίας]. He was impelled to cry out

[93] Josephus, *Ant.* 5.235–36; cf. 8.275–76.

The Theological Context: Consistency within Pauline Theology and Practice | 131

frequently in the presence of the masses, saying without disguise that truth had perished, justice had been abolished among men, and lies and malice prevailed and cast such a cloud over things that not even the greatest human sufferings were visible to erring men. Acting in this way, it would seem that he was incurring danger through his outspokenness, but his reasonableness moved all his hearers, who regarded him as meeting the occasion like a real man. For that reason everyone was glad to hear him say the things that he himself would have said, and while they were looking out for their own safety by keeping silence [σιγᾶν], they nevertheless approved of his outspokenness, for the expected tragedy forced everyone to speak about it.[94]

This second example shows the overlap with the infinitive form of σιγάω. It can be argued that ἡσυχία and σιγάω are being used interchangeably in this latter case. Therefore, it is more accurate to claim that the two terms have distinct meanings in certain contexts but overlap in meaning in other contexts.

In 1 Timothy 2, Paul used the term to refer to both tranquility (1 Tim 2:2), and silence (1 Tim 2:11–12). The reference in 1 Tim 2:2 refers to more of a "tranquility" due to the reference to one's life (βίος). The reference in 1 Tim 2:11–12 means more of a selective silence due to the teaching context. Some commentators conflate 1 Tim 2:2 with 2:11–12 and state that women's silence is more of a "quiet demeanor," but this combination does not appear valid.[95] In Greek literature, the same author can use ἡσυχία in different ways depending on the context. There are different contextual clues in 1 Tim 2:2 and 2:11–12 to show that a "quiet demeanor" is not necessarily the right translation in 1 Tim 2:11–12. Payne emphasizes the peaceful connotation in order to deny the meaning of silence in 1 Tim 2:11–12, writing that the term is "not silence but quietness-peace, the opposite of discord and disruption."[96] However, when the word itself is in dispute, an appeal to lexicons is not sufficient evidence.

In 1 Tim 2:2 ἡσυχία is combined with ἤρεμος ("quiet, tranquil").[97] Plutarch uses the latter term in reference to "the very dead [quietness] of night" (τῆς νυκτὸς τὸ ἐρημότατον).[98] The pairing of these two Greek terms in 1 Tim 2:2, along with the prepositional phrase "in all godliness and dignity" (ἐν πάσῃ εὐσεβείᾳ καὶ σεμνότητι), provides sufficient clues to the meaning of a "quiet life." Whenever the reader arrives at 1 Tim 2:11–12, Paul provides very different clues involving

---

94 Josephus, *Ant.* 16.375–78.
95 E.g., Gordon D. Fee, *1 and 2 Timothy, Titus*, NIBCNT (Peabody, MA: Hendrickson, 1988), 72.
96 Payne, *Man and Woman*, 314–15. Payne elaborates on this claim since he thinks silence is a contradiction in Paul.
97 BDAG, 439.
98 Plutarch, *Fort. Rom.* 325B.

learning, teaching, and authority. The parallel of ἐν ἡσυχίᾳ in 1 Tim 2:11 is ἐν πάσῃ ὑποταγῇ. Also, the contrast of silence in 1 Tim 2:12 is teaching and authority, which are speaking activities. From what has been shown above about the use of selective silence with ἡσυχία, the possibility of this usage in 1 Tim 2:11–12 must remain an open possibility.

Some writers attempt to combine meanings. Schlatter combines the ideas of tranquility and silence in order to argue that "the woman shall not speak until she can speak calmly."[99] Schlatter's view of a specific silence puts the emphasis on the manner of speaking. Similarly, Spicq appears to take a both/and approach in defining the term as not speaking and "being still."[100] In Greek literature ἡσυχία can simply mean "silence" when the context demands, and it does not necessarily have a "tranquil" connotation. The speaking in 1 Tim 2:11–12 is in relation to men and women in the church rooted in the creation of Adam and Eve (1 Tim 2:13). Silence demonstrates submission.[101] The second occurrence of ἡσυχία in 1 Tim 2:11–12 shows that the translation "silence" is more probable because the contrast with teaching and authority would be a specific silence and not just a demeanor. A specific silence contrasts with someone actually speaking or teaching.

First Timothy 2:11–12 is a fitting parallel to 1 Cor 14:34. Many writers have discussed ἡσυχία in relation to the context of 1 Timothy 2. When the term itself is in dispute, one must not rely only on Greek lexica but go back to the primary sources themselves. What has been considered above, though not exhaustive, is sufficient to demonstrate consistency regarding Paul's principles found in 1 Tim 2:11–12 and 1 Cor 14:34. Namely, Paul used silence in specific cases (regarding teaching men and judging prophecies in the assembly). What remains is an

---

99   Schlatter, *Kirche der Griechen im Urteil des Paulus*, 88: "Die Frau soll nicht reden, bis sie ruhig reden kann."

100 C. Spicq, *Saint Paul: Les Épitres Pastorales*, 4th ed., ÉBib (Paris: J. Gabalda et Cie, 1969), 1:380, writes, "What is significant is that a woman may not occupy a hierarchical position or teach in the church in any circumstance (the ban taken up by the fourth council of Carthage in 398); well to the contrary (ἀλλά in all its force is adversative) she is to keep quiet (ἐν ἡσυχίᾳ; vv. 2, 11; cf. *I Cor.* xiv, 34, σιγάτωσαν) without speaking and as 'being still' (as in Thucydide, ἡσυχία-ἡσυχάζειν = inaction, to rest in peace; as opposed to war, III, 6, 1; 12, 1; 66, 21; 71, 1; 106, 3)"; "Ce qui signifie qu'en aucune circonstance, une femme ne peut occuper une position hiérarchique et enseignante dans l'Église (interdiction reprise par le IVᵉ concile de Carthage en 398); bien au contraire (ἀλλά a toute sa force adversative), elle se tiendra tranquille (ἐν ἡσυχίᾳ; vv. 2, 11; cf. *I Cor.* xiv, 34, σιγάτωσαν) sans intervenir et comme « sans bouger » (dans Thucydide, ἡσυχία-ἡσυχάζειν = inaction, rester en paix; opposé à combat, III, 6, 1; 12, 1; 66, 21; 71, 1; 106, 3)." Spicq only discusses ἡσυχία in relation to Thucydides's work, which is a marked contrast to his later lexicon.

101 George W. Knight III, *The Pastoral Epistles: A Commentary on the Greek Text*, NIGTC (Grand Rapids: Eerdmans, 1992), 139; Köstenberger, *1–2 Timothy and Titus*, 114.

investigation into Paul's practice in order to see if Paul was consistent in his teaching about women and his working with them in the early church.

Lydia in Acts 16:11–15, 40

Paul wanted to go to the district of Macedonia to preach during one of his missionary journeys (Acts 16:9–10). Luke describes the scene involving Lydia:

> Now being put out to sea from Troas we ran a straight course to Samothrace, and on the next day to Neapolis and from there to Philippi, which is a leading city of the district of Macedonia, (and) a colony. Now we were spending some days in this city. And on the Sabbath day we went outside of the gate by a river where we were supposing there was a place of prayer, and when we sat down, we were speaking to the women who had gathered. And a certain woman with the name Lydia, a merchant dealing in purple cloth of the city of Thyatira, a God-fearer, was listening, whose heart the Lord opened to give heed to the words spoken by Paul. And as she was baptized and her household, she urged, saying, "If you have judged me to be faithful to the Lord, come and stay at my house." And she prevailed upon us. (Acts 16:11–15)[102]

Luke continues to narrate how Paul and Silas were put into prison following an exorcism of an evil spirit (16:16–24). Luke concludes with Paul and Silas's miraculous and public departure from prison: "And when they went out from the prison, they came to Lydia and they saw and encouraged the brothers and departed" (16:40). Lydia is named twice in this Lukan narrative. She is described religiously and socially. This section will examine the different views of Lydia and how they compare to Paul's view of women in the church.

Brian Capper argues that Lydia was an overseer by virtue of her physical support of Paul and connecting Lydia to the leaders addressed in Phil 1:1.[103] Capper writes, "If Sampley is correct to find the very explicit *societas* form of reciprocity in this letter, the consequence probably follows that Paul saw Lydia as his own *authoritative* representative amongst the converts whom he had left

---

102 On the challenging issue of πρώτη[ς] μερίδος τῆς Μακεδονίας πόλις in 16:12, see Metzger, *A Textual Commentary on the Greek New Testament*, 393–95. My translation follows Metzger's (i.e., the committee's) suggestion.
103 Brian J. Capper, "To Keep Silent, Ask Husbands at Home, and not to Have Authority over Men. Part I (I Corinthians 14:33–36 and I Timothy 2:11–12): The Transition from Gathering in Private to Meeting in Public Space in Second Generation Christianity and the Exclusion of Women from Leadership of the Public Assembly," *TZ* 61.2 (2005): 128–31.

behind in Philippi."[104] Capper, then, equates Lydia's financial support of Paul into authority among the Philippians. Capper's assertion is not able to be proven with the evidence available, and hence, he writes, "the consequence probably follows." Though Capper is cautious in his wording, we have already noted above in Chapter One how Capper views 1 Cor 14:33–36 as drastically compromising "the consistency of the New Testament witness concerning the proper role of women in the worship and leadership of the Christian assembly."[105] On the issue of women in early Christianity there is often a matter-of-fact claim, but when the details of each text are considered, there is more cautious language.

Reference to Lydia is sometimes interpreted in two different ways, either as a Christian who shows hospitality or a leader of a church in her home. I. Howard Marshall writes that Lydia "was thus quick not merely to follow the early Christian practice of being hospitable (Rom. 12:13; 1 Tim. 3:2; Heb. 13:2; 1 Pet. 4:9; 3 John 5–8), but also to share material goods with those who teach the Word (Gal. 6:6; cf. 1 Cor. 9:14)."[106] Commentators like Marshall do not feel compelled to make a case for Lydia as a church leader or pastor. Witherington does not attempt to move from Lydia's hospitality to church leadership, though he does mention the importance of the church in Philippi in relation to Lydia.[107]

By contrast, writers such as Gordon Fee attempt to make a case for Lydia's leadership in the church. While discussing Euodia and Syntyche, Fee argues that Lydia's hospitality "meant she was also a leader in the church, since heads of households automatically assumed the same role in the church that was centered in that household."[108] Fee provides no evidence for his conclusions. Also, some writers who make a case for Lydia's leadership in the church often use ambiguous language. John Polhill writes, "Priscilla and Lydia took an active role in the ministry of their churches."[109] There are contextual clues in Acts 16 regarding hospitality (Lydia's wealth, invitation, and Paul and Silas's visit) but not more specifically than this role. Fee's assertion is speculation, while Polhill's comments

---

104   Capper, "To Keep Silent, Part I," 130 (italics original).
105   Capper, "To Keep Silent, Part I," 114.
106   I. Howard Marshall, *The Book of Acts: An Introduction and Commentary*, TNTC (Grand Rapids: Eerdmans, 1980), 284. Cf. Mikeal C. Parsons, *Acts*, Paideia (Grand Rapids: Backer Academic, 2008), 230–31, 235; David G. Peterson, *The Acts of the Apostles*, PNTC (Grand Rapids: Eerdmans, 2009), 460–62, 474–75. Craig S. Keener discusses inns and places to stay in some of his comments on Lydia (*Acts: An Exegetical Commentary* [Grand Rapids: Baker Academic, 2014], 3:2414–16).
107   Ben Witherington III, *The Acts of the Apostles: A Socio-Rhetorical Commentary* (Grand Rapids: Eerdmans, 1998), 491–93, 499.
108   Gordon D. Fee, *Paul's Letter to the Philippians*, NICNT (Grand Rapids: Eerdmans, 1995), 390.
109   John B. Polhill, *Acts*, NAC 26 (Nashville: Broadman, 1992), 349.

Named Women in Romans 16:1–7

Paul refers to several women in his closing remarks in Rom 16:1–16. How does this passage compare with 1 Cor 14:34–35? Interestingly, Paul likely wrote the book of Romans from Corinth to the believers in Rome.[110] Paul writes,

> Now I recommend to you Phoebe our sister, who is [also] a deacon of the church in Cenchreae, that you may welcome her in the Lord in a manner worthy of saints and aid her in whatever matter she may have need of you. For she even became a patron[111] of many and of myself. Greet Prisca and Aquila, my fellow-workers in Christ Jesus, who risked their own necks for my life, for whom not only I give thanks but also all the Gentile churches, and the church in their home. Greet Epaenetus, my beloved, who is the first-fruit in Asia for Christ. Greet Mary, who greatly labored for you. Greet Andronicus and Junia my kinsmen and my fellow-prisoners, who are known[112] among the apostles, who also were in Christ before me. Greet Ampliatus, my beloved in the Lord. Greet Urbanus our fellow-worker in Christ and Stachys my beloved. Greet Apelles, approved in Christ. Greet those who belong to Aristobulus. Greet Herodion, my kinsman. Greet those who belong to Narcissus who are in the Lord. Greet Tryphena and Tryphosa who have labored in the Lord. Greet the beloved Persis, who greatly labored in the Lord. Greet Rufus chosen in the Lord and (chosen) by his mother and myself. Greet Asyncritus, Phlegon, Hermes, Patrobas, Hermas, and the brothers with them. Greet Philologus and Julia, Nereus and his sister, and Olympas and all the saints who are with them. Greet one another with a holy kiss. All the churches of Christ greet you. (Rom 16:1–16)

Women are mentioned in general terms in 1 Cor 14:34. Paul greets or recommends ten women in Rom 16:1–16. According to Roger Omanson the ten women are Phoebe, Priscilla, Mary, Junia, Tryphena, Tryphosa, Persis, the mother of Rufus,

---

110   John D. Harvey, *Romans*, EGGNT (Nashville: B&H Academic, 2017), 3–4.
111   Or, "of great assistance to many." BDAG, 885, "the relationship suggested by the term πρ[οστάτις] is not to be confused w[ith] the Rom. patron-client system, which was of a different order and alien to Gk. tradition."
112   BDAG, 378, "outstanding among the apostles."

Julia, and the sister of Nereus.[113] Writers often make ambiguous claims about women's leadership roles in the early church based upon Romans 16. Omanson concludes that "women played a prominent role of leadership in the churches which he [Paul] established."[114] Does he mean *every* leadership role? He does not elaborate or specify.[115] If the answer is every church leadership role, then Romans 16 would contradict 1 Cor 14:34. However, if Romans 16 refers to women in ministry in specific roles, then there is no contradiction with women being silent in some respects. The named women in Rom 16:1–7 will be considered below.

The Regular Citation of Inconsistency

Scholars regularly cite Rom 16:1–16 as inconsistent with 1 Cor 14:34. For instance, Pauline Hogan argues for non-Pauline authorship of 1 Cor 14:34–35 partially due to her overall understanding of Romans 16.[116] Andrie du Toit, after discussing most of the women in Romans 16, writes:

> To assume that all these women were, in the eyes of Paul, prominent and active gospel workers outside of the church gatherings, but must have sat quiet as mice in the gatherings of the congregation themselves, is too much to swallow! Already the warm and uninhibited way in which Paul enumerates this list of female coworkers in the Lord testifies of an entirely different spirit than in the synagogue concerning the place of the woman in the church. In light of this, it can hardly be denied that the absolute prohibition to speak in 1 Corinthians 14:33b–36 clashes with Paul's theology, and especially his view of the office, as it is presented elsewhere in his undisputed writings.[117]

Du Toit defines σιγάω here in absolute terms and assumes the women must have been "quiet as mice" if the regulation in 1 Cor 14:34 was followed. Defining σιγάω in this manner allows du Toit to claim that there is a "clash" with Paul's theology. Hans-Josef Klauck claims, "The silence regulation has almost completely displaced

---

113 Roger Omanson, "Who's Who in Romans 16? Identifying Men and Women among the People Paul Sent Greetings to." *BT* 49.4 (1998): 431. In the article Omanson identifies the feminine names but does not always explain how we know that they are feminine.
114 Omanson, "Who's Who in Romans 16?" 436.
115 The lack of precision is especially obvious when compared to his otherwise very precise statements on Bible translation.
116 Pauline Nigh Hogan, *No Longer Male and Female: Interpreting Galatians 3:28 in Early Christianity*, LNTS (New York: T&T Clark, 2008), 33–35, 41–42.
117 Andrie du Toit, "Die swyggebod van 1 Korintiërs 14:34–35 weer eens onder die loep," *HvTSt* 57 (2001): 182. A special thanks to Arjen Vreugdenhil for translating this Afrikaans article.

other evidence concerning enthusiastic speech and participation by women in the early church."[118] Klauck discusses Prisca, Phoebe, Junia, and Nympha but takes 1 Cor 14:34 as an interpolation.[119] Craig Keener claims that Romans 16 shows that women had teaching roles in the early church.[120] Keener maintains his claim by stating that Phoebe had a role of authority, Priscilla instructed Apollos privately, and Junia was an apostle (he appeals to other commentators as his evidence regarding Junia). Keener's comments on Euodia and Syntyche are tentatively based upon the situation in Philippi (utilizing cautious terminology that "it is possible" and "women may have been").[121] Keener's caution with Euodia and Syntyche is necessary from the limited information we have, but his caution here does not dissuade him from making definitive remarks about Romans 16 in his introduction.

Phoebe as a Deacon in Romans 16:1–2

In light of the above comments, it is necessary to take a closer look at Romans 16 to see if women actually publicly taught men in the church. The first woman Paul mentions is Phoebe. Capper states explicitly, "The New Testament figures Phoebe, Lydia and Nympha are clearly identifiable as part of this class of household-overseers."[122] Regarding Phoebe, Capper's reasons for identifying her in this way are "conventions of reciprocity," his own understanding of a deacon at this time, and Paul's commendation.[123] None of these reasons conclusively demonstrate that Phoebe was an overseer. Phoebe is specifically called a deacon (διάκονος) and a patron (προστάτις) in Rom 16:1–2. There is no evidence that a

---

118 Hans-Josef Klauck, *Gemeinde, Amt, Sakrament: Neutestamentliche Perspektiven* (Würzburg: Echter, 1989), 232: "Das Schweigegebot hat andere Zeugnisse über ein engagiertes Reden und Mitarbeiten von Frauen in urchristlichen Gemeinden fast völlig verdrängt."
119 Klauck, *Gemeinde, Amt, Sakrament*, 240: "The verses 34–35, with the framing in v. 33b and v. 36, are a later Pauline interpolation where the choice of the redactor of the Pauline letter inserted it into the joint work of the Corinthian correspondence either in the canonical letters around AD 100 or still a later gloss by aggrieved readers from the mark crowded into the text"; "Die Verse 34–35 mit der Rahmung in V. 33b und v. 36 sind eine nachpaulinische Interpolation, die entweder der Redaktor der Paulusbriefe einfügte bei der Zusammenarbeitung der korinthischen Korrespondenz zu den beiden kanonischen Briefen um 100 n. Chr. oder die noch später als Glosse eines ungehaltenen Lesers vom Rand aus in den Text eindrang."
120 Craig S. Keener, *Paul, Women, and Wives: Marriage and Women's Ministry in the Letters of Paul* (Peabody, MA: Hendrickson, 1992), 237–43 (esp. p. 237 n. 1).
121 Keener, *Paul, Women, and Wives*, 243.
122 Capper, "To Keep Silent, Part I," 127–28. Capper views Phil 1:1 "overseers and deacons" as referring to the same group by equating the terms exactly (p. 130).
123 Capper, "To Keep Silent, Part I," 128.

138 | *Paul, Women, and the Meaning of Silence*

διάκονος or a προστάτις taught authoritatively in the same way that an overseer did in the early church. To put another way, the two Greek terms do not refer to a pastor's role.

Payne goes to some length to make the case that Phoebe was both a church leader and also a teacher.[124] First, he argues that Paul would have submitted to local church leadership (in this case, Phoebe). He writes, "It should not be surprising that Paul, who calls all believers to submit to one another (Eph 5:21), should himself submit to the local leadership in churches he visited."[125] His appeal to Eph 5:21 as evidence is problematic since Eph 5:21 itself is debated on how exactly this submission was understood, especially in light of Paul being an apostle. There are at least five reasons why Paul would not have submitted to Phoebe. (1) There is no example of Paul submitting to other church leaders during his apostolic journeys. (2) Paul was an apostle (e.g., Rom 1:1), which was part of his authority to write Scripture for the churches. Paul wrote Scripture to overseers and deacons in order to instruct them (Phil 1:1). (3) The book of Philemon shows that Paul had the authority to command Philemon even though Philemon is described as a "fellow-worker" (Phlm 1).[126] (4) Paul's warning about visiting some churches shows his authority over them (1 Cor 5:21; 2 Cor 1:23–2:1). And (5) Paul guided the appointment of elders on occasion (Acts 14:23; Tit 1:5). Payne would need to explain how Eph 5:21 should be interpreted in light of how Paul's authority is described in Acts and his letters.

Second, Payne claims that the term προστάτις means a spiritual leader in the case of Phoebe. He appeals to sources in Horsley's *New Documents*.[127] Payne does not elaborate on how he views the specific references in Horsley to prove Phoebe was a church leader and teacher other than reference to προστάτις as the president of an association. Horsley's article does not give the president of an association as the only or main example. In fact, many of Horsley's references show that wealth and providing benefaction are often the emphasis. For example, Horsley states, "The link with Sophia should be clear: as with the similar honorific titles bestowed by a grateful citizenry, she has presumably been accorded the

---

124 Philip B. Payne, "Does the New Testament Name Only Men as Local Church Officers?" *Priscilla Papers* 26.3 (2012): 5–6.
125 Payne, "Does the New Testament Name Only Men as Local Church Officers?" 5.
126 Paul chose not to use his authority on occasion, but he clearly had the authority whether he used it or not (Phlm 1–2, 8–9, 21).
127 G. H. R. Horsley, "Sophia, 'The Second Phoibe,'" in *New Documents Illustrating Early Christianity: A Review of the Greek Inscriptions and Papyri Published in 1979*, The Ancient History Documentary Research Centre (North Ryde, NSW, Australia: Macquarie University, 1987), 4:239–44.

title 'Second Phoibe' because of benefactions provided (to her church?)."[128] The term προστάτις has a range of meaning in Greek literature, and so Payne needs to show contextually in Rom 16:1–2 how he applies Horsley's references (in addition to other Greco-Roman uses of the term).[129] Furthermore, Merkle explains, "She is said, however, to be the leader 'of many' (including Paul) rather than the leader 'of the church' (cf. v. 1)."[130] The Greek text indicates that Phoebe προστάτις πολλῶν ἐγενήθη καὶ ἐμοῦ αὐτοῦ ("became a patron of many and of myself"). As seen above, Payne views this construction to mean that Phoebe ruled over Paul on occasion. However, the reference to "many" and Paul himself points to Phoebe providing money to others in the work of ministry. Paul's submission to Phoebe is an unproven assumption by Payne, and thus, does not explain ἐμοῦ αὐτοῦ.

Third, Payne goes on to write, "Every meaning of every word in the New Testament related to the word Paul chose to describe Phoebe as a 'leader' (*prostatis*) that could apply in Rom 16:2 refers to leadership."[131] This argument does not explain the meaning of προστάτις itself. The term can refer to simple patronage.[132] Payne argues against the NRSV translation of "benefactor" by stating that it "is not listed by the lexicons Liddell Scott Jones (LSJ) or Bauer Arndt Gingrich (BAG). Additionally, Paul's companion Luke uses a different word for 'benefactor' in Luke 22:25, 'those in authority over them are called benefactors [*euergetai*].'"[133] However, as was seen in the study on ἡσυχία above, when the term itself is debated, there should be less reliance upon lexicons to prove a meaning. Nonetheless, in the case of προστάτις, Payne's comments relying upon an older version of BDAG could cause confusion to the average reader. Payne states in a footnote to this comment, "The Bauer, Danker, Arndt, and Gingrich (BDAG) lexicon, 885, does, however, list 'a woman in a supporting role, patron, benefactor,' citing Horsley, 'Phoibe,' 4:242–44. BDAG ignores Horsley's citations of instances where this word means 'guardian' (a person with legal authority) and 'president.'"[134] Payne provides in the main text of the journal support for his

---

128 Horsley, "Sophia, 'The Second Phoibe,'" 4:241.
129 Cf. the different shades of meaning in Dionysius, *Ant. rom.* 2.9–10 (financially taking care of another, among other descriptions); Josephus, *Life* 251 (governor); Josephus, *J.W.* 1.385 (protector); 1 Clem 36:1; 61:3; 64 (describing Jesus).
130 Benjamin L. Merkle, *The Elder and Overseer: One Office in the Early Church*, StBibLit 57 (New York: Peter Lang, 2003), 106.
131 Payne, "Does the New Testament Name Only Men as Local Church Officers?" 5.
132 Again, see Dionysius, *Ant. rom.* 2.9–10.
133 Payne, "Does the New Testament Name Only Men as Local Church Officers?" 5. Luke is quoting Jesus's words about benefactors.
134 Payne, "Does the New Testament Name Only Men as Local Church Officers?" 6 n. 12.

position, but then he relegates counter-evidence of his position to a footnote. Payne's method is inconsistent; that is, he relies upon lexicons when it supports his position, but then pushes the lexicon to a footnote whenever it does not support his position. Payne should not ultimately appeal to the authority of a lexicon in the first place if he is going to debate it in a footnote. His method is also problematic with the appeal to Luke to deny Paul a certain meaning of a term. Two authors can use two different terms, but still have the same meaning. Payne's method of word studies would change the face of Synoptic Gospel studies since the Gospel writers can refer to the same reference with different terms. For instance, Luke's version of "give to us our daily bread each day" uses καθ' ἡμέραν (Luke 11:3), whereas Matthew's version uses a different word with the same concept, "give to us our daily bread today" (σήμερον).[135] Matthew and Luke use different words to refer to the same general category of today or each day (slightly different meanings, but they are of the same category). So why could Paul not have used a different word as Luke and still refer to the same general category? Payne does not elaborate on the consistency of his method.

Fourth, Payne explains why Phoebe was not simply called an overseer or pastor. He writes, "Since Romans was written before any surviving reference to the office of a local church 'overseer,' 'deacon' *may have been* the only officially recognized title for a local church leader at that time and place."[136] He continues by claiming that deacon and προστάτις "*may have been* equivalent to the later-documented titles 'overseer,' 'elder,' and 'pastor.'"[137] Since there is no evidence for either of his claims, Payne is careful to state twice, "may have been." This caution, however, does not hinder him from concluding definitively that Phoebe was a "local church leader."[138] His comments neither elaborate on nor prove the timeline of how titles in the church evolved. One wonders how quickly Payne's historical reconstruction would have evolved between Romans and Philippians, where the latter mentions overseers and deacons (Phil 1:1).

Finally, Payne writes, "The scholarly consensus is that this indicates that Phoebe delivered the epistle to the Romans as Paul's emissary. As a result, she naturally would have answered the Romans' questions about it. Consequently . . .

---

135 If it is argued that my example from Matthew and Luke is actually quoting Jesus, and thus complicating the method further, Payne's own example also quotes Jesus in Luke 22:25. Additional examples could be provided (e.g., reference to church leaders using different terms between Paul and Peter in Phil 1:1 and 1 Pet 5:1).
136 Payne, "Does the New Testament Name Only Men as Local Church Officers?" 5 (italics added).
137 Payne, "Does the New Testament Name Only Men as Local Church Officers?" 5 (italics added).
138 Payne, "Does the New Testament Name Only Men as Local Church Officers?" 6.

Phoebe can properly be regarded as the first exegete of Paul's letter to the Romans."[139] Payne does not elaborate on how he jumps from Phoebe delivering the letter to Phoebe teaching the church at Rome. He simply states "as a result" and "consequently" without providing any data linking the assumption to the conclusion. Even if Phoebe delivered the letter, which is debatable, the delivery would not automatically make her the teaching pastor. The distinction in 1 Tim 3:1–13 between overseers and deacons has the overseers "skillful in teaching" (1 Tim 3:2) but not the deacons.[140] This fact should caution against all the lines of reasoning that Payne proposes. Craig Keener is closer to understanding Phoebe's role than Payne when Keener writes, "It thus seems safest to claim merely that she was a minister of some sort without defining the character of her ministry more specifically."[141] The text gives clues so that some specifics of Phoebe's ministry may be known as being hospitable and using her financial resources for the church in Cenchreae and abroad.[142] The combination of deacon (διάκονος) and a patron (προστάτις) easily fits within the idea of hospitality and using one's wealth for the benefit of a group. Paul does not contradict himself when he selectively silences women in 1 Corinthians 14 and also recognizes Phoebe as a servant and patron of men and women.[143] Writers should not appeal to Phoebe as evidence of women being teaching pastors in the early church.

Prisca and Aquila in Romans 16:3–5a

Paul called Prisca and Aquila his fellow-workers, and the book of Acts provides a glimpse of their lives (Acts 18:24–28). Does this couple contradict Paul's silencing women in 1 Cor 14:34? There is no evidence that Prisca publicly taught the church. The text in Acts shows the private nature of this teaching:

> Now a certain Jew with the name Apollos, from the nation Alexandria, an eloquent man, who was competent in the Scriptures, came to Ephesus. This one had been taught in the way of the Lord and with spiritual zeal he was speaking and teaching accurately the things about Jesus, though he only knew

---

139 Payne, "Does the New Testament Name Only Men as Local Church Officers?" 5–6.
140 Thomas R. Schreiner argues that Phoebe was a deacon but not with the same authority as an overseer (*Romans*, 2nd ed., BECNT [Grand Rapids: Baker Academic, 2018], 760 n. 7).
141 Craig S. Keener, *Romans*, NCCS 6 (Eugene, OR: Cascade, 2009), 183; cf. Scott W. Hahn, *Romans*, Catholic Commentary on Sacred Scripture (Grand Rapids: Baker Academic, 2017), 278.
142 Merkle, *The Elder and Overseer*, 106.
143 The argument here does not depend on if deacon is used in an official or non-official sense because both uses do not necessarily have pastoral authority attached. However, it is my opinion that 1 Tim 3:8–13 shows men were deacons and their wives assisted them.

the baptism of John. And this one began to speak fearlessly in the synagogue. And after hearing him Priscilla and Aquila took him aside, and they explained more accurately to him the way [of God]. And when he wanted to cross over to Achaia, when they urged (him) the brothers wrote to the disciples to receive him, who when he arrived helped many who had believed through grace. For he was confuting vigorously the Jews in public, showing through the Scriptures the Messiah to be Jesus. (Acts 18:24–28)

Prisca (or Priscilla), along with Aquila, privately took Apollos aside in order to teach him. The term προσλαμβάνω ("took aside") contrasts with Apollos's own teaching δημόσιος ("in public"). Keener explains that προσλαμβάνω meant bringing Apollos "into their home for food and discussion."[144] Craig Blomberg rightly states that "it goes well beyond what the text says to conclude that she is in any sense a formal leader or office holder in the church."[145] Still, writers like Keener will insert words like "leading" even though it is not in the text. Keener writes, "Paul's letters confirm that Priscilla and Aquila settled in Ephesus (1 Cor 16:19) and were still there leading a house church (16:19) at the height of Paul's ministry in Ephesus (16:8–9; Acts 19), probably sometime in the year before Acts 20:3."[146] Quite simply, Prisca and Aquila appear to have used their financial means to travel and assist churches, even hosting them, in the places that they went.[147]

---

144 Keener, *Acts*, 3:2808. Cf. Ceslas Spicq, "προσλαμβάνομαι," *TLNT* 3:198. Keener goes on to interpret this event as "Priscilla teaches privately, even if she takes the lead, and the public/private dichotomy was the primary cultural objection to women teaching publicly" (*Acts*, 3:2810).

145 Craig L. Blomberg, *From Pentecost to Patmos: An Introduction to Acts through Revelation* (Nashville: B&H Academic, 2006), 61. Blomberg clarifies that women may teach men "in at least some Christian contexts," but he does not expand on this statement. In his writings, Blomberg does not lean strongly in either direction of complementarian or egalitarian positions. He attempts to find a middle position and (often helpfully) to find weaknesses in both general viewpoints. He stops short of labeling exactly what his own position is (or exactly what he thinks Paul's position is), perhaps due to the difficulty in finding a middle position. See Craig L. Blomberg, "Neither Hierarchicalist nor Egalitarian: Gender Roles in Paul," in *Paul and His Theology*, ed. Stanley E. Porter (Leiden: Brill, 2006), 283–326, esp. p. 326; and Craig L. Blomberg, "Women in Ministry: A Complementarian Perspective," in *Two Views on Women in Ministry*, ed. James R. Beck, rev. ed. (Grand Rapids: Zondervan, 2005), 123–84, esp. p. 125.

146 Keener, *Acts*, 3:2808. Witherington likewise uses ambiguous language that opens the door to broader interpretations of women in early Christianity (*The Acts of the Apostles*, 338–39, 567). He uses "various roles" language, which sets the stage for other publications on women.

147 Cf. Schreiner, *Romans*, 768; James D. G. Dunn, *Romans 9–16*, WBC 38B (Dallas: Word, 1988), 892. Dunn discusses their business and hospitality, which surely appear correct, but he also says that they may have had teaching roles. Dunn appeals to Rom 16:3—συνεργοί and Acts 18:26. Richard N. Longenecker discusses their journey where they left Rome and then went to Corinth, then to Ephesus, and then returned to Rome at an unknown time (*The Epistle to the Romans: A Commentary on the Greek Text*, NIGTC [Grand Rapids: Eerdmans, 2016], 1066–68).

Junia in Romans 16:7

The interpretation of Rom 16:7 is significant for understanding how 1 Cor 14:34 fits within broader Pauline practice because silence is related to the idea of authority in the church. Does Rom 16:7 demonstrate that Junia had authority over men in the church? There are various points that could be examined, such as the gender of Junia's name.[148] However, this section will focus only on the significant phrase describing Andronicus and Junia as οἵτινές εἰσιν ἐπίσημοι ἐν τοῖς ἀποστόλοις (Rom 16:7). The discussion below will proceed in two main parts of explanation of the debate and analysis.

Literature on 1 Corinthians sometimes refers to Junia as evidence that Paul could not have silenced women in the church. For instance, Solomon O. Ademiluka writes, "In Romans 16:7, another woman, Junia, is listed with some apostles. In the opinion of Stegemann and Stegemann (1999: 395), the title of apostle probably characterises her as an envoy legitimated by an appearance of the resurrected Christ. Thus, she was one of 'the earliest itinerant missionaries, even before Paul himself.'"[149] Ademiluka goes from the ambiguous "listed with some apostles" to the definitive "title of apostle" and concludes the article by claiming this text contradicts 1 Cor 14:33b–36.[150] There is no mention of the debate of ἐπίσημοι ἐν τοῖς ἀποστόλοις in Ademiluka's article, which demonstrates that writers sometimes appeal to Junia without making an argument that Junia was an apostle.

The problem with simply referring to Junia with a brief cross-reference is that Michael Burer and Daniel Wallace have written an article presenting evidence that Junia was *not* an apostle, and Burer has written a follow-up article that provides additional evidence.[151] These two articles are so thorough that one is no longer able to assume Junia was an apostle without a detailed rebuttal. Even if one disagrees with Burer and Wallace, the evidence they present cannot be ignored. In essence, they contend that ἐπίσημος plus a genitive personal reference refers to being part of the group (labeled the *inclusive view* and would thus

---

148   For the argument that the name is feminine (Junia, Ἰουνίαν) and not masculine (Junias, Ἰουνιᾶν), see, e.g., Richard S. Cervin, "A Note Regarding the Name 'Junia(s)' in Romans 16:7," *NTS* 40 (1994): 464–70.
149   Solomon O. Ademiluka, "1 Corinthians 14:33b–36 in Light of Women and Church Leadership in Nigeria," *Verbum et Ecclesia* 38 (2017): 3.
150   Ademiluka, "1 Corinthians 14:33b–36," 7.
151   Michael H. Burer and Daniel B. Wallace, "Was Junia Really an Apostle? A Re-examination of Rom 16.7," *NTS* 47 (2001): 76–91; Michael Burer, "'ΕΠΙΣΗΜΟΙ ἘΝ ΤΟΙΣ ἈΠΟΣΤΟΛΟΙΣ in Rom 16:7 as 'Well Known to the Apostles': Further Defense and New Evidence," *JETS* 58.4 (2015): 731–55.

see Junia as included with the apostles), while ἐπίσημος plus ἐν and a personal dative refers to a distinction (labeled the *exclusive view* and would not see Junia or Andronicus as part of the apostles's group). They discuss these two constructions within Greek literature, and their discussions regularly refer to exclusive versus inclusive interpretations. After E. J. Epp, Richard Bauckham, and Linda Belleville countered by saying that Burer and Wallace did not provide enough data, Burer then reexamined the literature and presented additional evidence in a later, second article.[152] It is also worth noting that Epp, Bauckham, and Belleville did not always agree with one another about which texts should be interpreted as inclusive or exclusive when specific examples were discussed.[153] Belleville practically saw every ἐν + dative text as inclusive, though she did not engage every passage. Bauckham was balanced in his view where some ἐν + dative texts were inclusive and some were exclusive.

A number of commentators do not engage the arguments of Burer and Wallace even though they provide an interpretation of the debate. Before Burer and Wallace's original article, commentators typically took an inclusive view (i.e., Junia was included among the apostles), and they primarily based this interpretation on patristic evidence such as John Chrysostom.[154] Anthony Thiselton

---

152 The places for this complaint are found in: Eldon Jay Epp, *Junia: The First Woman Apostle* (Minneapolis: Fortress, 2005), 78; Richard Bauckham, *Gospel Women: Studies of the Named Women in the Gospels* (Grand Rapids: Eerdmans, 2002), 174; Linda Belleville, "Ἰουνιαν ... ἐπίσημοι ἐν τοῖς ἀποστόλοις: A Re-examination of Romans 16:7 in Light of Primary Source Materials," *NTS* 51 (2005): 246. So Burer rightly responds, "If the authors critiqued us because we did not offer enough evidence, one would think that part of their response would be to offer more evidence to the contrary, but that was not done" ("ἘΠΙΣΗΜΟΙ ἘΝ ΤΟΙΣ ἈΠΟΣΤΟΛΟΙΣ in Rom 16:7," 736). A reviewer agreeing with Burer and Wallace's overall thesis is Heath R. Curtis, "A Female Apostle?: A Note Reexamining the Work of Burer and Wallace Concerning ἐπισημος with ἐν and the Dative," *Concordia Journal* 28.4 (2002): 437–40. Curtis reexamines Lucian's *Salaried Posts in Great Houses* (*De mercede conductis*) 28 and argues that it proves Wallace and Burer's thesis (originally Burer and Wallace claimed that Lucian provided counter-evidence against their thesis in "Was Junia Really an Apostle?" 89). In Burer's follow-up article, he changes his position and agrees with Curtis's examination of the Lucian passage. In addition, Burer reevaluates and changes his position also on Josephus, *J.W.* 2.418 and Lucian, *Dial. mort.* 438 ("ἘΠΙΣΗΜΟΙ ἘΝ ΤΟΙΣ ἈΠΟΣΤΟΛΟΙΣ in Rom 16:7," 743–45).
153 The disagreement is especially noticeable among Bauckham and Belleville. Epp, *Junia*, 78, attempted to "put to rest" the exclusive view, but this strategy was both premature in light of Burer's second article and unpersuasive given the disagreements among Bauckham and Belleville.
154 C. E. B. Cranfield, *The Epistle to the Romans: A Critical and Exegetical Commentary*, ICC (London: T&T Clark, 1979; repr., 2002), 2:789; William Sanday and Arthur C. Headlam, *A Critical and Exegetical Commentary on the Epistle to the Romans*, ICC (Edinburgh: T&T Clark, 1895; repr., 1968), 423. Sanday and Headlam, in addition to patristic evidence, also argue for the inclusive view based upon the word ἐπίσημος itself and the wider use of ἀπόστολος. John Chrysostom wrote, "Think what great praise it was to be considered of note among the apostles. These two were of note because of their works and achievements. Think how great the devotion of this woman Junia must have been, that

and Robert Jewett both refer to Epp's book as the reason for adopting the inclusive view.[155] Neither writer appeals to Bauckham. This observation is significant because Jewett writes that Burer and Wallace's "examples are not compelling."[156] Bauckham did agree on some of Burer and Wallace's examples even if he did not agree with all the examples. Epp relied much on Bauckham and Belleville's assessments.[157] Epp's reliance upon Bauckham, and Bauckham's more even-handed analysis of the data, is important to keep in mind with the prominence given to Epp's work by later writers, such as Thiselton and Jewett. Richard Longenecker does not discuss Burer and Wallace at all, though he goes into detail about the gender of Junia's name.[158] Everett Harrison and Donald Hagner take an inclusive view but do not provide evidence or even mention Burer and Wallace.[159] Colin Kruse and John Harvey reviewed the debate and stated that they take an inclusive view.[160] However, they do not provide counter-evidence against Burer and Wallace. As will be seen below, the evidence is not so easily concluded in favor of the inclusive view.

Epp, Bauckham, and Belleville questioned the conclusions of Burer and Wallace but not their overall methodology. Burer and Wallace did arrive at the more likely interpretation with the exclusive view, but their method is not completely clear. They claim that the phrase ἐπίσημοι ἐν τοῖς ἀποστόλοις is exclusive due to lexical and syntactical evidence.[161] The lexical evidence is based upon the meaning of ἐπίσημος and the syntactical evidence is based upon the genitive versus ἐν + dative constructions. This way of framing the discussion is somewhat problematic. One simply is not able to prove an inclusive or an exclusive view by simply pointing to the lexical and syntactical evidence. They provide a clarification when they state that "the key to determining the meaning of the term

---

she should be worthy to be called an apostle! But even here Paul does not stop his praise, for they were Christians before he was" (Gerald Bray, ed. *Romans*, ACCS [Downers Grove, IL: InterVarsity Press, 1998], 372).

155 Anthony C. Thiselton, *Discovering Romans: Content, Interpretation, Reception* (Grand Rapids: Eerdmans, 2016), 257; Robert Jewett, *Romans: A Commentary*, Hermeneia (Minneapolis: Fortress, 2007), 963. It should be noted that Epp was the editor of Jewett's commentary.

156 Jewett, *Romans*, 963 n. 128.

157 Epp, *Junia*, 78, states, "This is supported by the critical evaluations by Bauckham and Belleville, both presenting more detailed critiques than I had...."

158 Longenecker, *The Epistle to the Romans*, 1060–61, 1068–70.

159 Everett F. Harrison and Donald A. Hagner, *Romans*, The Expositor's Bible Commentary, rev. ed., ed. Tremper Longman III and David E. Garland (Grand Rapids: Zondervan, 2008), 229.

160 Colin G. Kruse, *Paul's Letter to the Romans*, PNTC (Grand Rapids: Eerdmans, 2012), 562; John D. Harvey, *Romans*, EGGNT (Nashville: B&H Academic, 2017), 380.

161 Burer and Wallace, "Was Junia Really an Apostle?" 84.

[ἐπίσημος] in any given passage is both the general context and the specific collocation of this word with its adjuncts."[162] In other words, when one analyzes the plethora of Greek data in both of Burer's articles, then the exclusive versus inclusive interpretation is *not* based upon a genitive or dative form (or a preposition), but it is based upon broader context and whatever the related adjunct happens to be. Romans 16:7 must also be argued from a wider context.

It will be shown below that the Greek data is not uniform between the inclusive and exclusive views. The interpretations of the ancient texts depend upon the greater context and whatever the adjunct happens to be. By way of illustration, if I state, "Benedict Arnold is famous among the Americans," or "Benedict Arnold is famous among the British," then the broader context will show if Arnold is included or not within "American" or "British." Also, the specific adjunct "American" or "British" will play a role. But the term itself "famous" would not necessarily prove which group Arnold belonged to. Also, the word "among" in my sentence does not prove it either. The historical, wider context of Arnold's life shows the complexity of interpreting him inclusively or exclusively.

Relying on citations from Burer and Wallace, I will only focus on some of the personal references with the dative instead of impersonal references for a greater parallel with Rom 16:7.[163] Though Bauckham writes, "But we should also question the priority given [by Burer and Wallace] to the 'personal' texts: it is not at all clear why these should be grammatically different from those with impersonal referents."[164] However, since the passage in question in Rom 16:7 refers to Andronicus, Junia, and apostles, then it is reasonable to narrow the results down to personal referents. Bauckam does not explain the Romans passage in relation to his claim that "it is not at all clear." Burer and Wallace write, "Finally, to make sure we are 'comparing apples with apples', the substantival adjunct (i.e. either the noun in the genitive or the object of the preposition ἐν) should be *personal*. This

---

162 Burer and Wallace, "Was Junia Really an Apostle?" 84. Though I only slightly disagree with their article, I consider their work to be the best analysis to date. Before their article, many writers were simply appealing to other commentators for their position.

163 To my knowledge, no one has done another thorough, original search to confirm if there are additional passages that Burer and Wallace did not find. David Huttar claims "a fresh examination of the question," but he does not cite Wallace and Burer, nor does he tell us where he searched for his references. These omissions are significant since he also states, "I have been able to find only two examples of this construction [Person + ἐπίσημος + ἐν phrase]" ("Did Paul Call Andronicus an Apostle in Romans 16:7?" *JETS* 52.4 [2009]: 747, 750). Huttar mentions Euripides and Lucian as his two examples. However, Burer lists additional references that fit person + ἐπίσημος + ἐν phrase (e.g., *TAM* 2.905, *west wall coll.* 2.5.16–19).

164 Bauckham, *Gospel Women*, 178.

gives us the closest parallels to Rom 16:7. However, because of the potential paucity of data, both personal and impersonal constructions will be examined."[165] In light of Burer's second article providing additional data, we can limit the examination to personal references.[166]

Some texts do not fit Burer and Wallace's thesis. An inscription from Asia Minor about a person named Ὀπραμόας (Opramoas) has the personal elements but ἐπίσημος is found in the genitive form (unlike Rom 16:7): "[— — — — —, πατρὸς Ἀπολλων]ίου [δὶ]ς τοῦ Καλ[λιάδου οὐ μόνον ἐ]ν τῇ [π]ατρίδι πρώτου, ἀλλὰ [καὶ ἐν τῷ ἔθ]νει ἐπισήμου {ς} καὶ διαπρεποῦς."[167] The inscription reads, ". . . father Ἀπολλωνίου of Καλλιάδου who is not only first among his countrymen but also well-known and distinguished among the nation." This construction is inclusive, and would appear to go against Burer and Wallace's thesis.[168] The term ἔθνος consistently occurs throughout this lengthy inscription that confirms Ὀπραμόας was part of the nation.

However, other texts appear to support Burer and Wallace's thesis. For example, Euripides's *Hippolytus* states, "Yet she's revered and famous among mortals" (σεμνή γε μέντοι κἀπίσημος ἐν βροτοῖς).[169] A servant speaks these words to Hippolytus about Aphrodite. Aphrodite is distinct from mortals where the preposition ἐν + dative parallels Rom 16:7.[170] Belleville agrees that this text is exclusive, though she seeks to dismiss the relevancy of this text. She writes, "But it is also five centuries earlier than the other examples and at a time when ἐπίσημος had not yet acquired a comparative sense."[171] If Belleville were correct, one could see the change from a non-comparative

---

165 Burer and Wallace, "Was Junia Really an Apostle?" 85 (italics original).
166 At first glance, *Pss. Sol.* 2:6 (υἱοὶ καὶ θυγατέρες ἐν αἰχμαλωσίᾳ πονηρᾷ, ἐν σφραγίδι ὁ τράχηλος αὐτῶν, ἐν ἐπισήμῳ ἐν τοῖς ἔθνεσιν) appears to be a good parallel, but it does not have the subject of ἐπίσημος as personal. Greek text from Henry Barclay Swete, *The Psalms of Solomon with the Greek Fragments of the Book of Enoch* (Cambridge: Cambridge University Press, 1899), 2. R. B. Wright translates, "The sons and the daughters (were) in harsh captivity, their neck in a seal, a spectacle among the gentiles" ("Psalms of Solomon," in *OTP* 2:652). Burer later took the subject of ἐπίσημος as "in [a place] conspicuous" ("'ΕΠΙΣΗΜΟΙ ἘΝ ΤΟΙΣ ἈΠΟΣΤΟΛΟΙΣ in Rom 16:7," 736), while Belleville took it as "a slave-brand" ("Ἰουνιαν . . . ἐπίσημοι ἐν τοῖς ἀποστόλοις," 247). The repetition of ἐν is noteworthy in this instance.
167 *TAM* 2.905, *west wall coll.* 2.5.16–19. Greek texts of inscriptions are found at https://epigraphy.packhum.org.
168 So Belleville, "Ἰουνιαν . . . ἐπίσημοι ἐν τοῖς ἀποστόλοις," 245; contra Burer, "'ΕΠΙΣΗΜΟΙ ἘΝ ΤΟΙΣ ἈΠΟΣΤΟΛΟΙΣ in Rom 16:7," 740–41 and Bauckham, *Gospel Women*, 177. The genitive may not be significant since the nominative form is used in a similar construction that Burer also references: ἀνὴρ γένει καὶ ἀξίᾳ πρῶτος τῆς πόλεος [sic] ἡμῶν, ἐπίσημος δὲ καὶ ἐν τῷ ἔθνει (*TAM* 2.838.defg.3–4 [Burer references as *TAM* 2.1–3.838]).
169 Euripides, *Hipp.* 103.
170 Bauckham agrees (*Gospel Women*, 177).
171 Belleville, "Ἰουνιαν . . . ἐπίσημοι ἐν τοῖς ἀποστόλοις," 247 (Greek accent added). When Burer and Wallace sought to dismiss the relevance of two texts in their discussion, Belleville accused them of

sense to a comparative sense through the centuries. However, she does not seek to prove this change in meaning over time (only appealing to Bauckham, who also gives no evidence). In fact, Belleville's reliance upon Bauckham comes with a subtle shift. Belleville states definitively that Euripides was "at a time when ἐπίσημος had not yet acquired a comparative sense." But Bauckham was more cautious in his assessment that Euripides "*might have been* writing at a time when ἐπίσημος had not yet acquired a comparative sense."[172] Many of the texts cited by Burer and Wallace should be given closer consideration for the exclusive view.

There is a third category of texts that neither supports nor contradicts their thesis, but it leaves the question ambiguous. Harmonides said to his teacher Timotheus, "But the most important matter—the reason for my interest in the art of pipe-playing—I don't see how pipe-playing will ever bring me to it. I mean universal fame, being noticed in a crowd [καὶ τὸ ἐπίσημον εἶναι ἐν πλήθεσι], being pointed at, and on putting in an appearance anywhere having everyone turn towards me and say my name, 'That is Harmonides the outstanding piper.'"[173] The crowd is generic. On the one hand, one could say that Harmonides was different from the crowd (exclusive).[174] On the other hand, Harmonides wanted to be famous in the entire Greek world (possibly inclusive).[175] Another vague passage is Lucian's *On Salaried Posts in Great Houses* where he states, "If a whispering servant [ψιθυρὸς οἰκέτης] accuse you of being the only one who did not praise the mistress's page when he danced or played, there is no little risk in the thing. So you must raise your thirsty voice like a stranded frog, taking pains to be conspicuous among the claque [ὡς ἐπίσημος ἔσῃ ἐν τοῖς ἐπαινοῦσι] and to lead the chorus; and often when the others are silent you must independently let drop a well-considered word of praise that will convey great flattery."[176] Heath Curtis interprets this text as exclusive based upon Lucian's distinguishing Timocles from the other slaves.[177] Neither Epp nor Belleville interact with Curtis's article, where Curtis elaborates on the wider context and provides a different translation

---

"special pleading," yet Belleville does the same here with Euripides (in addition, the reasoning she gives for Burer and Wallace's dismissal of two texts did not accurately represent their argumentation).

172 Bauckham, *Gospel Women*, 178–79 (italics added for contrast).
173 Lucian, *Harmonides* 1.11–16.
174 So Burer and Wallace, "Was Junia Really an Apostle?" 89.
175 Lucian, *Harmonides* 1.3. Cf. Belleville, "Ἰουνιαν … ἐπίσημοι ἐν τοῖς ἀποστόλοις," 247, where she presses the Greek article to make her case instead of looking at the broader context.
176 Lucian, *Merc. cond.* 28.
177 Curtis, "A Female Apostle?" 439–40. Burer, "'ΕΠΙΣΗΜΟΙ ἘΝ ΤΟΙΣ ἈΠΟΣΤΟΛΟΙΣ in Rom 16:7," 743–44, agreed and changed his original position to Curtis's exclusive interpretation.

of the text.[178] Belleville interprets the passage as inclusive by focusing on all those who do the praising, though Belleville only offers a translation in defense.[179] The Lucian passage is not clear-cut if one is attempting to decide the relationship among Lucian's reader, Timocles, and the other slaves, as a look at the broader context will demonstrate. Lucian's work is an attempt to persuade Timocles to *not* enter into slavery.[180] The first lines of Lucian's text demonstrate the distinction, "'Where shall I make a beginning' my friend, 'and where make an end of relating' all that must be done and suffered by those who take salaried posts and are put on trial in the friendship of our wealthy men—if the name of friendship may be applied to that sort of slavery on their part?"[181] Lucian calls choosing this way of life "voluntary slavery" (ἐθελοδουλεία).[182] Here is how Lucian describes Timocles: "Since you were not brought up in the company of Slavery from your boyhood but made her acquaintance late and are getting your schooling from her at an advanced age, you will not be very successful or highly valuable to your master."[183] Lucian concludes, "The rest, my dear Timocles, is up to you; examine all the details with care and make up your mind whether it suits you to enter the pictured career [i.e., slavery] by these doors and be thrown out so disgracefully by that one opposite."[184] To equate Timocles with the other slaves in reality is incorrect. To equate Timocles with the other slaves within the story that Lucian was telling is debatable. Therefore, this text is ambiguous at best.

In light of the data from Burer and Wallace's work, I propose that Junia in Rom 16:7 cannot *definitively* be used to argue for a contradiction with 1 Cor 14:34. For any scholar to propose Junia's apostleship to be contrary to Paul's silencing of women, the burden of proof is on that writer to show the *certainty* of the inclusive view. Since Burer and Wallace have shown that at least some Greek texts prove the exclusive view exists with this construction, then certainty is not as likely. Neither the lexical meaning of ἐπίσημος nor the syntactical construction

---

178   Bauckham's work was published in the same year as Curtis's article, and so it is doubtful that Bauckham had access to it. But Epp and Belleville's work was published three years after Curtis's work.
179   Belleville, "Ἰουνιαν . . . ἐπίσημοι ἐν τοῖς ἀποστόλοις," 245.
180   Cf. A. M. Harmon, trans., *Lucian: On Salaried Posts in Great Houses*, LCL 130 (Cambridge: Harvard University Press, 1921), 3:411: "a Hogarthian sketch of the life led by educated Greeks who attached themselves to the households of great Roman lords—and ladies. Lucian feigns to be advising a young friend, whom he dubs Timocles (Master Ambitious), against such a career—a most effective stratagem, since by giving him a pretext for his criticism, it relieves him from all semblance of personal animus and even enables him to appear sympathetic toward the varlets while he dusts their jackets."
181   Lucian, *Merc. cond.* 1.
182   Lucian, *Merc. cond.* 5.
183   Lucian, *Merc. cond.* 23.
184   Lucian, *Merc. cond.* 42.

150 | *Paul, Women, and the Meaning of Silence*

of ἐν + dative prove or disprove the point. In the inscription about Opramoas the person is part of the nation due to the wider context. In Euripides we know that Aphrodite is not part of the mortals simply because of the meaning of "mortals" (i.e., because of the type of adjunct). There is nothing within Rom 16:7 itself that provides clues as to the inclusive versus the exclusive view. There are, however, several factors within the New Testament that cause the interpreter to lean towards the exclusive view: (1) Jesus chose twelve male apostles (Matt 10:1–4; Mark 3:13–19; Luke 6:12–16); (2) his choice was intentional (Mark 3:13; Luke 6:12–13); (3) the apostles, under God's guidance, chose another male to replace Judas, even though women were present (Acts 1:12–26); (4) in Romans the term ἀπόστολος is a technical term for Paul's apostleship (1:1; 11:13; cf. 1:5), just as the term is usually limited to a select group of individuals in the New Testament; (5) Paul referenced the wives of the other apostles, which implies that the other apostles were males (1 Cor 9:5); and (6) specific women are found in the New Testament as prophets (Acts 21:9), but no parallel reference is found concerning women apostles (if Rom 16:7 is found to be exclusive). In conclusion, I propose that ἐπίσημος plus ἐν plus the dative sometimes means exclusive and sometimes means inclusive. The wider context will determine the exclusive and inclusive view. Scholars who default to the inclusive view should not depend upon the lexical evidence itself or the Greek construction itself. Still, Burer and Wallace have provided a general framework that should not be ignored or easily dismissed. Romans 16:7 cannot be considered to contradict 1 Cor 14:34.

Euodia and Syntyche in Philippians 4:2–3

Paul and Timothy wrote to the church in Philippi, "I urge Euodia and I urge Syntyche to agree in the Lord. Yes, I also ask you, true comrade, support those who joined me in the gospel with both Clement and the rest of my fellow-workers, whose names are in the book of life" (Phil 4:2–3). Is Paul's silencing of women in the church consistent with his reference to Euodia and Syntyche? It should be noted that agreeing in the Lord is a theme in Philippians that applied to everyone in the local church. William Varner states, "The dominance of φρονέω language (1:7; 2:2, 5; 3:15, 19; 4:10) continues to convey the main theme of the letter."[185] Paul referred to the church generally, "Only live worthy of the gospel of Christ

---

185 William Varner, *Philippians: A Handbook on the Greek Text*, BHGNT (Waco, TX: Baylor University Press, 2016), 92.

in order that, whether I come and see you [ὑμᾶς] or being absent I hear about you, that you stand together in the faith of the gospel with one spirit, one mind" (Phil 1:27). Again he states, "Fulfill my joy that you agree, having the same love, united in spirit, having one mind" (2:2), and "think this way among yourselves which also was in Christ Jesus" (2:5). When Paul referred to the righteousness through faith in Christ and the power of his resurrection, he urged, "Therefore, whoever is mature, let us think this way, and if anyone thinks differently, God will also reveal this way to you" (3:15; cf. 3:9–10, 14). In light of several calls to agree together in the Philippian church, Paul calling for Euodia and Syntyche to agree together is not in itself evidence of being pastors or overseers or speaking in every situation of worship. The relationship of Phil 4:3 to 4:2 is not entirely clear. Paul addresses Euodia and Syntyche in Phil 4:2 and then addresses an unnamed individual in Phil 4:3 (καὶ σέ, γνήσιε σύζυγε).

Pheme Perkins, in her comments on 1 Cor 14:33b–36, writes, "The protests of modern readers that ... the women involved in Paul's wider missionary efforts must have instructed males (Phil. 4:2–3; Rom. 16:1–3) challenge those twenty-first-century churches that still silence women."[186] The contrast that Perkins attempts to make does not follow from Phil 4:2–3 or Rom 16:1–3. The reference to Euodia and Syntyche as those who "instructed males" is not in the passage of Phil 4:2–3. Cross-referencing Phil 4:2–3 and Rom 16:1–3 is part of a larger problem in hermeneutics. Scholars regularly cross-reference a text in order to prove a point in a different text. However, the argumentation sometimes ignores the actual wording in one of the passages and omits debates within the cross-referenced text. Perkins cannot appeal to Phil 4:2–3 in order to prove that women taught males because the cross-referenced text in Philippians does not state this point.

Scholars are divided on the role Euodia and Syntyche played in the church. Richard R. Melick rightly comments, "Nothing is known about these women or the dispute between them. Many scholars have attempted to identify them, but the conclusions are all conjecture, and the best course of action is to stay within the bounds of Scripture."[187] Likewise, Paul A. Holloway says, "We know nothing of them or of their disagreement except what Paul writes here."[188] Other scholars go beyond the evidence and argue that Euodia and Syntyche were church leaders

---

186 Pheme Perkins, *First Corinthians*, Paideia Commentaries on the New Testament (Grand Rapids: Baker Academic, 2012), 164–65.
187 Richard R. Melick, Jr., *Philippians, Colossians, Philemon*, NAC 32 (Nashville: Broadman, 1991), 146.
188 Paul A. Holloway, *Philippians: A Commentary*, Hermeneia (Minneapolis: Fortress, 2017), 182.

in Philippi. Strikingly, Bonnie Thurston and Judith Ryan write, "We do not know who Euodia and Syntyche were. Clearly they were women leaders in the church in Philippi, a church that was founded among women (see Acts 16) and that, historically, had prominent women leaders."[189] The juxtaposition of these two statements by Thurston and Ryan show an undefined jump from a lack of knowledge to a certainty that the women were church leaders. David Garland's evidence for their leadership in the church is from Paul's respect for the women.[190] However, Paul respected other women in the NT who did not necessarily hold a church office (e.g., the named women in Romans 16). Fee argues that overseers and deacons are mentioned in Phil 1:1 because "it seems more likely to be related to 4:2–3, where Euodia and Syntyche, who are most likely to be reckoned among these leaders, apparently are not in full accord with each other."[191] Since Fee does not provide a link between the overseers and deacons and Phil 4:2–3, then there is no way to prove or disprove his assertion. Some writers caution against making Euodia and Syntyche the main issue of the letter.[192] Philippians 4:2–3 cannot be interpreted as contradicting 1 Cor 14:34–35.

Nympha in Colossians 4:15

The final passage to be considered is Colossians 4:15 and Paul's reference to Nympha. Paul and Timothy wrote to the Christians in Colossae, "Greet the brothers in Laodicea and Nympha and the church in her home" (Col 4:15). Clearly there was some type of important role Nympha played in regard to a church meeting in her home. What the role was is not made explicit. It is worth noting that the Greek manuscripts of Col 4:15 are divided on two points. (1) The name Nympha is accented as the feminine Νύμφαν in B² 075 0278 6 81 1241ˢ 1739ᶜ 1881. It is accented as the masculine Νυμφᾶν in D² K L 104 326 365 630 1175 1505 1739* 2464 𝔐. Νυμφαν is without any accent in ℵ A B* C D* F G P Ψ 048 33. (2) The personal, possessive pronoun αὐτός is feminine singular (αὐτῆς)

---

189 Bonnie B. Thurston and Judith M. Ryan, *Philippians and Philemon*, SP 10 (Collegeville, MN: Liturgical, 2005), 140.
190 David E. Garland, "Philippians," in *The Expositor's Bible Commentary*, rev. ed., ed. Tremper Longman III and David E. Garland (Grand Rapids: Zondervan, 2006), 251.
191 Fee, *Paul's Letter to the Philippians*, 69; cf. 392 n. 34. Moisés Silva thinks the women were church leaders but does not know "the nature of their leadership" (*Philippians*, 2nd ed., BECNT [Grand Rapids: Baker Academic, 2005], 192).
192 E.g., John Reumann, *Philippians: A New Translation with Introduction and Commentary*, AB (New Haven: Yale University Press, 2008), 632–33.

in B 0278 6 1739 1881. It is masculine singular (αὐτοῦ) in D F G K L Ψ 365 630 1241ˢ 1505 𝔐. It is plural (αὐτῶν) in ℵ A C P 075 33 81 104 326 1175 2464. Bruce Metzger sums up the issue:

> Νυμφαν can be accented Νύμφαν, from the feminine nominative Νύμφα ("Nympha"), or Νυμφᾶν, from the masculine nominative Νυμφᾶς ("Nymphas"). The uncertainty of the gender of the name led to variation in the following possessive pronoun between αὐτῆς and αὐτοῦ. On the basis chiefly of the weight of B 6 424ᶜ 1739 1877 1881 syr^(h, palms) cop^(sa) Origen, the Committee preferred Νύμφαν ... αὐτῆς. The reading with αὐτῶν arose when copyists included ἀδελφούς in the reference.[193]

If one accepts the external evidence argument of Metzger, then the gender is feminine. Those who take a different text-critical approach than Metzger may find the gender to be masculine. Was it more likely that a scribe would change the pronoun from male to female, or female to male? Philip Comfort thinks that "it is far more likely that the pronoun 'her' was changed to 'his' than vice versa because it would be perceived that a man, not a woman, hosted the church."[194] Comfort does not provide evidence for this assertion, but he actually goes on to state that women did host churches.[195] Scholars should at least let readers know that the gender of Nympha is debatable in the textual tradition (though the comments below will assume Nympha was female).[196]

Capper states, "Of Nympha of Laodicea we know only that she entertained a church in her home (Col 4:15), but nothing in Paul's mention of her suggests any limitation of her role in this context."[197] The way Capper phrases his argument is similar to an argument from silence. Capper's admittance of the limited knowledge of Nympha stands in contrast to his earlier claim that "Phoebe, Lydia and Nympha are

---

193 Metzger, *A Textual Commentary on the Greek New Testament*, 560.
194 Philip W. Comfort, *New Testament Text and Translation Commentary: Commentary on the Variant Readings of the Ancient New Testament Manuscripts and How They Relate to the Major English Translations* (Carol Stream, IL: Tyndale House, 2008), 638.
195 Comfort, *New Testament Text and Translation Commentary*, 638. The position of Ulrich Huttner is ambiguous. On the one hand Huttner frames the external evidence in a way that leaves the reader thinking Nympha was male, but on the other hand Huttner discusses the later changing of the name from female to male (*Early Christianity in the Lycus Valley*, trans. David Green, ECAM 1 [Leiden: Brill, 2013], 95–96).
196 For additional reference to the gender of the name, see e.g., Eduard Lohse, *Colossians and Philemon: A Commentary on the Epistles to the Colossians and to Philemon*, trans. William R. Poehlmann and Robert J. Karris, Hermeneia (Philadelphia: Fortress, 1971), 174; and N. T. Wright, *The Epistles of Paul to the Colossians and to Philemon: An Introduction and Commentary*, TNTC 12 (Grand Rapids: Eerdmans, 2008), 163.
197 Capper, "To Keep Silent, Part I," 131.

154 | *Paul, Women, and the Meaning of Silence*

clearly identifiable as part of this class of householder-overseers."[198] How is Nympha "clearly identifiable" as an overseer? Capper does not provide evidence.

Some authors correctly admit that the NT provides limited knowledge about Nympha and her role.[199] Others still try to marshal evidence to prove Nympha was a church leader. On the one hand, Scot McKnight writes, "We know little about Nympha other than that she hosted a house church or that the church in Laodicea met in her home."[200] On the other hand, he writes,

> She must have been the household manager and a woman of means, and because she alone is mentioned, we can infer that she probably led that house church as an expression of the church of that city (like Lydia in Acts 16:11–40). If evidence were needed, it is worth noting that the "church" is not the building or the house but, as a gathering and fellowship of followers of Jesus, meets in a house. This text witnesses, at least indirectly, to the leadership of women, and in some ways creates tension with the household regulation's male-female ordering ([Col] 3:18–4:1).[201]

There are a number of issues in how McKnight argues. He speculates on Nympha's role despite his initial admission that "we know little." His reasoning of Nympha being mentioned alone ignores other possible reasons, such as being a widow. His equating of "evidence" with a definition of a house church does not itself prove who ("probably") led that church. He refers to this passage "indirectly" witnessing to women leaders, which is not the evidence needed to overturn other clear passages of Scripture on women in the church. He gives a vague reference to the passage "in some ways" creating tension. What ways? His reference to the tension with Col 3:18–4:1 would be due to wives submitting to their husbands, but he does not elaborate on his balancing of the different passages. Why not allow the clear passage of Col 3:18–4:1 inform the brief reference in Col 4:15? The brief reference to Nympha does not demand a church leadership position, just as in Acts 16 with Lydia. Paul mentions other names in his letter, and every

---

198   Capper, "To Keep Silent, Part I," 128.
199   Melick, Jr. *Philippians, Colossians, Philemon*, 332; David W. Pao, *Colossians and Philemon*, ZECNT (Grand Rapids: Zondervan, 2012), 319–20.
200   Scot McKnight, *The Letter to the Colossians*, NICNT (Grand Rapids: Eerdmans, 2018), 394–95.
201   McKnight, *The Letter to the Colossians*, 395. There are other writers who claim that Nympha was a church leader but do not provide the reasoning like McKight does for his position. See Robert W. Wall, *Colossians and Philemon*, IVP New Testament Commentary (Downers Grove, IL: InterVarsity Press, 1993), 174; R. McL. Wilson, *Colossians and Philemon: A Critical and Exegetical Commentary*, ICC (London: T&T Clark, 2005), 305; and James D. G. Dunn, *The Epistles to the Colossians and to Philemon: A Commentary on the Greek Text*, NIGTC (Grand Rapids: Eerdmans, 1996), 285.

name mentioned would not have necessarily been a church leader. For instance, Epaphras is mentioned as a teacher in Col 1:7 (καθὼς ἐμάθετε ἀπὸ Ἐπαφρᾶ). Both Onesimus and Epaphras are referred to as "from you [Colossians]" (ἐξ ὑμῶν; 4:9, 12). Finally, Archippus is mentioned in closing about his ministry (διακονία) in Col 4:17. In light of the brief reference to Nympha, there is no clear evidence that her role might contradict a specific silence of women in 1 Cor 14:34.

Conclusion

Some writers claim that Paul would not have silenced women in the church in 1 Cor 14:34–35 because this command would have contradicted his other statements about women and his regular practice of working with women in ministry. Scholars regularly refer to a few specific New Testament passages regarding women in order to make this claim. The passages often cited are Gal 3:28; 1 Tim 2:9–14; Acts 16:11–15, 40; Rom 16:1–7 (with Acts 18:24–28); Phil 4:2–3; and Col 4:15.

Paul writes in Gal 3:28, "There is neither Jew nor Gentile, there is neither slave nor free, there is not male and female, for you all are one in Christ Jesus." Does this principle contradict the silence of women in 1 Cor 14:34? It has been argued above that the original context of Gal 3:28 is salvation, and therefore, Paul does not contradict himself. In addition, certain views of Gal 3:28 were critiqued for methodological consistency. If Gal 3:28 can make gender obsolete in regard to ministry, why not also for the moral question of homosexuality? Paul's other key reference to men and women is in 1 Tim 2:8–15. In this study, the focus was placed upon Paul's silencing of women in 1 Tim 2:11–12. There is some overlap in meaning between ἡσυχία in 1 Tim 2:11–12 and σιγάω in 1 Cor 14:34. Both Greek terms can mean selective silence in some contexts. The comparison of 1 Tim 2:11–12 and 1 Cor 14:34 sees consistency of women's selective silence in light of male authority in the church.

The remaining New Testament passages (Acts 16:11–15, 40; 18:24–28; Rom 16:1–7; Phil 4:2–3; Col 4:15) include named women in the churches who served in various capacities. However, none of the passages refer to a woman exercising authority over a man in any church. Each passage's context was considered to discover the original meaning. This method brought clarity to generalized cross-references about women in the churches for the scholarly debates of 1 Cor 14:34. Scholars sometimes state that women exercised their gifts in church leadership positions without proving their claims exegetically in each passage. None of the

156 | *Paul, Women, and the Meaning of Silence*

New Testament passages show women in the position of an elder or apostle. Therefore, Paul is theologically consistent in commanding women to be silent during the judgment of prophecy in 1 Cor 14:34. Paul's own principles and practice were consistent throughout his writings. He was also consistent in his practice of working with women in the advancement of the gospel. Paul's letters have also shown the many crucial ways women served the church even as they exemplified a submissive spirit. Scholars should no longer appeal to the broader theological context of the New Testament in order to diminish the original meaning of 1 Cor 14:34–35 and its applicability today.

General Conclusion

Paul instructed God's church in Corinth, "Women in the churches are to be silent [σιγάτωσαν], for it is not permit for them to speak, but to be in submission, just as also the law says. And if they want to learn anything, let them ask their own husbands at home, for it is shameful for a woman to speak in church" (1 Cor 14:34–35). This study has argued that Paul's intended meaning in 1 Cor 14:34–35 is consistent with the context of 1 Corinthians and the rest of Pauline theology and practice. Literary, historical, and theological contexts have been examined in order to demonstrate consistency in Paul's silence of women in the church. Some scholars have argued that 1 Cor 14:34–35 is inconsistent with either Paul or the rest of the New Testament. The charge of inconsistency has included a contradiction with women praying and prophesying in 1 Cor 11:5, the gifting of the church in 1 Cor 14:26, or the role of the Spirit and spiritual gifts in 1 Cor 12–14. Paul's reference to women in his other letters and the appeal to the law in 1 Cor 14:34 are also used to claim contradiction. Some of the proposed solutions to the perceived inconsistency include the interpolation theory, a reference to a Corinthian slogan, a reference to married women only, or a limited application to Corinthian women or women in the broader Greco-Roman world.

Summary

The literary context was examined first. Claims of contradiction often assume a definition of silence (σιγάω). The range of usage for σιγάω can be defined based upon the over 5,700 uses of the term in Greek literature. This study has narrowed the data down to occurrences between 5 BC to AD 1. The range of σιγάω includes absolute silence, temporary silence (specific silence), secret/conceal,

The Theological Context: Consistency within Pauline Theology and Practice | 157

proverbial silence, silence of nature, and submission. The vast majority (75.9%) of cases for σιγάω refer to a temporary silence for a specific instance (see the Appendix). The definition of silence in 1 Cor 14:34 was reexamined, especially in light of the previous, specific, uses of silence in 1 Cor 14:28 and 14:30. Scholars who claimed the text of 1 Cor 14:34–35 contradicts Paul's theology and practice usually assumed σιγάω is defined as absolute silence. Absolute silence could, then, be used to contradict passages like women praying and prophesying in 1 Cor 11:5. Some scholars relied upon Greek lexicons, but the lexicons themselves needed to be regularly reexamined, as with any Greek term. A reexamination of the literary context of 1 Corinthians 11–14 with a specific definition of σιγάω demonstrated some of the weaknesses of other theories. When each context of each passage was closely examined, 1 Cor 14:34–35 was seen to be in line with other passages throughout Paul's first letter to the Corinthians. For example, Paul allowed women to pray and prophesy in 1 Cor 11:5, but he silenced women in the judging of men's prophecies in 1 Cor 14:34–35.

The interpolation theory should no longer be a sure dogma of scholarship because silence can no longer be assumed to be absolute. Since every extant Greek manuscript that includes 1 Corinthians 14 includes 1 Cor 14:34–35, then the interpolation theory must be abandoned. The theory that Paul was quoting the Corinthians in 1 Cor 14:34–35 (or a variant thereof) was also shown to be unconvincing. This study looked at slogans throughout the first letter to the Corinthians. Although Paul did cite slogans of the Corinthians in some contexts (e.g., 1 Cor 1:12; 3:4; 15:12), the text of 1 Cor 14:34–35 does not have the same textual clues.

Claiming that women could not be silenced in any manner in the church because the Spirit gifts both men and women assumes that Paul could never at any time have silenced women in the church. However, the same letter that silenced women and men is the same letter that speaks regularly of the Spirit's gifting. If the logic of some scholars were correct in appealing to the Spirit, then Paul could never, at any time, have silenced women. When scholars appealed to the work of the Spirit in order to reinterpret the meaning of silence, they usually assumed the definition of silence to be absolute. Furthermore, others (e.g., in queer studies) also claimed that they have the right interpretation simply because they refer to the work of the Spirit. Therefore, appeal to the Spirit in itself does not prove one's interpretation because many different interpreters claim to be led by the Spirit.

The examination of the historical context began by questioning vague and generic references to ancient culture. Scholars sometimes made brief and general references to the Greco-Roman culture in order to explain a biblical passage. A closer look at the ancient world causes the reader to ask, "Which culture?" Ancient cultures, like modern cultures, were mixed and diverse. Even specific references to women's education and public speaking were more complicated upon closer inspection. Sweeping assertions about women's education is not the reason for Paul's words to silence women given both the complex ancient context of education and Paul's own reason for his instructions (i.e., the law). It has been shown that Paul intended his words to move beyond Corinth, and so interpretations that limit meaning and application to Corinth alone are insufficient. Paul rooted his instructions in the law, presumably from Genesis 1–2, and so the debate must be decided on the basis of a theology of the law. This study has also shown that Paul was consistent not only with his use of silence but also with his use of the law.

The examination of the theological context sought to prove consistency within Pauline theology and practice. By examining each individual context, Paul's teaching about women in 1 Cor 14:34–35 was shown to cohere with his teaching about male and female in Gal 3:28. Since the contexts between Galatians and 1 Corinthians addressed different issues, there is no reason to think these two texts are inconsistent regarding women's freedom and women's specific silence. In contrast to Gal 3:28, the context of 1 Tim 2:11–12 is similar to the context of 1 Cor 14:34–35. A study of silence in both passages revealed significant overlap. Other passages that reference women, such as Romans 16, showed no mention of a woman in the position of church elder or exercising authority over men. The specific type of silencing that Paul communicates in 1 Cor 14:34–35 could easily have applied to women such as Lydia, Nympha, Phoebe, Junia, and the rest. These women served in various capacities for the good of the church, but none of them are explicitly mentioned as exercising authority over men. Paul was also consistent in his practice within the church. In 1 Cor 14:26–40, Paul addressed order in the church regarding speaking gifts. He began with the problem of everyone speaking in church, and he reminded the Corinthians of the edification principle (1 Cor 14:26). Paul explained selective silence in regard to tongues and prophecies (14:27–30), which included the evaluation of prophets (14:29). While everyone—men and women—may prophesy in turn, the evaluation process must also include the principle of submission (14:31–32). These instructions are rooted in a knowledge of God as the God of peace, just as he is in every church (14:33). Paul then silenced women regarding the evaluation of prophecies (14:34). The Corinthians could easily have interpreted σιγάω as selective silence in light of (1) the typical Greek usage; (2) the pervasive language of evaluation throughout 1 Cor 14:26–40; and (3) the instructions of Paul elsewhere on women, including

1 Cor 11:5. Paul's reference not to permit the women to speak referred to some type of speaking gift, as λαλέω does in 1 Cor 14:27–29, 39. Interpreters sometimes assumed the reference to the law in 1 Cor 14:34 referred directly to silence; however, the nearest reference to the law is submission. This observation shows that the speaking gifts in Corinth were ultimately connected to the question of submission within the local assembly and as taught in the Old Testament law (i.e., Genesis 1–2). Wayne Grudem, then, explains Paul's teaching on asking their husbands at home (1 Cor 14:35): "Then such questioning could be used as a platform for expressing in none-too-veiled form the very criticisms Paul forbids. Paul anticipates this possible evasion and writes, 'If there is anything they desire to know, let them ask their husbands at home. For it is shameful for a woman to speak [that is, question prophecies] in church.'"[202] Paul viewed the Corinthian church as under the same authority and teaching as other churches (1 Cor 14:36). This reminder continued the theme of "all the churches" (14:33–34). Paul concluded with a call to recognize the truth of what he says and to speak in church in an orderly manner (14:37–40).

Implications

This study has implications for both scholarship and the church. The benefit for scholarship includes support for Pauline authorship and the need to reexamine lexicography within Pauline debates. A contextual reading of σιγάω and other Pauline references to women are consistent with Pauline authorship in 1 Cor 14:34–35. The goal of this study was not to prove Pauline authorship but to prove Pauline consistency. However, Pauline consistency is part of the broader discussion on Pauline authorship. Scholars should no longer assume Paul did not write 1 Cor 14:34–35 on the basis of inconsistency alone. Scholars who do assert that 1 Cor 14:34–35 is inconsistent with the rest of Paul must prove their assertion using a contextual definition of σιγάω based upon all Greek data. As has been shown above, many scholars simply assume a definition of σιγάω instead of proving a definition. The assumptions over definition in 1 Corinthians literature motivated a reexamination of lexical data. Therefore, lexicography itself needs to be continually questioned within debates over Paul's intended meaning. For instance, more work remains to be done on ἡσυχία and its cognates in regard to Greek literature. With a large quantity of primary source data, scholars should

---

202 Wayne Grudem, "Prophecy—Yes, But Teaching—No: Paul's Consistent Advocacy of Women's Participation without Governing Authority," *JETS* 30 (1987): 22.

no longer rely only on lexicons if the debate centers around the definition of the term itself. This point of reliance upon lexicons is especially crucial in commentary writing. If a commentator is making a judgment on a debate, but the debate is over a term that has not been sufficiently examined by anyone, then judgment should be suspended. This study has sought to provide enough data on σιγάω so that readers can make informed judgments of definition and meaning (see the Appendix). Other words within Pauline texts, such as ἡσυχία, still need more lengthy treatments. Some debates that appear to be settled and closed should always be reopened if primary source data has not yet been fully considered.

This study is helpful for the church in regard to consistently applying Paul's words to women today. The church can benefit by seeking a consistent method of interpretation even on highly debated topics such as the role of women in the church. The method used here was to take standard hermeneutical principles and apply them to the highly debated text of 1 Cor 14:34–35. The church may be able to move towards unity when discussing consistent methods of interpretation. The church should be able to find a consistent message for women in the church today based upon God's word given through Paul to the ancient church in 1 Cor 14:34–35. This study has shown that Paul's words to women—then and now—are neither overly restrictive nor completely permissive. Paul intended a specific silence in the church service within the context of women using their spiritual gifts. This book also has implications for interpreters to carefully cross-reference other Bible passages in order to avoid wrong application.

This study has examined the literary, historical, and theological context of silence in Paul's instructions for women in the church. The research has sought to demonstrate consistency in Pauline theology and practice. God's word remains the same.

Appendix: ΣΙΓΑΩ in Greek Literature

There are more than 5,700 occurrences of σιγάω in Greek literature (as of May, 2019). The references and dates come from the TLG (most fragments not included).[1] The Appendix has been limited to when σιγάω is found approximately 5 BC–AD 1.[2] The Appendix below will include the reference (centered) with

---

1. It is doubtful that citing every fragment would dramatically change the current conclusions. While some fragments are cited below, fragments referenced by the TLG but not included in this Appendix include the following authors: Euripides, Ion, Cratinus, Epicharmus, Isocrates, Plato, Gorgias, Xenocrates, Speusippus, Menander, Zeno, Cleanthes, Megasthenes, Timon, Erasistratus, Bion, Chrysippus, Apollodorus, Philodemus, Philoxenus, Dorotheus, and Apion.
2. The TLG occasionally lists a work within this time period but upon closer review does not appear to fit the specific time-frame. The TLG lists Clemens *Homiliae* and *Pseudo-Clementina* as first century sources. However, it is unlikely that these documents are that early. See, e.g., Massimo Fusillo, "Pseudo-Clementine Literature," *BNP* 12:114–15, who lists the *Homiliae* as fourth century AD from Syria. Also, the dating of the *Life of Aesop* is uncertain (σιγάω is in Vita G). Only two of the various views will be mentioned here. B. E. Perry, *Studies in the Text History of the Life and Fables of Aesop*, Philological Monographs 7 (Haverford, PA: The American Philological Association, 1936), 25, writes, "I think it probable, however, in view of the general character of the book, that the archetype of which we have been speaking was composed sometime in the second century after Christ." Cf. Jeremy B. Lefkowitz, "Ugliness and Value in the *Life of Aesop*," in *KAKOS: Badness and Anti-Value in Classical Antiquity*, ed. Ineke Sluiter and Ralph M. Rosen, Mnemosyne Supplements: Monographs on Greek and Roman Language and Literature 307 (Leiden: Brill, 2008), 62 n. 12. By contrast Francisco R. Adrados, "The 'Life of Aesop' and the Origins of Novel in Antiquity," *Quaderni Urbinati di Cultura Classica* 1 (1979): 98, thinks it was written in the first century. The Greek text can be found in Ben Edwin Perry,

the symbol key showing my interpretation of the quotation. Then the English translation will be given quotation marks in order to allow the reader to confirm my interpretation. My own comments about the context of some quotations will come last and marked off by the word "comment." The inflected Greek term will be in brackets. Unless otherwise noted, English translations and references are from the Loeb Classical Library. Brackets found in any LCL translation are maintained in the quoted text to show that it is textually suspect.

Symbol Key:

AS = Always Silent/Absolute Silence
SS = Sometimes Silent/Silent in a Specific Instance
SE = Secret/Conceal
SU = Submission
P = Proverbial Statement
D = Descriptive of nature or poetry
N/A = Not applicable due to no context provided

[SS] Thucydides *History* (5 BC) 8.66.2.2–6

"And no search was made for those who did the deed, nor if they were suspected was any legal prosecution held; on the contrary, the populace kept quiet and were in such consternation that he who did not suffer any violence, even though he never said a word [σιγῴη], counted that a gain."

Comment: They kept quiet on any change to the government or the death of one who spoke against the conspiracy. In other words, silent in this particular case. The populace obviously spoke of other matters.

[P] Euripides *Fragments* (5 BC) Fragment 29

"A thinking man is better silent [σιγᾶν] than when fallen into company. I wish I may be neither friend nor companion to the man who believes his thoughts are self-sufficient while deeming his friends slaves."

Comment: Fragments are like proverbs where there is a limited context in which to read the statements.

[P] Euripides *Fragments* (5 BC) Fragment 126

"You do not speak [σιγᾷς]? But silence is a poor interpreter of words."

ed., *Aesopica: A Series of Texts Relating to Aesop or Ascribed to Him or Closely Connected with the Literary Tradition that Bears His Name* (Urbana: The University of Illinois Press, 1952), 1:42–43, 63.

[P] Euripides *Fragments* (5 BC) Fragment 334

"I've stood beside many a man, and been truly indignant at any who, though honourable, was like base men in coming out for a contest of wild words. What proved past hearing or bearing, however, was listening in silence [σιγᾶν] to dreadful abuse from baser men."

Comment: Some of Euripides's proverbs can be taken as sometimes silent in a particular case, such as in Fragment 334.

[P] Euripides *Fragments* (5 BC) Fragment 410

"A wife should always be served by such a woman as will not be silent [σιγήσεται] over what is right, but who hates what is shameful and keeps it before the eyes."

[SE] Euripides *Fragments* (5 BC) Fragment 411

"And let no one know these things which ought to be kept quiet [σιγᾶσθαι]. Just as one could set fire to the slopes of Ida from a small torch, so from one's word to a single man all citizens could find out (what one ought to conceal)."

[SS] Euripides *Fragments* (5 BC) Fragment 413

"I know all that one well-born should, to keep silent [σιγᾶν] where necessary and to speak where safe, and to see what is necessary and not to see what is unfitting . . . and to control appetite; for though I am in the midst of troubles, I have been schooled in freeborn ways."

Comment: This text is a very clear example of sometimes silent and speaking at other times. The relevant phrase is σιγᾶν θ' ὅπου δεῖ.

[P] Euripides *Fragments* (5 BC) Fragment 690

"[Y]our very appearance, though you are silent [σιγῶντος], declares that you would not be obedient, but would prefer giving instructions to being instructed."

[AS] Euripides *Fragments* (5 BC) Fragment 706

"Agamemnon, not even if someone with an axe in his hands were about to strike it on my neck, shall I keep silent [σιγήσομαι]; for I have a just reply to make."

[SE] Euripides *Fragments* (5 BC) Fragment 781 lines 11–13

"O Helios with your beautiful light, you have destroyed me and Phaethon here! You are rightly called Apollo among men, where any knows the unspoken meaning [σιγῶντ'] of gods' names!"

[SS] Euripides *Fragments* (5 BC) Fragment 1008

"Why are you silent [σιγᾷς]? You've not committed some bloodshed?"

[D] Euripides *Phaethon* (5 BC) Lines 81–84

"(Escort us,) breeze, our mistress, on a calm voyage with quiet [σιγώντων] winds (towards) our dear (children) and wives'; and the canvas comes close to the forestay's middle."

Comment: Sailors describe the winds as silent.

[SS] Euripides *Cyclops* (5 BC) Line 82

"Silence [σιγήσατ'], my sons! Order your attendants to drive the flocks into the rocky cave!"

Comment: Silence may have the nuance of submission here from Silenus to the chorus. In any case, Silenus is commanding them to simultaneously be silent and speak ("order your attendants").

[SS] Euripides *Cyclops* (5 BC) Line 476

"Then hold your tongue [σιγᾶτέ]—you now know my plan— and when I give the word, do what the master builder tells you."

Comment: Odysseus says to the chorus leader to be silent for a certain duration of time.

[SS] Euripides *Cyclops* (5 BC) Line 488

"Hush [σίγα]! Hush [σίγα]! For now the Cyclops, drunk and making graceless melody, comes forth from the rocky cave, a singer who is inept and who shall pay dearly."

Comment: The chorus leader says this statement to himself because just previous to this statement there is a stage direction note about "singing within."[3] So the chorus leader can command himself to be silent for a short duration of time.

[SS] Euripides *Cyclops* (5 BC) Line 568

"See, I'm pouring. Just be quiet [σίγα]."

---

3   David Kovacs, ed., *Euripides: Cyclops*, LCL 12 (Cambridge: Harvard University Press, 1994), 1:115.

Comment: Odysseus says this statement to Cyclops while giving him a drink. They continue to have a conversation.

[SS] Euripides *Cyclops* (5 BC) Line 624

"Silence [σιγᾶτε], you savages, for heaven's sake quiet! Let your lips be shut fast! I forbid anyone even to breath or to blink or to clear his throat lest the monster wake up before the Cyclops' eye can have its contest with the fire."

Comment: The specific moment is intended as absolute silence but not in the broader context.

[SS] Euripides *Cyclops* (5 BC) Line 629

"We hold our peace [σιγῶμεν], gulping down the air with our mouths."

Comment: The chorus leader responds to Odysseus's request. The chorus leader will later speak again.

[SS] Euripides *Alcestis* (5 BC) Lines 77–78

"What means this stillness before the palace? Why is the house of Admetus wrapped in silence [σεσίγηται]?"

Comment: The silent house is due to no mourners and the circumstance for Alcestis. Though servants come later to weep. Absolute silence during a specific moment.

[SS] Euripides *Alcestis* (5 BC) Lines 703–05

"Hold your tongue [σίγα]! Consider that if you love life, so do all men. If you continue to insult me, you shall hear reproaches many and true."

Comment: Pheres, the father of Admetus, was silencing his son regarding Admetus's insults to him.

[SS] Euripides *Alcestis* (5 BC) Lines 1008–1010

"One should speak frankly to a friend, Admetus, and not silently [σιγῶντ'] store up reproaches in the heart."

Comment: Silently storing up is the opposite here of the same person speaking frankly.

166 | *Appendix*

[SS] Euripides *Alcestis* (5 BC) Line 1088

"Hush [σίγησον]! What a shocking thing you have said! I should never have thought it of you."

Comment: Admetus silences Heracles's previous sentence that he disagrees with.

[SS] Euripides *Medea* (5 BC) Lines 80–81

"But you, hold your peace (since it is not the right time for your mistress to know this) and say nothing [σίγα] of this tale."

[SE] Euripides *Medea* (5 BC) Lines 259–263

"And so I shall ask this much from you as a favor: if I find any means or contrivance to punish my husband for these wrongs [and the bride's father and the bride], keep my secret [σιγᾶν]."

[SS] Euripides *Medea* (5 BC) Lines 314–15

"For although I have been wronged, I will hold my peace [σιγησόμεσθα], yielding to my superiors."

Comment: Medea is speaking to Creon, king of Corinth. She is silent on going into exile, but spoke clearly on other matters. See *Medea* Line 338.

[SS] Euripides *Children of Heracles* (5 BC) Lines 951–52

"I say nothing [σιγῶ] of all the other troubles you contrived for him, for my tale would become too long."

Comment: Alcmene is silent on certain troubles but speaks otherwise.

[SS] Euripides *Hippolytus* (5 BC) Line 273

"Tis all one: on all these questions she is mute [σιγᾷ]."

Comment: Phaedra is silent here on what is wrong with her.

[AS] Euripides *Hippolytus* (5 BC) Lines 293–300

"If your malady is one of those that are unmentionable, here are women to help set it to rights. If your misfortune may be spoken of to men, speak so that the thing may be revealed to doctors. (*Phaedra is silent.*) Well, why are you silent [σιγᾷς]? You ought not to be silent [σιγᾶν], child, but should either refute me if I have said something amiss or agree with what has been said aright. (*She remains silent.*) Say something!"

Comment: Phaedra is absolutely silent in the immediate context. In the broader context, she speaks.

[SS] Euripides *Hippolytus* (5 BC) Lines 311–12

"You are killing me, Nurse, and I beg you by the gods never to say [σιγᾶν] anything of this man again!"

Comment: Phaedra wants the Nurse to be silent regarding Hippolytus.

[SS] Euripides *Hippolytus* (5 BC) Line 336

"I'll be silent [σιγῶμ']. Henceforth it is your turn to speak."

Comment: After Phaedra answers, the nurse once again speaks and continues the dialogue.

[SE] Euripides *Hippolytus* (5 BC) Lines 391–94

"I shall also tell you the way my thoughts went. When love wounded me, I considered how I might best bear it. My starting point was this, to conceal my malady in silence [σιγᾶν]."

[SS] Euripides *Hippolytus* (5 BC) Line 565

"Silence [σιγήσατ'], women! I am done for!"

Comment: Phaedra calls for silence for the moment so that she can hear what is being said through the door.

[SS] Euripides *Hippolytus* (5 BC) Line 568

"I hold my peace [σιγῶ]. But what you say bodes ill."

Comment: The chorus leader is silent while Phaedra listens through the door. The chorus continues to speak afterwards.

[SS] Euripides *Hippolytus* (5 BC) Line 603

"Silence [σίγησον], my son, before someone hears your shout!"

Comment: The nurse wants Hippolytus to be silent about what he has just heard.

[SS] Euripides *Hippolytus* (5 BC) Line 604

"I have heard dread things: I cannot now be silent [σιγήσομαι]."

Comment: Hippolytus speaks about not being silent specifically on what he has just heard.

[SS] Euripides *Hippolytus* (5 BC) Lines 685–86

"Did I not warn you—did I not guess your purpose—to say nothing [σιγᾶν] of the things now causing me disgrace?"

Comment: Phaedra specifies the parts she is silent on.

[SS] Euripides *Hippolytus* (5 BC) Lines 909–11

"What has happened to her? How did she die? Father, I want to learn this from you. What, silent [σιγᾷς]? Silence is no use in misfortune."

Comment: Hippolytus wonders at his father's silence on the occasion of his wife's death.

[SS] Euripides *Hippolytus* (5 BC) Lines 1428–30

"The practice skill of poetry sung by maidens will for ever make you its theme, and Phaedra's love for you shall not fall nameless and unsung [σιγηθήσεται]."

Comment: The non-silence here concerns Phaedra's love in particular.

[SS] Euripides *Andromache* (5 BC) Lines 678–79

"And when you mention my generalship, you help my case more than by saying nothing [σιγῶν]."

Comment: Menelaus, speaking to Peleus, refers to silence in regards to a point Peleus could mention or be silent on.

[SS] Euripides *Hecuba* (5 BC) Lines 529–33

"He nodded to me to call for silence from the whole Achaean army. Standing before them I said, 'Silence [Σιγᾶτ'], you Achaeans; let the whole army keep silence; hold your peace [σίγα], be still!' And I brought the multitude into a windless calm."

Comment: Silence is called for during the sacrifice of Polyxena.

[SS] Euripides *Hecuba* (5 BC) Lines 724–25

"But since I see Agamemnon, your master, approaching, let us now hold our peace [σιγῶμεν]."

Comment: The chorus leader calls for silence during Agamemnon's entrance.

[SS] Euripides *Hecuba* (5 BC) Lines 1066–70

"O Helios, would that you might heal, might heal, my bloodied lids and take away the blindness of my eyes! Ah, ah! Soft there [σίγα]! I hear the stealthy footsteps of the women."

Comment: The translation can also be "silent" as Polymestor, now blind, hears the footsteps coming.

[SS] Euripides *Suppliant Women* (5 BC) Lines 297–300

"I shall not hold my peace and then at some later time reproach myself for my present silence, nor, since it is a useless thing for women to be eloquent, shall I, out of fear, let go of the noble task that is mine."

Comment: The LCL does not translate σιγάω here. The Greek text is: οὔτοι σιωπῶσ'εἶτα μέμψομαί ποτε τὴν νῦν σιωπὴν ὡς ἐσιγήθη κακῶς, οὐδ᾽, ὡς ἀχρεῖον τὰς γυναῖκας εὖ λέγειν δείσασ᾽ἀφήσω τῷ φόβῳ τοὐμὸν καλόν. There should be the added phrase "a silence wrongly kept."[4] Aethra, mother of Theseus, king of Athens, speaks to Theseus about what she thinks he should do regarding burying the dead.

[SS] Euripides *Suppliant Women* (5 BC) Lines 438–41

"Freedom consists in this: 'Who has a good proposal and wants to set it before the city?' He who wants to enjoys fame, while he who does not holds his peace [σιγᾷ]. What is fairer for a city than this?"

Comment: Theseus replies to the herald concerning a debate over the nature of government. So the one holding his peace is doing so in a particular instance here.

[SS] Euripides *Suppliant Women* (5 BC) Lines 668–72

"Theseus' herald spoke as follows to all: 'Silence [σιγᾶτε], men at arms, be still, you ranks of Cadmeans, and listen! We have come for the dead, wishing to bury them! We are upholding the law of all the Greeks! It is not our desire to shed blood!' "

Comment: This reference is silence during his speech, for the next line states, "Creon made no proclamation in answer to this speech but sat near his weapons in silence" (*Supplices* 673–74). In other words, Creon could have been silent

---

4 So Frank William Jones, trans., "The Suppliant Women," in *Euripides IV*, The Complete Greek Tragedies, ed. David Grene and Richmond Lattimore (Chicago: The University of Chicago Press, 1992), 149.

during the speech and then have given an answer to the proclamation of Theseus without ignoring Theseus's intention.

[SS] Euripides *Electra* (5 BC) Line 1122

"I will be silent [σιγῶ]. My fear of him is as it is."

Comment: Electra is silent on a specific subject but continues the dialogue with Clytaemestra.

[SS] Euripides *Electra* (5 BC) Lines 1245–46

"And Phoebus, Phoebus—but no, since he is my lord, I hold my peace [σιγῶ]. Still, wise god though he is, his oracle to you was not wise."

Comment: Castor speaks here at length and continues to dialogue.

[SS] Euripides *Heracles* (5 BC) Lines 222–23

"I have no word of praise for Greece either (I shall never keep silent [σιγῶν] on this point), since I have found her disloyal toward my son."

Comment: Amphitryon specifies the type of silence concerning his view of Greece in regards to his son, Heracles.

[SS] Euripides *Heracles* (5 BC) Lines 760–61

"Old friends, the godless man is no more: the house is silent [σιγᾷ]. Let us turn ourselves to dancing."

Comment: Silence here is referring to the effects of Lycus's death.

[SS] Euripides *Trojan Women* (5 BC) Lines 105–10

"Ah me, ah me! What lament is there that I cannot utter, unlucky woman that I am? My country is gone, my children, my husband! Great pride of my ancestors, now cut short, how slight a thing you were after all! What should I wrap in silence [σιγᾶν], what should I not wrap in silence [σιγᾶν]?"

Comment: Hecuba is grieving and wondering what should and should not be said.

[SS] Euripides *Trojan Women* (5 BC) Lines 383–85

"[This is the praise the army deserves. Better to say nothing [σιγᾶν] of disgraceful matters: may my Muse not be a singer who hymns disaster.]"

Comment: Cassandra, a prophetess, is speaking here.

[SS] Euripides *Trojan Women* (5 BC) Lines 398–99

"Paris married Zeus's daughter, and had he not done so, he would have had a wife in his house no one talked of [σιγώμενον]."

Comment: Cassandra is still speaking here.

[SS] Euripides *Trojan Women* (5 BC) Lines 732–39

"For these reasons I want you not to be enamored of a fight or to do anything either undignified or hateful or yet to hurl curses at the Greeks. If you say anything to anger the army, this boy might not receive the mercy of a burial. But if you keep still [σιγῶσα] and bear your misfortunes well, you will not leave this boy's corpse behind unburied, and you yourself will win the favor of the Achaeans."

Comment: Talthybius is speaking. Being silent here is the opposite of saying something that would anger the army.

[SS] Euripides *Iphigeneia at Tauris* (5 BC) Lines 35–41

"And therefore in accordance with the custom in which the goddess Artemis delights, the custom of the feast whose name alone is fair (its other aspects I pass over in silence [σιγῶ] for fear of the goddess) [I sacrifice, since this was also formerly the custom for the city], I consecrate as victim any Greek who comes to this land, but the slaying is the concern of others [, secret sacrifices within this temple of the goddess]."

Comment: Iphigenia, daughter of Agamemnon, specifies the aspects she is silent on.

[SS] Euripides *Iphigeneia at Tauris* (5 BC) Lines 456–60

"But here come the two men with their hands bound together, a fresh sacrifice for the goddess. Keep silence [σιγᾶτε], my friends! The finest offering of Greece draws near to our temple."

[SS] Euripides *Iphigeneia at Tauris* (5 BC) Lines 723–24

"Enough [σίγα]! Phoebus' words do me no good: here comes the woman out of the house."

Comment: Orestes is speaking to Pylades. Later they will continue to dialogue.

[AS] Euripides *Iphigeneia at Tauris* (5 BC) Lines 759–64

"Well, here is what I shall do (for more precautions mean more success): all that is contained in the folds of the tablet I shall tell you in words so that you can tell my loved ones. That way lies safety. If you keep the tablet unharmed, all by itself it will silently [σιγῶσα] communicate what it contains. But if this letter is lost at sea, by saving yourself you also will save my message for me."

Comment: Iphigenia is speaking to Pylades in response to the possibility of being lost at sea and losing the tablet. "Silently communicate" is the opposite of Pylades verbally speaking the message.

[SS] Euripides *Iphigeneia at Tauris* (5 BC) Line 925

"Let us not speak [σιγῶμεν] of them: I was avenging my father."

Comment: This conversation between Iphigenia and Orestes shows that silence is in regard to the previously stated "terrible deeds against our mother" (*Iphigenia Taurica* 924).

[SS] Euripides *Iphigeneia at Tauris* (5 BC) Line 928

"I say nothing [σιγῶ]. But does Argos now look to you as its ruler?"

Comment: As in line 925 above, this statement is also about the previous reference, in this case the "mother's deeds" (*Iphigenia Taurica* 927).

[SE] Euripides *Iphigeneia at Tauris* (5 BC) Line 938

"Orders to do what? Can it be revealed or not [σιγώμενον]?"

[SS] Euripides *Iphigeneia at Tauris* (5 BC) Lines 939–44

"I will tell you: this was the beginning of many troubles for me. When the wrongs against my mother that I do not describe [σιγῶμεν] had polluted my hands, the Erinyes pursued me as I fled headlong on my delirious course until Loxias sent me to Athens to stand trial before the nameless goddesses."

[SE] Euripides *Iphigeneia at Tauris* (5 BC) Lines 1063–64

"Keep our secret [σιγήσαθ'] and help us make our escape."

[SE] Euripides *Iphigeneia at Tauris* (5 BC) Lines 1075–77

"Courage, dear mistress! Just get safely home! For, as Zeus is my witness, I will keep the secret [σιγηθήσεται] you ask me to keep."

Comment: The chorus leader is responding to Iphigenia's previous request (previous reference above in lines 1063–64).

[SS] Euripides *Ion* (5 BC) Lines 256–57

"It's nothing. I have let my shaft fly. As for what my words imply, I say nothing [σιγῶ], and you too should think no more of it."

Comment: Creusa is speaking to Ion in response to his concern for her unhappiness and what Creusa is remembering from her past. Creusa and Ion continue the extended dialogue.

[SS] Euripides *Ion* (5 BC) Line 362

"I say no more [σιγῶ]. But bring to completion what I asked you about."

Comment: Creusa's reference of saying no more refers to not bringing up a memory that would make Ion weep.

[SS] Euripides *Ion* (5 BC) Lines 392–97

"But I see my noble husband Xuthus nearby, just come from the cave of Trophonius. Say nothing [σίγα] to him, stranger, about what I have said so that my secret errand may not bring me into disgrace and the story reach other ears than I intended."

Comment: Creusa is speaking and clarifies the silence in regard to "what I have said" as Xuthus enters the scene.

[SE] Euripides *Ion* (5 BC) Line 432

"Or does she have a secret [σιγῶσ'] that must be kept quiet?"

[SS] Euripides *Ion* (5 BC) Lines 582–84

"Silence [σιγᾷς]? Why do you keep your eyes fixed on the ground? Why begin to worry? Why change from joy and make your father afraid?"

Comment: Ion is silent when Xuthus speaks, but Ion will later speak to Xuthus.

[SS] Euripides *Ion* (5 BC) Lines 598–601

"As for all those who are of good character and have an aptitude for wisdom but live quietly [σιγῶσι] and do not exert themselves in public affairs, they will think I am laughably foolish not to keep quiet in a city full of fear."

174 | *Appendix*

Comment: Though this passage is textually suspect, it still provides a glimpse into a writer's usage. Living quietly is the opposite of forcing oneself into public affairs.

[SS] Euripides *Ion* (5 BC) Lines 666–67

"You servants, say nothing [σιγᾶν] about these matters: the penalty for telling my wife is death."

[SS] Euripides *Ion* (5 BC) Line 758

"Shall we speak or be silent [σιγῶμεν]? What are we to do?"

Comment: The chorus leader is questioning whether to say anything about Ion, not about being silent in general.

[SS] Euripides *Ion* (5 BC) Lines 866–69

"Though I wished to achieve these hopes by saying nothing [σιγῶσα, 2x] of the rape or of my tearful childbirth, I could not."

Comment: Creusa clearly specifies the exact topics of her silence.

[SS] Euripides *Ion* (5 BC) Lines 1382–83

"If some slave woman bore me, it is worse to find my mother than to say nothing [σιγῶντ'] and let matters be."

Comment: Ion's reference here is to saying nothing about a slave mother.

[AS] Euripides *Ion* (5 BC) Line 1396

"Quiet [σίγα]! You caused me grief before as well."

Comment: Ion says this word to Creusa as he looks at the cradle. Absolute silence may be Ion's intention in this moment.

[SS] Euripides *Helen* (5 BC) Lines 151–57

"But leave this land quickly before Proteus' son, the country's ruler, sees you! He is away hunting wild beasts with his hounds, but he kills every Greek he catches. Just why, you should not try to learn, and I will not tell you [σιγῶ]. What good would it do you?"

Comment: Helen is speaking to Teucer.

Appendix

[SS] Euripides *Helen* (5 BC) Lines 1017–23

"To make my tale brief: I shall keep silent [σιγήσομαι], as you have begged me to do, and never help my brother's folly with my counsel. I am doing him a good turn (though he might not think so) if I cause him to be god-fearing instead of impious. So you yourselves find some way of escape: I shall stand out of the way and hold my peace [σιγήσομαι]."

Comment: Theonoe, sister of the king of Egypt, is speaking to Menelaus and Helen.

[SS] Euripides *Helen* (5 BC) Lines 1045–46

"His sister would never allow you [σιγήσειεν]: she would tell him that you intended to kill him."

Comment: Helen speaks to Menelaus that Theonoe would not be silent about such a plot.

[SS] Euripides *Phoenician Women* (5 BC) Lines 344–49

"I did not kindle for you the blazing torch that custom requires [in marriages], as befits a mother blessed. The Ismenus River made this alliance without the luxurious bath, and in the city of Thebes none cried aloud [ἐσίγαθεν] at the entrance of your bride."

[SE] Euripides *Phoenician Women* (5 BC) Line 908

"He is my son and will keep any secrets [σιγήσεται] he must."

Comment: Creon is speaking to Teiresias, seer of Thebes, about if Menoeceus should hear the prophecies.

[SS] Euripides *Phoenician Women* (5 BC) Line 925

"... say nothing [σίγα]: do not tell the city these prophecies!"

Comment: Creon states this word to Teiresias concerning the prophecy of Menoeceus's death.

[SS] Euripides *Phoenician Women* (5 BC) Lines 960–61

"Creon, why are you silent [σιγᾷς], uttering no sound? I am no less startled than you."

176 | *Appendix*

Comment: The chorus leader speaks to Creon after the exchange between Creon and Teiresias. Creon has been speaking before and after, but was silent for shocking moment.

[SS] Euripides *Orestes* (5 BC) Lines 16–18

"To Atreus (I pass over [σιγῶ] intervening events) were born Agamemnon the glorious, if indeed glorious he is, and Menelaus: their mother was the Cretan Aërope."

[SS] Euripides *Orestes* (5 BC) Lines 579–81

"In the gods' name—it is untimely of me to mention the gods, who sit in judgment over murder, but still—if I had acquiesced [σιγῶν] in my mother's actions, what would the dead man have done to me?"

Comment: Orestes, attempting to defend his own actions, is speaking specifically of if he had been silent regarding his mother's deeds.

[SS] Euripides *Orestes* (5 BC) Line 789

"Clearly better to say nothing [σιγᾶν]."

Comment: Orestes is speaking to Pylades on whether to tell his sister about their decision.

[SS] Euripides *Orestes* (5 BC) Line 1103

"Softly [σίγα] then: I have little confidence in women."

Comment: Pylades and Orestes continue to speak to one another. In this case, Pylades is silencing Orestes on his previous statement about revenge.

[SS] Euripides *Orestes* (5 BC) Line 1128

"Yes, and any who won't keep quiet [σιγῶντ'] we must kill."

Comment: Orestes is speaking with Pylades about the attendants during their murder plot against Helen. The silence is during the period which they plan to lock the attendants up in different places in the palace.

[SS] Euripides *Orestes* (5 BC) Line 1311

"Silence [σιγᾶτε], silence [σιγᾶτ']! I heard someone's footfall, someone coming along the path near the palace!"

[AS] Euripides *Orestes* (5 BC) Lines 1347–52

"No more talk [σιγᾶν]! You have come to save our lives, not yours! Take hold, take hold of her! Place the sword again her neck and bide your time, so that Menelaus may see that he has met with real men, not cowardly Phrygians, and has fared as a coward ought to fare!"

Comment: Electra says this statement to Hermione during the murder plot.

[SS] Euripides *Orestes* (5 BC) Lines 1366–68

"But the bars of the palace gate are clanging. Hush [σιγήσατ'], here comes one of the Phrygians, from whom we shall learn how matters stand indoors."

Comment: The chorus leader is calling for silence as the one from the Phrygians enters.

[SS] Euripides *Orestes* (5 BC) Line 1403–07

"One was said to have the general for his father, the other was the son of Strophius, a guileful fellow like Odysseus, silently [σιγᾷ] crafty, but loyal to friends, bold for the fight, skilled in war, and a deadly snake: a curse on his cooling plan, that villain!"

Comment: Phrygian is describing the son of Strophius, using Odysseus as a comparison. A person can both speak one moment and be silently crafty another moment.

[AS] Euripides *Orestes* (5 BC) Line 1599

"Say no more [σίγα] then and endure the bad fortune you have deserved!"

Comment: Orestes is speaking to Menelaus as he holds a sword to his daughter's throat.

[AS] Euripides *Bacchae* (5 BC) Lines 800–01

"What an impossible foreigner I'm grappling with here! Whether he's the doer or the sufferer, he won't keep quiet [σιγήσεται]!"

Comment: Pentheus, king of Thebes, is speaking to Dionysus.

[D] Euripides *Bacchae* (5 BC) Lines 1084–85

"The upper air was still [σίγησε], the leaves of the wooded glade kept silence, and no sound of beast could be heard."

[SS] Euripides *Iphigeneia at Aulis* (5 BC) Line 655

"(*to himself*) Ah me, how hard to hold my tongue [σιγᾶν]! (*aloud*) I thank you, daughter."

Comment: Agamemnon is trying to keep quiet about what is in store for Iphigenia as they dialogue.

[SS] Euripides *Iphigeneia at Aulis* (5 BC) Lines 1141–43

"I know all: I have learned what you intend to do to me. Your very silence [σιγᾶν] and your groans are a sign that you admit it. You need not trouble yourself to make a long reply."

Comment: Clytaemestra is speaking to Agamemnon. It is interesting that silence and sounds (groaning) are discussed together. Nonetheless, Clytaemestra speaks of his silence all the while he is dialoguing with her.

[SS] Sophocles *Fragments* (5 BC) Fragment 314 line 103

"Quiet [σῖγα]! A god is leading our expedition!"

Comment: The expedition is a search for cattle.

[SS] Sophocles *Fragments* (5 BC) Fragment 314 lines 135–44

"SI: Why are you now silent [σιγᾶθ], you who used to talk so much?
CH: No, be quiet!
SI: What is it there that you keep turning away from?
CH: Listen, do!
SI: How can I listen when I hear no one's voice?
CH: Do what I say!
SI: A lot of help you will give me in my chase!
CH: Listen yourself for a moment, father, and learn what sort of noise terrifies us here and maddens us; no mortal ever heard it yet!"

[SS] Sophocles *Fragments* (5 BC) Fragment 314 lines 203–04

"Father, why are you silent [σιγᾷς]? Didn't we speak the truth? Can't you hear the noise, or are you deaf?"

Comment: The continued dialogue demonstrates a momentary silence.

[SS] Sophocles *Fragments* (5 BC) Fragment 653 line 2

"Do not spread abroad to many your prevailing fortune; it is fitter to keep silent [σιγώμενος] about it as you lament it."

Comment: The silence is specifically about one's fortune.

[SE] Sophocles *Fragments* (5 BC) Fragment 679 lines 1–2

"Be sympathetic and maintain silence [σιγῶσαι]! For a woman should cover up what brings shame on women."

Comment: The editor of this edition states, "Evidently Phaedra is asking the Chorus not to reveal her secret."[5]

[SE] Sophocles *Fragments* (5 BC) Fragment 757 lines 1–4

"Tongue that has remained silent [σιγήσασα] for so long, how shall you endure to bring out this matter? Indeed nothing is weightier than necessity, which shall force you to reveal the secret of the palace."

[SS] Sophocles *Fragments* (5 BC) Fragment 815 line 1

"Listen, silence [σίγα]! What is this cry inside the house?"

[SS] Sophocles *Fragments* (5 BC) Fragment 930 lines 1–2

"But when one has been caught red-handed in a theft, one must keep silent [σιγᾶν], even if one carries about a chattering tongue."

[SS] Sophocles *Ajax* (5 BC) Lines 87–88

"Athena: Then stand in silence [σίγα] and remain as you are.
Odysseus: I shall remain; but I wish I were not here."

Comment: In this scene, Athena has Odysseus remain quiet while she calls Ajax out to speak to him. Then when Ajax leaves, Athena and Odysseus continue the dialogue.

[SS] Sophocles *Ajax* (5 BC) Lines 975–76

"Be silent [σίγησον]! for I think I hear the voice of Teucer, crying out in a strain that has regard to this disaster."

Comment: The chorus is calling for silence as Teucer enters.

---

5   Hugh Lloyd-Jones, ed., in *Sophocles Fragments*, LCL 483 (Cambridge: Harvard University Press, 1996), 3:325.

[SS] Sophocles *Electra* (5 BC) Line 1238

"It is best to keep silent [σιγᾶν], in case anyone inside should hear."

Comment: Orestes is speaking to Electra, and they continue to dialogue.

[SS] Sophocles *Electra* (5 BC) Lines 1322–23

"I counsel silence [σιγᾶν]; for I hear at the door one of the people within is coming."

Comment: Orestes is speaking to Electra.

[SS] Sophocles *Oedipus Tyrannus* (5 BC) Line 569

"I do not know; when I do not understand I like to say nothing [σιγᾶν]."

Comment: Creon is speaking. This quotation is a clear example of selective silence.

[SS] Sophocles *Antigone* (5 BC) Lines 87–88

"Ah, tell them all! I shall hate you far more if you remain silent [σιγῶσ'], and do not proclaim this to all."

Comment: Antigone is speaking to Ismene about the burial of Polynices.

[SS] Sophocles *Trachiniae* (5 BC) Lines 731–33

"As to the rest of the story you should be silent [σιγᾶν], unless you are going to say something to your son; for he who had gone to look for his father is now present."

[SS] Sophocles *Trachiniae* (5 BC) Lines 813–14

"Why do you depart in silence? Do you not know that your silence [σιγῶσα] seconds the accuser?"

Comment: The chorus asks these questions about Deianeira, who was previously speaking and then leaves in silence after Hyllus accuses and curses her.

[SS] Sophocles *Trachiniae* (5 BC) Lines 974–75

"Quiet [σῖγα], my son, do not arouse the savage pain of your stern father!"

Comment: The doctor is speaking to Hyllus to be quiet for the moment.

[SS] Sophocles *Trachiniae* (5 BC) Line 1126

"Yes, for things stand so with her that silence [σιγᾶν] would be wrong."

Comment: Hyllus, speaking to Heracles, refers to being silent about his mother.

[SS] Sophocles *Philoctetes* (5 BC) Lines 804–05

"What do you say, boy? What do you say? Why are you silent [σιγᾷς]? Where are you, my son?"

Comment: Philoctetes is speaking to Neopteolemus. They dialogue before and after this statement. Perhaps a temporary silence by Neoptolemus occurs during Philoctetes's speech.

[SS] Sophocles *Philoctetes* (5 BC) Lines 865–66

"I tell you to be silent [σιγᾶν], and not to lose your wits! For the man is beginning to see and is raising his head!"

Comment: Neoptolemus is speaking to the chorus, calling for silence as Philoctetes speaks again.

[SS] Sophocles *Oedipus Coloneus* (5 BC) Lines 111–16

"Antigone: Be silent [σίγα]! For here come some men advanced in age, to spy out your seat!
Oedipus: I will be silent [σιγήσομαι], and do you hide me in the grove, away from the road, until I know what words they will utter; for if we are to act cautiously we must find out!"

Comment: Oedipus is silent while the men enter the scene.

[SS] Sophocles *Oedipus Coloneus* (5 BC) Lines 978–81

"And are you not ashamed, you wretch, of forcing me to speak of my marriage with my mother, seeing that she was your sister, when it was such as I shall now describe; for I shall not keep silent [σιγήσομαι], now that you have gone so far, unholy mouth!"

Comment: The reference to not being silent is specifically about the events surrounding his father and mother.

[SS] Sophocles *Oedipus Coloneus* (5 BC) Lines 1271–72

"Why are you silent [σιγᾷς]? Say some word, father! Do not turn away from me!"

Comment: Polynices is asking why his father is silent at this time while Polynices is speaking.

182 | *Appendix*

[SS] Herodotus *Histories* (5 BC) 1.88.5–8

"Presently he turned and said (for he saw the Persians sacking the city of the Lydians), 'O King, am I to say to you now what is in my mind, or keep silence [σιγᾶν]?'"

Comment: Croesus is asking Cyrus about speaking about the plundering.

[SE] Herodotus *Histories* (5 BC) 3.82.8–11

"Nothing can be found better than the rule of the one best man; his judgment being like to himself, he will govern the multitude with perfect wisdom, and best conceal [σιγῷτό] plans made for the defeat of enemies."

[SE] Herodotus *Histories* (5 BC) 5.22.1–2

"Thus was the death of these Persians suppressed and hidden in silence [ἐσιγήθη]."

[SS] Herodotus *Histories* (5 BC) 7.104.26–29

"If this that I say seems to you but foolishness, then let me hereafter hold my peace [σιγᾶν]; it is under constraint that I have now spoken. But may your wish, O king! be fulfilled."

[SS] Herodotus *Histories* (5 BC) 8.26.10–18

"Then Tigranes son of Artabanus uttered a most noble saying (but the king deemed him a coward for it); when he heard that the prize was not money but a crown, he could not hold his peace [σιγῶν], but cried, 'Zounds, Mardonius, what manner of men are these that you have brought us to fight withal? 'tis not for money they contend but for glory of achievement!' Such was Tigranes' saying."

Comment: Tigranes could not be silent specifically about the prize.

[SS] Herodotus *Histories* (5 BC) 8.61.1–7

"Thus said Themistocles; but Adimantus the Corinthian attacked him again, saying that a landless man should hold his peace [σιγᾶν], and that Eurybiades must not suffer one that had no city to vote; let Themistocles (said he) have a city at his back ere he took part in council,—taunting him thus because Athens was taken and held by the enemy."

Comment: Holding one's peace here is parallel to not voting for what they were going to do militarily.

[SS] Herodotus *Histories* (5 BC) 8.65.28–33

"Demaratus replied thereto, 'Keep silence [σῖγα], and speak to none other thus; for if these words of yours be reported to the king, you will lose your head, and neither I nor any other man will avail to save you.'"

Comment: Demaratus is speaking to Dicaeus, who had just explained the meaning (from his perspective) of the cry they heard.

[SE] Herodotus *Histories* (5 BC) 8.110.5–10

"Having won them over, Themistocles straightway sent men in a boat whom he could trust not to reveal [σιγᾶν] under any question whatsoever the message which he charged them to deliver to the king; of whom one was again his servant Sicinnus."

[SS] Herodotus *Histories* (5 BC) 9.42

"None withstood this argument, so that his opinion prevailed; for it was he and not Artabazus who was generalissimo of the army by the king's commission. He sent therefore for the leaders of the battalions and the generals of those Greeks that were with him, and asked them if they knew any oracle which prophesied that the Persians should perish in Hellas. They that were summoned said nought [σιγώντων], some not knowing the prophecies, and some knowing them but deeming it perilous to speak; then said Mardonius himself: 'Since, therefore, you either have no knowledge or are afraid to declare it, hear what I tell you out of the full knowledge that I have. There is an oracle that Persians are fated to come to Hellas and there all perish after they have plundered the temple at Delphi. We, therefore, knowing this same oracle, will neither approach that temple nor essay to plunder it; and in so far as destruction hangs on that, none awaits us. Wherefore as many of you as wish the Persians well may rejoice for that, as knowing that we shall overcome the Greeks.' Having thus spoken he gave command to have all prepared and set in fair order for the battle that should be joined at the next day's dawn."

Comment: I quote this entire section due to the combination of σιγάω and prophecy, which is similar to the context of 1 Cor 14.

[N/A] Crates *Fragments* (5 BC) Fragment 4 line 1

"You must be quiet [σιγᾶν] and not utter a peep."

Comment: There is no context.

[SS] Isocrates *On the Banker* (5–4 BC) 10.1–7

"Thus beset on every side by misfortunes so dire, what, think you, was my state of mind? If I kept silent [σιγῶντι] I should be defrauded of my money by Pasion here; if I should make this complaint, I was none the more likely to recover it and I should bring myself and my father into the greatest disrepute with Satyrus. The wisest course, therefore, as I though, was to keep silent."

Comment: Being silent here refers to the decision of bringing the complaint to a jury.

[SS] Isocrates *Ad Demonicum* (5–4 BC) 41

"Always when you are about to say anything, first weigh it in your mind; for with many the tongue outruns the thought. Let there be but two occasions for speech—when the subject is one which you thoroughly know and when it is one on which you are compelled to speak. On these occasions alone is speech better than silence; on all others, it is better to be silent [σιγᾶν] than to speak."

[SS] Isocrates *Busiris* (5–4 BC) 29.1–8

"For so greatly did he surpass all others in reputation that all the younger men desired to see their sons staying in his company than attending to their private affairs. And these reports we cannot disbelieve; for even now persons who profess to be followers of his teaching are more admired when silent [σιγῶντας] than are those who have the greatest renown for eloquence."

Comment: The statement is a general statement of silence versus speaking eloquently. There is no evidence that these followers remained absolutely silent in life.

[AS] Aristophanes *Acharnians* (5–4 BC) Line 59

"Sit down and be quiet [σῖγα]!"

Comment: The herald is speaking to Dicaeopolis. The conflict in the scene shows that he wants him silenced absolutely.

[AS] Aristophanes *Acharnians* (5–4 BC) Line 64

"Silence [σῖγα]!"

Comment: This quote is a continuation of line 59 above between the herald and Dicaeopolis.

[AS] Aristophanes *Acharnians* (5–4 BC) Line 123

"Sit down and be quiet [σίγα]!"

Comment: Again, the herald wanting Dicaeopolis to stop talking.

[AS] Aristophanes *Clouds* (5–4 BC) Line 1088

"I'll shut up [σιγήσομαι]; what else could I do?"

Comment: Better Argument and Worse Argument are debating here. Better Argument says he will be silenced if he is out performed on a given point of debate.

[SS] Aristophanes *Wasps* (5–4 BC) Lines 85–86

"You're getting nowhere with all this hot air; you'll never find the answer. If you really want to know, then be quiet [σιγᾶτέ]."

Comment: The two slaves Xanthias and Sosias are speaking. Xanthias speaks to Sosias as the two trade guesses as to what is wrong with their master Bdelycleon (Loathecleon).

[SS] Aristophanes *Wasps* (5–4 BC) Lines 512–14

"Sure, because you're addicted to that kind of fun. But if you'll hold your tongue [σιγῶν] and open your mind to what I have to say, I think I'll enlighten you about the total error of your ways."

Comment: Bdelycleon, the son, is speaking to his father, Philocleon (Lovecleon) as they debate the merits of the father being a juror.

[SS] Aristophanes *Wasps* (5–4 BC) Lines 741–42

"But I can't help being displeased that he's silent [σιγᾷ] and won't so much as grunt."

Comment: Bdelycleon speaks about Philocleaon during a turning point in their debate.

[SS] Aristophanes *Wasps* (5–4 BC) Line 905

"Sit down and be quiet [σίγα]. You, take the stand and begin the prosecution."

Comment: Bdelycleon speaks to Xanthias so that the "prosecutor" (the Demadogue) can begin his speech.

[SS] Aristophanes *Peace* (5–4 BC) Lines 60–61

"What's that? Be quiet [σιγήσαθ']; I think I hear a voice."

Comment: Trygaeus enters the scene for the first time. The second slave, speaking in general, calls for silence as he hears the voice of Trygaeus.

[SS] Aristophanes *Peace* (5–4 BC) Line 91

"Be quiet [σίγα], be quiet [σίγα]!"

Comment: Trygaeus speaks to his second slave after the slave calls him deranged. It is more likely that Trygaeus is calling for silence from being called deranged because they continue to dialogue. See more context below, in lines 96–101.

[SS] Aristophanes *Peace* (5–4 BC) Lines 96–101

"You must speak auspiciously and make no foolish noise, but raise a cheer; and bid mankind be quiet [σιγᾶν], and wall off with fresh bricks the privies and alleyways, and lock up their arseholes!"

Comment: Trygaeus speaks to the second slave. Trygaeus is not calling for the absolute silence of all mankind.

[SS] Aristophanes *Peace* (5–4 BC) Lines 102–03

"There's no way I'll be quiet [σιγήσομ'] unless you tell me where you mean to fly."

Comment: This quote continues the dialogue where the second slave called Trygaeus deranged (see line 91 above).

[SS] Aristophanes *Birds* (5–4 BC) Lines 1505–06[6]

"Be quiet [σίγα], don't mention my name. You'll be the death of me, if Zeus sees me here."

Comment: Prometheus tries to quiet down Peisetaerus from shouting, especially shouting his name.

---

6   Aristophanes, *Av.* 1196, contains a textual issue on whether σιγάω is original. The LCL has chosen not to include the term in the Greek or English text. Lines 1189–98 read, "War is begun, inexpressive war, War is begun twixt the Gods and me! Look out, look out, through the cloud-wrapt air Which erst the Darkness of Erebus bare, Lest a God slip by, and we fail to see. Glance eager-eyed on every side, For close at hand the winged sound I hear Of some Immortal hurtling through the Sky." The critical edition of N. G. Wilson simply places in brackets σιγᾶτε σῖγ but does not provide anything in the apparatus. See N. G. Wilson, *Aristophanis Fabulae*, Scriptorum Classicorum Bibliotheca Oxoniensis (Oxford: E Typographeo Clarendoniano, 2007), 1:403. Neither is the variant referenced by John Williams White and Earnest Cary, "Collations of the Manuscripts of Aristophanes' Aves," *Harvard Studies in Classical Philology* 29 (1918): 77–131, esp. 117. Therefore, the reference is not included in the statistics for this study.

[SS] Aristophanes *Birds* (5–4 BC) Lines 1683–84

"Very well, you two negotiate the terms of a settlement; if that's your decision, I'll keep quiet [σιγήσομαι]."

Comment: Poseidon will be quiet about the conclusion of their negotiation and its settlement, which is about the Princess.

[SS] Aristophanes *Lysistrata* (5–4 BC) Lines 69–70

"I hope we're not too late, Lysistrata. What do you say? Why don't you say something [σιγᾷς]?"

Comment: Lysistrate is speaking throughout this section. She was simply silent to Myrrhine because she arrived late.

[AS] Aristophanes *Lysistrata* (5–4 BC) Lines 507–20

"Lysistrata: Gladly. Before now, and for quite some time, we maintained our decorum and suffered [in silence] whatever you men did, because you wouldn't let us make a sound. But you weren't exactly all we could ask for. No, we knew only too well what you were up to, and many a time we'd hear in our homes about a bad decision you'd made on some great issue of state. Then, masking the pain in our hearts, we'd put on a smile and ask you, 'How did the Assembly go today? Any decision about a rider to the peace treaty?' And my husband would say, 'What's that to you? Shut up [σιγήσει]!' And I'd shut up [σίγων].
First Old Woman: I wouldn't have shut up [ἐσίγων]!
Magistrate: If you hadn't shut up [σίγας] you'd have got a beating!
Lysistrata: Well, that's why I did shut up [ἐσίγων]—then. But later on we began to hear about even worse decisions you'd made, and then we would ask, 'Husband, how come you're handling this so stupidly?' And right away he'd glare at me and tell me to get back to my sewing if I didn't want major damage to my head: 'War shall be the business of menfolk,' unquote."

Comment: The husband's aggressive stance shows that he intended absolute silence from the wife concerning "business of menfolk." Though the responses of the First Old Woman and the later speech of Lysistrata show that silence in the ancient world was practiced in different ways.

[SS] Aristophanes *Lysistrata* (5–4 BC) Lines 587–90

"Magistrate: Isn't it awful how these women go like this with their sticks, and like that with their bobbins, when they share none of the war's burdens?

Lysistrata: None? You monster! We bear more than our fair share, in the first place by giving birth to sons and sending them off to the army—
Magistrate: Enough of that [σίγα]! Don't open old wounds."

Comment: Lysistrate and the Magistrate continue to dialogue. Context shows that the silence is for the topics that "open old wounds."

[SS] Aristophanes *Lysistrata* (5–4 BC) Lines 765–73

"Lysistrata: Just be patient, good ladies, and put up with this only a little bit longer. There's an oracle predicting victory for us, but only if we stick together. Here's the oracle right here.
Third Wife: Tell us what is says.
Lysistrata: Be quiet [σιγᾶτε], then. yea, when the swallows hole up in a single home, fleeing the hoopoes and leaving the phallus along, then are their problems solved, and high-thundering Zeus shall reverse what's up and what's down—
Third Wife: You mean *we'll* be lying on top?"

Comment: The Third Wife continues to speak with Lysistrata, and the silence was for the moment of reading the oracle.

[SS] Aristophanes *Lysistrata* (5–4 BC) Lines 1003–06

"Herald: We're hard up! We walk around town hunched over, like men carrying lamps. The women won't let us even touch [σιγῆν] their cherries till all of us unanimously agree to make peace with the rest of Greece."

Comment: Loeb Classical Library does not translate σιγάω as silence in this text. The Greek phrase is ταὶ γὰρ γυναῖκες οὐδὲ τῶ μύρτω σιγῆν ἐῶντι.

[SS] Aristophanes *Thesmophoriazusae* (5–4 BC) Lines 25–30

"Kinsman: Now what?
Euripides: Do you see that doorway?
Kinsman: By Heracles, I believe I do!
Euripides: Be quiet now [σίγα].
Kinsman: I'm being quiet about the doorway.
Euripides: Listen.
Kinsman: I'm listening and being quiet about the doorway.
Euripides: This happens to be the dwelling of the renowned tragic poet Agathon.
Kinsman: What Agathon do you mean?"

Appendix | 189

[SS] Aristophanes *Thesmophoriazusae* (5–4 BC) Lines 45–47

"Kinsman: Blah!
Euripides: Shhh [σίγα]! What's he say?
Slave: Let the feathered tribes lie down in rest, and the paws of wild beasts that course the woods be checked—
Kinsman: Blah blah blah!"

Comment: Euripides is trying to get the Kinsmans to be quiet while the slave speaks.

[SS] Aristophanes *Thesmophoriazusae* (5–4 BC) Lines 90–95

"Euripides: To attend the women's assembly and say whatever's necessary on my behalf.
Kinsman: Openly or in disguise?
Euripides: In disguise, dressed up like a woman.
Kinsman: A pretty cute bit, and just your style. We take the cake for craftiness!
Euripides: Shh [σίγα]!
Kinsman: What?
Euripides: Agathon's coming out."

[SS] Aristophanes *Thesmophoriazusae* (5–4 BC) Line 99

"Shh [σίγα]; he's getting ready to sing his aria."

Comment: Euripides wants Kinsman to be silent during Agathon's song.

[SS] Aristophanes *Thesmophoriazusae* (5–4 BC) Lines 144–45

"Well? Why don't you answer [σιγᾷς]? Or must I find you out from your song, since you yourself refuse to speak?"

Comment: Agathon had just finished his song. Kinsman then asks Agathon a series of questions and ends with lines 144–45 before Agathon answers.

[SS] Aristophanes *Thesmophoriazusae* (5–4 BC) Lines 381–82

"Quiet [σίγα]! Silence! Pay attention, because she's clearing her throat just like the politicians. She'll probably be making a long speech."

[SS] Aristophanes *Thesmophoriazusae* (5–4 BC) Lines 571–73

"Stop abusing each other! A woman is heading for our meeting in a hurry. Before this gets to be a brawl I want you quiet [σιγᾶθ'], so we can hear what she has to say in an orderly fashion."

[SS] Aristophanes *Frogs* (5–4 BC) Line 832

"Why so quiet [σιγᾷς], Aeschylus? You hear what he says."

Comment: Dionysus speaks to Aeschylus, who then speaks.

[SS] Aristophanes *Frogs* (5–4 BC) Lines 914–15

"And while they sat there in silence [ἐσίγων], his chorus would rattle off four suites of choral lyric one after another without a break."

Comment: Benjamin Rogers explains the reference, "He is referring to two lost tragedies of Aeschylus, the *Phrygians or the Ransom of Hector* and the *Niobe*. In the former, Achilles was introduced, wrapped in sullen gloom for the loss of Patroclus, and refusing all food and consolation. In the latter, Niobe was shown, dumb with sorrow for her six sons and six daughters, whom Apollo and Artemis had slain."[7]

[SS] Aristophanes *Wealth* (5–4 BC) Lines 18–21

"Well, I certainly don't intend to keep quiet [σιγήσομαι], master, not unless you tell me why we're following this fellow; I'll just give you a hard time. And you wouldn't dare beat me when I'm wearing a wreath."

Comment: Cario opens the play with this speech stating that he will not be quiet unless Chremylus tells him why he is following a blind man.

[SE] Aristophanes *Wealth* (5–4 BC) Lines 78–79

"You scum of the earth, you weren't going to tell us [ἐσίγας] that you're Wealth?"

[SS] Aristophanes *Wealth* (5–4 BC) Lines 664–671

"Wife: Were there any other patients at the shrine?
Cario: One was Neocleides, who's blind but has a sharper eye than the sighted when it comes to stealing; and there were many others, with all kinds of illnesses. Then the temple servant put out the lamps and told us all to go to sleep, and to be quiet [σιγᾶν] if we heard any noise, and we all lay there in good order."

---

7   Benjamin Bickley Rogers, trans., in *Aristophanes: The Peace, The Birds, The Frogs*, LCL (Cambridge: Harvard University Press, 1924; repr., 1996), 2:378 n. a.

[SS] Xenophon *Hellenica* (5–4 BC) 3.4.7–3.4.8

"[A]nd for this reason a very great crowd was continually courting and following him, so that Agesilaus appeared to be a man in private station and Lysander king. Now Agesilaus showed afterwards that he also was enraged by these things; but the thirty Spartiatae with him were so jealous that they could not keep silence [ἐσίγων], but said to Agesilaus that Lysander was doing an unlawful thing in conducting himself more pompously than royalty."

[SS] Xenophon *Memorabilia* (5–4 BC) 3.5.6

"The behaviour of sailors is a case in point. So long as they have nothing to fear, they are, I believe, an unruly lot, but when they expect a storm or an attack, they not only carry out all orders, but watch in silence [σιγῶσι] for the word of command like choristers."

[AS] Xenophon *Memorabilia* (5–4 BC) 4.2.39

"'I am forced to agree once more,' cried Euthydemus, 'evidently by my stupidity. I am inclined to think I had better hold my tongue [σιγᾶν], or I shall know nothing at all presently.' And so he went away very dejected, disgusted with himself and convinced that he was indeed a slave."

Comment: Euthydemus speaks to Socrates after their dialogue.

[SS] Xenophon *Anabasis* (5–4 BC) 5.6.25–26

"It was ridiculous, he said, when there was plenty of fertile land in Greece, to be hunting for it in the domain of the barbarians. 'And until you reach that spot,' he continued, 'I also, like Timasion, promise you regular pay.' All this he said with full knowledge of what the Heracleots and the Sinopeans were promising Timasion for getting the army to sail away. Xenophon meanwhile was silent [ἐσίγα]."

Comment: The Greek text has that Xenophon was silent specifically ἐν τούτῳ.

[SS] Xenophon *Cyropaedia* (5–4 BC) 1.4.15

"Thereupon, Astyages gave his consent and from his position he watched them rushing in rivalry upon the beasts and vying eagerly with one another in giving chase and in throwing the spear. And he was pleased to see that Cyrus was unable to keep silence [σιγᾶν] for delight, but, like a well-bred hound, gave tongue whenever he came near an animal and urged on each of his companions by name."

[SS] Xenophon *Cyropaedia* (5–4 BC) 1.6.40

"And you yourself from behind shouting with a cry that kept right up with the hare would frighten him so that he would lose his wits and be taken; those in front, on the other hand, you had instructed to keep silent [σιγᾶν] and made them lie concealed in ambush."

Comment: Silence here is related to a moment in time during hunting the hare.

[SS] Xenophon *Cyropaedia* (5–4 BC) 4.5.19

"On hearing the messenger, therefore, the Medes were silent [ἐσίγησαν], for they were at a loss how they could disobey him when he summoned them, and they asked themselves in fear how they could obey him when he threatened so, especially as they had experience of his fury."

[SS] Xenophon *Cyropaedia* (5–4 BC) 5.5.20–21

"To this Cyaxares said nothing [ἐσίγα]. So Cyrus went on again: 'Well, seeing that it suits you better to be silent than to reply to this question, tell me whether you thought you were wronged in any way because, when you did not think it safe to pursue, I excused you from a share in that peril and asked you to let some of your cavalry go with me. For if I did wrong also in asking that, and that, too, when I had previously given you my own services as an ally that is yours to prove.' And as Cyaxares again said nothing [ἐσίγα], Cyrus resumed: 'Well, seeing that you do not choose to answer that either, please tell me then if I did you wrong in the next step I took.'"

Comment: Cyaxares was specifically silent πρὸς τοῦτο (a phrase used in both occurrences here of silence for the question if Cyrus was selfish or Cyaxares was wronged). Cyaxares does speak to Cyrus both before and after this section.

[SS] Plato *Apology of Socrates* (5–4 BC) 24C–D

"Socrates: 'Come up here, Meletus, and tell me: do you think there is nothing of greater importance than how our young people are to be the best possible?'
Meletus: 'I Do.'
Socrates: 'Then come on and tell these people: who makes them better? It's clear you know: after all you do care. Having discovered who it is who corrupts them, me, as you claim, you bring me forward and accuse me in front of these people. So come on and say who makes them better and point out to them who it is. Do you see, Meletus, you're silent [σιγᾷς] and have nothing to say? And yet don't

you think it's a disgrace and sufficient evidence of what I'm saying that you've never cared about this. Well tell us, like the good man you are, who makes them better?'

Meletus: 'The laws.'"

Comment: Socrates continues to question Meletus, and Meletus continues to answer.

[SS] Plato *Apology of Socrates* (5–4 BC) 37E

"Perhaps someone may say: 'If you keep silent [σιγῶν] and lead a quiet life, Socrates, won't you be able to carry on living away from us in exile?' This is the most difficult thing of all to convince some of you of."

Comment: Silence here is equivalent to a quiet life where one does speak but not speak in a way as to challenge his hearers.

[SS] Plato *Theaetetus* (5–4 BC) 146A

"Why are you silent [σιγᾶτε]? I hope, Theodorus, I am not rude, through my love of discussion and my eagerness to make us converse and show ourselves friends and ready to talk to one another."

Comment: Socrates asks this question in the middle of his speech. Theodorus and Theaetetus are speaking to Socrates before and after this statement. Socrates is commenting on a momentary silence.

[SS] Plato *Theaetetus* (5–4 BC) 161E

"Must we not believe that Protagoras was 'playing to the gallery' in saying this? I say nothing [σιγῶ] of the ridicule that I and my science of midwifery deserve in that case,—and, I should say, the whole practice of dialectics, too."

[SS] Plato *Phaedrus* (5–4 BC) 275D

"Writing, Phaedrus, has this strange quality, and is very like painting; for the creatures of painting stand like living beings, but if one asks them a question, they preserve a solemn silence [σιγᾷ]. And so it is with written words; you might think they spoke as if they had intelligence, but if you question them, wishing to know about their sayings, they always say only one and the same thing."

Comment: The analogy here seems to be that painting "speaks" and is "silent" in select ways, and so also written words.

[SS] Plato *Phaedrus* (5–4 BC) 276A

"The word which is written with intelligence in the mind of the learner, which is able to defend itself and knows to whom it should speak, and before whom to be silent [σιγᾶν]."

Comment: This statement is a continuation of the discussion above (*Phaedrus* 275D). However, Socrates had just asked, "Now tell me; is there not another kind of speech, or word, which shows itself to be the legitimate brother of this bastard one, both in the manner of its begetting and in its better and more powerful nature" (276A).

[SS] Plato *Alcibiades I* (5–4 BC) 106A

"You seem to me far more extraordinary, Socrates, now that you have begun to speak, then before, when you followed me about in silence [σιγῶν]; though even then you looked strange enough."

Comment: Alcibiades is speaking after Socrates mentioned that the god had prevented him from talking to him. So in this case Socrates is silent for a period of time to a particular person.

[SS] Plato *The Lovers* (5–4 BC) 133A

"Then the two striplings, overhearing us speak somewhat like this, were silent [ἐσιγησάτην], and ceasing from their own contention they became listeners to ours."

Comment: Two boys were speaking in the school among themselves, and then they stop to listen to Socrates and the two lovers. Later the boys "were delighted and laughed their approval" (134B).

[SS] Plato *The Lovers* (5–4 BC) 134A

"Here I felt it was time to stir up the lover of athletics, in order that he might give me the support of his athletic experience; so I proceeded to ask him: And you then, pray, why are you silent [σιγᾷς], excellent sir, while your friend here is speaking thus? Do you agree that men are in good bodily condition through much exercise, or is it rather through moderate exercise?"

Comment: The lover of athletics had spoken at the beginning of this debate (132B) but after that had been silent until this point in the debate.

[SS] Plato *The Lovers* (5–4 BC) 139A

"On my saying this the cultivated youth was silent [ἐσίγησεν], feeling ashamed for what he had said before, while the unlearned one said it was as I stated; and the rest of the company praised the argument."

Comment: The youth was silenced concerning the specific topic being debated.

[SS] Plato *Lysis* (5–4 BC) 222A

"And in a case where one person desires another, my boys, or loves him, he would never be desiring or loving or befriending him, unless he somehow belonged to his beloved either in soul, or in some disposition, demeanour or cast of soul. Yes, to be sure, said Menexenus; but Lysis was silent [ἐσίγησεν]."

Comment: Lysis had spoken previously but is silent about this point.

[SS] Plato *Euthydemus* (5–4 BC) Stephanus 286B

"At this Ctesippus was silent [ἐσίγησεν]; but I, wondering at the argument, said: How do you mean, Dionysodorus?"

Comment: Ctesippus is speaking both before and after this statement about his silence. Ctesippus was momentarily silent about the previous question that was posed (see "at this" in the translation).

[SS] Plato *Euthydemus* (5–4 BC) 299C–D

"At this Euthydemus was silent [ἐσίγησεντ]; then Dionysodorus asked some questions on Ctesippus' previous answers, saying: Well now, gold is in your opinion a good thing to have?"

Comment: This quote is the same usage of silence as 286B, above.

[SS] Plato *Euthydemus* (5–4 BC) 300A–D

> "Tell me, said Euthydemus, do the Scythians and men in general see things possible of sight, or things impossible?
> Possible, I presume.
> And you do so too?
> I too.
> Then you see our cloaks?
> Yes.
> And have they power of sight?
> Quite extraordinarily, said Ctesippus.
> What do they see? he asked.

Nothing. Perhaps you do not think they see—you are such a sweet innocent. I should say, Euthydemus, that you have fallen asleep with your eyes open and, if it be possible to speak and at the same time say nothing, that this is what you are doing.

Why, asked Dionysodorus, may there not be a speaking of the silent [σιγῶντα]?

By no means whatever, replied Ctesippus.

Nor a silence [σιγᾶν] of speaking?

Still less, he said.

Now, when you speak of stones and timbers and irons, are you not speaking of the silent [σιγῶντα]?

Not if I walk by a smithy, for there, as they say, the irons speak and cry aloud, when they are touched; so here your wisdom has seduced you into nonsense. But come, you have still to propound me your second point, how on the other hand there may be a silence [σιγᾶν] of speaking. (It struck me that Ctesippus was specially excited on account of his young friend's presence.)

When you are silent [σιγᾷς], said Euthydemus, are you not making a silence [σιγᾷς] of all things?

Yes, he replied.

Then it is a silence [σιγᾷς] of speaking things also, if the speaking are among all things.

What, said Ctesippus, are not all things silent [σιγᾷ]?

I presume not, said Euthydemus.

But then, my good sire, do all things speak?

Yes, I suppose, at least those that speak.

But that is not what I ask, he said: are all things silent [σιγᾷ] or do they speak?

Neither and both, said Dionysodorus, snatching the word from him: I am quite sure that is an answer that will baffle you!"

Comment: The very fact that there is debate over the meaning of words, such as silence here, shows that more time should be given to a contextual definition of silence than is often granted in the interpretation of 1 Corinthians.

[SS] Plato *Protagoras* (5–4 BC) 360D

"Here he could no longer bring himself to nod agreement, and remained silent [ἐσίγα]. Then I proceeded: Why is it, Protagoras, that you neither affirm nor deny what I ask you?"

Comment: Protagoras is silent on the previous question posed to him. Protagoras continues the debate after this moment.

[SS] Plato *Lesser Hippias* (5–4 BC) 363A

"Why, then, are you silent [σιγᾷς], Socrates, when Hippias has been delivering such a fine display?"

Comment: Eudicus is speaking at the opening of *Hippias minor*. Socrates was silent after Hippias's speech, and Eudicus wanted Socrates to "join us in praising some part of his speech" or "refute him" (363A).

[SS] Plato *Laws* (5–4 BC) 788C

"Hence, while it is impossible to pass over these practices in silence [σιγᾶν], it is difficult to legislate concerning them."

Comment: In the context of children's nurture and education, "these practices" refer to certain things done privately by a family.

[SS] Plato *Laws* (5–4 BC) 792A

"When nurses are trying to discover what a baby wants, they judge by these very same signs in offering it things. If it remains silent [σιγᾷ] when the thing is offered, they conclude that it is the right thing, but the wrong thing if it weeps and cries out. Thus infants indicate what they like by means of weepings and outcries—truly no happy signals!—and this period of infancy lasts not less than three years, which is no small fraction of one's time to spend ill or well."

[SS] Plato *Laws* (5–4 BC) 876B

"It will be best to make the following statement next,—that in a State where the courts are poor and dumb and decide their cases privily, secreting their own opinions, or (and this is a still more dangerous practice) when they make their decisions not silently [σιγῶντα] but filled with tumult, like theatres, roaring out praise or blame of each speaker in turn,—then the whole State, as a rule, is faced with a difficult situation."

[SS] Plato *Letters* (5–4 BC) 311B–C[8]

"Now my object in saying all this is to make it clear, that when we ourselves die men's talk about us will not likewise be silenced [σεσιγήσονται]; so that we must

---

8   Plato, *Ep.* 310D–E states, "Now as for you and me, the relation in which we stand towards each other is really this. There is not a single Greek, one may say, to whom we are unknown, and our intercourse is a matter of common talk [σιγᾶται]; and you may be sure of this, that it will be common talk [σιγηθήσεται] also in days to come, because so many have heard tell of it owing to its duration and its publicity." This usage appears to be an anomaly in how σιγάω is used.

be careful about it. We must necessarily, it seems, have a care also for the future, seeing that, by some law of nature, the most slavish men pay no regard to it, whereas the most upright do all they can to ensure that they shall be well spoken of in the future."

Comment: Even if the men still living were silent in this case (see "talk about us"), they would still be speaking about other matters.

[D] Plato *Epigrammata* (5–4 BC) Book 9 epigram 823[9]

"Let the cliff clothed in greenery of the Dryads keep silence [σιγάτω], and the fountains that fall from the rock, and the confused bleating of the ewes newly lambed; for Pan himself plays on his sweet-toned pipe, running his pliant lips over the joined reeds, and around with their fresh feet they have started the dance, the Nymphs, Hydriads, and Hamadryads."[10]

[SS] Plato *Republic* (5–4 BC) 378A

"Even if they were true I should not think that they ought to be thus lightly told to thoughtless young persons. But the best way would be to bury them in silence [σιγᾶσθαι], and if there were some necessity for relating them, that only a very small audience should be admitted under pledge of secrecy and after sacrificing, not a pig, but some huge and unprocurable victim, to the end that as few as possible should have heard these tales."

Comment: The topic is censorship of stories such as ones from Hesiod and Homer.

[SS] Plato *Republic* (5–4 BC) 514B–515A

"'See also, then, men carrying past the wall implements of all kinds that rise above the wall, and human images and shapes of animals as well, wrought in stone and wood and every material, some of these bearers presumably speaking and others silent [σιγῶντας].' 'A strange image you speak of,' he said, 'and strange prisoners.'"

Comment: This reference is the famous scene of the allegory of the cave.

9   See W. R. Paton, trans., *The Greek Anthology*, LCL 84 (Cambridge: Harvard University Press, 1983), 3:442–43.
10 The reference in TLG of Plato *Epigrammata* (5–4 BC) Epigram 26 is a duplicate of the same Greek text.

[SS] Plato *Republic* (5–4 BC) 615D–616A

"But there were some of private station, of those who had committed great crimes. And when these supposed that at last they were about to go up and out, the mouth would not receive them, but it bellowed when anyone of the incurably wicked or of those who had not completed their punishment tried to come up.... And then, though many and manifold dread things had befallen them, this fear exceeded all—lest each one should hear the voice when he tried to go up, and each went up most gladly when it had kept silence [σιγήσαντος]."

[SS] Lysias *In Eratosthenem* (5–4 BC) 13

"Peison came up and urged me to keep silent [σιγᾶν] and have no fear, as he was coming on to that place."

Comment: To save his own life, Lysias bribed Peison. It is concerning this plan that Peison urges silence when Melobius and Mnesitheides came to them. Lysias continues to speak of other matters.

[AS] Hippocrates *Epidemics* (5–4 BC) 3.1.154–58

"She had a cough with signs of coction, but brought up nothing. No appetite for any food the whole time, nor did she desire anything. No thirst, and she drank nothing worth mentioning. She was silent [σιγῶσα], and did not converse at all. Depression, the patient despairing of herself."

Comment: This medical case is about a maiden daughter of Euryanax who had died from her condition. The emphasis on not conversing is οὐδὲν διελέγετο.

[AS] Hippocrates *Epidemics* (5–4 BC) 3.17.305–10

"*First day.* Acute fever with shivering; painful heaviness of head and neck. Sleepless from the first, but silent [σιγῶσα], sulky and refractory. Urine thin and of no colour; thirsty; nausea generally; bowels irregularly disturbed with constipation following."

[SS] Hippocrates *Epidemics* (5–4 BC) 3.15.318–36

"In Thasos the wife of Delearees, who lay sick on the plain, was seized after a grief with an acute fever with shivering. From the beginning she would wrap herself up, and throughout, without speaking a word [σιγῶσα], she would fumble, pluck, scratch, pick hairs, weep and then laugh, but she did not sleep; though stimulated, the bowels passed nothing. She drank a little when the attendants suggested it. Urine thin and scanty; fever slight to the touch; coldness of the extremities. *Ninth day*. Much wandering followed by return of reason; silent [σιγῶσα].... *Twenty-first day*. Death. The respiration of this patient throughout was rare and large; took no notice of anything; she constantly wrapped herself up; either much rambling or silence [σιγῶσα] throughout."

Comment: The final occurrence of σιγάω demonstrates that the same patient alternated between being silent and rambling (λόγοι πολλοί). TLG lists this reference as 3.17(15).

[SS] Hippocrates *Epidemics* (5–4 BC) 6.3.19

"When it is necessary to prevent thirst, keep the mouth closed, do not speak [σιγᾶν], inhale cold wind with drink."

Comment: Hippocrates thinks that the solution of being silent (among other actions) is during the time when "it is necessary to prevent thirst."

[SU] Hippocrates *In the Surgery* (5–4 BC) 6

"Let those who look after the patient present the part for operation as you want it, and hold fast the rest of the body so as to be all steady, keeping silence [σιγῶντες] and obeying their superior."

[SS] Hippocrates *On Joints* (5–4 BC) 50.19–26

"It is well to reduce the diet, keep the body at rest as far as possible, avoid sexual intercourse, rich foods and those which excite coughing, and all strong nourishment; to open a vein at the elbow, observe silence [σιγᾶν] as much as possible, dress the contused part with pads not much folded, but numerous, and extending in every direction a good way beyond the contusion."

Comment: There is a parallel in Greek here:
ἀτρεμεῖν τε τῷ σώματι ὡς μάλιστα, "keep the body at rest as far as possible."
σιγᾶν τε ὡς μάλιστα, "observe silence as much as possible."

[SS] Hippocrates *The Oath* (5–4 BC) 29–32

"And whatsoever I shall see or hear in the course of my profession, as well as outside my profession in my intercourse with men, if it be what should not be published abroad, I will never divulge [σιγήσομαι], holding such things to be holy secrets."

Comment: This oath is a way of life and silence specifically for "what should not be published abroad."

[SS] Hippocrates *Coan Prenotions* (5–4 BC) 65

"Silent [σιγῶσαι] trances during fevers, in a patient who has not lost his speech, are a fatal sign."

[SS] Hippocrates *Coan Prenotions* (5–4 BC) 476

"Patients with silent [σιγῶσαι] derangements of the mind, who are not at peace, who gaze about with their eyes, and who expel their breath forcefully, are doomed; these conditions bring about chronic paralyses, and also mania."

[N/A] Hippocrates *Diseases of Women II* (5–4 BC) 44 (328)

"To such patients, if later their uterus fails to remain in place but moves around, give hellebore. If such measures are not effective, also induce vomiting, forbid bathing, and have the patient stay still and quiet [σιγᾶν]."

Comment: It may not be possible to determine with much certainty the degree of quietness here. It is stated simply in general terms without any elaboration.

[SS] Hippocrates *The Physician* (5–4 BC) 1

"The dignity of a physician requires that he should look healthy, and as plump as nature intended him to be; for the common crowd consider those who are not of this excellent bodily condition to be unable to take care of others. Then he must be clean in person, well dressed, and anointed with sweet-smelling unguents that are beyond suspicion. For all these things are pleasing to people who are ill, and he must pay attention to this. In matters of the mind, let him be prudent, not only with regard to silence [σιγᾶν], but also in having a great regularity of life, since this is very important in respect of reputation; he must be a gentleman in character, and being this he must be grave and kind to all."

Comment: This quotation is the opening statement of the book. It charges a physician with a certain way of life—knowing when to be silent and when to speak.

[SS] Demosthenes *On the Peace* (4 BC) 9–10

"But you will find that I neither took part in this deception, nor passed it over in silence [σιγήσας], but spoke out boldly, as I am sure you remember, saying that I had neither knowledge nor expectation of such results and that all such talk was nonsense."

Comment: In context Demosthenes references very specific promises and "false hopes."

[SS] Demosthenes *3 Philippic* (4 BC) 61

"When the democrats of Oreus saw this, instead of rescuing him and knocking the others on the head, they showed no resentment against them and gloated over Euphraeus, saying that he deserved all he had got. Then having all the liberty of action they desired, they intrigued for the capture of the city and prepared to carry out their plot, while any of the common folk who saw what they were at were terrorized into silence [ἐσίγα], having the fate of Euphraeus before their eyes. And so abject was their condition that, with this danger looming ahead, no one dared to breathe a syllable until the enemy, having completed their preparations, were approaching the gates; and then some were for defence, the others for surrender."

Comment: The common people were silent about anything that would bring against them the same fate as Euphraeus.

[SS] Demosthenes *On the Crown* (4 BC) 23

"Yet if I had really intrigued with Philip to stop a Panhellenic coalition, it was your business not to hold your peace [σιγῆσαι], but to cry aloud, to protest, to inform the people. You did nothing of the sort."

[SS] Demosthenes *On the Crown* (4 BC) 189

"That is the salient difference between the statesman and the charlatan, who are indeed in all respects unlike one another. The statesman declares his judgment before the event, and accepts responsibility to his followers, to fortune, to the chances of the hour, to every critic of his policy. The charlatan holds his peace [σιγήσας] when he ought to speak, and then croaks over any untoward result."

[SS] Demosthenes *False Embassy* (4 BC) 31

"These documents will satisfy you that I did not hold my peace [σιγήσας] then, to run away from my actions now,—for I was laying my complaint, and trying to forecast results, at the first opportunity; and also that the Council, not being debarred from hearing the truth from me, did not give these men either a vote of thanks, or an invitation to the public dinner in the Town Hall."

[SS] Demosthenes *False Embassy* (4 BC) Section 33

"For it is clear that, if the evil-doer could hold his peace [σιγᾶν], escape immediate detection, and never afterwards allow himself to be called to account, that was good enough for him; whereas the man with a good conscience bethought himself that it would be very hard if by keeping silence he should become a reputed accomplice in scandalous and wicked actions. Well, then, it was I who denounced these men from the outset, and none of them denounced me."

[SS] Demosthenes *False Embassy* (4 BC) 255

"Now here, now there, they raven, rob and seize
Heedless of Justice and her stern decrees,
Who silently [σιγῶσα] the present and the past
Reviews, whose slow revenge o'ertakes at last."

Comment: Demosthenes is quoting Solon for his purpose against Aeschines. The picture is of Justice silently reviewing the deeds of "dishonest demagogues."

[SS] Demosthenes *Against Aristocrates* (4 BC) 57

"Let us suppose that a fate that has doubtless befallen others before now should befall him,—that he should withdraw from Thrace and come and live somewhere in a civilized community; and that, though no longer enjoying the licence under which he now commits many illegalities, he should be driven by his habits and his lusts to attempt the sort of behavior I have mentioned, will not a man be obliged to allow himself to be insulted by Charidemus in silence [σιγῶντα]? It will not be safe to put him to death, nor, by reason of this decree, to obtain the satisfaction provided by law."

Comment: The context is the possibility that Charidemus could mistreat a man, and silence would be equivalent to the "man whom he insults has been defrauded of his legal remedy" (59).

[SE] Aeschines *Against Timarchus* (4 BC) 107

"And in his treatment of the wives of free men he showed such licentiousness as no other man ever did. Of these men I call no one into court to testify publicly to his own misfortune, which he has chosen to cover in silence [σιγᾶν], but I leave it to you to investigate this matter."

[SS] Aeschines *On the Embassy* (4 BC) 34–35

"Now when I had said this and more beside, at last came Demosthenes' turn to speak.... So when all were thus prepared to listen, this creature mouthed forth a proem—an obscure sort of thing and as dead as fright could make it; and getting on a little way into the subject he suddenly stopped speaking [ἐσίγησε] and stood helpless; finally he collapsed completely. Philip saw his plight and bade him take courage, and not to think, as though he were an actor on the stage, that his collapse was an irreparable calamity, but to keep cool and try gradually to recall his speech, and speak it off as he had prepared it. But he, having been once upset, and having forgotten what he had written, was unable to recover himself; nay, on making a second attempt, he broke down again. Silence followed; then the herald bade us withdraw."

Comment: Demosthenes is speaking and then silent. It is noteworthy that he made a "second attempt" at speaking, and that Philip wanted him to continue speaking after being silent even though Demosthenes was unable to do so.

[SE] Aeschines *On the Embassy* (4 BC) 86

"And my accuser has dared to tell you that it was I who drove Critobulus, Cersobleptes' ambassador, from the ceremony—in the presence of the allies, under the eyes of the generals, after the people had voted as they did! Where did I get all that power? How could the thing have been hushed up [ἐσιγήθη]? If I had really dared to undertake such a thing, would you have suffered it, Demosthenes?"

[SS] Aeschines *On the Embassy* (4 BC) 162–63

"And so it seems that among all these I was conspicuous, not by my silence, but by joining in the singing—for Demosthenes says so, who was not there himself, and presents no witness from among those who were. Who would have noticed me, unless I was a sort of precentor and led the chorus? Therefore if I was silent [ἐσίγων], your charge is false; but if, with our fatherland safe and no harm done to my fellow citizens, I joined the other ambassadors in singing the paean when the god was being magnified and the Athenians in no wise dishonoured, I was doing a pious act and no wrong, and I should justly be acquitted."

Comment: The first sentence "not by my silence" is οὐκ ὑποσιγῶν. The topic here is whether or not Aeschines was silent during the singing.

[SS] Aeschines *Against Ctesiphon* (4 BC) 4

"The result of all this is that we have ceased to hear [σεσίγηται] that wisest and most judicious of all the proclamations to which the city was once accustomed, 'Who of the men above fifty years of age wishes to address the people,' and then who of the other Athenians in turn."

Comment: Aeschines specifies the proclamation that is being silenced (the proclamation here quoted).

[SS] Aeschines *Against Ctesiphon* (4 BC) 165–66

"Pray set forth to us, Demosthenes, what in the world there was that you did then, or what in the world there was that you said. I will yield the platform to you, if you wish, until you have told us. You are silent [σιγᾷς]. I can well understand your embarrassment. But what you said then, I myself will tell now."

Comment: Aeschines's rhetoric needs to be kept in mind here between his disputes and speeches against Demosthenes.

[SS] Aeschines *Against Ctesiphon* (4 BC) 218

"As to my silence, Demosthenes, it has been caused by the moderation of my life. For a little money suffices me, and I have no shameful lust for more. Both my silence [σιγῶ *or* σιωπῶ] and my speech are therefore the result of deliberation, not of the impulse of a spendthrift nature. But you, I think, are silent [σιγᾷς *or* σεσίγηκας] when you have gotten, and bawl aloud after you have spent; and you speak, not when your judgment approves, and not what you wish to speak, but whenever your pay-masters so order."

Comment: The passage is textually different between the TLG and LCL. I have provided both Greek terms in each case. Nonetheless, the passage puts silence and speech together for both Aeschines and Demosthenes.

[SS] Aeschines *Against Ctesiphon* (4 BC) Section 225

"I say nothing [σιγῶ] of forged letters and the arrest of spies, and torture applied on groundless charges, on your assertion that I with certain persons was seeking a revolution."

[SS] Aeneas *On the Defense of Fortified Positions* (4 BC) 22.12–14

"During the dark winter nights stone after stone should be thrown over the walls, and, as if persons were seen, let the guard ask, 'Who goes there?', for any who might be approaching would thus be recognized without more ado. If it should seem best, this could be done also inside the city. Some, however, say this is dangerous, for a party of the enemy which might be approaching in the darkness are made aware in advance that they must not attack at this point, by the noise of the patrols and the throwing of stones, but rather at the point where there is no noise [σιγώμενον]. The best plan, however, on such nights is to have dogs tied outside the wall to keep watch."

Comment: There is a specific point in this scenario where there is silence (εἰς τὸν σιγώμενον τόπον).

[SS] Aristoteles *Sophistical Refutations* (4 BC) 166A

"The following examples are connected with ambiguity: 'To wish me the enemy to capture,' and 'when a man knows something, surely there is knowledge of this'; for it is possible by this expression to signify both the knower and the things known as knowing. And 'what a man sees, surely that (he) sees: a man a pillar sees, therefore the pillar sees.' Again, 'Surely you insist on being what you insist on being. You insist on a stone being: therefore, you insist on being a stone.' Again 'Surely speaking is possible of the silent [σιγῶντα].' 'Speaking of the silent [σιγῶντα]' can also be taken in two ways, either that the speaker is silent [σιγᾶν] or the things spoken of are silent."

Comment: Like Plato's *Euthydemus* (300A–D), Aristotle's illustration using σιγάω demonstrates that the term can have different meanings depending on the contextual use. For Aristotle to discuss ambiguity here means that one cannot assume a single definition. This theme of using silence as an illustration will continue in the examples below.

[SS] Aristoteles *Sophistical Refutations* (4 BC) 171A

"It is quite absurd to discuss refutation without previously discussing proof.... In the argument that 'the silent [σιγῶντα] speaks,' the refutation lies in the contradiction, not in the proof; in the argument that 'a man can give away what he has not got,' it lies in both; in the argument that 'Homer's poetry is a figure' because it forms a 'cycle,' it lies in the proof. The argument that errs in neither respect is a true proof."

[SS] Aristoteles *Sophistical Refutations* (4 BC) 171A

"But to resume from the point whence the argument digressed, Are mathematical arguments always applied to the thought or not...? Further, if the name has several meanings but the answerer does not think or imagine that this is so, has not the questioner reasoned against his thought? Or how else must the question be asked except by offering a distinction? In which case one will ask, 'Is it or is it not possible for a man to speak when silent [σιγῶντα], or is the answer in one sense 'No,' in another 'Yes'?'"

[SS] Aristoteles *Sophistical Refutations* (4 BC) 171A

"But if one claims to make distinctions, saying, 'by 'the silent [σιγῶντα] speaking' I mean sometimes one thing and sometimes another,' this claim is, in the first place, absurd (for sometimes the question does not seem to involve any ambiguity, and it is impossible to make a distinction where no ambiguity is suspected); and, secondly, what else will didactic argument be but this? For it will make clear the position to one who neither has considered nor knows nor conceives that a second meaning is possible."

[SS] Aristoteles *Sophistical Refutations* (4 BC) 177A

"Of the refutations which hinge upon equivocation and ambiguity some involve a question which bears more than one sense, while others have a conclusion which can bear several meanings; for example, in the argument about 'the speech of the silent [σιγῶντα],' the conclusion has a double meaning, and in the argument that 'a man who knows is not conscious of what he knows,' one of the questions involves ambiguity. Also, that which has a double meaning is sometimes true and sometimes false, the term 'double' signifying that which is party true and partly untrue."

[SS] Aristoteles *Sophistical Refutations* (4 BC) 177A

"At the beginning, therefore, one ought to reply to an ambiguous term or expression in the following manner, that 'in one sense it is so and in another it is not so'; for example 'the speaking of the silent [σιγῶντα]' is possible in one sense but not in another. Or again, 'what needs must is to be done sometimes and not at other times'; for the term 'what needs must' can bear several meanings. If one does not notice the ambiguity, one should make a correction at the end by adding to the questioning: 'Is the speaking of the silent [σιγῶντα] possible?' 'No, but speaking of this particular man when he is silent [σιγῶντα] is possible.'"

[D] Theocritus *Idylls* (4–3 BC) Idyll 2.38–41

"Look, still is the sea and still [σιγῶντι] are the breezes; but the pain in my heart is not still. The whole of me is burning for the man who made me disgraced—wretch that I am—and no longer a virgin, instead of his wife."

[SS] Theocritus *Idylls* (4–3 BC) Idyll 15.96–99

"Stop talking [σίγη], Praxinoa; the Argive woman's daughter is going to sing the hymn to Adonis, that talented singer who did best in the lament last year. She'll give an excellent performance, I'm sure. She's just clearing her throat."

Comment: Gorgo is telling her friend to be quiet while they listen to the hymn. Interestingly, Praxinoa had just told a man why she would not stop chatting with her friend Gorgo since he was not her master (15.87–95). The form σίγη is unexpected in this sentence. Bernard Grenfell and Arthur Hunt explain the textual tradition, "σιγη: so K; σίγα other MSS."[11]

[SE] Theocritus *Idylls* (4–3 BC) Idyll 16.48–57

"Who would have ever known of the leaders of the Lycians or the long-haired sons of Priam or Cycnus, whose complexion was like a girl's, if poets had not celebrated the battles of men of old? Odysseus, who wandered for six score months all through the world, and went to farthest Hades while still alive, and escaped from the cave of the terrible Cyclops, would not have had long-lasting fame, and Eumaeus the swineherd and Philoetius who looked after the herding of cattle, and greathearted Laertes himself would have been unknown [ἐσιγάθη] if the songs of the Ionian bard had not benefited them."

Comment: It appears that Eumaeus, Philoetius, and Laertes would be silenced (or concealed, kept secret) were it not for poets making them known for later generations. M. J. Chapman translates that they would "had been in a perpetual silence pent, But for that old Ionian eloquent."[12]

[N/A] Menander *Sententiae e codicibus Byzantinis* (4–3 BC) Line 258
(so also Sententia Mono Section 1 line 387)

"Sometimes it is better to be silent [σιγᾶν] than to speak."[13]

Comment: W.G. Arnott writes, "Throughout later antiquity collections were made of those individual lines from Menander's plays which could stand on their own as aphorisms. In the course of time the text of many of these now contextless lines became badly garbled, and the genuinely Menandrean material was augmented with much that was spurious."[14]

[N/A] Menander *Sententiae e codicibus Byzantinis* (4–3 BC) Line 521
(so also Sententia Mono Section 1 line 375)

"Now it is more fitting to be silent [σιγᾶν] than to speak."[15]

---

11 Bernard P. Grenfell and Arthur P. Hunt, *The Oxyrhynchus Papyri*, Part 13 (London: Egypt Exploration Fund, 1919), 179.
12 M. J. Chapman, trans., *The Greek Pastoral Poets: Theocritus—Bion—Moschus*, 3rd, rev. ed. (London: Saunders, Otley, and Co., 1866).
13 My translation. The Greek text of Menander taken from Siegfried Jäkel, ed., *Menandri Sententiae*, BSGRT (Lipsiae: Teubner, 1964).
14 W. G. Arnott, ed., *Menander*, LCL 132 (Cambridge: Harvard University Press, 1979), 1:xxv.
15 My translation.

[N/A] Menander *Sententiae e codicibus Byzantinis* (4–3 BC) Line 555 (so also Sententia Mono Section 1 line 401)

"As a guest it is better to be silent [σιγᾶν] than to cry."[16]

[N/A] Menander *Sententiae e codicibus Byzantinis* (4–3 BC) Line 566 (so also Sententia Mono Section 1 line 417)

"It is not shameful to be silent [σιγᾶν] but to speak in vain."[17]

[N/A] Menander *Sententiae e codicibus Byzantinis* (4–3 BC) Line 710 (so also Sententia Mono Section 1 line 484)

"It is better to be silent [σιγᾶν] than to speak what is not fitting."[18]

[N/A] Menander *Sententiae e papyris* (4–3 BC) Sententia 4 line 7

"Σιγᾶν δύνασθαι λ [οι] δορούμενον καλό[ν]."

Comment: The sentence is fragmentary.

[N/A] Menander *Sententiae e papyris* (4–3 BC) Sententia 13 lines 14–15

"Sometimes it is better to be silent [σιγᾶν] than to speak."[19]

Comment: The context is fragmentary though the idea appears to be selective silence.

[SS] Apollonius Rhodius *Argonautica* (3 BC) 2.254–56

"Thus he spoke. The old man opened his blank eyes and directed them straight up at him, and answered with these words: 'Hush [σίγα]! Please do not put such thoughts in your head, my son.'"

Comment: He is silencing Zetes who had just spoken. *Argonautica* 2.430–34 later states, "And Zetes, still drawing hard breath after his toil, spake among the eager listeners, telling them how far they had driven the Harpies and how Iris prevented their slaying them, and how the goddess of her grace gave them pledges, and how those others in fear plunged into the vast cave of the Dictaean cliff."

---

16 My translation.
17 My translation.
18 My translation.
19 My translation.

[N/A] Asclepiades *Epigrammata* (3 BC) Book 5 epigram 167

"There was rain and darkness and that third burden for lovers, wine. There was also a cold north wind, find I was alone. But lovely Moschus was stronger yet: you too would have gone forth, not pausing in even one doorway. Standing there drenched, I shouted this: 'How long, Zeus? Silence [σίγησον] please, Zeus; you too learned to love.'"[20]

[N/A] Posidippus *Epigrammata* (3 BC) Book 5 epigram 134[21]

"Sprinkle, Cecropian jug, the moist dew of Bacchus; sprinkle, and bedew the toast that I contribute. Let Zeno, that philosophical swan, and Cleanthes' Muse, keep silent [σιγάσθω], and bittersweet Love be our topic."[22]

[SE] Polybius *The Histories* (3–2 BC) 9.13

"Therefore in such enterprises commanders must be careful about every detail. The first and foremost requisite is to keep silence [σιγᾶν], and never either from joy if some unexpected hope shall present itself, or from fear, or from familiarity with or affection for certain persons, to reveal one's design to anyone unconcerned in it, but to communicate it only to those without whom it cannot be put in execution, and even to these not earlier than when the need of their services renders it imperative. And we must keep not only our tongues tied [σιγᾶν] but even more so our minds. For many who have kept their own counsel have revealed their projects either by the expression of their faces or by their actions."

Comment: Polybius writes about how a commander can be successful. In this case, the same person can keep a secret from one group of people and to another group "communicate it."

[SS] Exodus (3 BC/AD 3) 14:14 LXX

"The Lord will fight for you, and you yourselves be silent [σιγήσετε]."[23]

Comment: The people of Israel simply needed to be silent during the Lord's battle against the Egyptians. Of course, Israel would sing to the Lord after the battle.

---

20   Text and translation from Kathryn J. Gutzwiller, *Poetic Garlands: Hellenistic Epigrams in Context* (Berkeley: University of California Press, 1998), 140.
21   See W. R. Paton, trans., *The Greek Anthology*, rev. ed., Michael A. Tueller, LCL 67 (Cambridge: Harvard University Press, 2014), 1:290–91.
22   The second reference in TLG of Posidippus *Epigrammata* (3 BC) Epigram 123 line 3 is a duplicate of the same Greek text.
23   My translation. LXX texts used in this section are the Göttingen text (where available) and Rahlfs-Hanhart.

[SS] 1 Esdras (3 BC/AD 3) 3:23/3:24 LXX

"O men, is not wine the strongest since it compels people to act so? And he was silent [ἐσίγησεν] after thus speaking."[24]

Comment: The setting is the contest between the three bodyguards on what is the strongest (wine, the king, or women/truth). The first bodyguard gave his speech and then was silent for the second bodyguard to speak.

[SS] 1 Esdras (3 BC/AD 3) 4:12 LXX

"O men, how is the king not strongest since he is thus obeyed? And he was silent [ἐσίγησεν]."[25]

Comment: The second bodyguard gave his speech and then was silent for the third bodyguard to speak.

[SS] Tobit (Codex B, Codex A) (3BC/AD 3) 10:6–7a LXX

"And Tobit said to her, 'Quiet [σίγα], you have no reason, he is fine.' And she said to him, 'Quiet [σίγα], do not deceive me. My child has perished.'"[26]

Comment: Tobit and his wife are shushing each other over the question of why Tobias has not arrived yet.

[SS] 1 Maccabees (3 BC/AD 3) 11:5 LXX

"And they notified the king of what Jonathan had done in order to blame him, but the king was silent [ἐσίγησεν]."[27]

Comment: The king was silent in regards to the attempted blame of Jonathan.

[SS] Psalm (3 BC/AD 3) 31:3 LXX

"Because I was silent [ἐσίγησα], my bones decayed from my crying the entire day."[28]

Comment: David was silent over his sins, but in Psalm 31:5 LXX he confesses them to the Lord.

---

24 My translation.
25 My translation.
26 My translation. There is an expansion in Codex Sinaiticus, but there is no major difference for Tob 10:6–7 regarding σιγάω. Tobit 5:23/6:1 in Codex Sinaiticus has καὶ ἐσίγησεν κλαίουσα (as opposed to καὶ ἐπαύσατο κλαίουσα). Robert J Littman, who translates this phrase as "she grew silent from her crying," summarizes some of the critical issues (*Tobit: The Book of Tobit in Codex Sinaiticus*, ed. Stanley E. Porter, Richard S. Hess, and John Jarick, Septuagint Commentary Series [Leiden: Brill, 2008], 106).
27 My translation.
28 My translation.

[SS] Psalm (3 BC/AD 3) 38:3 LXX

"I was speechless and humbled and silent [ἐσίγησα] from good things, and my grief was revived."[29]

Comment: David will go on to describe how he then spoke (Psalm 38:4 LXX).

[SS] Psalm (3 BC/AD 3) 49:21 LXX

"You did these things, and I was silent [ἐσίγησα]. You suppose in lawlessness that I will be like you. I will rebuke you and I will show you to yourself."

Comment: Clearly, God is not absolutely silent, by his very nature. He was "silent" for a moment but now will rebuke the wicked.

[SS] Psalm (3 BC/AD 3) 82:2 LXX

"O God, who is like you? Do not be silent [σιγήσῃς] or softened, O God."[30]

Comment: The topic in this case is not to be "silent" in regard to his enemies. God can at the same time be speaking to his people and be "silent" against his enemies.

[D] Psalm (3 BC/AD 3) 106:29 LXX

"And he commanded the storm and stopped the wind, and its waves were silenced [ἐσίγησαν]."[31]

[SS] Ecclesiastes (3 BC/AD 3) 3:7b LXX

"There is a time to be silent [σιγᾶν] and a time to speak."[32]

Comment: The context is that "for all things there is a time, and a time for every matter under heaven" (Ecc 3:1 LXX).

[SS] Wisdom of Solomon (3 BC/AD 3) 8:12 LXX

"When I am silent [σιγῶντά] they will wait for me, and when I speak they will give heed; if I speak at greater length, they will put their hands on their mouths."[33]

Comment: The author is referring to speaking with wisdom.

---

29 My translation.
30 My translation.
31 My translation.
32 My translation.
33 NRSV.

[P] Sirach/Ecclesiasticus (3 BC/3 AD) 13:23ab LXX

"The rich speaks, and everyone is silent [ἐσίγησαν]. And his speech they exalt to the clouds."[34]

Comment: People will stop and listen to what a rich person says simply because he is rich.

[P] Sirach/Ecclesiasticus (3 BC/3 AD) 20:7 LXX

"A wise man will be silent [σιγήσει] until the time, but the boastful and foolish person oversteps the time."[35]

[N/A] Amos (3 BC/AD 3) 6:10 LXX

"And they will take hold of the members of their households and will prevail upon them to bring out their bones from the house and will say to the heads of the house, 'Is he still with you?' And he will say, 'No longer.' And he will say, 'Quiet [σίγα], that you may not name the name of the Lord.'"[36]

Comment: The Lord through Amos is declaring future exile. This passage shows the people's reaction during God's judgment. I have labeled the passage as N/A to show the inconclusive nature of this passage for our current purpose. There are contextual factors that would indicate both absolute silence and specific silence.

[N/A] Isaiah (3 BC/AD 3) 32:5 LXX

"And no longer will one say to the foolish to rule, and no longer will helpers say of you, 'Quiet [σίγα].'"[37]

Comment: The reference and intent of the speaker(s) are unclear in the LXX translation.

---

34 My translation.
35 My translation.
36 My translation.
37 My translation.

[SS] Lamentations (3 BC/AD 3) 3:49–50 LXX

"My eyes are swallowed up with tears, and I will not be silent [σιγήσομαι] to be calm until when the Lord stoops and sees from heaven."[38]

Comment: The context is the destruction of Jerusalem. Being silent or not corresponds to whether or not he continues weeping.[39]

[AS] Moschus *Lament for Bion* (2 BC) Lines 98–107

"Begin, Sicilian Muses, begin your grieving song.
Alas! When garden mallows die back, or green parsley, or the flourishing curly anise, they live again and grow another year; but we men, great and strong and wise, as soon as we die, unhearing in the hollow earth we sleep a long, an endless, an unwaking sleep. And so you, surrounded by silence [σιγᾷ], will be in the earth, while the Nymphs deem it right for the frog to croak for ever. But I feel no envy: that song is not a good one."

Comment: This text may be labeled absolute silence since the context is about Bion's death.

[SS] Agatharchides *On the Erythraean Sea* (2 BC) Section 107

"In discussing the tides the author adduces various explanations and rejects all of them as in no way true. 'That all of these are empty verbiage that ought to be shamed into silence [σιγᾶν] as they have no connection with any fact capable of shedding light on the subject under discussion,' he says, 'is easy to discern.'"[40]

Comment: Specific "explanations" of the tides are said to need silencing.

[AS] *Sibylline Oracles* (2 BC–AD 4) 3.470–73

"But when a destructive man comes from Italy then, Laodicea, dashed down headlong by the wonderful water of Lycus, beautiful town of the Carians, you will bemoan your famous parent and be silent [σιγήσεις]."[41]

---

38 My translation. Helpful are Bernard A. Taylor, *Analytical Lexicon to the Septuagint*, exp. ed. (Peabody, MA: Hendrickson, 2009), and T. Muraoka, *A Syntax of Septuagint Greek* (Leuven: Peeters, 2016). In the latter, see esp. p. 295 n. 2.

39 F. B. Huey, Jr. writes, "The poet would weep unceasingly until God answered from heaven" (*Jeremiah, Lamentations*, NAC 16 [Nashville: Broadman, 1993], 477).

40 Translation from Agatharchides of Cnidus, *On the Erythraean Sea*, ed. and trans. Stanley M. Bursteign, Hakluyt Society, 2nd series, no. 172 (London: Hakluyt Society, 1989), 172. Greek text from Karl Müller, ed., *Geographi Graeci Minores*, vol. 1 (Paris: Ambrosio Firmin Didot, 1855).

41 Translation of the Sibylline Oracles taken from *OTP*.

Comment: A number of clues in the context are intended to speak of great destruction. So the silence here is in response to "dashed down headlong."

[D] *Sibylline Oracles* (2 BC–AD 4) 5.54–59

"First, indeed, around the steps of your much-lamented temple maenads will dart, and you will be in bad hands on that day, when the Nile traverses the whole land of Egypt up to sixteen cubits, so as to flood the whole land and drench it with streams. The beauty of the land and glory of its appearance will disappear [σιγήσει]."

[N/A] *Sibylline Oracles* (2 BC–AD 4) 5.90–91

"You will make retribution for pride, the things you formerly did. You will be silent [σιγήσεις] for a long age, and the day of return."

Comment: The text is not complete.

[AS] *Sibylline Oracles* (2 BC–AD 4) 5.179–83

"Now again, Egypt, I will bewail your fate. Memphis, you will be leader of labors, smitten on the ankles. In you the pyramids will utter a shameless sound. Python, rightly called 'double-city' of old, be silent [σίγησον] forever, so that you may desist from wickedness."

[AS] *Sibylline Oracles* (2 BC–AD 4) 5.394–96

"Be silent [σίγησον], most lamentable evil city, which indulges in revelry. For no longer in you will virgin maidens tend the divine fire of sacred nourishing wood."

[SS] *Sibylline Oracles* (2 BC–AD 4) 8.290–94

"Then he will stretch out his back and give it to the whips (for he will hand over to the world the holy virgin). Beaten, he will be silent [σιγήσει], lest anyone recognize who he is, whose son, and whence he came, so that he may speak to the dead; and he will wear the crown of thorns."

Comment: The reference here is back to Jesus and his crucifixion.

[SS] *Sibylline Oracles* (2 BC–AD 4) 8.366–71

"For I myself fashioned the forms and minds of men, and I gave right reason, and I taught understanding, I who formed eyes and ears, seeing and hearing and knowing every thought, and sharing the knowledge of all. Being within, I am silent [σιγῶ], and later I myself will test and bring about."

Comment: The text breaks off, but since God is the assumed speaker, then the silence must be specific.

[AS] *Sibylline Oracles* (2 BC–AD 4) 8.419–23

"Whoever are convicted in the trial because they were exalted and stopped the mouth of all so that they in envy could equally subject those who act in holy manner, ordering them to be silent [σιγᾶν], pressing on for gain, will all depart then, as not approved by me."

Comment: Those who would have oppressed others for gain would naturally have intended an absolute silence from those they were oppressing.

[N/A] Ptolemaeus ΠΕΡΙ ΔΙΑΦΟΡΑΣ ΛΕΞΕ΄ΩΝ
(2 BC/AD 2) Page 396 lines 1–2[42]

"To be quiet is to keep your entire body calm, but to be silent [σιγᾶν] is not to speak."

Comment: There is little context to allow a lengthy discussion of the difference between uses of σιγάω and ἡσυχάζω, but the quotation does show some distinction at times.

[SS] Dionysius of Halicarnassus *Roman Antiquities* (1 BC) 8.41.1

"Having said this and shed many tears, she became silent [ἐσίγησεν]. And when the other women also lamented and added many entreaties, Veturia, after pausing a short time and weeping, said.. . ."

Comment: Valeria had just spoken to Veturia when she became silent. Veturia then makes a speech. Later Dionysius writes, "Then Valeria again indulged in fresh entreaties that were long and affecting, and all the rest of the women who were connected by friendship or kindred with either of them remained there, beseeching her and embracing her knees, till Veturia, not seeing how she could help herself in view of their lamentations and their many entreaties, yielded and promised to perform the mission in behalf of her country, taking with her the wife of Marcius and his children and as many matrons as wished to join them" (8.43.2). Thus, Valeria was silent simply for Veturia's reply.

---

42 My translation. Greek text from G. Heylbut, "ΠΕΡΙ ΔΙΑΦΟΡΑΣ ΛΕΞΕ΄ΩΝ," *Hermes* 22.3 (1887): 388–410.

[SS] Dionysius of Halicarnassus *On the Style of Demosthenes* (1 BC) 1.10–16

"For these men were endowed with a valour that was divine, but a mortality that was human, and they far preferred practical equity to rigid justice, and integrity of speech to the exactitude of the law, considering that the most divine and universal law is to speak, to be silent [σιγᾶν] and to act, each rightly and at the right time."

[AS] Dionysius of Halicarnassus *On the Style of Demosthenes* (1 BC) 26.13–16

"It is right that the good be lauded with the finest songs, for this is the only tribute which approaches that accorded the immortals. For when spoken of, <a deed, even when small, lives forever>, but even a noble deed perishes if condemned to silence [σιγαθὲν]."

Comment: There is a textual issue here. See LCL.

[SS] Dionysius of Halicarnassus *On Literary Composition* (1 BC) 11.101–10

"Many lines of verse illustrate this, but none better than the lyric which Euripides makes Electra address to the Chorus in the *Orestes*:
Be silent [σῖγα]! Silent [σῖγα]! Let the sandal's tread
Be light, no jarring sound.
Depart ye hence afar, and from his bed withdraw.
In these lines the words σῖγα σῖγα λευκόν are sung on one note; and yet each of the three words has both low and high pitch."

[N/A] Philo *Who Is the Heir?* (1 BC–AD 1) 4.14 (474–75)

"For the ignorant then it is well to keep silence, but for those who desire knowledge and also love their master, frank speech is a most essential possession. Thus we read in Exodus, 'The Lord will war for you and ye shall be silent [σιγήσετε],' and at once there follows a divine oracle in these words, 'What is it that thou shoutest to me?' (Ex. xiv. 14, 15). The meaning is that those should keep silent who have nothing worth hearing to say, and those should speak who have put their faith in the God-sent love of wisdom, and not only speak with ordinary gentleness but shout with a louder cry."

Comment: I have listed this text as not applicable due to the way Philo interprets Exodus. The quotation from Exodus is a specific silence in its original context (see above on the LXX examples), but Philo interprets it as the ignorant keeping silent (which could be taken as absolute silence). See Philo's different use of Exodus below.

[SS] Philo *On Dreams* (1 BC–AD 1) 2.265 (693–94)

"Again when amid the wars and ills of life you see the merciful hand and power of God extended over you as a shield, be still. For that Champion needs no ally, and we have a proof of this in the words which Holy Scripture keeps amid its treasures, 'The Lord shall war for you and ye shall be silent [σιγήσεσθε]' (Ex. xiv. 14)."

[SS] Philo *That Every Good Person Is Free* (1 BC–AD 1) 15.101 (461)

"Hermes, for example, in answer to the question whether Heracles is worthless says:
Worthless? far from it, quite the contrary:
His bearing's dignified, no meanness here,
Not slave-like overstocked with fat, and look
How smart his dress—and he can wield a club.
To which the other replies:
Who wants to buy a stronger than himself,
And bring him home as master of the house?
It fairly frightens one to look at you,
Eyes full of fire—you look just like a bull
Watching a lion's onset.
Then he continues:
Your looks alone are evidence enough,
Though you say nothing [σιγῶντος], that you won't obey—
Giving, not taking, orders is your line."

[SS] Strabo *Geography* (1 BC–AD 1) 1.2.29

"And so it is proved, on many grounds, that Homer both knows and expressly says what is to be said, and that he keeps silent [σιγῶν] about what is too obvious to mention, or else alludes to it by an epithet."

[SS] Strabo *Geography* (1 BC–AD 1) 4.4.3

"But now they give heed, for the most part, to the commands of the Romans. There is a procedure that takes place in their assemblies which is peculiar to them: if a man disturbs the speaker and heckles him, the sergeant-at-arms approaches him with drawn sword, and with threat commands him to be silent [σιγᾶν]; if he does not stop, the sergeant-at-arms does the same thing a second time, and also a third time, but at last cuts off enough of the man's 'sagus' to make it useless for the future."

Comment: The silence is intended during the speech of the speaker in the assembly. The sagus is "a kind of coarse cloak."[43]

[SS] Strabo *Geography* (1 BC–AD 1) 9.2.10

"Near Oropus is a place called Graea, and also the temple of Amphiaraüs, and the monument of Narcissus the Eretrian, which is called 'Sigelus's,' because people pass it in silence [σιγῶσι]."

[SS] Strabo *Geography* (1 BC–AD 1) 12.3.27

"Nor yet, surely, was he ignorant of peoples that were equally near, some of which he names and some not; for example he names the Lycians and the Solymi, but not the Milyae; nor yet the Pamphylians or Pisidians; and though he names the Paphlagonians, Phrygians, and Mysians, he does not name Mariandynians or Thynians or Bithynians or Bebryces; and he mentions the Amazons, but not the White Syrians or Syrians, or Cappadocians, or Lycaonians, though he repeatedly mentions the Phoenicians and the Egyptians and the Ethiopians. And although he mentions the Alëian plain and the Arimi, he is silent [σιγᾷ] as to the tribe to which both belong."

[SS] Strabo *Geography* (1 BC–AD 1) 15.1.39

"He says, then, that the population of India is divided into seven castes: the one first in honour, but the fewest in number, consists of the philosophers; and these philosophers are used, each individually, by people making sacrifice to the gods or making offerings to the dead, but jointly by the kings at the Great Synod, as it is called, at which, at the beginning of the new year, the philosophers, one and all, come together at the gates of the king; and whatever each man has drawn up in writing or observed as useful with reference to the prosperity of either fruits or living beings or concerning the government, he brings forward in public; and he who is thrice found false is required by law to keep silence [σιγᾶν] for life, whereas he who has proved correct is adjudged exempt from tribute and taxes."

Comment: Though it is possible that this reference is an absolute silence, the practicality of being absolutely silent for life is unlikely. It is more likely that the silence was regarding the role as philosopher.

---

43   Horace Leonard Jones, ed., *The Geography of Strabo*, LCL (Cambridge: Harvard University Press, 1988), 2:240 n. 6.

[AS] *The Life of Adam and Eve* (1 BC–AD 1) 12:1–2

"Seth said to the beast, 'Shut your mouth and be silent [σίγα], and keep away from the image of God until the day of judgment.' Then the beast said to Seth, 'See, I stand off, Seth, from the image of God.' Then the beast fled and left him wounded and went to its dwelling."[44]

Comment: There is the additional emphasis on absolute silence with κλεῖσαί σου τὸ στόμα.

[SS] Josephus *Jewish Antiquities* (AD 1) 1.265–66

"Of Isaac's two children, Esau, the favourite of his father, at the age of forty married Ada and Alibame, daughters respectively of Helon and Eusebeon, Canaanite chieftains; these marriages he contracted on his own responsibility without consulting his father, for Isaac would never have permitted them, had his advice been sought, having no desire to form ties of affinity with the indigenous population. However, not wishing to become at enmity with his son through ordering him to separate himself from these women, he resolved to hold his peace [σιγᾶν]."

[SU] Josephus *Jewish Antiquities* (AD 1) 2.60

"Joseph, on his side, committing his cause entirely to God, sought neither to defend himself nor yet to render a strict account of what had passed, but silently [σιγῶν] underwent his bonds and confinement, confident that God, who knew the cause of his calamity and the truth, would prove stronger than those who had bound him; and of His providence he had proof forthwith."

[SS] Josephus *Jewish Antiquities* (AD 1) 4.118–19

"But when Balak fumed and accused him of transgressing the covenant whereunder, in exchange for liberal gifts, he had obtained his services from his allies—having come, in fact, to curse his enemies, he was now belauding those very persons and pronouncing them the most blessed of men—'Balak,' said he, 'hast thou reflected on the whole matter and thinkest thou that it rests with us at all to be silent [σιγᾶν] or to speak on such themes as these, when we are possessed by the spirit of God? For that spirit gives utterance to such language and words as it will, whereof we are all unconscious.'"

---

44 Translation from *OTP*. For the Greek text with variants, see Johannes Tromp, *The Life of Adam and Eve in Greek: A Critical Edition*, Pseudepigrapha Veteris Testamenti Graece 6 (Leiden: Brill, 2005), 132–34.

Comment: Josephus is describing Balak and Balaam from the book of Numbers. Balaam's reference to silence is specifically for περὶ τῶν τοιούτων (the blessing or cursing of Israel).

[SE] Josephus *Jewish Antiquities* (AD 1) 5.310

"And then this woman, with whom Samson was continually consorting, would say that she took it ill that he had not confidence enough in her affection for him to tell her just what she desired, as though she would not conceal [σιγησομένης] what she knew must in his interests not be divulged."

[SS] Josephus *Jewish Antiquities* (AD 1) 13.315–16

"Thereupon a cry went up from those who saw this that the servant had spilled the blood there deliberately, and when Aristobulus heard it, he asked what the reason for it was, and as they did not tell him, he became still more determined to find out, for in such cases men naturally suspect the worst in what is covered by silence [σιγώμενα]. But when, under his threats and the constraint of fear, they told him the truth, he was stricken in mind by his consciousness of guilt."

Comment: The context is Aristobulus's murder of his brother, and Aristobulus's blood spilled in the same spot as his brother's blood.

[SS] Josephus *Jewish Antiquities* (AD 1) 16.378

"For that reason everyone was glad to hear him say the things that he himself would have said, and while they were looking out for their own safety by keeping silence [σιγᾶν], they nevertheless approved of his outspokenness, for the expected tragedy forced everyone to speak about it."

Comment: The individual who spoke out is Tiro concerning Herod and his sons and whether to put the sons to death.

[SS] Josephus *Jewish Antiquities* (AD 1) 17.309

"Moreover, about the corrupting of their virgin daughters and the debauching of their wives, victims of drunken violence and bestiality, they were silent [σιγᾶν] only because those who suffer such indignities are just as pleased to have them remain undisclosed as they are not to have had them happen at all. For Herod had inflicted such outrages upon them as not even a beast could have done if it possessed the power to rule over men."

Comment: The context is "when permission to speak was given to the Jewish envoys, who were waiting to ask for the dissolution of the kingdom, they applied themselves to accusing Herod of lawless acts" (17.304).

[SS] Josephus *Jewish Antiquities* (AD 1) 19.39

"Clemens was silent [σιγήσαντος], but by his look and blush showed how ashamed he was of the emperor's orders; out of regard for his own safety, however, he did not think it right to refer openly to the emperor's madness."

Comment: Chaerea and Clemens are speaking to one another. The quoted text below (19.44) shows that Clemens speaks up after Chaerea's speech.

[SS] Josephus *Jewish Antiquities* (AD 1) 19.44

"Clemens, it was evident, approved the resolve of Chaerea, but bade him keep silent [σιγᾶν], lest as the story spread more widely and reports got abroad of what should properly be concealed, the plot might be discovered before they succeeded in its execution, and so they would be punished."

[SS] Josephus *Jewish Antiquities* (AD 1) 19.92

"When Cluvius replied that he had perceived no indication of this, Bathybius said, 'Well then, Cluvius, the programme for to-day will include assassination of a tyrant.' Cluvius answered, 'Be silent [σίγα], good sir, lest some other of the Achaeans hear the word.'"

[SS] Josephus *The Life* (AD 1) 174–75

"The Tiberians, discovering, on my arrival at Tarichaeae, the trick which I had played upon them, were amazed at the manner in which I had checked their arrogance without bloodshed. I now sent for my Tiberian prisoners, among whom were Justus and his father Pistus, and made them sup with me. During the entertainment I remarked that I was well aware myself of the unrivalled might of the Roman arms, but, on account of the brigands, kept my knowledge [σιγῴην] to myself."

[SS] Josephus *Jewish War* (AD 1) 1.496

"He, accordingly, had the prince suddenly arrested and imprisoned, and then proceeded to put his friends to the torture. Many died silent [σιγῶντες], without saying anything beyond what they knew; but some were driven by their sufferings to falsehood and declared that Alexander and his brother Aristobulus were conspiring against him and were watching for an opportunity to kill him, while out hunting, meaning then to escape to Rome."

[AS] Josephus *Jewish War* (AD 1) 1.622

"Herod burst out upon him to be silent [σιγᾶν] and then addressed Varus: 'That you, Varus, and every honest judge will condemn Antipater as an abandoned criminal, I am fully persuaded.'"

Comment: From Herod's point-of-view he may have intended absolute silence for Antipater. It should be noted, however, that Antipater later made a speech (1.629–36).

[SS] Josephus *Jewish War* (AD 1) 1.639

"Varus then called on Antipater for his defence. But he would say no more than 'God is witness of my innocence' and remained prostrate and silent [σιγῶν]."

[SS] Josephus *Jewish War* (AD 1) 2.333

"However, the magistrates of Jerusalem, on their side, did not remain silent [ἐσίγησαν]: they, too, wrote to Cestius, as did also Bernice, on the subject of the iniquities perpetrated upon the city by Florus."

Comment: The issue is over crimes or loyalty to Rome.

[SE] Josephus *Jewish War* (AD 1) 5.413–14

"Nay, an honourable man will fly from a wanton house and abhor its inmates, and can you persuade yourselves that God still remains with his household in their iniquity—God who sees every secret thing and hears what is buried in silence [σιγωμένων]? And what is there veiled in silence [σιγᾶται] or secrecy among you? Nay, what has not been exposed even to your foes? For you parade your enormities and daily contend who shall be the worst, making an exhibition of vice as though it were virtue."

Comment: Josephus is appealing to the Jews to surrender to the Romans.

[SS] Apollonius of Tyana *Letters* (AD 1) 8.1–2 (in Philostratus)

"To the same: Would you, too, indict me? If only you were honorable enough to do so. You could make these hackneyed, easy charges: 'Apollonius avoids every bathing establishment.' Yes, and he never emerges from his house, and keeps his feet safe.... 'He speaks little and briefly.' Yes, because he has the power to be silent [σιγῆσαι]."

224 | Appendix

[SS] Apollonius of Tyana *Letters* (AD 1) 92–94 (in Philostratus)

"Apollonius to his pupils: Take great care not to say what you should not. For it is the absolute mark of an uncultured person not to be unable to stay silent [σιγεῖν] and to blurt out improprieties. Apollonius to the same. Talkativeness causes many a mistake, but silence [σιγᾶν] is safe. Apollonius to Euphrates. The best people use the fewest words. That is why, if chatterers felt as much annoyance as they cause, they would not make long speeches."

[SS] Gaius Musonius Rufus *Dissertationum a Lucio digestarum reliquiae* (AD 1) Discourse 9 line 97[45]

"But that it seems to me one ought to speak what is good, not thereafter to shun freedom of speech, where it seems to you [i.e., Euripides] that freedom of speech is not to be silent [σιγᾶν] with anything one happens to think."

Comment: The context is freedom of speech (παρρησία). Silence here is part of that nuanced discussion.

[SS] Clement of Rome *1 Clement* (AD 1) 35.7–12

"For the Scripture says, 'God says to the sinner, 'Why do you declare my righteous deeds and receive my covenant in your mouth? For you despised discipline and tossed my words aside. When you saw a robber, you ran along with him; and you joined forces with adulterers. Your mouth multiplied evil and your tongue wove threads of deceit. You sat and spoke slanders against your brother and caused the son of your mother to stumble. You did these things and I was silent [ἐσίγησα]. You have supposed, oh lawless one, that I will be like you. I will convict you and set you up against your own face. So, understand these things, you who forget about God—lest like a lion he seize you, and there be no one to deliver you. A sacrifice of praise will glorify me; there is the path I will show him as the salvation of God.'"

Comment: I have quoted this text at some length since it is also a letter to the Corinthians similar to Paul's letters. For the OT quotation, see comments above on Psalms 49:21 LXX.

---

45 My translation. Greek text from Otto Hense, ed., *C. Musonii Rufi Reliquiae* (Leipzig: Teubner, 1905), 48.

[SS] Plutarch *Caius Marcius Coriolanus* (AD 1) 36.1, 3–4

"While Volumnia was saying this, Marcius listened without making any answer, and after she had ceased also, he stood a long time in silence. Volumnia therefore began once more: 'Why art thou silent [σιγᾷς], my son . . .?' And with these words she threw herself at his feet, together with his wife and children. Then Marcius, crying out 'What hast thou done to me, my mother!' lifted her up, and pressing her right hand warmly, said: 'Thou art victorious, and thy victory means good fortune to my country, but death to me; for I shall withdraw vanquished, though by thee alone.'"

Comment: Marcius was silent for "a long time," but eventually he is heard "crying out."

[SS] Plutarch *Brutus* (AD 1–2) 45.7

"Brutus had nothing to say [ἐσίγα], being concerned about other matters, but Messala Corvinus gave his opinion that they should be publicly flogged and then sent back naked to the enemy's generals, in order to let these know what sort of boon companions they required on their campaigns."

Comment: Brutus was in command over two camps at this time (45.3). His friends had brought two people to him, but Brutus had nothing specifically to say in this case ("being concerned about other matters"). Then immediately Casca speaks to Brutus, and Brutus replies (45.7–9).

[SS] Plutarch *The Education of Children* (AD 1–2) 10E–F

"The control of the tongue, then, still remains to be discussed of the topics I suggested. If anybody has the notion that this is a slight and insignificant matter, he is very far from the truth. For timely silence is a wise thing, and better than any speech. And this is the reason, as it appears to me, why the men of olden time established the rites of initiation into the mysteries, that we, by becoming accustomed to keep silence there, may transfer that fear which we learned from the divine secrets to the safe keeping of the secrets of men. For, again, nobody was ever sorry because he kept silent, but hundreds because they talked. Again, the word unspoken [σιγηθὲν] can easily be uttered later; but the spoken word cannot possibly be recalled. I have heard of countless men who have fallen into the greatest misfortunes through intemperate speech."

226 | *Appendix*

[SS] Plutarch *The Education of Children* (AD 1–2) 13E–F

"Though our slaves often suffer from a headache in the morning, we do not force them to confess a debauch.... 'He once took away a yoke of cattle from the field, he once came home with breath reeking from yesterday's debauch; ignore it. Or smelling of perfume; do not say a word [σίγησον].' In this fashion is restive youth gradually broken to harness."

Comment: The context is advice for fathers with their children. He uses an argument of how one treats slaves in these situations (and so no less should they with their children).

[D] Plutarch *How the Young Man Should Study Poetry* (AD 1–2) 17F–18A

"We shall steady the young man still more if, at his first entrance into poetry, we give a general description of the poetic art as an imitative art and faculty analogous to painting. And let him not merely be acquainted with the oft-repeated saying that 'poetry is articulate painting, and painting is inarticulate [σιγῶσαν] poetry,' but let us teach him in addition that when we see a lizard or an ape or the face of Thersites in a picture, we are pleased with it and admire it, not as a beautiful thing, but as a likeness."

[SE] Plutarch *How a Man May Become Aware of His Progress in Virtue* (AD 1–2) 81A

"It is therefore the mark of a man who is making progress, not only when he has given to a friend or done a kindness to an acquaintance to refrain from telling of it to others, but also when he has given an honest judgement amidst a numerous and dishonest majority ... or when he has fought a good fight, like Agesilaus, against a kiss of a lovely girl or youth, to keep all this to himself and put the seal of silence [σιγῆσαι] on it."

[SS] Plutarch *Advice about Keeping Well* (AD 1–2) 125C–D

"Whenever, then, someone of those rare and notorious means of enjoyment is afforded us, we ought to take more pride in abstinence than in enjoyment, remembering that just as Simonides used to say that he had never been sorry for having kept silent [σιγήσαντι], but many a time for having spoken, so we have never been sorry either for having put a dainty to one side, or for having drunk water instead of Falernian wine, but the opposite; not only ought Nature not to be forced, but if anything of this sort is offered her even when she has need of it, the appetite ought to be often diverted from it towards the plain and familiar food for the sake of habituation and training."

[P] Plutarch *Sayings of Spartans* (AD 1–2) 220B

"In a council meeting he was asked whether it was due to foolishness or lack of words that he said nothing. 'But a fool,' said he, 'would not be able to hold his tongue [σιγᾶν].'"

[SS] Plutarch *Sayings of Spartans* (AD 1–2) 229E

"In answer to a man who said that he commended him and was very fond of him, he said 'I have two oxen in a field, and although they both may utter no sound [σιγώντων], I know perfectly well which one is lazy and which one is the worker.'"

Comment: Oxen may not utter a sound at this moment. They may make a sound at another time.

[SE] Plutarch *Concerning Talkativeness* (AD 1–2) 505F

"No spoken word, it is true, has ever done such service as have in many instances words unspoken; for it is possible at some later time to tell what you have kept silent [σιγηθέν], but never to keep silent what once has been spoken—*that* has been spilled, and has made its way abroad."

[SS] Plutarch *Concerning Talkativeness* (AD 1–2) 506C

"And Ino in Euripides, speaking out boldly concerning herself, says that she knows how to be 'Silent [σιγᾶν] in season, to speak where speech is safe.' For those who have received a noble and truly royal education learn first to be silent [σιγᾶν], and then to speak."

[SS] Plutarch *Concerning Talkativeness* (AD 1–2) 508E–F

"Still speaking his head was mingled with the dust. But if the man had remained silent [ἐσίγησε] at that time and had mastered himself for a little while, when the king later won success and regained power, he would have earned, I fancy, an even larger reward for his silence than for his hospitality."

[SS] Plutarch *On Exile* (AD 1–2) 606A

"These initial assumptions are wrong and untrue. In the first place it is not a slave's part 'not to speak one's mind,' but that of a man of sense on occasions and in matters that demand silence and restraint of speech, as Euripides himself has elsewhere put it better: 'Silence [σιγᾶν] in season, speech where speech is safe.' In the next place we are compelled to bear 'the folly of the mighty' no less at home than in exile; indeed, those who remain behind are often in even greater terror of men who wield unjust power in cities through chicane or violence than those who have taken their departure."

[SS] Plutarch *Lives of the Ten Orators* (AD 1–2) 836F–837A

"In his boyhood he was as well educated as any Athenian, for he attended the lectures of Prodicus of Ceos, Gorgias of Leontini, Teisias of Syracuse, and the orator Theramenes; and when the last-named was in danger of being arrested by the Thirty and had fled for safety to the alter of Hestia Boulaea, everyone else was terrified, but Isocrates alone arose to speak in his aid; and at first he was silent [ἐσίγησε] for a long time, then afterwards he was urged to be silent by Theramenes himself, who said that his misfortune would be more painful if any of his friends should share it."

[SS] Plutarch *Fragments* (AD 1–2) Fragment 157.1

"Ancient natural science, among both Greeks and foreign nations, took the form of a scientific account hidden in mythology, veiled for the most part in riddles and hints, or of a theology such as is found in mystery-ceremonies: in it what is spoken is less clear to the masses than what is unsaid [σιγωμένων], and what is unsaid [σιγώμενα] gives cause for more speculation than what is said. This is evident from the Orphic poems and the accounts given by Phrygians and Egyptians."

Comment: Hans Dieter Betz writes about fragment 157, "Descriptions of the cult of Hera, its ceremonies, myths, and philosophic interpretations seems to have made up the content of the treatise which is significant for its cultic and otherwise religious terminology"; and then about σιγάω, "The uninitiated masses do not understand the meaning of the mystery cult language."[46]

[SS] Plutarch *Fragments* (AD 1–2) Fragment 207

"Plutarch:
Homers approval of 'holding the tongue' is clearly shown by the following lines: he writes,
Thersites, unconsidered are your words;
Keep quiet, ready speaking though you be,
Nor wish alone to wrangle with the king.

---

46   Hans Dieter Betz, "Fragmenta 21–23, 157–158, 176–178," in *Plutarch's Theological Writings and Early Christian Literature*, ed. Hans Dieter Betz, Studia ad Corpus Hellenisticum Novi Testamenti (Leiden: Brill, 1975), 318.

And when Telemachus said,

> Some god's within, a dweller in wide heaven,
> his father restrained him with the words,
> Silence [σίγα]! Repress your thought and ask no questions:
> The dwellers in Olympus have this right.
> The Pythagoreans called this 'firm silence,' and gave no answer

to those who, recklessly and without qualms, put indiscriminate questions about the gods."

Comment: The reference is to Homer's *The Odyssey*, which states, "Then at last Telemachus spoke to his father: 'Father, surely this is a great marvel that my eyes behold; certainly the walls of the house and the lovely panels and the crossbeams of fir and the pillars that reach on high glow in my eyes as if with the light of blazing fire. Surely some god is within, one of those who hold broad heaven.' Then resourceful Odysseus answered him, and said: 'Hush, check your thought, and ask no question; this, I tell you, is the way of the gods who hold Olympus. But go and take your rest and I will remain behind here, that I may stir yet more the minds of the maids and of your mother; and she with weeping will ask me of each thing separately'" (19.35–46).

Bibliography

Abbott-Smith, G. *A Manual Greek Lexicon of the New Testament*. 3rd ed. Edinburgh: T&T Clark, 1937.

Adelakun, Adewale J. "Complementarians versus Egalitarians: An Exegesis of Galatians 3:28 from Nigerian Cultural Perspective." *Ogbomoso Journal of Theology* 17 (2012): 77–95.

Ademiluka, Solomon O. "1 Corinthians 14:33b–36 in Light of Women and Church Leadership in Nigeria." *Verbum et Ecclesia* 38 (2017): 1–8.

Adrados, Francisco R. "The 'Life of Aesop' and the Origins of Novel in Antiquity." *Quaderni Urbinati di Cultura Classica* 1 (1979): 93–112.

Aeneas Tacticus. *On the Defense of Fortified Positions*. Pages 26–199. Translated by The Illinois Greek Club. LCL. Cambridge: Harvard University Press, 1923. Repr., 1962.

Aeschines. *Against Timarchus; On the Embassy; Against Ctesiphon*. Translated by Charles Darwin Adams. LCL. Cambridge: Harvard University Press, 1919.

Agatharchides of Cnidus. *On the Erythraean Sea*. Edited and translated by Stanley M. Bursteign. Hakluyt Society. 2nd series, no. 172. London: Hakluyt Society, 1989.

Aland, Barbara, Kurt Aland, Johannes Karavidopoulos, Carlo M. Martini, and Bruce Metzger, eds. *The Greek New Testament*. 5th ed. Institute for New Testament Textual Research. Stuttgart: United Bible Societies, 2014.

Aland, Barbara, Kurt Aland, Johannes Karavidopoulos, Carlo M. Martini, and Bruce M. Metzger, eds. *Novum Testamentum Graece*. 28th ed. Institute for New Testament Textual Research. Stuttgart: Deutsche Bibelgesellschaft, 2012.

Bibliography

Aland, Kurt, and Barbara Aland. *The Text of the New Testament: An Introduction to the Critical Editions and to the Theory and Practice of Modern Textual Criticism*. Translated by Erroll F. Rhodes. 2nd ed. Grand Rapids: Eerdmans, 1981.

Albrecht, Ruth. "Woman." Pages 694–710 in vol. 15 of *Brill's New Pauly: Encyclopaedia of the Ancient World*. Edited by Hubert Cancik and Helmuth Schneider. 22 vols. Leiden: Brill, 2010.

Allo, E.-B. *Saint Paul: Première épitre aux Corinthiens*. 2nd ed. Études Bibliques. Paris: Gabalda, 1956.

Amadi-Azuogu, Adolphus Chinedu. *Gender and Ministry in Early Christianity and the Church Today*. Lanham, MD: University Press of America, 2007.

Amphoux, Christian-Bernard. "Codex Vaticanus B: Les Points Diacritiques des Marges de Marc." *Journal of the Evangelical Theological Society* 58.2 (2007): 440–66.

Apolonnius Rhodius. *Argonautica*. Edited and translated by William H. Race. LCL. Cambridge: Harvard University Press, 2008.

Arichea, Daniel C. "The Silence of Women in the Church: Theology and Translation of 1 Corinthians 14.33b–36." *The Bible Translator* 46.1 (1995): 101–12.

Aristophanes. *Acharnians*. Pages 56–217. Edited and translated by Jeffrey Henderson. Vol. 1. LCL. Cambridge: Harvard University Press, 1998. Repr., 2018.

Aristophanes. *Birds; Lysistrata; Women at the Thesmophoria*. Edited and translated by Jeffrey Henderson. Vol. 3. LCL. Cambridge: Harvard University Press, 2000. Repr., 2018.

Aristophanes. *Clouds; Wasps; Peace*. Edited and translated by Jeffrey Henderson. Vol. 2. LCL. Cambridge: Harvard University Press, 1998.

Aristophanes. *Frogs; Assemblywomen; Wealth*. Edited and translated by Jeffrey Henderson. Vol. 4. LCL. Cambridge: Harvard University Press, 2002.

Aristotle. *On Sophistical Refutations*. Pages 10–155. Translated by E. S. Forster. LCL. Cambridge: Harvard University Press, 1955. Repr., 1965.

Arnott, W. G., ed. *Menander*. Vol. 1. LCL. Cambridge: Harvard University Press, 1979.

Assis, Elie. "The Alphabetic Acrostic in the Book of Lamentations." *Catholic Biblical Quarterly* 69.4 (2007): 710–24.

Bailey, Kenneth E. *Paul through Mediterranean Eyes: Cultural Studies in 1 Corinthians*. Downers Grove, IL: IVP Academic, 2011.

Bailey, Kenneth E. "The Structure of 1 Corinthians and Paul's Theological Method with Special Reference to 4:17." *Novum Testamentum* 25.2 (1983): 152–81.

Baker, J. Wayne. "Musculus, Wolfgang." Pages 103–4 in vol. 3 of *The Oxford Encyclopedia of the Reformation*. Edited by Hans J. Hillerbrand. 4 vols. New York: Oxford University Press, 1996.

Balz, Horst, and Gerhard Schneider, eds. *Exegetical Dictionary of the New Testament*. 3 vols. Grand Rapids: Eerdmans, 1990–93.

Barclay, John M. G. "1 Corinthians." Pages 91–126 in *The Oxford Bible Commentary: The Pauline Epistles*. Edited by John Muddiman and John Barton. Oxford: Oxford University Press, 2001.

Barclay, John M. G. "Mirror-Reading a Polemical Letter: Galatians as a Test Case." *Journal for the Study of the New Testament* 31 (1987): 73–93.

Barrett, C. K. *The First Epistle to the Corinthians*. Black's New Testament Commentary. Peabody, MA: Hendrickson, 1993.

Barton, Stephen C. "Paul's Sense of Place: An Anthropological Approach to Community Formation in Corinth." *New Testament Studies* 32.2 (1986): 225–46.

Bauckham, Richard. *Gospel Women: Studies of the Named Women in the Gospels.* Grand Rapids: Eerdmans, 2002.

Bauer, Walter, Frederick William Danker, W. F. Arndt, and F. W. Gingrich. *A Greek-English Lexicon of the New Testament and Other Early Christian Literature.* 3rd ed. Chicago: University of Chicago Press, 2000.

Bauer, Walter, William F. Arndt, F. Wilbur Gingrich. *A Greek-English Lexicon of the New Testament and Other Early Christian Literature.* Chicago: University of Chicago Press, 1957.

Bauer, Walter, William F. Arndt, F. Wilbur Gingrich, and Frederick W. Danker. *A Greek-English Lexicon of the New Testament and Other Early Christian Literature.* 2nd ed. Chicago: University of Chicago Press, 1979.

Beale, G. K. *The Book of Revelation: A Commentary on the Greek Text.* The New International Greek Testament Commentary. Grand Rapids: Eerdmans, 1999.

Belleville, Linda. "Ἰουνιαν . . . ἐπίσημοι ἐν τοῖς ἀποστόλοις: A Re-examination of Romans 16:7 in Light of Primary Source Materials." *New Testament Studies* 51 (2005): 231–49.

Betz, Hans Dieter. "Fragmenta 21–23, 157–158, 176–178." Pages 317–24 in *Plutarch's Theological Writings and Early Christian Literature.* Edited by Hans Dieter Betz. Studia ad Corpus Hellenisticum Novi Testamenti. Leiden: Brill, 1975.

Betz, Hans Dieter. *Galatians: A Commentary on Paul's Letter to the Churches in Galatia.* Hermeneia. Philadelphia: Fortress, 1979.

Biraschi, Anna Maria. "Strabo and Homer: A Chapter in Cultural History." Pages 73–85 in *Strabo's Cultural Geography: The Making of a Kolossourgia.* Edited by Daniela Dueck, Hugh Lindsay, and Sarah Pothecary. Cambridge: Cambridge University Press, 2005.

Blampied, Anne B. "Paul and Silence for 'the Women' in 1 Corinthians 14:34–35." *Studia Biblica et Theologica* 13 (1983): 143–65.

Blomberg, Craig L. *1 Corinthians.* The NIV Application Commentary. Grand Rapids: Zondervan, 1994.

Blomberg, Craig L. "Applying 1 Corinthians in the Early Twenty-First Century." *Southwestern Journal of Theology* 45 (2002): 19–38.

Blomberg, Craig L. *From Pentecost to Patmos: An Introduction to Acts through Revelation.* Nashville: B&H Academic, 2006.

Blomberg, Craig L. "Neither Hierarchicalist nor Egalitarian: Gender Roles in Paul." Pages 283–326 in *Paul and His Theology.* Edited by Stanley E. Porter. Leiden: Brill, 2006.

Blomberg, Craig L. "Women in Ministry: A Complementarian Perspective." Pages 123–84 in *Two Views on Women in Ministry.* Edited by James R. Beck. Rev. ed. Grand Rapids: Zondervan, 2005.

Bock, Darrell L. *Acts.* Baker Exegetical Commentary on the New Testament. Grand Rapids: Baker Academic, 2007.

Bock, Darrell L. *Luke 9:51–24:53.* Vol. 2. Baker Exegetical Commentary on the New Testament. Grand Rapids: Baker Academic, 1996.

Bonnard, Pierre. *L'Épitre de Saint Paul aux Galates.* Commentaire du Nouveau Testament 9. Neuchatel, Paris: Delachaux & Niestlé, 1953.

Bray, Gerald, ed. *Romans*. Ancient Christian Commentary on Scripture. Downers Grove, IL: InterVarsity Press, 1998.

Brewer, D. Instone. "1 Corinthians 9:9–11: A Literal Interpretation of 'Do Not Muzzle the Ox.'" *New Testament Studies* 38 (1992): 554–65.

Brookins, Timothy A., and Bruce W. Longenecker. *1 Corinthians 1–9: A Handbook on the Greek Text*. Baylor Handbook on the Greek New Testament. Waco, TX: Baylor University Press, 2016.

Brookins, Timothy A., and Bruce W. Longenecker. *1 Corinthians 10–16: A Handbook on the Greek Text*. Baylor Handbook on the Greek New Testament. Waco, TX: Baylor University Press, 2016.

Brooten, B. J. *Women Leaders in the Ancient Synagogue: Inscriptional Evidence and Background Issues*. Atlanta: Scholars, 2020.

Bruce, F. F. *1 and 2 Corinthians*. New Century Bible. Grand Rapids: Eerdmans, 1971. Repr., 1983.

Bruce, F. F. *The Book of Acts*. Rev. ed. The New International Commentary on the New Testament. Grand Rapids: Eerdmans, 1988.

Bruce, F. F. *The Epistle to the Galatians: A Commentary on the Greek Text*. The New International Greek Testament Commentary. Grand Rapids: Eerdmans, 1982.

Bryce, David W. "'As in All the Churches of the Saints': A Text-Critical Study of 1 Corinthians 14:34, 35." *Lutheran Theological Journal* 31 (1997): 31–39.

Burer, Michael H. "ΕΠΙΣΗΜΟΙ ἘΝ ΤΟΙΣ ἈΠΟΣΤΟΛΟΙΣ in Rom 16:7 as 'Well Known to the Apostles': Further Defense and New Evidence." *Journal of the Evangelical Theological Society* 58 (2015): 731–55.

Burer, Michael H., and Daniel B. Wallace. "Was Junia Really an Apostle?: A Re-examination of Rom 16:7." *New Testament Studies* 47 (2001): 76–91.

Burton, Keith A. "1 Corinthians 11 and 14: How Does a Woman Prophesy and Keep Silence at the Same Time?" *Journal of the Adventist Theological Society* 10 (1999): 268–84.

Cancik, Hubert, and Helmuth Schneider, eds. *Brill's New Pauly: Encyclopaedia of the Ancient World*. 22 vols. Leiden: Brill, 2002–2011.

Capper, Brian J. "To Keep Silent, Ask Husbands at Home, and not to Have Authority over Men. Part I (I Corinthians 14:33–36 and I Timothy 2:11–12): The Transition from Gathering in Private to Meeting in Public Space in Second Generation Christianity and the Exclusion of Women from Leadership of the Public Assembly." *Theologische Zeitschrift* 61.2 (2005): 113–31.

Capper, Brian J. "To Keep Silent, Ask Husbands at Home, and not to Have Authority over Men. Part II (I Corinthians 14:33–36 and I Timothy 2:11–12): The Transition from Gathering in Private to Meeting in Public Space in Second Generation Christianity and the Exclusion of Women from Leadership of the Public Assembly." *Theologische Zeitschrift* 61.4 (2005): 301–19.

Carson, D. A. "'Silent in the Churches': On the Role of Women in 1 Corinthians 14:33b–36." Pages 140–53 in *Recovering Biblical Manhood and Womanhood: A Response to Evangelical Feminism*. Edited by John Piper and Wayne Grudem. Wheaton: Crossway, 1991.

The Center for the Study of New Testament Manuscripts. www.csntm.org.

Cervin, Richard. "A Note Regarding the Name 'Junia(s)' in Romans 16:7." *New Testament Studies* 40 (1994): 464–70.

Chapman, M. J., trans. *The Greek Pastoral Poets: Theocritus—Bion—Moschus*. 3rd, Rev. ed. London: Saunders, Otley, and Co., 1866.
Charlesworth, James H., ed. *The Old Testament Pseudepigrapha*. 2 vols. Garden City, NY: Doubleday & Company, 1983–1985.
Cho, Ho Hyung. "Another Look at ἔννομος Χριστοῦ in 1 Corinthians 9:21." *Expository Times* 130.2 (2018): 62–71.
Chow, John K. *Patronage and Power: A Study of Social Networks in Corinth*. Journal for the Study of the New Testament Supplement Series 75. Sheffield: Sheffield Academic Press, 1992.
Ciampa, Roy E., and Brian S. Rosner. "1 Corinthians." Pages 695–752 in *Commentary on the New Testament Use of the Old Testament*. Edited by G. K. Beale and D. A. Carson. Grand Rapids: Baker Academic, 2007.
Ciampa, Roy E., and Brian S. Rosner. *The First Letter to the Corinthians*. The Pillar New Testament Commentary. Grand Rapids: Eerdmans, 2010.
Clark, Gillian. "The Women at Corinth." *Theology* 85 (1982): 256–62.
Clarke, Graham. "'As in All the Churches of the Saints' (1 Corinthians 14.33)." *The Bible Translator* 52 (2001): 144–47.
Cleaver, Richard. *Know My Name: A Gay Liberation Theology*. Louisville: Westminster John Knox, 1995.
Clement of Rome. *The Apostolic Fathers: 1 Clement*. Pages 34–151. Edited and translated by Bart D. Ehrman. Vol. 1. LCL. Cambridge: Harvard University Press, 2003.
Coggins, Richard J. *Sirach*. Guides to Apocrypha and Pseudepigrapha. Sheffield: Sheffield Academic, 1998.
Cohick, Lynn H. *Women in the World of the Earliest Christians: Illuminating Ancient Ways of Life*. Grand Rapids: Baker Academic, 2009.
Collins, Raymond F. *First Corinthians*. Edited by Daniel J. Harrington, S. J. Sacra Pagina Series 7. Collegeville, MN: The Liturgical Press, 1999.
Comfort, Philip W. *New Testament Text and Translation Commentary: Commentary on the Variant Readings of the Ancient New Testament Manuscripts and How They Relate to the Major English Translations*. Carol Stream, IL: Tyndale House, 2008.
Conzelmann, Hans. *1 Corinthians*. Edited by George W. MacRae, S. J. Translated by James W. Leitch. Hermeneia. Philadelphia: Fortress, 1975.
Cranfield, C. E. B. *The Epistle to the Romans: A Critical and Exegetical Commentary*. Vol. 2. The International Critical Commentary. Edinburgh: T&T Clark, 1979. Repr., 2002.
Crates. "Fragment 4." Page 211 in *Fragments of Old Comedy: Alcaeus to Diocles*. Edited and translated by Ian C. Storey. Vol. 1. LCL. Cambridge: Harvard University Press, 2011.
Cross, F. L., and E. A. Livingstone, eds. "Colet, John." Page 375 in *The Oxford Dictionary of the Christian Church*. 3rd ed. Oxford: Oxford University Press, 1997.
Crüsemann, Marlene. "Irredeemably Hostile to Women: Anti-Jewish Elements in the Exegesis of the Dispute about Women's Right to Speak (1 Cor. 14.34–35)." *Journal for the Study of the New Testament* 79 (2000): 19–36.
Curtis, Heath R. "A Female Apostle?: A Note Re-examining the Work of Burer and Wallace Concerning ἐπίσημος with ἐν and the Dative." *Concordia Journal* 28.4 (2002): 437–40.

Cutler, Caroline Schleier. "New Creation and Inheritance: Inclusion and Full Participation in Paul's Letters to the Galatians and Romans." *Priscilla Papers* 30.2 (2016): 21–29.

Daniels, Debra Bendel. "Evangelical Feminism: The Egalitarian-Complementarian Debate." PhD diss., University of Wisconsin-Madison, 2003.

Dautzenberg, Gerhard. *Urchristliche Prophetie: Ihre Erforschung, ihre Voraussetzungen im Judentum und ihre Struktur im ersten Korintherbrief*. Beiträge zur Wissenschaft vom Alten und Neuen Testament. Stuttgart: W. Kohlhammer, 1975.

Davis, John Jefferson. "Some Reflections on Galatians 3:28, Sexual Roles, and Biblical Hermeneutics." *Journal of the Evangelical Theological Society* 19 (1976): 201–8.

de Boer, Martinus C. *Galatians: A Commentary*. New Testament Library. Louisville: Westminster John Knox, 2011.

Delobel, Joël. "Textual Criticism and Exegesis: Siamese Twins?" Pages 98–117 in *New Testament Textual Criticism, Exegesis, and Early Church History: A Discussion of Methods*. Edited by Barbara Aland and Joël Delobel. Contributions to Biblical Exegesis and Theology. Kampen, The Netherlands: Kok Pharos, 1994.

de M. Johnson, J., Victor Martin, and Arthur S. Hunt, eds. *Catalogue of the Greek Papyri in the John Rylands Library Manchester*. Vol. 2. Manchester: Manchester University Press, 1915.

Demosthenes. *Against Aristocrates*. Pages 214–367. Translated by J. H. Vince. Vol. 3. LCL. Cambridge: Harvard University Press, 1935. Repr., 1964.

Demosthenes. *De Corona; De Falsa Legatione; Books 18–19*. Translated by C. A. Vince and J. H. Vince. Vol. 2. LCL. Cambridge: Harvard University Press, 1926. Repr., 1971.

Demosthenes. *On the Peace; Book 5*. Pages 104–19 in *Olynthiacs; Philippics; Minor Public Speeches; Speeches against Leptines*. Translated by J. H. Vince. Vol. 1. LCL. Cambridge: Harvard University Press, 1930. Repr., 1962.

Demosthenes. *The Third Philippic; Book 9*. Pages 224–65 in *Olynthiacs; Philippics; Minor Public Speeches; Speeches against Leptines*. Translated by J. H. Vince. Vol. 1. LCL. Cambridge: Harvard University Press, 1930. Repr., 1962.

deSilva, David A. *Galatians: A Handbook on the Greek Text*. Baylor Handbook on the Greek New Testament. Waco, TX: Baylor University Press, 2014.

Deslauriers, Marguerite. "Women, Education, and Philosophy." Pages 343–53 in *A Companion to Women in the Ancient World*. Edited by Sharon L. James and Sheila Dillon. Chichester, West Sussex, UK: Wiley Blackwell, 2012.

Dewailly, L.-M. "Mystère et silence dans Rom 16:25." *New Testament Studies* 14 (1967): 111–18.

Diggle, J., B. L. Fraser, P. James, O. B. Simkin, A. A. Thompson, and S. J. Westripp. *The Cambridge Greek Lexicon*. Vol. 2. Cambridge: Cambridge University Press, 2021.

Dinkler, Michal Beth. *Silent Statements: Narrative Representations of Speech and Silence in the Gospel of Luke*. Beihefte zur Zeitschrift für die neutestamentliche Wissenschaft 191. Berlin: Walter de Gruyter, 2013.

Dio Chrysostom. "To the People of Alexandria." Pages 172–271 in *Discourses 31–36*. Translated by J. W. Cohoon and H. Lamar Crosby. Vol. 3. LCL. Cambridge: Harvard University Press, 1940.

Dionysius of Halicarnassus. *On Literary Composition*. Pages 14–243 in *The Critical Essays*. LCL. Translated by Stephen Usher. Vol. 2. LCL. Cambridge: Harvard University Press, 1985.

Dionysius of Halicarnassus. *On the Style of Demosthenes*. Pages 238–455 in *The Critical Essays*. Translated by Stephen Usher. Vol. 1. LCL. Cambridge: Harvard University Press, 1974.

Dionysius of Halicarnassus. *The Roman Antiquities; Books 1–2*. Translated by Earnest Cary. Vol. 1. LCL. Cambridge: Harvard University Press, 1937.

Dionysius of Halicarnassus. *The Roman Antiquities; Books 3–4*. Translated by Earnest Cary. Vol. 2. LCL. Cambridge: Harvard University Press, 1939.

Dionysius of Halicarnassus. *The Roman Antiquities; Books 8–9.24*. Translated by Earnest Cary. Vol. 5. LCL. Cambridge: Harvard University Press, 1945.

Doran, Robert. *2 Maccabees: A Critical Commentary*. Hermeneia. Minneapolis: Fortress, 2012.

Dunn, James D. G. *Romans 9–16*. Word Biblical Commentary 38B. Dallas: Word, 1988.

Dunn, James D. G. *The Epistles to the Colossians and to Philemon: A Commentary on the Greek Text*. The New International Greek Testament Commentary. Grand Rapids: Eerdmans, 1996.

Dutch, Robert S. *The Educated Elite in 1 Corinthians: Education and Community Conflict in Graeco-Roman Context*. Journal for the Study of the New Testament Supplement Series 271. London: T&T Clark, 2005.

du Toit, Andrie. "Die swyggebod van 1 Korintiërs 14:34–35 weer eens onder die loep." *Hervormde Teologiese Studies* 57 (2001): 172–86.

du Toit, Philip la Grange. "Paul's Reference to the 'Keeping of the Commandments of God' in 1 Corinthians 7:19." *Neotestamentica* 49.1 (2015): 21–45.

Ebeling, Heinrich. *Griechisch-deutsches Wörterbuch zum Neuen Testamente*. Hannover: Hahnsche, 1913.

Eckstein, Hans-Joachim. *Christus in Euch: Von der Freiheit der Kinder Gottes: Eine Auslegung des Galaterbriefes*. Neukirchener Theologie. Göttingen: Vandenhoeck & Ruprecht, 2017.

Edsall, Benjamin A. *The Reception of Paul and Early Christian Initiation: History and Hermeneutics*. Cambridge: Cambridge University Press, 2019.

Elliott, J. K. *A Bibliography of Greek New Testament Manuscripts*. 3rd ed. Supplements to Novum Testamentum 160. Leiden: Brill, 2015.

Ellis, E. E. "The Silenced Wives of Corinth (1 Cor. 14.34–35)." Pages 213–20 in *New Testament Criticism: Its Significance for Exegesis: Essays in Honour of Bruce M. Metzger*. Edited by Eldon Jay Epp and Gordon D. Fee. Oxford: Clarendon, 1981.

Epp, Eldon Jay. *Junia: The First Woman Apostle*. Minneapolis: Fortress, 2005.

Epp, Eldon Jay. "Text-Critical, Exegetical, and Socio-Cultural Factors Affecting the Junia/Junias Variation in Romans 16,7." Pages 227–92 in *New Testament Textual Criticism and Exegesis: Festschrift J. Delobel*. Edited by A. Denaux. Bibliotheca Ephemeridum Theologicarum Lovaniensium 161. Leuven: Leuven University Press, 2002.

Eriksson, Anders. "'Women Tongue Speakers, Be Silent': A Reconstruction through Paul's Rhetoric." *Biblical Interpretation* 6 (1998): 80–104.

Estep, Jr., James Riley. "Women in Greco-Roman Education and Its Implications for 1 Corinthians 14 and 1 Timothy 2." Pages 80–93 in *Women in the Biblical World: A Survey of Old and New Testament Perspectives*. Edited by Elizabeth A. McCabe. Vol. 2. Lanham: University Press of America, 2011.

Euripides. *Bacchae; Iphigenia at Aulis; Rhesus*. Edited and translated by David Kovacs. Vol. 6. LCL. Cambridge: Harvard University Press, 2002.

Bibliography

Euripides. *Children of Heracles; Hippolytus; Andromache; Hecuba*. Edited and translated by David Kovacs. Vol. 2. LCL. Cambridge: Harvard University Press, 1995. Repr., 2005.

Euripides. *Cyclops; Alcestis; Medea*. Edited and translated by David Kovacs. Vol. 1. LCL. Cambridge: Harvard University Press, 1994. Repr., 2001.

Euripides. *Fragments: Aegeus–Meleager*. Edited and translated by Christopher Collard and Martin Cropp. Vol. 7. LCL. Cambridge: Harvard University Press, 2008.

Euripides. *Fragments: Oedipus–Chrysippus; Other Fragments*. Edited and translated by Christopher Collard and Martin Cropp. Vol. 8. LCL. Cambridge: Harvard University Press, 2008.

Euripides. *Helen; Phoenician Women; Orestes*. Edited and translated by David Kovacs. Vol. 5. LCL. Cambridge: Harvard University Press, 2002.

Euripides. *Suppliant Women; Electra; Heracles*. Edited and translated by David Kovacs. Vol. 3. LCL. Cambridge: Harvard University Press, 1998.

Euripides. *Trojan Women; Iphigenia Among the Taurians; Ion*. Edited and translated by David Kovacs. Vol. 4. LCL. Cambridge: Harvard University Press, 1999.

Evans, Craig A., and Stanley E. Porter, eds. *Dictionary of New Testament Background*. Downers Grove, IL: IVP Academic, 2000.

Fee, Gordon D. *1 and 2 Timothy, Titus*. New International Biblical Commentary on the New Testament. Peabody, MA: Hendrickson, 1988.

Fee, Gordon D. *Galatians: Pentecostal Commentary*. Pentecostal Commentary Series. Blandford Forum: Deo, 2007.

Fee, Gordon D. *Gospel and Spirit: Issues in New Testament Hermeneutics*. Peabody, MA: Hendrickson, 1991.

Fee, Gordon D. "On Women Remaining Silent in the Churches: A Text-critical Approach to 1 Corinthians 14:34–35." Pages 173–88 in *Evangelical Scholarship, Retrospects and Prospects: Essays in Honor of Stanley N. Gundry*. Edited by Dirk R. Buursma, Katya Covrett, and Verlyn D. Verbrugge. Grand Rapids: Zondervan, 2017.

Fee, Gordon D. *Paul's Letter to the Philippians*. The New International Commentary on the New Testament. Grand Rapids: Eerdmans, 1995.

Fee, Gordon D. *The First Epistle to the Corinthians*. Rev ed. The New International Commentary on the New Testament. Grand Rapids: Eerdmans, 2014.

Fellows, Richard G. "Are There Distigme-Obelos Symbols in Vaticanus." *New Testament Studies* 65 (2019): 246–51.

Fiorenza, Elisabeth Schüssler. *In Memory of Her: A Feminist Theological Reconstruction of Christian Origins*. New York: Crossroad, 1983.

Fiorenza, Elisabeth Schüssler. "Women in the Pre-Pauline and Pauline Churches." *Union Seminary Quarterly Review* 33.3 (1978): 153–66.

Fish, John H. III. "Women Speaking in the Church: The Relationship of 1 Corinthians 11:5 and 14:34–36." *Emmaus Journal* 1.3 (1992): 214–51.

Fitzer, Gottfried. *Das Weib schweige in der Gemeinde: Über den unpaulinischen Charakter der mulier-taceat-Verse in 1. Korinther 14*. Theologische Existenz heute 110. München: Chr. Kaiser, 1963.

Fitzmyer, Joseph A., S. J. *First Corinthians: A New Translation with Introduction and Commentary*. The Anchor Yale Bible 32. New Haven: Yale University Press, 2008.

Flanagan, Neal M., and Edwina H. Snyder. "Did Paul Put Down Women in 1 Cor 14:34–36?" *Foundations* 24.3 (1981): 216–20.

Forbes, Christopher. *Prophecy and Inspired Speech: In Early Christianity and its Hellenistic Environment.* Peabody, MA: Hendrickson, 1995.

France, R. T. *Women in the Church's Ministry: A Test Case for Biblical Interpretation.* Grand Rapids: Eerdmans, 1995.

Fung, Ronald Y. K. *The Epistle to the Galatians.* The New International Commentary on the New Testament. Grand Rapids: Eerdmans, 1988.

Furnish, Victor Paul. *The Moral Teaching of Paul.* Nashville: Abingdon, 1979.

Fusillo, Massimo. "Pseudo-Clementine Literature." Pages 114–16 in vol. 12 of *Brill's New Pauly: Encyclopaedia of the Ancient World.* Edited by Hubert Cancik and Helmuth Schneider. 22 vols. Leiden: Brill, 2008.

Gardner, Paul. *1 Corinthians.* Zondervan Exegetical Commentary on the New Testament. Edited by Clinton E. Arnold. Grand Rapids: Zondervan, 2018.

Garland, David E. *1 Corinthians.* Baker Exegetical Commentary on the New Testament. Grand Rapids: Baker Academic, 2003.

Garland, David E. "Philippians." Pages 177–261 in *The Expositor's Bible Commentary.* Rev. ed. Edited by Tremper Longman III and David E. Garland. Grand Rapids: Zondervan, 2006.

George, Timothy. *Galatians.* Christian Standard Commentary. Nashville: Holman, 2020.

Gera, Deborah. *Judith.* Commentaries on Early Jewish Literature. Berlin: de Gruyter, 2014.

Glenny, W. Edward. *Amos: A Commentary Based on Amos in Codex Vaticanus.* Septuagint Commentary Series. Leiden: Brill, 2013.

Goodrich, John K. "'As Long as the Heir Is a Child': The Rhetoric of Inheritance in Galatians 4:1–2 and P. Ryl. 2.153." *Novum Testamentum* 55 (2013): 61–76.

Goshen-Gottstein, Moshe H., ed. *The Book of Isaiah.* Vol 2. The Hebrew University Bible Project. Jerusalem: Hebrew University, 1981.

Gravely, Edward D. "The Text Critical Sigla in Codex Vaticanus." PhD diss., Southeastern Baptist Theological Seminary, 2009.

Green, Joel B., and Lee Martin McDonald, eds. *The World of the New Testament: Cultural, Social, and Historical Contexts.* Grand Rapids: Baker Academic, 2013.

Greenbury, James. "1 Corinthians 14:34–35: Evaluation of Prophecy Revisited." *Journal of the Evangelical Theological Society* 51.4 (2008): 721–31.

Grenfell, Bernard P., and Arthur S. Hunt, eds. *The Oxyrhynchus Papyri.* Part 13. London: Egypt Exploration Fund, 1919.

Groothuis, Rebecca Merrill. *Good News for Women: A Biblical Picture of Gender Equality.* Grand Rapids: Baker, 1997.

Grosheide, F. W. *Commentary on the First Epistle to the Corinthians: The English Text with Introduction, Exposition and Notes.* The New International Commentary on the New Testament. Grand Rapids: Eerdmans, 1953.

Grudem, Wayne. "1 Corinthians 14.20–25: Prophecy and Tongues as Signs of God's Attitude." *Westminster Theological Journal* 41.2 (1979): 381–96.

Grudem, Wayne. "Does ΚΕΦΑΛΗ ('Head') Mean 'Source' or 'Authority Over' in Greek Literature? A Survey of 2,336 Examples." *Trinity Journal* 6 (1985): 38–59.

Grudem, Wayne. "Prophecy—Yes, But Teaching—No: Paul's Consistent Advocacy of Women's Participation without Governing Authority." *Journal of the Evangelical Theological Society* 30.1 (1987): 11–23.

Gutzwiller, Kathryn J. *Poetic Garlands: Hellenistic Epigrams in Context*. Berkeley: University of California Press, 1998.

Hansen, G. Walter. *Galatians*. IVP New Testament Commentary Series. Downers Grove, IL: InterVarsity Press, 1994.

Harman, Allan M. *Commentary on the Psalms*. Mentor. Scotland: Christian Focus Publications, 1998.

Harmon, A. M., trans. *Lucian: On Salaried Posts in Great Houses*. Vol. 3. LCL. Cambridge: Harvard University Press, 1921.

Harrill, J. A. "Slavery." Pages 1124–27 in *Dictionary of New Testament Background*. Edited by Craig A. Evans and Stanley E. Porter. Downers Grove, IL: IVP Academic, 2000.

Harris, Murray J. *Slave of Christ: A New Testament Metaphor for Total Devotion to Christ*. New Studies in Biblical Theology. Downers Grove, IL: IVP Academic, 1999.

Harrison, Everett F., and Donald A. Hagner. *Romans*. The Expositor's Bible Commentary. Rev. ed. Edited by Tremper Longman III and David E. Garland. Grand Rapids: Zondervan, 2008.

Harrisville, Roy A. *1 Corinthians*. Augsburg Commentaries on the New Testament. Minneapolis, MN: Augsburg, 1987.

Harvey, John D. *Romans*. Exegetical Guide to the Greek New Testament. Edited by Andreas J. Köstenberger and Robert W. Yarbrough. Nashville: B&H Academic, 2017.

Hasitschka, Martin. "'Die Frauen in den Gemeinden sollen schweigen': 1 Kor 14,33b–36—Anweisung des Paulus zur rechten Ordnung im Gottesdienst." *Studien zum Neuen Testament und seiner Umwelt* 22 (1997): 47–56.

Hays, Richard B. *First Corinthians*. Interpretation: A Bible Commentary for Teaching and Preaching. Louisville: John Knox, 1997.

Hense, Otto, ed. *C. Musonii Rufi Reliquiae*. Leipzig: Teubner, 1905.

Hensley, Adam. "σιγαω, λαλεω, and ὑποτασσω in 1 Corinthians 14:34 in their Literary and Rhetorical Context." *Journal of the Evangelical Theological Society* 55.2 (2012): 343–64.

Héring, Jean. *La première épître de saint Paul aux Corinthiens*. Commentaire du Nouveau Testament 7. Neuchatel: Delachaux & Niestlé, 1949.

Héring, Jean. *The First Epistle of Saint Paul to the Corinthians*. Translated by A. W. Heathcote and P. J. Allcock. London: Epworth, 1962.

Herodotus. *Histories; Books 1–9*. Translated by A. D. Godley. 4 vols. LCL. Cambridge: Harvard University Press, 1920–22, 1925. Repr., 1966, 1971, 1969.

Heylbut, G. "ΠΕΡΙ ΔΙΑΦΟΡΑΣ ΛΕΞΕ'ΩΝ." *Hermes* 22.3 (1887): 388–410.

Hippocrates. *Coan Prenotions*. Pages 108–269. Edited and translated by Paul Potter. Vol. 9. LCL. Cambridge: Harvard University Press, 2010.

Hippocrates. *Diseases of Women II*. Pages 262–451. Edited and translated by Paul Potter. Vol. 11. LCL. Cambridge: Harvard University Press, 2018.

Hippocrates. *Epidemics; Book 3*. Pages 218–87. Translated by W. H. S. Jones. Vol. 1. LCL. Cambridge: Harvard University Press, 1923.

Hippocrates. *Epidemics; Book 6*. Pages 206–75. Translated by Wesley D. Smith. Vol. 7. LCL. Cambridge: Harvard University Press, 1994.

Hippocrates. *In the Surgery*. Pages 58–81. Translated by E. T. Withington. Vol. 3. LCL. Cambridge: Harvard University Press, 1928.

Hippocrates. *On Joints*. Pages 200–397. Translated by E. T. Withington. Vol. 3. LCL. Cambridge: Harvard University Press, 1928.

Hippocrates. *Physician*. Pages 296–311. Edited and translated by Paul Potter. Vol. 8. LCL. Cambridge: Harvard University Press, 1995.

Hippocrates. *The Oath*. Pages 298–301. Translated by W. H. S. Jones. Vol. 1. LCL. Cambridge: Harvard University Press, 1923.

Hiu, Elim. *Regulations Concerning Tongues and Prophecy in 1 Corinthians 14.26–40: Relevance Beyond the Corinthian Church*. The Library of New Testament Studies 406. New York: T&T Clark, 2010.

Hluan, Anna Sui. "Silence in Translation: Interpreting 1 Corinthians 14:34–35 in Myanmar." PhD diss., University of Otago, 2017.

Hogan, Pauline Nigh. *No Longer Male and Female: Interpreting Galatians 3:28 in Early Christianity*. The Library of New Testament Studies 380. New York: T&T Clark, 2008.

Hollander, Harm W. "The Meaning of the Term 'Law' (NOMOS) in 1 Corinthians." *Novum Testamentum* 40 (1998): 117–35.

Holloway, Paul A. *Philippians: A Commentary*. Hermeneia. Minneapolis: Fortress, 2017.

Holmes, J. M. *Text in a Whirlwind: A Critique of Four Exegetical Devices at 1 Timothy 2.9–15*. Journal for the Study of the New Testament Supplement Series 196. Sheffield: Sheffield Academic, 2000.

Holmyard, Harold R. III. "Does 1 Corinthians 11:2–16 Refer to Women Praying and Prophesying in Church?" *Bibliotheca Sacra* 154 (1997): 461–72.

Horrell, David G. *The Social Ethos of the Corinthians Correspondence: Interests and Ideology from 1 Corinthians to 1 Clement*. Edinburgh: T&T Clark, 1996.

Horsley, G. H. R. "Sophia, 'The Second Phoibe.'" Pages 239–44 in *New Documents Illustrating Early Christianity: A Review of the Greek Inscriptions and Papyri Published in 1979*. Vol. 4. The Ancient History Documentary Research Centre. North Ryde, NSW, Australia: Macquarie University, 1987.

House, Paul R. *Lamentations*. Word Biblical Commentary 23B. Nashville: Thomas Nelson, 2004.

Huey, Jr., F. B. *Jeremiah, Lamentations*. New American Commentary 16. Nashville: Broadman, 1993.

Hurley, James B. "Did Paul Require Veils or the Silence of Women? A Consideration of I Cor. 11:2–16 and I Cor. 14:33b–36." *Westminster Theological Journal* 35 (1973): 190–220.

Huttar, David. "Did Paul Call Andronicus an Apostle in Romans 16:7?" *Journal of the Evangelical Theological Society* 52.4 (2009): 747–78.

Huttner, Ulrich. *Early Christianity in the Lycus Valley*. Translated by David Green. Early Christianity in Asia Minor 1. Leiden: Brill, 2013.

Hylen, Susan E. "Modest, Industrious, and Loyal: Reinterpreting Conflicting Evidence for Women's Roles." *Biblical Theology Bulletin* 44 (2014): 3–12.

Institute for New Testament Textual Research. http://ntvmr.uni-muenster.de.
Isocrates. *Busiris: Oration 9*. Pages 102–31. Translated by Larue van Hook. Vol. 3. LCL. Cambridge: Harvard University Press, 1945. Repr., 1968.
Isocrates. *To Demonicus: Oration 1*. Pages 4–35. Translated by George Norlin. Vol. 1. LCL. Cambridge: Harvard University Press, 1928. Repr., 1966.
Isocrates. *Trapeziticus: Oration 17*. Pages 212–49. Translated by Larue van Hook. Vol. 3. LCL. Cambridge: Harvard University Press, 1945. Repr., 1968.
Jäkel, Siegfried, ed. *Menandri Sententiae*. Bibliotheca Scriptorum Graecorum et Romanorum Teubneriana. Lipsiae: Teubner, 1964.
Jenkins, Claude. "Origen on 1 Corinthians, IV." *Journal of Theological Studies* 10.37 (1908): 29–51.
Jervis, L. Ann. "1 Corinthians 14:34–35: A Reconsideration of Paul's Limitation of the Free Speech of Some Corinthian Women." *Journal for the Study of the New Testament* 58 (1995): 51–74.
Jewett, Paul K. *Man as Male and Female: A Study in Sexual Relationships from a Theological Point of View*. Grand Rapids: Eerdmans, 1975.
Jewett, Paul K. *Romans: A Commentary*. Hermeneia. Minneapolis: Fortress, 2007.
Johnson, Alan F. *1 Corinthians*. IVP New Testament Commentary. Downers Grove, IL: InterVarsity Press, 2004.
Johnson, Luke Timothy. *The First and Second Letters to Timothy: A New Translation with Introduction and Commentary*. Anchor Bible. New York: Doubleday, 2001.
Jones, Frank William, trans. "The Suppliant Women." Pages 137–84 in *Euripides*. The Complete Greek Tragedies. Vol. 4. Chicago: The University of Chicago Press, 1992.
Jones, Horace Leonard, ed. *The Geography of Strabo*. Vol. 2. LCL. Cambridge: Harvard University Press, 1988.
Josephus. *Jewish Antiquities; Books 1–4*. Translated by H. St. J. Thackeray. Vol. 4. LCL. Cambridge: Harvard University Press, 1930. Repr., 1967.
Josephus. *Jewish Antiquities; Books 5–8*. Translated by H. St. J. Thackeray and Ralph Marcus. Vol. 5. LCL. Cambridge: Harvard University Press, 1934. Repr., 1966.
Josephus. *Jewish Antiquities; Books 12–14*. Translated by Ralph Marcus. Vol. 7. LCL. Cambridge: Harvard University Press, 1943. Repr., 1966.
Josephus. *Jewish Antiquities; Books 15–17*. Translated by Ralph Marcus. Vol. 8. LCL. Cambridge: Harvard University Press, 1963. Repr., 1969.
Josephus. *Jewish Antiquities; Books 18–19*. Translated by Louis H. Feldman. Vol. 12. LCL. Cambridge: Harvard University Press, 1965. Repr., 2000.
Josephus. *The Jewish War; Books 1–3*. Translated by H. St. J. Thackeray. Vol. 2. LCL. Cambridge: Harvard University Press, 1927. Repr., 1967.
Josephus. *The Jewish War; Books 4–7*. Translated by H. St. J. Thackeray. Vol. 3. LCL. Cambridge: Harvard University Press, 1928. Repr., 1968.
Josephus. *The Life*. Pages 2–159. Translated by H. St. J. Thackeray. Vol. 1. LCL. Cambridge: Harvard University Press, 1926. Repr., 1966.
Kamphuis, Bart L. F., Jan L. H. Krans, Silvia Castelli, and Bert Jan Lietaert Peerbolte. "Sleepy Scribes and Clever Critics: A Classification of Conjectures on the Text of the New Testament." *Novum Testamentum* 57 (2015): 72–90.

Karris, Robert J. "Women in the Pauline Assembly: To Prophesy but Not to Speak?" Pages 205–8 in *Women Priests: A Catholic Commentary on the Vatican Declaration*. Edited by Leonard Swidler and Arlene Swindler. New York: Paulist, 1977.

Kaster, Robert A. "Notes on 'Primary' and 'Secondary' Schools in Late Antiquity." *Transactions of the American Philological Association* 113 (1983): 323–46.

Keener, Craig S. *1–2 Corinthians*. The New Cambridge Bible Commentary. Cambridge: Cambridge University Press, 2005.

Keener, Craig S. *Acts: An Exegetical Commentary*. 4 vols. Grand Rapids: Baker Academic, 2012–2015.

Keener, Craig S. *Galatians: A Commentary*. Grand Rapids: Baker Academic, 2019.

Keener, Craig S. "Learning in the Assemblies: 1 Corinthians 14:34–35." Pages 161–71 in *Discovering Biblical Equality: Complementarity without Hierarchy*. Edited by Ronald W. Pierce and Rebecca Merrill Groothuis. Downers Grove, IL: InterVarsity Press, 2004.

Keener, Craig S. "Man and Woman." Pages 583–92 in *Dictionary of Paul and His Letters: A Compendium of Contemporary Biblical Scholarship*. Edited by Gerald F. Hawthorne and Ralph P. Martin. Downers Grove, IL: IVP Academic, 1993.

Keener, Craig S. *Paul, Women and Wives: Marriage and Women's Ministry in the Letters of Paul*. Peabody, MA: Hendrickson, 1992.

Keener, Craig S. *Romans*. New Covenant Commentary 6. Eugene, OR: Cascade, 2009.

Keener, Craig S. "Women's Education and Public Speech in Antiquity." *Journal of the Evangelical Theological Society* 50 (2007): 747–59.

Kelly, J. N. D. *A Commentary on the Pastoral Epistles: Timothy I and II, Titus*. San Francisco: Harper & Row, 1960.

Kent, John Harvey. *Corinth: The Inscriptions 1926–1950*. Vol 8, Part 3. Princeton: The American School of Classical Studies at Athens, 1966.

Kistemaker, Simon J. *Exposition of the First Epistle to the Corinthians*. Grand Rapids: Baker, 1993.

Klaiber, Walter. *Der erste Korintherbrief*. Die Botschaft des Neuen Testaments. Göttingen: Neukirchener Theologie, 2011.

Klauck, Hans-Josef. *Gemeinde, Amt, Sakrament: Neutestamentliche Perspektiven*. Würzburg: Echter, 1989.

Klauck, Hans-Josef. *1. Korintherbrief*. Neue Echter Bibel. Würzburg: Echter, 1984.

Kloha, Jeffrey John. "A Textual Commentary on Paul's First Epistle to the Corinthians." 4 vols. PhD diss., The University of Leeds, 2006.

Knight, George W. "A Response to Problems of Normativeness in Scripture: Cultural Versus Permanent." Pages 243–53 in *Hermeneutics, Inerrancy, and the Bible*. Edited by Earl D. Radmacher and Robert D. Preus. Grand Rapids: Zondervan, 1984.

Knight, George W. *The Pastoral Epistles: A Commentary on the Greek Text*. The New International Greek Testament Commentary. Grand Rapids: Eerdmans, 1992.

Köstenberger, Andreas J. *1–2 Timothy and Titus*. Evangelical Biblical Theology Commentary. Bellingham, WA: Lexham, 2020.

Köstenberger, Andreas J. "Gender Passages in the NT: Hermeneutical Fallacies Critiqued." *Westminster Theological Journal* 56 (1994): 259–83.

Köstenberger, Andreas J., Benjamin L. Merkle, and Robert L. Plummer. *Going Deeper with New Testament Greek: An Intermediate Study of the Grammar and Syntax of the New Testament*. Rev. ed. Nashville: B&H Academic, 2020.

Köstenberger, Andreas J., L. Scott Kellum, and Charles L. Quarles. *The Cradle, the Cross, and the Crown: An Introduction to the New Testament*. 2nd ed. Nashville: B&H Academic, 2016.

Köstenberger, Andreas, and Raymond Bouchoc. *The Book Study Concordance of the Greek New Testament*. Nashville: Broadman & Holman, 2003.

Köstenberger, Andreas J., and Thomas R. Schreiner, eds. *Women in the Church: An Interpretation and Application of 1 Timothy 2:9–15*. 3rd ed. Wheaton: Crossway, 2016.

Köstenberger, Andreas J., Thomas R. Schreiner, and H. Scott Baldwin, eds. *Women in the Church: A Fresh Analysis of 1 Timothy 2:9–15*. Grand Rapids: Baker, 1995.

Köstenberger, Margaret Elizabeth. *A Critique of Feminist and Egalitarian Hermeneutics and Exegesis: With Special Focus on Jesus' Approach to Women*. ThD diss., University of South Africa, 2006.

Kovacs, David, ed. *Euripides: Cyclops*. Vol. 1. LCL. Cambridge: Harvard University Press, 1994.

Kowalski, Waldemar. "Does Paul Really Want All Women to be Silent? 1 Corinthians 14:34–35." *Asian Journal of Pentecostal Studies* 20.2 (2017): 171–81.

Krans, Jan. "Paragraphos, Not Obelos, in Codex Vaticanus." *New Testament Studies* 65 (2019): 252–57.

Kraus, Thomas J. "'Uneducated', 'Ignorant', or even 'Illiterate'? Aspects and Background for an Understanding of ΑΓΡΑΜΜΑΤΟΙ (and ΙΔΙΩΤΑΙ) in Acts 4.13." *New Testament Studies* 45 (1999): 434–49.

Kroeger, Catherine Clark. "1 Corinthians." Pages 646–64 in *The IVP Women's Bible Commentary*. Edited by Catherine Clark Kroeger and Mary J. Evans. Downers Grove, IL: InterVarsity Press, 2002.

Kroeger, Richard C., and Catherine Kroeger. "Strange Tongues or Plain Talk?" *Daughters of Sarah* 12 (1986): 10–13.

Kruse, Colin G. *Paul's Letter to the Romans*. The Pillar New Testament Commentary. Grand Rapids: Eerdmans, 2012.

Laney, J. Carl. "Gender Based Boundaries for Gathered Congregations: An Interpretive History of 1 Corinthians 14:34–35." *The Journal for Biblical Manhood and Womanhood* 7.1 (2002): 4–13.

Lang, Friedrich. *Die Briefe an die Korinther*. Das Neue Testament Deutsch 7. Göttingen: Vandenhoeck and Ruprecht, 1986.

Lategan, Bernard C. "Reconsidering the Origin and Function of Galatians 3:28." *Neotestamentica* 46 (2012): 274–86.

Lavrinoviča, Aļesja. "1 Cor 14.34-5 without 'in All the Churches of the Saints': External Evidence." *New Testament Studies* 63 (2017): 370–89.

Lee, John A. L. *A History of New Testament Lexicography*. Studies in Biblical Greek 8. New York: Peter Lang, 2003.

Lefkowitz, Jeremy B. "Ugliness and Value in the *Life of Aesop*." Pages 59–81 in *KAKOS: Badness and Anti-Value in Classical Antiquity*. Edited by Ineke Sluiter and Ralph M. Rosen. Mnemosyne Supplements: Monographs on Greek and Roman Language and Literature 307. Leiden: Brill, 2008.

Lefkowitz, Mary R., and Maureen B. Fant. *Women's Life in Greece and Rome: A Source Book in Translation.* 3rd ed. Baltimore, MD: Johns Hopkins University Press, 2005.

Li, Soeng Yu. *Paul's Teaching on the Pneumatika in 1 Corinthians 12–14: Prophecy as the Paradigm of ta Charismata ta Meizona for the Future-Oriented Ekklēsia.* Wissenschaftliche Untersuchungen zum Neuen Testament 455. Tübingen: Mohr Siebeck, 2017.

Liddell, Henry George, Robert Scott, and Henry Stuart Jones. *A Greek-English Lexicon.* Oxford: Clarendon, 1996.

Lindemann, Andreas. *Der erste Korintherbrief.* Handbuch zum Neuen Testament 9. Tübingen: Mohr Siebeck, 2000.

Litke, Wayne. "Beyond Creation: Galatians 3:28, Genesis and the Hermaphrodite Myth." *Studies in Religion* 24 (1995): 173–78.

Littman, Robert J. *Tobit: The Book of Tobit in Codex Sinaiticus.* Edited by Stanley E. Porter, Richard S. Hess, and John Jarick. Septuagint Commentary Series. Leiden: Brill, 2008.

Livy. *History of Rome; Books 31–34.* Edited and translated by J. C. Yardley. Vol. 9. LCL. Cambridge: Harvard University Press, 2017.

Lloyd-Jones, Hugh, ed. *Sophocles Fragments.* Vol. 3. LCL. Cambridge: Harvard University Press, 1996.

Lockwood, Gregory J. *1 Corinthians.* Concordia Commentary. Saint Louis: Concordia, 2000.

Lohse, Eduard. *Colossians and Philemon.* Edited by Helmut Koester. Translated by William R. Poehlmann and Robert J. Karris. Hermeneia. Philadelphia: Fortress, 1971.

Longenecker, Richard N. *New Testament Social Ethics for Today.* Grand Rapids: Eerdmans, 1984. Repr., Vancouver: Regent College Bookstore, 1995.

Longenecker, Richard N. *The Epistle to the Romans: A Commentary on the Greek Text.* The New International Greek Testament Commentary. Grand Rapids: Eerdmans, 2016.

Louw, Johannes P., and Eugene A. Nida. *Greek-English Lexicon of the New Testament: Based on Semantic Domains.* 2nd ed. 2 vols. New York: United Bible Societies, 1989.

Lucian. *On Salaried Posts in Great Houses.* Pages 411–80. Translated by A. M. Harmon. Vol. 3. LCL. Cambridge: Harvard University Press, 1921.

Lucian. *Harmonides.* Pages 216–225. Translated by K. Kilburn. Vol. 6. LCL. Cambridge: Harvard University Press, 1959.

Lysias. *In Eratosthenem: Oration 12.* Pages 226–77. Translated by W. R. M. Lamb. LCL. Cambridge: Harvard University Press, 1930. Repr., 1967.

MacGregor, Kirk R. "1 Corinthians 14:33b–38 as a Pauline Quotation-Refutation Device." *Priscilla Papers* 32.1 (2018): 23–28.

Manetsch, Scott M., ed. *1 Corinthians.* Reformation Commentary on Scripture: New Testament 9a. Downers Grove, IL: IVP Academic, 2017.

Manetsch, Scott M. "(Re)Constructing the Pastoral Office: Wolfgang Musculus's Commentaries on 1 and 2 Corinthians." Pages 253–66 in *On the Writing of New Testament Commentaries: Festschrift for Grant R. Osborne on the Occasion of His 70th Birthday.* Edited by Stanley E. Porter and Eckhard J. Schnabel. Texts and Editions for New Testament Study 8. Leiden: Brill, 2013.

Manus, Chris Ukachukwu. "The Subordination of the Women in the Church. 1 Cor 14:33b–36 Reconsidered." *Revue Africaine de Théologie* 8 (1984): 183–95.

Marchal, Joseph A. "Bodies Bound for Circumcision and Baptism: An Intersex Critique and the Interpretation of Galatians." *Theology and Sexuality* 16.2 (2010): 163–82.

Marshall, I. Howard. *Acts: An Introduction and Commentary.* Tyndale New Testament Commentaries 5. Downers Grove, IL: IVP Academic, 1980.

Marshall, Jill E. *Women Praying and Prophesying in Corinth: Gender and Inspired Speech in First Corinthians.* Wissenschaftliche Untersuchungen zum Neuen Testament 448. Tübingen: Mohr Siebeck, 2017.

Martin, Dale B. *Sex and the Single Savior: Gender and Sexuality in Biblical Interpretation.* Louisville: Westminster John Knox, 2006.

Martin, Faith McBurney. "Galatians 3:28." *Priscilla Papers* 9 (1995): 1–3.

Martin, Troy W. "The Covenant of Circumcision (Genesis 17:9–14) and the Situational Antitheses in Galatians 3:28." *Journal of Biblical Literature* 122 (2003): 111–25.

Massey, Preston T. "Women, Talking and Silence: 1 Corinthians 11.5 and 14.34–35 in the Light of Greco-Roman Culture." *Journal of Greco-Roman Christianity and Judaism* 12 (2016): 127–60.

Mathews, Kenneth. *Genesis 1–11:26.* New American Commentary 1A. Nashville: B&H, 1996.

McKnight, Scot. *The Letter to the Colossians.* The New International Commentary on the New Testament. Grand Rapids: Eerdmans, 2018.

McQuilkin, J. Robertson. "Problems of Normativeness in Scripture: Cultural Versus Permanent." Pages 219–40 in *Hermeneutics, Inerrancy, and the Bible.* Edited by Earl D. Radmacher and Robert D. Preus. Grand Rapids: Zondervan, 1984.

McRay, J. R. "Corinth." Pages 227–31 in *Dictionary of New Testament Background.* Edited by Craig A. Evans and Stanley E. Porter. Downers Grove, IL: IVP Academic, 2000.

McWilliams, David B. *Galatians.* A Mentor Commentary. Ross-shire, Great Britain: Mentor, 2009.

Meeks, Wayne A. "The Image of the Androgyne: Some Uses of a Symbol in Earliest Christianity." *History of Religions* 13 (1974): 165–208.

Melick, Jr., Richard R. *Philippians, Colossians, Philemon.* New American Commentary 32. Nashville: Broadman, 1991.

Meritt, Benjamin Dean. *Corinth: Greek Inscriptions 1896–1927.* Vol. 8, Part 1. Cambridge: The American School of Classical Studies at Athens, Harvard University Press, 1931.

Merkle, Benjamin L. "Are the Qualifications for Elders or Overseers Negotiable?" *Bibliotheca Sacra* 171 (2014): 172–88.

Merkle, Benjamin L. *Ephesians.* Exegetical Guide to the Greek New Testament. Nashville: B&H Academic, 2016.

Merkle, Benjamin L. "Paul's Argument from Creation in 1 Corinthians 11:8–9 and 1 Timothy 2:13–14: An Apparent Inconsistency Answered." *Journal of the Evangelical Theological Society* 49.3 (2006): 527–48.

Merkle, Benjamin L. *The Elder and Overseer: One Office in the Early Church.* Studies in Biblical Literature 57. New York: Peter Lang, 2003.

Metzger, Bruce M. *A Textual Commentary on the Greek New Testament.* 2nd ed. Stuttgart: United Bible Societies, 1994.

Miller, Clint. "A Comparative Analysis of Wayne Grudem's Complementarian Position and Gordon Fee's Egalitarian Position within the Gender Debate." PhD diss., New Orleans Baptist Theological Seminary, 2011.

Miller, J. Edward. "Some Observations on the Text-Critical Function of the Umlauts in Vaticanus, with Special Attention to 1 Corinthians 14:34–35." *Journal for the Study of the New Testament* 26 (2003): 217–36.

Mitchell, Margaret M. "1 Cor 14:33B–36: Women Commanded to Be 'Silent' in the Assemblies." Pages 477–78 in *Women in Scripture: A Dictionary of Named and Unnamed Women in the Hebrew Bible, the Apocryphal/Deuterocanonical Books, and the New Testament*. Edited by Carol Meyers. Grand Rapids: Eerdmans, 2000.

Moffatt, James. *The First Epistle of Paul to the Corinthians*. Moffatt New Testament Commentary. New York: Harper and Brothers, 1900.

Montague, George T. *First Corinthians*. Catholic Commentary on Sacred Scripture. Grand Rapids: Baker Academic, 2011.

Moo, Douglas J. "1 Timothy 2:11–15: Meaning and Significance." *Trinity Journal* 1 (1980): 62–83.

Moo, Douglas J. *Galatians*. Baker Exegetical Commentary on the New Testament. Grand Rapids: Baker Academic, 2013.

Moo, Douglas J. *The Epistle to the Romans*. 2nd ed. The New International Commentary on the New Testament. Grand Rapids: Eerdmans, 2018.

Moo, Douglas J. "The Interpretation of 1 Timothy 2:11–15: A Rejoinder." *Trinity Journal* 2 (1981): 198–222.

Morris, Leon. *The First Epistle of Paul to the Corinthians: An Introduction and Commentary*. Rev. ed. Tyndale New Testament Commentaries. Grand Rapids: Eerdmans, 1985.

Moschus. *Lament for Bion*. Pages 468–81. Edited and translated by Neil Hopkinson. LCL. Cambridge: Harvard University Press, 2015.

Mounce, Robert H. *The Book of Revelation*. Rev. ed. The New International Commentary on the New Testament. Grand Rapids: Eerdmans, 1977.

Mounce, William D. *Pastoral Epistles*. Word Biblical Commentary 46. Nashville: Thomas Nelson, 2000.

Moxnes, Halvor. "Honor and Shame." Pages 19–40 in *The Social Sciences and New Testament Interpretation*. Edited by Richard L. Rohrbaugh. Peabody, MA: Hendrickson, 1996.

Müller, Karl, ed. *Geographi Graeci Minores*. Vol. 1. Paris: Ambrosio Firmin Didot, 1855.

Muraoka, T. *A Greek-English Lexicon of the Septuagint*. Louvain: Peeters, 2009.

Muraoka, T. *A Syntax of Septuagint Greek*. Leuven: Peeters, 2016.

Murphy-O'Connor, Jerome. *1 Corinthians*. New Testament Message 10. Wilmington, DE: Michael Glazier, 1979.

Murphy-O'Connor, Jerome. "Interpolations in 1 Corinthians." *Catholic Biblical Quarterly* 48 (1986): 81–94.

Murphy-O'Connor, Jerome. "The Corinth that Saint Paul Saw." *Biblical Archaeologist* 47 (1984): 147–59.

Naselli, Andrew David. *How to Understand and Apply the New Testament: Twelve Steps from Exegesis to Theology*. Phillipsburg: P&R, 2017.

Nash, Robert Scott. *1 Corinthians*. Smyth and Helwys Bible Commentary. Macon, GA: Smyth and Helwys, 2009.

Nelson, James B. *Embodiment: An Approach to Sexuality and Christian Theology*. Minneapolis: Augsburg, 1978.

Neusner, Jacob, trans. *Pesiqta deRab Kahana: An Analytical Translation*. Vol. 2. Brown Judaic Studies 123. Atlanta: Scholars, 1987.

Neusner, Jacob, trans. *Song of Songs Rabbah: An Analytical Translation*. Vol. 2. Brown Judaic Studies 198. Atlanta: Scholars, 1989.

Neutel, Karin B. "Women's Silence and Jewish Influence: The Problematic Origins of the Conjectural Emendation on 1 Cor 14.33b–35." *New Testament Studies* 65 (2019): 477–95.

Ngunga, Abi T., and Joachim Schaper. "Isaiah." Pages 456–68 in *The T&T Clark Companion to the Septuagint*. Edited by James K. Aitken. London: Bloomsbury, 2015.

Niccum, Curt. "The Voice of the Manuscripts on the Silence of Women: The External Evidence for 1 Corinthians 14:34–35." *New Testament Studies* 43 (1997): 242–55.

Nicole, Roger. "Biblical Hermeneutics: Basic Principles and Questions of Gender." Pages 355–63 in *Discovering Biblical Equality: Complementarity without Hierarchy*. Edited by Ronald W. Pierce and Rebecca Merrill Groothuis. Downers Grove, IL: InterVarsity Press, 2004.

Noll, Sonja. *The Semantics of Silence in Biblical Hebrew*. Studies in Semitic Languages and Linguistics 100. Leiden: Brill, 2020.

Odell-Scott, D. W. "Editorial Dilemma: The Interpretation of 1 Corinthians 14:34–35 in the Western Manuscripts of D, G and 88." *Biblical Theology Bulletin* 30 (2000): 68–74.

Odell-Scott, D. W. "In Defense of an Egalitarian Interpretation of 1 Cor 14:34–36: A Reply to Murphy-O'Connor's Critique." *Biblical Theology Bulletin* 17.3 (1987): 100–3.

O'Kelly, Bernard, and Catherine A. L. Jarrot. *John Colet's Commentary on First Corinthians: A New Edition of the Latin Text, with Translation, Annotations, and Introduction*. Binghamton, New York: Medieval & Renaissance Texts & Studies, 1985.

Omanson, Roger L. "The Role of Women in the New Testament Church." *Review and Expositor* 83 (1986): 15–25.

Omanson, Roger L. "Who's Who in Romans 16? Identifying Men and Women among the People Paul Sent Greetings to." *The Bible Translator* 49.4 (1998): 430–36.

Oropeza, B. J. *1 Corinthians*. A New Covenant Commentary. Eugene, OR: Cascade, 2017.

Osborne, Grant R. "Hermeneutics and Women in the Church." *Journal of the Evangelical Theological Society* 20 (1977): 337–52.

Osborne, Grant R. *Revelation*. Baker Exegetical Commentary on the New Testament. Grand Rapids: Baker Academic, 2002.

Osburn, Carroll. "Interpretation of 1 Cor. 14:34–35." Pages 219–42 in *Essays on Women in Earliest Christianity*. Edited by Carroll Osburn. Vol. 1. Eugene, OR: Wipf & Stock, 1993.

Osiek, Carolyn. "Women in the Ancient Mediterranean World: State of the Question New Testament." *Biblical Research* 39 (1994): 57–61.

Oswalt, John N. "חרשׁ." Pages 296–97 in vol. 2 of *New International Dictionary of Old Testament Theology and Exegesis*. Edited by Willem A. VanGemeren. Grand Rapids: Zondervan, 1997.

Packard Humanities Institute. https://epigraphy.packhum.org.

Paige, Terence. "The Social Matrix of Women's Speech at Corinth: The Context and Meaning of the Command to Silence in 1 Corinthians 14:33b–36." *Bulletin for Biblical Research* 12.2 (2002): 217–42.

Pao, David W. *Colossians and Philemon*. Zondervan Exegetical Commentary on the New Testament. Grand Rapids: Zondervan, 2012.

Parsons, Mikeal C. *Acts*. Paideia. Grand Rapids: Backer Academic, 2008.

Paton, W. R., trans. *The Greek Anthology; Books 1–5*. Vol. 1. Revised by Michael A. Tueller. LCL. Cambridge: Harvard University Press, 2014.

Paton, W. R. *The Greek Anthology; Book 9*. Vol. 3. LCL. Cambridge: Harvard University Press, 1917.

Payne, Philip B. "Does the New Testament Name Only Men as Local Church Officers?" *Priscilla Papers* 26.3 (2012): 5–6.

Payne, Philip B. "Fuldensis, Sigla for Variants in Vaticanus, and 1 Cor 14.34–5." *New Testament Studies* 41 (1995): 240–62.

Payne, Philip B. "Is 1 Corinthians 14:34–35 a Marginal Comment or a Quotation? A Response to Kirk MacGregor." *Priscilla Papers* 33.2 (2019): 24–30.

Payne, Philip B. "Libertarian Women in Ephesus: A Response to Douglas J. Moo's Article, '1 Timothy 2:11–15: Meaning and Significance.'" *Trinity Journal* 2 (1981): 169–97.

Payne, Philip B. *Man and Woman, One in Christ: An Exegetical and Theological Study of Paul's Letters*. Grand Rapids: Zondervan, 2009.

Payne, Philip B. "MS. 88 as Evidence for a Text without 1 Cor 14.34–35." *New Testament Studies* 44 (1998): 152–58.

Payne, Philip B. https://www.pbpayne.com.

Payne, Philip B. "The Interpretation of 1 Timothy 2:11–15: A Surrejoinder." Pages 96–115 in *What Does the Scripture Teach about the Ordination of Women: A Study Commissioned by the Committee on Ministerial Standing*. Part 2. Minneapolis: The Evangelical Free Church of America, 1986.

Payne, Philip B. "The Text-critical Function of the Umlauts in Vaticanus, with Special Attention to 1 Corinthians 14.34–35: A Response to J. Edward Miller." *Journal for the Study of the New Testament* 27 (2004): 105–12.

Payne, Philip B. "Vaticanus Distigme-obelos Symbols Marking Added Text, Including 1 Corinthians 14.34–5." *New Testament Studies* 63.4 (2017): 604–25.

Payne, Philip B., and Paul Canart. "The Originality of Text-Critical Symbols in Codex Vaticanus." *Novum Testamentum* 42.2 (2000): 105–13.

Peisker, C. H. "Ἡσυχία, ἡσυχάζω, ἡσύχιος." Page 125 in vol. 2 of *Exegetical Dictionary of the New Testament*. Edited by Horst Balz and Gerhard Schneider. Grand Rapids: Eerdmans, 1991.

Penner, Ken. M. "Ancient Names for Hebrew and Aramaic: A Case for Lexical Revision." *New Testament Studies* 65 (2019): 412–23.

Perkins, Pheme. *First Corinthians*. Paideia Commentaries on the New Testament. Grand Rapids: Baker Academic, 2012.

Perry, B. E., ed. *Aesopica: A Series of Texts Relating to Aesop or Ascribed to Him or Closely Connected with the Literary Tradition that Bears His Name*. Vol. 1. Urbana: The University of Illinois Press, 1952.

Perry, B. E. *Studies in the Text History of the Life and Fables of Aesop*. Philological Monographs 7. Haverford, PA: The American Philological Association, 1936.

Peterson, David G. *The Acts of the Apostles*. The Pillar New Testament Commentary. Grand Rapids: Eerdmans, 2009.

Petzer, J. H. "Reconsidering the Silent Women of Corinth—A Note on 1 Corinthians 14:34–35." *Theologia Evangelica* 26 (1993): 132–38.

Philip, Finny. "1 Corinthians." Pages 1555–84 in *South Asia Bible Commentary*. Edited by Brian Wintle. Rajasthan, India: Open Door Publications, 2015.

Philo. *On Dreams*. Pages 294–579. Translated by F. H. Colson and G. H. Whitaker. Vol. 5. LCL. Cambridge: Harvard University Press, 1934. Repr., 1968.

Philo. *That Every Good Person Is Free*. Pages 10–101. Translated by F. H. Colson. Vol. 9. LCL. Cambridge: Harvard University Press, 1941. Repr., 1967.

Philo. *That the Worse Is Wont to Attack the Better*. Pages 202–319. Translated by F. H. Colson and G. H. Whitaker. Vol. 2. LCL. Cambridge: Harvard University Press, 1929. Repr., 1968.

Philo. *Who Is the Heir?* Pages 284–447. Translated by F. H. Colson and G. H. Whitaker. Vol. 4. LCL. Cambridge: Harvard University Press, 1932. Repr., 1968.

Philostratus. *Apollonius of Tyana: Letters of Apollonius*. Pages 10–79. Edited and translated by Christopher P. Jones. Vol. 3. LCL. Cambridge: Harvard University Press, 2006.

Pickering, John. *A Comprehensive Lexicon of the Greek Language*. Boston: Wilkins, Carter, and Company, 1847.

Pierce, Ronald W., and Rebecca Merrill Groothuis, eds. *Discovering Biblical Equality: Complementarity without Hierarchy*. Downers Grove, IL: InterVarsity Press, 2004.

Pietersma, Albert, and Benjamin G. Wright, eds. *A New English Translation of the Septuagint: And the Other Greek Translations Traditionally Included under that Title*. New York: Oxford University Press, 2007.

Plato. *Alcibiades I*. Pages 98–223. Translated by W. R. M. Lamb. LCL. Cambridge: Harvard University Press, 1927. Repr., 1964.

Plato. *Apology*. Pages 106–93. Edited and translated by Chris Emlyn-Jones and William Preddy. Vol. 1. LCL. Cambridge: Harvard University Press, 2017.

Plato. *Epistles*. Pages 394–627. Translated by R. G. Bury. LCL. Cambridge: Harvard University Press, 1929. Repr., 1966.

Plato. *Euthydemus*. Pages 378–505. Translated by W. R. M. Lamb. Vol. 2. LCL. Cambridge: Harvard University Press, 1924. Repr., 1967.

Plato. *Laws; Books 7–12*. Translated by R. G. Bury. Vol. 11. LCL. Cambridge: Harvard University Press, 1926. Repr., 1968.

Plato. *Lesser Hippias*. Pages 428–75. Translated by H. N. Fowler. Vol. 4. LCL. Cambridge: Harvard University Press, 1926. Repr., 1970.

Plato. *Lysis*. Pages 6–71. Translated by W. R. M. Lamb. Vol. 3. LCL. Cambridge: Harvard University Press, 1925.

Plato. *Phaedrus*. Pages 412–579. Translated by Harold North Fowler. Vol. 1. LCL. Cambridge: Harvard University Press, 1914.

Plato. *Protagoras*. Pages 92–257. Translated by W. R. M. Lamb. Vol. 2. LCL. Cambridge: Harvard University Press, 1924. Repr., 1967.

Plato. *Theaetetus*. Pages 6–257. Translated by Harold North Fowler. Vol. 7. LCL. Cambridge: Harvard University Press, 1921. Repr., 1967.

Plato. *The Lovers*. Pages 312–39. Translated by W. R. M. Lamb. Vol. 12. LCL. Cambridge: Harvard University Press, 1927. Repr., 1955.

Plato. *The Republic; Books 1–10*. Translated by Paul Shorey. Vols. 5–6. LCL. Cambridge: Harvard University Press, 1930, 1935. Repr., 1994, 1999.

Plutarch. *Advice about Keeping Well*. Pages 216–93. Translated by Frank Cole Babbitt. Vol. 2. LCL. Cambridge: Harvard University Press, 1928. Repr., 1962.

Plutarch. *Advice to Bride and Groom*. Pages 298–343. Translated by Frank Cole Babbitt. Vol. 2. LCL. Cambridge: Harvard University Press, 1928. Repr., 1962.

Plutarch. *Brutus*. Pages 126–247 in *Lives*. Translated by Bernadotte Perrin. Vol. 6. LCL. Cambridge: Harvard University Press, 1918. Repr., 1970.

Plutarch. *Concerning Talkativeness*. Pages 396–467. Translated by W. C. Helmbold. Vol. 6. LCL. Cambridge: Harvard University Press, 1939. Repr., 1962.

Plutarch. *Coriolanus*. Pages 118–219 in *Lives*. Translated by Bernadotte Perrin.. Vol. 4. LCL. Cambridge: Harvard University Press, 1916. Repr., 1968.

Plutarch. "Fragments from Other Named Works." Pages 88–339 in *Moralia*. Translated by F. H. Sandbach. Vol. 15. LCL. Cambridge: Harvard University Press, 1969.

Plutarch. *How a Man May Become Aware of His Progress in Virtue*. Pages 400–57. Translated by Frank Cole Babbitt. Vol. 1. LCL. Cambridge: Harvard University Press, 1927. Repr., 1969.

Plutarch. *How the Young Man Should Study Poetry*. Pages 74–197. Translated by Frank Cole Babbitt. Vol. 1. LCL. Cambridge: Harvard University Press, 1927. Repr., 1969.

Plutarch. *Lives of the Ten Orators*. Pages 344–457. Translated by Harold North Fowler. Vol. 10. LCL. Cambridge: Harvard University Press, 1936. Repr., 1969.

Plutarch. *On Exile*. Pages 518–71. Translated by Phillip H. de Lacy and Benedict Einarson. Vol. 7. LCL. Cambridge: Harvard University Press, 1959. Repr., 1968.

Plutarch. *On the Fortune of the Romans*. Pages 322–77. Translated by Frank Cole Babbitt. Vol. 4. LCL. Cambridge: Harvard University Press, 1936.

Plutarch. *Sayings of Spartans*. Pages 242–421. Translated by Frank Cole Babbitt. Vol. 3. LCL. Cambridge: Harvard University Press, 1931. Repr., 1968.

Plutarch. *The Education of Children*. Pages 4–69. Translated by Frank Cole Babbitt. Vol. 1. LCL. Cambridge: Harvard University Press, 1927. Repr., 1969.

Polhill, John B. *Acts*. New American Commentary 26. Nashville: Broadman, 1992.

Polybius. *The Histories*. Translated by W. R. Paton. Vol. 4. LCL. Cambridge: Harvard University Press, 1925. Repr., 1968.

Powell, Benjamin. "Greek Inscriptions from Corinth." *American Journal of Archaeology* 7.1 (1903): 26–71.

Punt, Jeremy. "Power and Liminality, Sex and Gender, and Gal 3:28: A Postcolonial, Queer Reading of an Influential Text." *Neotestamentica* 44.1 (2010): 140–66.

Quintilian. *The Orator's Education: Books 1–2*. Edited and translated by Donald A. Russell. Vol. 1. LCL. Cambridge: Harvard University Press, 2001.

Radl, W. "σιγάω; σιγή." Page 242 in vol. 3 of *Exegetical Dictionary of the New Testament*. Edited by Horst Balz and Gerhard Schneider. Grand Rapids: Eerdmans, 1993.

Rahlfs, Alfred, and Robert Hanhart. *Septuaginta*. Stuttgart: Deutsche Bibelgesellschaft, 2006.

Rambau, Leonce F. "Paul and His Co-Workers: Equality in Pauline Letters." PhD diss., The University of Notre Dame, 2014.

Reumann, John. *Philippians: A New Translation with Introduction and Commentary*. The Anchor Yale Bible. New Haven: Yale University Press, 2008.

Richardson, William Edward. "Liturgical Order and Glossolalia: 1 Corinthians 14:26c–33a and its Implications." PhD diss., Andrews University Seventh-day Adventist Theological Seminary, 1983.

Riches, John. *Galatians Through the Centuries*. Wiley-Blackwell Bible Commentaries. Oxford: Wiley-Blackwell, 2013.

Richter, Philip. "Social-Scientific Criticism of the New Testament: An Appraisal and Extended Example." Pages 266–309 in *Approaches to New Testament Study*. Edited by Stanley E. Porter and David Tombs. Journal for the Study of the New Testament Supplement Series 120. Sheffield: Sheffield Academic Press, 1995.

Riddlebarger, Kim. *1 Corinthians*. The Lectio Continua. Powder Springs, GA: Tolle Lege, 2013.

Roberts, J. J. M. *First Isaiah*. Hermeneia. Minneapolis: Fortress, 2015.

Robertson, Archibald, and Alfred Plummer. *A Critical and Exegetical Commentary on the First Epistle of St Paul to the Corinthians*. 2nd ed. International Critical Commentary. Edinburgh: T&T Clark, 1953.

Rogers, Benjamin Bickley, trans. *Aristophanes: The Peace, The Birds, The Frogs*. Vol. 2. LCL. Cambridge: Harvard University Press, 1924. Repr., 1996.

Rosner, Brian S. *Paul and the Law: Keeping the Commandments of God*. New Studies in Biblical Theology. Downers Grove, IL: InterVarsity Press, 2013.

Ross, J. M. "Floating Words: Their Significance for Textual Criticism." *New Testament Studies* 38 (1992): 153–56.

Rowe, Arthur. "Silence and the Christian Women of Corinth: An Examination of 1 Corinthians 14:33b–36." *Communio Viatorum* 33.1 (1990): 41–84.

Salters, R. B. *A Critical and Exegetical Commentary on Lamentations*. International Critical Commentary. London: Bloomsbury, 2014.

Sampley, J. Paul. "The First Letter to the Corinthians." Pages 771–1004 in *The New Interpreter's Bible*. Vol. 10. Nashville: Abingdon, 2002.

Sanday, William, and Arthur C. Headlam. *A Critical and Exegetical Commentary on the Epistle to the Romans*. The International Critical Commentary. Edinburgh: T&T Clark, 1895. Repr., 1968.

Schemm, Peter R. "Galatians 3:28: Prooftext or Context?" *Journal for Biblical Manhood and Womanhood* 8 (2003): 23–30.

Schlatter, A. *Kirche der Griechen im Urteil des Paulus: Eine Auslegung seiner Briefe an Timotheus und Titus*. 2nd ed. Stuttgart: Calwer, 1958.

Schnabel, Eckhard J. *Der erste Brief des Paulus an die Korinther*. Historisch-theologische Auslegung, Neues Testament 4. Wuppertal: Brockhaus, 2006.

Schottroff, Luise. *Der erste Brief an die Gemeinde in Korinth*. Theologischer Kommentar zum Neuen Testament. Stuttgart: W. Kohlhammer, 2013.

Schrage, Wolfgang. *Der erste Brief an die Korinther*. Vol. 3. Evangelisch-Katholischer Kommentar zum Neuen Testament. Zürich: Benziger, 1999.
Schreiner, Thomas R. *1 Corinthians: An Introduction and Commentary*. Tyndale New Testament Commentaries 7. Downers Grove, IL: IVP Academic, 2018.
Schreiner, Thomas R. *40 Questions About Christians and Biblical Law*. Edited by Benjamin L. Merkle. 40 Questions. Grand Rapids: Kregel, 2010.
Schreiner, Thomas R. *Galatians*. Zondervan Exegetical Commentary on the New Testament. Grand Rapids: Zondervan, 2010.
Schreiner, Thomas R. *Romans*. 2nd ed. Baker Exegetical Commentary on the New Testament. Grand Rapids: Baker Academic, 2018.
Semler, Johann Salomo. *Paraphrasis in Primam Pavli ad Corinthios Epistolam: Cvm Notis, et Latinarvm Translationvm Excerptis*. Halae Magdebvrgicae: Impensis Carol. Herm. Hemmerde, 1770.
Senft, Christophe. *La première épitre de Saint Paul aux Corinthiens*. 2nd ed. Commentaire du Nouveau Testament. Genève: Labor et Fides, 1990.
Septuaginta. *Vetus Testamentum Graecum*. 20 vols. Auctoritate Academiae Scientiarum Gottingensis. Göttingen: Vandenhoeck & Ruprecht, 1931–.
Shack, Jennifer. "A Text without 1 Corinthians 14.34–35? Not According to the Manuscript Evidence." *Journal of Greco-Roman Christianity and Judaism* 10 (2014): 90–112.
Sigountos, James G., and Myron Shank. "Public Roles for Women in the Pauline Church: A Reappraisal of the Evidence." *Journal of the Evangelical Theological Society* 26.3 (1983): 283–95.
Siker, Jeffrey S. "Gentile Wheat and Homosexual Christians: New Testament Directions for the Heterosexual Church." Pages 137–51 in *Biblical Ethics and Homosexuality: Listening to Scripture*. Edited by Robert L. Brawley. Louisville: Westminster, 1996.
Silva, Moisés, ed. *New International Dictionary of New Testament Theology and Exegesis*. 2nd ed. 5 vols. Grand Rapids: Zondervan, 2014.
Silva, Moisés. *Philippians*. 2nd ed. Baker Exegetical Commentary on the New Testament. Grand Rapids: Baker Academic, 2005.
Silva, Moisés. Review of *Greek-English Lexicon of the New Testament: Based on Semantic Domains*, by Johannes P. Louw and Eugene A. Nida. *Westminster Theological Journal* 51 (1989): 163–67.
Simon, Stephen J. "Women Who Pleaded Causes Before the Roman Magistrates." *Classical Bulletin* 66 (1990): 79–81.
Smelik, Willem F. "The Use of הזכיר בשם in Classical Hebrew: Josh 23:7; Isa 48:1; Amos 6:10; Ps 20:8; 4Q504 III 4; 1QS 6:27." *Journal of Biblical Literature* 118 (1999): 321–32.
Smith, Gary V. *Isaiah 1–39*. New American Commentary 15A. Nashville: B&H, 2007.
Smith, Jay E. "Slogans in 1 Corinthians." *Bibliotheca Sacra* 167 (2010): 68–88.
Smith, Travis Lee. "Towards Establishing Criteria for Identifying Corinthian Slogans and Their Application to 1 Corinthians 14:34–35 and 15:29." ThM thesis, Dallas Theological Seminary, 2006.
Soards, Marion L. *1 Corinthians*. Understanding the Bible Commentary. Grand Rapids: Baker, 2011.
Sophocles. *Ajax; Electra; Oedipus Tyrannus*. Edited and translated by Hugh Lloyd-Jones. Vol. 1. LCL. Cambridge: Harvard University Press, 1994. Repr., 1997.

Sophocles. *Antigone; The Women of Trachis; Philoctetes; Oedipus at Colonus*. Edited and translated by Hugh Lloyd-Jones. Vol. 2. LCL. Cambridge: Harvard University Press, 1994. Repr., 1998.

Sophocles. *Fragments*. Edited and translated by Hugh Lloyd-Jones. Vol. 3. LCL. Cambridge: Harvard University Press, 1996. Repr., 2003.

Spicq, Ceslas. *Saint Paul: Les Épitres Pastorales*. 4th ed. Études bibliques. Paris: J. Gabalda et Cie, 1969.

Spicq, Ceslas. *Theological Lexicon of the New Testament*. Translated and edited by James D. Ernest. 3 vols. Peabody, MA: Hendrickson, 1994.

Stendahl, Krister. *The Bible and the Role of Women: A Case Study in Hermeneutics*. Translated by Emilie T. Sander. Biblical Series 15. Philadelphia: Fortress, 1966.

Stettler, C. "The 'Command of the Lord' in 1 Cor 14,37—a Saying of Jesus?" *Biblica* 87 (2006): 42–51.

Stott, John R. W. *The Message of Galatians*. The Bible Speaks Today. Downers Grove, IL: InterVarsity Press, 1968.

Strabo. *The Geography of Strabo*. Translated by Horace Leonard Jones. Vol. 1. LCL. Cambridge: Harvard University Press, 1917. Repr., 1969.

Strabo. *The Geography of Strabo*. Translated by Horace Leonard Jones. Vol. 2. LCL. Cambridge: Harvard University Press, 1923. Repr., 1969.

Strabo. *The Geography of Strabo*. Translated by Horace Leonard Jones. Vol. 3. LCL. Cambridge: Harvard University Press, 1924. Repr., 1967.

Strabo. *The Geography of Strabo*. Translated by Horace Leonard Jones. Vol. 4. LCL. Cambridge: Harvard University Press, 1927. Repr., 1961.

Strabo. *The Geography of Strabo*. Translated by Horace Leonard Jones. Vol. 5. LCL. Cambridge: Harvard University Press, 1928. Repr., 1969.

Strabo. *The Geography of Strabo*. Translated by Horace Leonard Jones. Vol. 7. LCL. Cambridge: Harvard University Press, 1930. Repr., 1966.

Stuart, Douglas. *Hosea–Jonah*. Word Biblical Commentary 31. Waco, TX: Word, 1987.

Swete, Henry Barclay. *The Psalms of Solomon with the Greek Fragments of the Book of Enoch*. Cambridge: Cambridge University Press, 1899.

Taylor, Bernard A. *Analytical Lexicon to the Septuagint*. Exp. ed. Peabody, MA: Hendrickson, 2009.

Taylor, Mark. *1 Corinthians*. New American Commentary 28. Nashville: B&H, 2014.

Thayer, Joseph H. *A Greek-English Lexicon of the New Testament*. Grand Rapids: Baker, 1977.

Theocritus. *Idyll*. Pages 18–409. Edited and translated by Neil Hopkinson. LCL. Cambridge: Harvard University Press, 2015.

Thielman, Frank. "The Coherence of Paul's View of the Law: The Evidence of First Corinthians." *New Testament Studies* 38 (1992): 235–53.

Thiselton, Anthony C. *Discovering Romans: Content, Interpretation, Reception*. Grand Rapids: Eerdmans, 2016.

Thomas, Robert L. "The Structure of the Apocalypse: Recapitulation or Progression?" *The Master's Seminary Journal* 4 (1993): 45–66.

Thrall, Margaret E. *I and II Corinthians*. Cambridge Bible Commentary. Cambridge: Cambridge University Press, 1965.

Thucydides. *History of the Peloponnesian War; Books 7–8*. Translated by Charles Forster Smith. Vol. 4. LCL. Cambridge: Harvard University Press, 1923. Repr., 1965.

Thurston, Bonnie B., and Judith M. Ryan. *Philippians and Philemon*. Sacra Pagina 10. Collegeville, MN: Liturgical, 2005.

Tischendorf, Constantinus. *Novum Testamentum Graece*. Vol. 2. 8th ed. Lipsiae: Giesecke & Devrient, 1872.

Tolmie, D. Francois. "Tendencies in the Interpretation of Galatians 3:28 Since 1990." *Acta Theologica* 34 (2014): 105–29.

Tomson, Peter J. *Paul and the Jewish Law: Halakha in the Letters of the Apostle to the Gentiles*. Compendia Rerum Iudaicarum ad Novum Testamentum. Minneapolis: Fortress, 1990.

Trick, Bradley R. *Abrahamic Descent, Testamentary Adoption, and the Law in Galatians: Differentiating Abraham's Sons, Seed, and Children of Promise*. Supplements to Novum Testamentum 169. Leiden: Brill, 2016.

Tromp, Johannes. *The Life of Adam and Eve in Greek: A Critical Edition*. Pseudepigrapha Veteris Testamenti Graece 6. Leiden: Brill, 2005.

Van der Kooij, Arie. "The Septuagint of Isaiah and the Issue of Coherence. A Twofold Analysis of LXX Isaiah 31:9B–32:8." Pages 33–48 in *The Old Greek of Isaiah: Issues and Perspectives: Papers read at the Conference on the Septuagint of Isaiah, held in Leiden 10–11 April 2008*. Edited by Arie van der Kooij and Michaël N. van der Meer. Contributions to Biblical Exegesis and Theology 55. Leuven: Peeters, 2010.

VanGemeren, Willem A., ed. *New International Dictionary of Old Testament Theology and Exegesis*. 5 vols. Grand Rapids: Zondervan, 1997.

Van Neste, Ray. *Cohesion and Structure in the Pastoral Epistles*. Journal for the Study of the New Testament Supplement Series 280. London: T&T Clark International, 2004.

Varner, William. *Philippians: A Handbook on the Greek Text*. Baylor Handbook on the Greek New Testament. Waco, TX: Baylor University Press, 2016.

Vatican Library. https://digi.vatlib.it.

Walde, Christine. "Silence." Pages 454–56 in vol. 13 of *Brill's New Pauly: Encyclopaedia of the Ancient World*. Edited by Hubert Cancik and Helmuth Schneider. 22 vols. Leiden: Brill, 2008.

Wall, Robert W. *Colossians and Philemon*. IVP New Testament Commentary. Downers Grove, IL: InterVarsity Press, 1993.

Wallace, Daniel B. *Greek Grammar Beyond the Basics: An Exegetical Syntax of the New Testament*. Grand Rapids: Zondervan, 1996.

Watson, Duane F. "1 Corinthians 10:23–11:1 in the Light of Greco-Roman Rhetoric: The Role of Rhetorical Questions." *Journal of Biblical Literature* 108.2 (1989): 301–18.

Webb, William J. "Gender Equality and Homosexuality." Pages 401–13 in *Discovering Biblical Equality: Complementarity without Hierarchy*. Edited by Ronald W. Pierce and Rebecca Merrill Groothuis. Downers Grove, IL: InterVarsity Press, 2004.

Webb, William J. *Slaves, Women, and Homosexuals: Exploring the Hermeneutics of Cultural Analysis*. Downers Grove, IL: InterVarsity Press, 2001.

Webb, William J. "The Limits of a Redemptive-Movement Hermeneutic: Focused Response to T. R. Schreiner." *Evangelical Quarterly* 75.4 (2003): 327–42.

Weeks, Noel. "Of Silence and Head Covering." *Westminster Theological Journal* 35 (1972): 21–27.
Weiss, Johannes. *Der erste Korintherbrief.* Göttingen: Vandenhoeck and Ruprecht, 1910.
Wettlaufer, Ryan Donald. *No Longer Written: The Use of Conjectural Emendation in the Restoration of the Text of the New Testament, the Epistle of James as a Case Study.* New Testament Tools, Studies and Documents 44. Leiden: Brill, 2013.
White, John Williams, and Earnest Cary. "Collations of the Manuscripts of Aristophanes' Aves." *Harvard Studies in Classical Philology* 29 (1918): 77–131.
Wilson, N. G. *Aristophanis Fabulae.* Vol. 1. Scriptorum Classicorum Bibliotheca Oxoniensis. Oxford: E Typographeo Clarendoniano, 2007.
Wilson, R. McL. *Colossians and Philemon: A Critical and Exegetical Commentary.* The International Critical Commentary. London: T&T Clark, 2005.
Winter, Bruce W. *Roman Wives, Roman Widows: The Appearance of New Women and the Pauline Communities.* Grand Rapids: Eerdmans, 2003.
Wire, Antoinette C. *Corinthian Women Prophets: A Reconstruction through Paul's Rhetoric.* Minneapolis: Fortress, 1990.
Witherington, Ben III. *The Acts of the Apostles: A Socio-Rhetorical Commentary.* Grand Rapids: Eerdmans, 1998.
Witherington, Ben III. *Conflict and Community in Corinth: A Socio-Rhetorical Commentary on 1 and 2 Corinthians.* Grand Rapids: Eerdmans, 1995.
Witherington, Ben III. *Grace in Galatia: A Commentary on Paul's Letter to the Galatians.* Grand Rapids: Eerdmans, 1998.
Witherington, Ben III. *Letters and Homilies for Hellenized Christians: A Socio-Rhetorical Commentary on Titus, 1–2 Timothy and 1–3 John.* Downers Grove, IL: IVP Academic, 2006.
Witherington, Ben III. "Rite and Rights for Women—Galatians 3:28." *New Testament Studies* 27 (1981): 593–604.
Wolff, Christian. *Der erste Brief des Paulus an die Korinther.* Theologischer Handkommentar zum Neuen Testament 7. Leipzig: Evangelische, 1996.
Wolff, Hans Walter. *Joel and Amos.* Edited by S. Dean McBride, Jr. Translated by Waldemar Janzen, S. Dean McBride, Jr., and Charles A. Muenchow. Hermeneia. Philadelphia: Fortress, 1977.
Woodruff, Marguerite. "Underlying Factors Contributing to Paul's Teaching Concerning Women." PhD diss., Southwestern Baptist Theological Seminary, 1950.
Wright, N. T. *The Epistles of Paul to the Colossians and to Philemon: An Introduction and Commentary.* Tyndale New Testament Commentaries 12. Grand Rapids: Eerdmans, 2008.
Xenophon. *Anabasis.* Translated by Carleton L. Brownson. Revised by John Dillery. Vol. 3. LCL. Cambridge: Harvard University Press, 1998. Repr., 2001.
Xenophon. *Cyropaedia; Books 1–8.* Translated by Walter Miller. Vols. 5–6. LCL. Cambridge: Harvard University Press, 1914. Repr., 1968.
Xenophon. *Hellenica; Books 1–4.* Translated by Carleton L. Brownson. LCL. Cambridge: Harvard University Press, 1918. Repr., 1997.
Xenophon. *Memorabilia.* Pages 2–359. Translated by E. C. Marchant. Vol. 4. LCL. Cambridge: Harvard University Press, 1923. Repr., 1968.
Yarbrough, Robert W. *The Letters to Timothy and Titus.* The Pillar New Testament Commentary. Grand Rapids: Eerdmans, 2018.

Zamfir, Korinna. "Women Teaching—Spiritually Washing the Feet of the Saints? The Early Christian Reception of 1 Timothy 2:11–12." *Annali di Storia dell'esegesi* 2 (2015): 353–79.

Zeller, Dieter. *Der erste Brief an die Korinther.* Kritisch-exegetischer Kommentar über das Neue Testament 5. Göttingen: Vandenhoeck & Ruprecht, 2010.

Ziegler, Joseph. *Untersuchungen zur Septuaginta des Buches Isaias.* Alttestamentliche Abhandlungen 12.3. Münster: Aschendorffschen, 1934.

Zuntz, G. *The Text of the Epistles: A Disquisition upon the Corpus Paulinum.* The Schweich Lectures of the British Academy 1946. London: Oxford University Press, 1953.

Index

absolute silence. *See also* Corinthians
    Aristophanes view, 186–187
    contextual clues and meaning, 24
    definition of, 10, 39
    1 Cor 14:34–35 on, 13, 24–25, 47, 57, 67, 122–123, 156–157
    Euripides' view, 165, 174
    First Corinthians 14:27–30, 39–40
    Greek literature, 25
    Herod's perspectives, 26, 223
    in Amos, 31, 213
    in New Testament, 24–28, 32–36
    lexical work, 21–23
    Luke's Gospel, 33
    Moschus on, 214
    Old Testament, 29–32
    other terms, 23
    Payne, Philip's view, 11
    Philo's on 218
    Seth and the beast example, 56, 220
    Sibylline Oracles, 216
    Strabo on, 219
    symbol key, 162
    1 Tim 2:11–12, 121–122
    usage in Old Testament, 31–32
    women in church leadership, 44
Achaeans, 168, 171, 222
Achaia, 43, 142
Achilles, 190
Acts
    4:13, 75
    12:17; 15:12–13, 32
    16:11–15, 17–18, 155
    18:9, 32
    21:40, 22, 35
    22:2, 124
    Herod's imprisoning of Peter, 33
    Jesus choosing male apostles, 150
    Lydia, 19, 133–135, 154
    Paul's ministry in Ephesus, 142
    Paul's writings, 2, 107–108
    Payne on silence, 123, 138
    Prisca and Aquila, 141
    women in church, 152
    women in the book of Acts, 82
Adelakun, Adewale, 117

Index

Admetus, 165–166
Aeschines
  Against Ctesiphon, 204–205
  On the Embassy, 203–204
Aeneas, *On the Defense of Fortified Positions*, 205
Aeschylus, 190
Aesop, 161–162
Aethra, 169
Agamemnon, 163, 168, 171, 178
Agatharchides, *On the Erythraean Sea*, 214
Agathon, 188–189
Agesilaus, 191, 226
Alcimus, 127–128
Alexander, 130, 222
Amos, 29, 31, 213
Amphiaraüs, temples of, 219
Amphitryon, 170
Ampliatus, 135
Ancherimphis, 80
ancient education, 69, 73–75, 105
ancient world, 14, 18, 70–74, 77, 79, 81, 87, 105, 107
Andronicus, 4, 143–144, 146
  and Junia, 143
Apelles, 135
Aphrodite, 47, 150
Apollonius Rhodius, *Argonautica*, 209
Apollonius of Tyana, *Letters*, 223–224
Apollos, 38, 72, 88, 142, 163, 190
Aquila, 108, 135, 141–142
Aramaic, 30
Aristobulus, 135, 221
Aristocrates, 203
Aristophanes, 66
  Acharnians, 184–185
  Birds, 186–187
  Clouds, 185
  Frogs, 190
  Lysistrata, 187–188
  Peace, 186
  Thesmophoriazusae, 188–189
  Wasps, 185
  Wealth, 190
Aristoteles, *Sophistical Refutations*, 206–207
Artabanus, 182
Artabazus, 183
Artemas, 88
Artemis, 171, 190
Asclepiades, *Epigrammata*, 210
Astyages, 191
Asyncritus, 135
Atreus, 176

baptism, 109–110, 142
barbarians, 111, 191
believers, 12, 102, 116, 135, 138
Bible, 81–84, 118, 160
bride, 166, 175

charlatan, 202
chorus, 148, 164, 167, 179–181, 190, 204, 217
  leader, 164–165, 167, 173–174, 176–177
Christian assembly, 4, 134
Christians, 15, 53, 86, 104, 114, 120, 152
Christian Women, 11, 14, 18, 26
Chrysostom, John, 15, 144
church
  leadership, 13, 111, 134, 143
  service, 37, 39, 54–55, 92, 160
circumcision, 103, 113–114, 117
Clement of Rome, *1 Clement*, 224
Colossians, 4, 108
  Nympha in, 152–155
  and Philemon, 153–154
commentators, 12, 44, 48, 55, 72–75, 124, 134, 137, 144
congregations, 8, 18–19, 45, 76, 107, 109, 122, 136

contextual clues, 24, 26, 45, 131, 134
Corinthian Church, 42, 75, 91–92, 101, 106, 159
Corinthians
  1 Corinthians 1:12; 3:4; 15:12, 48–49
  1 Corinthians 7:1, 48
  1 Corinthians, 7:4, 3
  1 Corinthians, 11:5, 54–58, 67
  1 Corinthians, 11:11, 3
  1 Corinthians, 11–14, 21
  1 Corinthians, 12:11, 51–54
  1 Corinthians, 12–14, 36, 51–53, 67, 94
  1 Corinthians 14, 26, 28, 32, 37–39, 67
  1 Corinthians 14:27–30, 39–42
  1 Corinthians 14:31–33, 42–44
  1 Corinthians 14:33–34, 91
  1 Corinthians 14:34, 44–47
  1 Corinthians 14:34–35, 6–14, 18, 45–46, 59, 69, 88
  1 Corinthians 14:35–36, 47–50
  1 Corinthians 14:37–40, 50–51
  1 Corinthians 16:15–18, 43
  comparable use of the law, 100, 104–105
  cultural and transcultural statements, 86
  definition of σιγάω, 157
  ethics, 102
  Junia, reference in, 143
  literary relationship, 121–122, 158–159
  male and female problem, 90–97
  Oropeza's introduction, 90
  Pastoral Epistles and, 64
  Paul's first letter to the Corinthians, 106
  statements on women, 72
  theme of boasting, 103
  Pauline theology, 1, 17, 38, 93–97, 100, 136, 141, 156
Crates, *Fragments*, 183
creation, 10, 17–18, 101, 104, 111–114, 132
culture, 2, 14, 18, 70, 73, 82–84, 87
  ancient, 70, 83, 105, 157–158
  cultural arguments, 2, 15, 69, 83–84, 105, 117

dative, forms of, 57, 144, 146
day of judgment, 56, 220
deacons, 138, 140–141, 152
Demetrius, 127–128
Demosthenes, 201–205, 217
  3 Philippic, 202
  Against Aristocrates, 203
  Against Timarchus, 203
  False Embassy, 202–203
  On the Crown, 202
  On the Peace, 201
Deuteronomy, 44, 79, 103, 105
Dio Chrysostom, 15–16
Dionysius of Halicarnassus
  On Literary Composition, 217
  Roman Antiquities, 125–126, 216
  On the Style of Demosthenes, 217
Dionysodorus, 195–196
dispute, 5, 11, 26, 131–132, 151, 205

Early Christianity, 19, 109, 134
early church, 7, 17, 70, 112, 133, 136–139, 141
early Pauline communities, 3, 66
Ecclesiastes, 29, 40, 212
edification, 12, 36–38, 67, 92, 95
eloquence, 73–74, 184
Ephesians, 87
Ephesus, 122–23
1 Esdras, 211
ethics, 41, 102, 113, 116
Euripides, 48, 99
  Alcestis, 165–166
  Andromache, 168
  Bacchae, 177
  Children of Heracles, 166
  Cyclops, 164–165
  Electra, 170
  Fragments, 77, 162–164
  Hecuba, 168–169
  Helen, 174–175
  Heracles, 170

262 | Index

Hippolytus, 166–168
Ion, 173–174
Iphigeneia at Aulis, 178
Iphigeneia at Tauris, 171–173
Medea, 166
Orestes, 176–177
Phaethon, 164
Phoenician Women, 175–176
Suppliant Women, 169–170
Trojan Women, 170–171
Euthydemus, 191, 195–196, 206, 250
evangelism, 76, 111
Exodus, 210, 217–218

faith, 33–34, 36, 99, 113–115, 151, 217
food laws, 102
foolishness, 28, 182, 227
freedom of speech, 224

Gaius Musonius Rufus *Dissertationum a Lucio digestarum reliquiae*, 224
Galatians
   3:28, 3, 108–116
   on homosexuality, 118–120
   male problems, 117
   women's freedom
gender
   egalitarian conclusions, 81
   Galatians view, 109–110, 115–118, 155
   homosexuality, 82, 84
   Junia in Romans, 143, 145
   of Nympha, 153
   Paul's central point in 1 Corinthians, 12–13, 76
   spiritual gifts, 51–53
Genesis
   Adam's leadership, 52, 99
   creation narratives, 101
   on circumcision, 113
   on women, 83–84
   Pauline theology, 158–159
genitive, 143, 145–147
Gentiles, 33, 110, 119

gifts, 12–14, 36–37, 51–53, 67, 95, 110, 155–160, 220
Greco-Roman, 2, 15, 44, 69, 73, 76–77, 81, 89–90, 94–95, 98, 105

Hamadryads, 198
head covering, 57
Hebrew, 29–30, 35, 125
Heracleots, 191
Heracles, 166, 180, 218
Hermas, 135
Hermeneutics, 21, 81–82, 116–117, 151
Hermes, 135, 218
Herod, 26, 221–223
Herodotus, *Histories*, 182–183
heterosexuality, 112
Hippocrates, 24, 28
   Coan Prenotions, 201
   Diseases of Women II, 201
   Epidemics, 24, 199–200
   On Joints, 200
   The Oath, 200
   The Physician, 201
   In the Surgery, 200
Homer, 27, 198, 218
homosexuality, 53, 82–85, 105–106, 117–119, 155
hospitality, 134, 141–142, 227
households, 14, 31, 43, 65, 133–134, 137, 154, 213

inheritance, 109–110, 113–117
interpreters, 4, 7, 14, 45, 55, 62, 91, 94, 97, 110, 116, 157, 159
Isaiah, 29–30, 101, 213
Isocrates
   Ad Demonicum, 184
   Busiris, 184
   On the Banker, 184

Jerusalem Council in Acts, 114
Jewish Law, 104

Jews, 75, 95, 100, 142, 223
Josephus, 26, 28, 126, 130–131
  Jewish Antiquities, 129–130, 220–222
  The Life, 222
  Jewish War, 222–223
Judas, 128, 150
judgment, 35–36, 41, 47, 56, 58, 87, 156, 160, 176, 187, 202, 205, 213, 220
  of prophecy, 41, 44–45, 54, 67, 156
Junia, 4, 135, 137, 143–146, 149, 158
justice, 74, 131, 203, 217

kinsman, 135, 188–189

Lamentations, 30, 126, 214, 216
law of God, 100–102
law of love, 98, 102–103
law of Moses, 100, 104–105, 114
law of sin and death, 99
leadership, 4, 12–13, 18–19, 43–44, 51, 89, 99, 110–111, 120, 134, 136, 138–139, 152, 155
The Life of Adam and Eve, 220
Lucian, 148–149
Luke, 22, 32–33, 35, 64, 124–25, 133, 139–140, 150
Lysias, *In Eratosthenem*, 199

Maccabees, 127–128, 211
manuscript tradition, 6–8, 11, 32, 63–64
marriages, 175, 181, 220
married women, 6, 14, 80, 156
  First Corinthians 14:34– 35, 14
Menander
  Sententiae e codicibus Byzantinis, 208–209
  Sententiae e papyris, 209
mortals, 147, 150, 178
Mosaic law, 99–102, 104
Moschus *Lament for Bion*, 24, 214
Moses, 100, 102, 104–105, 114, 125, 129

New Testament, 2, 4, 17–19, 21–24, 32, 49–50, 57–59, 111–112, 150–151, 155–156
  on absolute silence, 24–28, 32–36
Nympha, 19, 137, 152–155, 158
Nymphs, 24, 198, 214

Old Testament, 70, 84, 97, 99, 101, 105–106, 115, 159
  on absolute silence, 29–32
  laws, 2, 73, 77, 92, 100–101, 104

Pastoral Epistles, 64–65
patriarchy, 17, 83, 90, 118
Patrobas, 135
Pauline authorship, 8, 48, 58, 65–67, 97, 99, 104, 159
  criticism, 58–62
  interpolated version, 62–67
Paul, silencing women, 70–72
  consistent pattern, 85–90
  cultural situation, 81–85
  intended meaning in 1 Cor 14:34–35, 69
  lack of education argument, 72–77
  lack of public speaking argument, 77–81
  use of the law, 97–105
Pauline theology
  Euodia and Syntyche in Philippians 4:2–3, 150–152
  Galatians 3:28, 108–116
  First Timothy 2:11–12, 120–132
  hermeneutical criteria, 116–120
  Junia in Romans 16:7, 143–150
  Lydia in Acts 16:11–15; 16:40, 133–135
  Nympha in Colossians 4:15, 152–155
  Prisca and Aquila in Romans 16:3–5a, 141–143
  regular citation of inconsistency, 136–137
  Romans 16:1–7, 135–141
Paul's Letters, 25, 65, 88–89, 96, 115, 123, 142, 145, 152, 156, 224
Philippians, Euodia and Syntyche in, 150–152

264 | Index

Philo, Worse, 125
   Who Is the Heir?, 217–218
   On Dreams, 218
   That Every Good Person Is Free, 218
Phlegon, 135
Phrygians, 16, 27, 177, 190, 219, 228
Plato
   Alcibiades, 194
   Apology of Socrates, 192–193
   Epigrammata, 198
   Euthydemus, 195–196, 206
   Laws, 197
   Lesser Hippias, 197
   Letters, 197–198
   The Lovers, 194–195
   Lysis, 195
   Phaedrus, 193–194
   Protagoras, 196
   Republic, 198–199
   Theaetetus, 193
Plutarch, 15–16, 26–28, 71, 78, 131
   Advice about Keeping Well, 226
   Brutus, 225
   Caius Marcius Coriolanus, 225
   Concerning Talkativeness, 26, 227
   On Exile, 227–228
   The Education of Children, 225–226
   Fragments, 228–229
   How the Young Man Should Study Poetry, 226
   How a Man May Become Aware of His Progress in Virtue, 226
   Lives of the Ten Orators, 228
   Sayings of Spartans, 227
Polybius, *The Histories*, 210
Posidippus, *Epigrammata*, 210
prayer, 31, 35, 47, 54, 57–58, 126, 133
Prisca and Aquila, 108, 141–142
prohibitions, 2, 11–12, 16, 24, 26, 71, 85, 136
prophecy
   building church, 36
   evaluation, 50

judgment, 41, 44, 67, 89, 156
Law of Moses, 104
male church leadership, 43
on silence, 5, 45–47
Paul's discussion, 65, 91
practice of tongues, 101
as spiritual gift, 51
women's prayer, 54–55, 57–58
prophets
   evaluation, 50, 158
   female/women, 41, 56, 92
   ministry of gay and lesbian, 52
   New Testament, 150
   Old Testament, 99, 101
   on silence, 46–47, 56, 96
   speech, 54
   spirits of, 41–43, 45
   use of church, 95
   writing, 34
proverbs, 128, 162
Psalm, 28–29, 211–212, 224
Ptolemaeus ΠΕΡΙ, 216
public affairs, 173–174
Pylades, 171–172, 176
   and Orestes, 176
Pythagoreans, 229
Python, 215
queer, 110, 116–118, 120

Quintilian, 73–74
quotation formula, 97–98

Rabbinic tradition, 98
restrictions, 11, 15–16, 51, 85–86, 110
revelation, 12, 34–39, 47, 67, 76, 92, 96
rhetorical questions, 3, 49
   function of, 49
right of land and property inheritance, 115
Romans, 34, 82, 102
   16:1–2, 137–141
   16:1–7, 135–137

Junia in, 143–150
Prisca and Aquila in, 141–142
and Philippians, 140
Rufus, 135–136

Sabbath day, 133
saints, 12, 35, 43, 47, 86, 93–94, 96, 121, 135
salvation, 10, 109–10, 112–16, 155, 224
Samaritan woman, 111
selective silence, 24, 26, 29, 31, 67, 125, 128, 131, 155, 158, 180, 209
Septuagint, 29–30
sexual immorality, 91, 103
shame, 1, 13–14, 16, 45, 89, 96, 156, 163, 179
Sibylline Oracles, 214–216
Sirach/Ecclesiasticus, 78, 213
slogans, 10, 48–49, 157
Sophocles
  Ajax, 179
  Antigone, 180
  Electra, 180
  Fragments, 178–179
  Oedipus Coloneus, 181
  Oedipus Tyrannus, 180
  Philoctetes, 181
  Trachiniae, 180–181
soteriology, 109, 116
spiritual gifts, 12, 14, 36–37, 51–52, 67, 94, 101, 156, 160
Strabo *Geography*, 27, 218–219
synagogue, 16, 73, 136, 142

temple, 75, 128, 171, 183, 219
Theocritus, *Idylls*, 207–208
Thucydides, *History*, 162
Timothy, 18, 88, 94
  2:11–12, 120–128, 132
  2:19, 85
Titus, 23, 88, 116–117

Tobias, 211
Tobit, 211
tongues, 54, 95, 101, 158, 210
  and prophecies, 51, 101, 158
Torah, 10

umlauts, 60–61
unbelievers, 36
uncircumcision, 103
uncultured person, 77, 224

victory, 72, 78, 188, 225
violence, 13, 162, 221, 228
virgin, 207, 215, 221

Wisdom of Solomon, 212
witnesses, 52, 60, 78–79, 103, 172, 204
women in the churches. *See also* Pauline theology
  cultural ideals, 15–16
  lack of education, 15–16
  literary context, 6–14
  Paul's writing and practice, 1–5, 16–19
  research history, 6, 16–17
  theological context, 17

Xanthias, 185
Xenophon
  Anabasis, 191
  Cyropaedia, 191–192
  Hellenica, 191
  Memorabilia, 191
Xuthus, 173

Yahweh, 31

Zenas, 88
Zeno, 210
Zetes, 209
Zeus, 172, 186, 188, 210
Zuntz, 3–4

Studies in Biblical Literature

This series invites manuscripts from scholars in any area of biblical literature. Both established and innovative methodologies, covering general and particular areas in biblical study, are welcome. The series seeks to make available studies that will make a significant contribution to the ongoing biblical discourse. Scholars who have interests in gender and sociocultural hermeneutics are particularly encouraged to consider this series.

For further information about the series and for the submission of manuscripts, contact:

Peter Lang Publishing
Acquisitions Department
80 Broad Street, 5th floor
New York, NY 10004

To order other books in this series, please contact our Customer Service Department:

peterlang@presswarehouse.com (within the U.S.)
orders@peterlang.com (outside the U.S.)

or browse online by series at:

WWW.PETERLANG.COM

Made in the USA
Columbia, SC
12 April 2023

880e289e-8de1-4ea2-a5bb-cdc285169f3bR02